DATE DUE

OC 1 0 '01			
OC 2 4 '02			
SE 24 '02			
OC 24 '02			
SE 1 6 '05			
OC 2 4 '06			
OC 25 '06			
NO 0 6 '08			
OC 29 '08			
10/21			

Demco, Inc. 38-293

Experts in Action

LONGMAN SERIES IN
PUBLIC COMMUNICATION

SERIES EDITOR: RAY ELDON HIEBERT

EXPERTS IN ACTION

Inside Public Relations

Bill Cantor

Edited by
Chester Burger

LONGMAN INC.
New York & London

The character of a man can be easily judged by the way he treats those from whom he may not benefit

This book is dedicated to the most important people in my life: my wife, Jeanne, and my sons, David and Bill.

Experts in Action
Inside Public Relations

Longman Inc., 1560 Broadway, New York, N.Y. 10036
Associated companies, branches, and representatives
throughout the world.

Copyright © 1984 by Longman Inc.
Chapter 16, "Speechwriting," by John B. McDonald. Copyright © 1984 John B. McDonald.

Developmental Editor: Gordon T.R. Anderson
Editorial and Design Supervisor: Thomas Bacher
Interior Designer: The Antler & Baldwin Design Group
Production/Manufacturing Ferne Y. Kawahara
Composition: Graphicraft Typesetters, Ltd.
Printing and Binding: Maple-Vail Book Manufacturing Group

Library of Congress Cataloging in Publication Data
Cantor, Bill, 1931–
    Experts in Action.
    (Longman series in public communication)
    Includes index.
    1. Public relations — United States — Addresses, essays,
lectures.   2. Public relations consultants — United States
— Addresses, essays, lectures.   3. Industrial publicity —
Addresses, essays, lectures.   I. Burger, Chester.
II. Title.   III. Series.
HM263.C253   1984   659.2   83-17558
ISBN 0-582-28437-6
ISBN 0-582-28438-4 (pbk.)

Manufactured in the United States of America
Printing: 9 8 7 6 5 4 3 2   Year: 92 91 90 89 88 87 86 85 84

CONTENTS

PROLOGUE

Edward L. Bernays

John Milton summed it all up when he wrote, "So celebrated in the mouths of wisest men; that to the public good private respects must yield."

Obviously John Milton did not refer specifically to public relations. But his poetic wisdom certainly foreshadowed it hundreds of years before the profession came to be.

Certainly the French Revolution too had something to do with bringing public relations about. For in this revolution, people power manifested itself in a decisive way; the dictatorial monarch was relieved of his power and people power was substituted.

Our own revolutionary period in the United States was a splendid example of people power and its strength. American patriots wanted to free themselves from the rule of Great Britain. They propagandized their publics into a new united nation of men and women, dedicated to freedom, equality, and orderly justice. Committees of correspondence played their part. Samuel Adams became the press agent of the Revolution. Thomas Jefferson in the Declaration of Independence, a public relations document, declared the country's liberty. And people power expressed itself in the Revolutionary War and won.

The early years of the new Republic were geared to expansion and development. Distance and lack of communication and transportation facilities left little basis for communications between the citizens of the new country and for the creation of a cohesive public opinion and people power.

The basis for strengthened people power soon arose. New speeded-up communications methods developed. In 1832 de Toqueville, the French observer of the new United States, wrote, "The newspaper is the only

Edward L. Bernays created and named the profession of "counsel on public relations." In 1923 he wrote the seminal book on the subject, *Crystallizing Public Opinion* , which laid down the principles, practices, and ethics of the profession. A nephew of Sigmund Freud, he pioneered the application of the social sciences to public relations. Simon & Schuster published his memoirs, *Biography of an Idea* (1965), and F. W. Faxon Company published a bibliography of Bernays's, *Public Relations The Edward L. Bernayses and the American Scene* (1978). He has become a legend in his own lifetime.

instrument by which the same thought can be dropped into a thousand homes at the same moment." The invention of the telegraph took place the same year. Other inventions such as steam railroads and boats speeded up transportation and shortened distances in time. In 1863, invention made it possible to print both sides of a sheet of paper.

The divisiveness caused by slavery brought with it many pro-and-con efforts at persuasion of publics. The Civil War preserved the union and confirmed we were one people, with goals of freedom, equality, and orderly justice — the foundation values of the republic.

Nationwide industrial development came after the war. Behavior determined mainly by personal interest, which deplored the interest of others, developed in this country. Business interests, the railroads, public utilities, trusts, and monopolies of varied kinds functioned on the basis mainly of their private interest. The period was characterized by the response William H. Vanderbilt of the New York Central Railroad gave to an inquiring reporter, "the public be damned." This subsequently was the name given to the years 1865 to 1900.

In the late 1890s came change. The farmers, the new labor movement, the Christian Socialists, and others protested the goings-on. At the turn of the century, the muckrakers played a leading role in social change. They emphasized the values of the public interest, convenience, and necessity and the vital importance of the public and the private interest coinciding. Ida Tarbell, Lincoln Steffens, Stewart Edward White, and others in *Everybody's*, *McClure's*, and other periodicals by the people stressed the shame of the cities, the monopolies, and trusts in a free country. They educated, persuaded, and rallied public opinion to fight to ensure that the public interest would be maintained in private enterprise and in the public sector, where selfish interest had ruled. They gave strength to President Theodore Roosevelt's "Square Deal" and made it possible for him to wield "the big stick" on behalf of the public. I vividly remember that period and was heavily impressed by how one man in his leadership strategies and tactics both reflected and affected public opinion and public action.

John Donne, the English seer, centuries before had stated that no man is an island unto himself. We are indeed all part of a whole. Now laws were being put on the statute books that private action must be in accord with the public interest.

During a coal strike in 1902, George F. Baer, a mine owner, in a widely circulated statement announced that "God in His Infinite Wisdom has given control of the property interest of the country" to the George F. Baers. This had stirred up antagonism. In a subsequent coal strike, the mine owners engaged a young publicity man, Ivy Lee. He introduced a new period of public information about private interests. A member of the publicity firm of Parker and Lee, he advised the coal operators that the public was no longer to be ignored, in the traditional manner of business. The public was to be informed. The innovation was followed by many business interests at that time.

Theodore Newton Vail, president of the American Telephone and Telegraph Company, also gave the concept of the public interest impetus. In August 1913, he issued a statement to the effect that "We have found . . . that our interests were best served when the public interests were best served; and we believe that such success as we have had has been because our business has been conducted along these lines."

The outbreak of World War I brought a recognition to the warring nations concerning how vital public opinion was to the success of their efforts. Ideas and their distribution became weapons and words became bullets. War publicity became an essential part of the war effort. The problem of informing and persuading people in one's own country, in neutral countries, and enemy countries challenged policy makers in all countries.

President Woodrow Wilson's power to dramatize ideas had a powerful effect. Only one week after the United States entered World War I on April 6, 1917, the United States Committee on Public Information was set up under the direction of George Creel, former editor of the *Rocky Mountain News* of Denver. Other members were the secretaries of war, navy, and state. The committee had two sections, foreign and domestic.

I was a staff member of the U.S. Committee on Public Information in the foreign service here and at the Peace Conference in Paris. Our efforts were directed to make the world safe for democracy and make this the war to end all wars. We worked also to publicize the Fourteen Points and found people power was essential in meeting our national goals. Freedom of the seas won over the neutral Swiss. Independence for ethnic entities gained us the support of the Latvians, Estonians, and Lithuanians.

When I returned from Paris, I recognized that people power had become the most significant force in the world. I recognized that all institutions of the society, if they were to carry on, depended on the coincidence of the public and the private interest. In cooperation with my future wife, Doris E. Fleischman, I opened an office in New York.

I called our work "publicity direction." But soon the nature and title of our work was changed to "counsel on public relations." The private and the public interest must coincide in actions. Words were ancillary to deeds. To publicize the vocation, I wrote in 1923 what was the first book on public relations, *Crystallizing Public Opinion*; and to give the activity status, I gave the first course on the subject at an institution of higher learning, New York University, in that year.

The spread of the activity of counsel on public relations surged ahead. In the United States over 10,000 men and women are members of the Public Relations Society of America, and there are many special associations of public relations. Throughout the free world, there are professional public relations men and women. The International Public Relations Association has over 600 members in 60 countries. They advise on how to develop coincidence between the particular employer or client and the public.

Fundamentally, public relations is today a profession. By definition, a profession is an art applied to a science, in which the public interest rather than pecuniary motivation is the primary objective. Public relations has a literature of some 16,000 items, another criterion of a profession. It has its associations, where members may exchange principles, techniques, and methods. It has a code of ethics defined by its associations. And it has its educational facilities both in the United States and other parts of the world.

But unfortunately in the United States, words have the stability of soap bubbles and Belgian lace unless they are defined by law. The two words "public relations" are in the public domain. This is contrary to criteria of other professions. In other professions, the criteria are defined by law, with economic sanctions for those who transgress. In the United States, on the other hand, anyone can call himself or herself a public relations practitioner and often does, with disadvantage to public and profession alike.

Registration and licensing, with economic sanctions to wrongdoers, will ensure that as in the case of other professions, such as medicine, law, and architecture, public and profession alike will be protected against charlatans and other antisocial practitioners who today misuse the words "public relations practitioner."

Speeded-up communication and transportation have already made one room of the entire country and of the world. The revolution brought about by radio, television, and motion pictures is now being followed by new electronic media.

Cable television, satellite transmission, and reception, computerism, interacting TV systems, and videotapes will have influence on people's attitudes and behavior. More people will be exposed to more ideas, actions, and facts. My considered opinion is that this will not change the present situation greatly, except to make more people more informed and people power stronger. One possible danger may come from monopoly control of media, limiting the free flow of fact and viewpoint. But the United States thus far has handled the monopoly problem.

Public relations should continue to grow as long as our democratic society remains. In our fluid democracy, competition of ideas, services, and things will carry on. The practitioner of the future will be a generalist and a specialist, oriented to society as a whole and to one special segment of it. Educational training for public relations, so chaotic today because of the lack of definition, will fortunately conform to licensing and registration standards. It will prepare for the broad functions of the profession.

As our society grows increasingly complex with increased literacy, technology, and more sophisticated viewpoints, the societal technician in public relations should become an increasingly important professional as an adviser to achieve social goals with publics. Practitioners and the profession should reap rewards in status and other values. And so should society.

PREFACE

Bill Cantor

President
The Cantor Concern, Inc.

In the last two decades, more than a few managers of public and private institutions, and the public relations professionals who report to them, have seen their business plans collapse in the face of unforeseen social change. Others have benefited, often unwittingly, from the same unanticipated changes. Whether winners or losers, they have learned that those who do not manage for change may become its victims: those who do not take the actions necessary to establish the correct public perception of their institutions can see that image tarnished by others and the ability of that institution to function impaired.

For that reason, managers who elect to chart a clear course for their institutions through the complex maze of today's changing social forces know they must demand the most sophisticated counsel, plans, and programs from their public relations professionals. Those professionals who can respond to that challenge become invaluable to their institutions; those who cannot do not survive.

Having witnessed these rapid changes and the creative response to them by sophisticated public relations people, and having spent many years providing counsel as well as executive search services to the public relations field, I felt it my obligation to collect the best that the public relations field has to offer in the way of its thoughts about the profession: how it works, how it must face the future, how it should be managed, and what skills it has and needs. Those thoughts, ideas, and experiences are presented here by many of the leading professionals. I believe what they have to say will be of benefit to the next generation, which must continue to help guide our most valuable institutions into the future.

This is not, then, a book for beginners. It was not meant to be one. It is, instead, a book for those who know something about the field, who work with public relations professionals, who manage, or seek to manage, public relations departments. For these people, too, I have included a section that attempts to provide standards and descriptions of public relations functions. That is my own particular contribution, a contribution arising from my years of working to help my own clients understand what they really need in the people they seek to hire and the jobs they seek to fill — rather than what they thought they needed.

The two tasks of this book, then, are Herculean. The first is to provide real information about what public relations is, does, and should do. The second is to provide an idea of what kinds of people the profession has and should have. Completing these tasks to everyone's satisfaction may not be possible, but if the professionals whose work is gathered here cannot do it, I suspect no one can.

The preparation of this book has been a labor of love and respect. I have, for many years, considered myself privileged to work with and for the people of public relations. By virtue of their sensitivity, intellect, pragmatism, and exceptional communications skills, public relations people have enriched my working life. If I can give something back to the field, something that will help it and its people understand themselves and be better understood by others, then this will begin to repay my debt to them.

There's a special reason why I have enjoyed working on this book. This is one of my first joint efforts with my friend and partner, Chester Burger, since the Cantor Concern merged with Chester Burger & Company, Inc., in 1982.

I hope you find this book stimulating, meaningful, and useful.

There have been literally hundreds of people who unknowingly inspired me to develop this book and for a variety of reasons — some because of their knowledge, others because of their lack of knowledge, and still others because of their thirst for knowledge.

To a select few, I am compelled to express my sincere appreciation:

First and most important, I extend my unlimited gratitude to my business partner, my very best friend, and my wife, Jeanne. Her loving patience, support, understanding, and stabilizing influence helped me, as so often in the past, move from adversity to success. Without her personal involvement and major contributions this book would not have been completed.

To my public relations counsel, Kenneth Virch, president of Kenneth Virch Associates, who expended an inordinate amount of time and energy on this project, sharing with me his vast wisdom to help steer my course of action; I can but acknowledge his contribution in this effort as monumental.

To Henry Fiur, a topflight public relations professional and friend, who unselfishly donated hour on hour of precious evenings and weekends for conceptualization, analysis, and guidance so that I might attain the objectives of this book. Those objectives were clearly determined by the collected efforts of myself, Henry, and Bob Ferrante, who since his initial involvement in this book has become one of my partners in Chester Burger & Company, Inc. Bob's perceptions took us to new avenues of exploration and were instrumental in broadening our road to include a greater audience.

To Don Bates, president of Don Bates & Associates, Inc., and administrator of the Foundation for Public Relations Research and Education, one of the first professionals from whom I sought and received much appreciated counsel.

My heartfelt appreciation to Jan Van Meter, Mike Tabris, Bill Cox, and Merton Fiur, who in addition to contributing their own chapters to the book were always available for counsel and input. Their efforts will long be remembered.

And finally, many thanks to my partner, Chet Burger, for his encouragement, enthusiasm, and invaluable and professional expertise.

INTRODUCTION

Ray E. Hiebert

President
Communication Research Associates, Inc.

Public relations has often been misunderstood by the public at large, and yet it is indispensable to modern democratic society. The profession bears some of the responsibility for this misunderstanding, since its leaders have not always clearly explained their work.

This book helps to correct that problem because it is a book about the profession for its professionals. *Experts in Action* deals with the functions, tools, and techniques of the profession. In doing so, this work demonstrates clearly that there is nothing sinister, tricky, or underhanded about successful public relations.

To begin the discussion, I would like to put the practice of public relations into some philosophical perspective.

First, public relations operates on the *fundamental rights* of freedom of speech and freedom of the press. Everyone in a democratic society should have an equal right to be heard. This freedom does not only apply to the owners and operators of newspapers and broadcast stations. Unfortunately, the news media have appropriated this notion as their own, for their own protection, and they have taken the initiative in fighting for these freedoms, often using public relations as the whipping boy, as if public relations practitioners were opposed to freedoms of speech and of the press. In truth, public relations exists because of those freedoms, could not exist without them, and in fact, helps to preserve those freedoms by providing the techniques whereby anyone can be heard. Each individual and each insitution has a right to use public relations counsel.

Ray E. Hiebert is president of Communication Research Associates, Inc., and a professor at the Unviersity of Maryland. He has been a communication consultant in the Washington, D.C., area for more than twenty years. He has written and edited a number of books in the communication field, including *Mass Media*, a widely used college textbook. He is coeditor of *The Voice of Government* and *Informing the People*, two public affairs handbooks, and is editor of the *Public Relations Review*, a quarterly journal and the *Social Science Monitor*

A second point is that public relations is *essential* in modern democracies with mass societies and mass communications. In Thomas Jefferson's time, when most people lived in rural areas or small towns, every voice that was raised could be heard. Getting on a soapbox in the village square was sufficient to ensure that one's neighbors in the community would listen. But by Teddy Roosevelt's era, we had become a mass society, with most people living in large metropolitan areas, and to be heard one had to take his message to the people through the growing and increasingly impersonal mass media. Media workers became the gatekeepers that decided who and what should be heard. They didn't arrogate that role unto themselves; circumstances forced it upon them. But it was — and is — antithetical to democracy to allow one group to dictate what can and cannot be communicated to the masses. The techniques of public relations, which grew out of industrialization and mass communication, today provide a method for all individuals and groups to state their messages in such a way that they have some chance of being heard by others.

A third point is that public relations, as defined by the profession and in this book, can exist *only* in democratic societies. It cannot and does not exist (in the way it is described here) in authoritarian, dictatorial, or totalitarian regimes. In governments in which one party, or one leader, decides public policy, there can be no legitimate role for public relations. The party or the leader might use communication techniques to keep the people in line, but there would be no need for professionals to practice those techniques on behalf of those who wanted to propose different ideas or policies or procedures. In fact, such practice would be clearly subversive and obviously outlawed in non-democratic societies.

Fourth, public relations exists in a democracy because *everyone has a right to his or her own version of the truth*. There is no *one* truth; absolute truth only exists in totalitarian societies. We all see the world with our own eyes, from our own unique angle of vision. The wonderful thing about democracy is that it protects our right to our own vision.

Take for example a modern American university. It is composed of students, faculty, administration, and staff, but it also is of direct concern to alumni, taxpayers, community neighbors, parents of students, professional, scientific, and scholarly organizations, and local, state, and national governmental agencies. Each of these groups has its own view of what the university should be and do. Students might want the university to train them for a job, or provide them with a sound basis for life, or in the extreme, get them out of the draft. Faculty might want the university to provide a place to do research and pursue the "truth." Administration and staff might want the university to be a well-run organization. Alumni might want the university to guarantee the validity of their diploma for career advancement. Taxpayers might want the university to increase the economic well-being of the region. Neighbors might want the university to be clean, orderly, and inconspicuous in order that property values are maintained. Parents might want the university to provide an easy transition for their children to adulthood. Professional organizations might want the university to further the cause of their professions. Governments might want the university to stimulate economic growth and development.

Whose view should prevail? In authoritarian regimes, there would be no question. The person or persons in authority would have the final say. (In many non-democratic countries, as a matter of fact, the head of government is also the head of the university.) But in a democracy, it is very difficult — even at the university level — for any one faction or person (even the university president) to have absolute power and control over the institution.

In a democracy, we have to convince the majority of the views that should prevail. It is the majority view that wins. Even in institutions where votes are not taken on all issues and where power is distributed among a variety of interest groups, where there are no plebiscites or roll calls, institutions manage on the basis of the good will of their constituent publics. And all individuals and groups of individuals have a right to their own view of what is right.

Fifth, as a result of this kind of democracy, "truth" is *the will of the majority*. Whether right or wrong from any one individual's perspective, if the majority goes one way or the other, that way becomes the law that governs all. What this means is that in a democracy, public opinion is the ultimate law, the real king, or, as Ivy Lee told the American Railroad Guild in 1914, "The people now rule. We have substituted for the divine right of kings, the divine right of the multitude. The crowd is enthroned."

In a democratic society, no one — not even the president — can succeed without the majority of the public behind him. Abraham Lincoln understood this even before he became president. In one of his famous debates with Stephen Douglas in 1858, he said: "Public sentiment is everything. With public sentiment nothing can fail; without it, nothing can succeed. Consequently, he who molds public sentiment goes deeper than he who enacts statutes or pronounces decisions. He makes statutes or decisions possible or impossible to be executed."

The public relations professional is the person who molds public sentiment. One hundred and twenty-five years after Lincoln made his statement, we are finally beginning to understand what Lincoln knew — the importance of that molding function.

The final point is that if *public opinion is the law*, then we need new kinds of lawyers — in addition to those who are concerned with statutes. Lawyers advise their clients on what they can do within the limits of the law and advocate their clients' positions before the courts. Public relations professionals advise their clients on what they can do within the limits of public opinion and advocate their clients' positions before the court of public opinion. Public relations practitioners cannot tell their publics what to do or what to think any more than lawyers can tell the court what it must do or think. For both, it is a two-way proposition. Lawyers must interpret the law to their clients and their clients to the court of law. Public relations professionals must interpret publics and public opinion to their clients and their clients to their publics.

This book is about the many ways that have been developed to do just that. The functions, tools, and techniques are described here by professionals who have tested them in their work over years of practice. They have stood the test of time. And this description should in the long run help develop a theoretical foundation for public relations and lead to clear requirements for professional education and career development.

This book has an added dimension so crucial to the successful understanding and, ultimately, the practice of public relations. In discussing the techniques, the tools and the theories, it describes the kinds of people the profession has and should have. The individual authors themselves are the best examples of what the public relations professional should be.

For assembling this eminent array of authors, we are indebted to Bill Cantor who occupies a unique and special place in our field.

PART

I

PUBLIC RELATIONS— WHAT IT IS AND WHAT IT DOES

An Overview

Loet A. Velmans

Chairman, President, and Chief Executive Officer
Hill & Knowlton, Inc.

Any definition of public relations must proceed from a single fact that is important to remember and, seemingly, easy to forget. That is, very simply, that every act of an institution and every inaction is a form of communication that can and often does affect the way its various publics perceive it.

This fact of human and institutional life is true for any society. But its implications for public relations, as a contemporary profession, only apply to democracies. Indeed, public relations can only exist in open societies where business and government are both amenable to freely expressed opinion and

Loet A. Velmans is chairman and president of Hill & Knowlton, Inc., the world's largest public relations firm. He also became chief executive officer in 1979. He joined Hill & Knowlton in 1953. Shortly thereafter, he established the firm's first European office, in Paris.

He was born in Amsterdam, where he received his early education. At the outbreak of World War II he joined the Dutch army and served in the Far East, where he was taken prisoner. At war's end, he became information officer for his government in Singapore. He served as associate editor of a Dutch newspaper in Southeast Asia and became a correspondent in the area for several Dutch and Australian newspapers. Returning to the Netherlands in 1947, he subsequently joined a Dutch advertising agency, becoming a vice president a year later.

1

where the public itself has the power to alter proposed and existing policies. While, in the rest of this introduction, I shall talk about public relations in the corporate world, what I say applies to any organization in an open society, whether governmental, nonprofit, or free enterprise.

In such a socio-political environment, then, public relations is the way in which a corporation communicates to all its audiences, whether internal or external.

Public relations is also to whom a corporation communicates, actively or passively, openly or tacitly, aggressively or not at all (since not communicating still says something very loudly).

Public relations is also what a corporation communicates about itself explicitly, as well as what it communicates in the products and services it produces, in the way it operates its factories and offices, in the way it deals with its employees, and in the way it perceives and deals with the issues that affect it and society as a whole.

This is what public relations is—what its mission is. In fact, this mission has not changed substantially over the almost 60-year history of public relations. What has changed is the scope of that mission and the means by which that mission is undertaken. What has also changed is the degree of recognition of its integral importance to overall corporate goals.

That public relations should have changed so in scope and means is not surprising. After all, public relations exists only in the interaction between the corporate institution and the democratic public. The evolution of public relations had to take place if it was to keep up with the changes occurring on each side of that interaction.

Since World War II, those business and societal changes have been rapid and increasingly so. In the business world, we have seen, for example:

- The growth of whole new industries, especially in the financial, service, and information areas.
- The development of a world market and vast international trade.
- The coming of age of the multinational corporation.
- The emergence of new world competitors outside the European-American sphere.
- The invention of new technologies which have dramatically altered economics and social relations.

In the world "external" to business, the changes have been equally drastic and have affected both society and business alike in dramatic ways:

- A profound public mistrust of all large institutions—whether governmental or corporate—a distrust first made manifest in the United States by the antiwar movement of the Vietnam era, but of far older origins in Europe.

- A public belief that organized citizens movements were the only real way that governmental or corporate policy could be affected. This belief was a direct outcome of the minority rights, antiwar, and antinuclear movements of the 1960s and 1970s throughout the industrialized West.
- The proliferation of special interest groups, first on the liberal side of the political spectrum and then on the conservative side, with highly developed skills in publicity gathering and in confrontation techniques.
- A growing public realization that corporate policies as well as governmental policies have profound implications for the public's economic and noneconomic lives—for good as well as ill.
- A major demographic change in the population as a whole and in the work force, creating a very different kind of corporate and national citizen. Impatient with or indifferent to traditional authority, younger and better educated than work forces in the past, employees demand different treatment than in the past. The same holds true for citizens of local communities, politicians, and shareholders.
- A structural change in the nature of the industrialized economies of the world that is making the service and information industries dominant while reducing the importance of the traditional heavy industries.
- Increased vulnerability of the private enterprise corporation to events which were once considered wholly extraneous. The women's rights movement and conservationism, once only represented by entries on bestseller lists, have profoundly altered the way companies hire, promote, operate, and relate to the public and to government.

And these are only a few, though perhaps the most important few, of the changes. That they have altered the manner in which business, government, and the public interact is obvious. What is not so obvious is that they have also forced a major diversification in the ways in which corporations had to communicate and, thus, in the ways in which public relations could carry out its historical mission.

Today, public relations is no longer just a company spokesman telling a newspaper editor what the company has to say. Public relations has come to include every form of communications except product advertising.

Public relations is still corporate publicity, but it is also shareholder relations, financial relations, environmental and consumer affairs, internal communications, labor relations, broadcasting, community affairs, government relations at all levels, issue advertising, corporate identification, corporate graphics, issue response management . . . the list is nearly endless.

That is a brief sketch of what public relations *is*, but it says nothing about what public relations *does.* What public relations does is:

- Assist in creating and/or maintaining an organization's reputation;
- Help ensure an organization's short- and long-term survival; and

• Enhance an organization's ability to operate profitably and productively within the limits of the national and international economy.

Public relations performs these three vital functions by communicating; by explaining an organization's positions, problems, and solutions; by marketing an organization's products and services; and by enhancing the organization's relationships with all those who affect or who are affected by it.

The best delineation of who those publics are has been done by the former chairman of Cummins Engine Company, Irwin Miller. He has defined what he calls "corporate stakeholders," those groups who, in one way or another, have a stake in the actions of a corporation. Those stakeholders can be viewed as concentric circles which begin at the center with the stakeholder groups of employees and shareholders. Next come its customers/consumers, suppliers, plant communities, and headquarters communities. Next are the state governments where it operates, and then its national publics: the federal government, the financial community, peer companies in its own industry, and companies of similar size. Last, for many companies, are the international governmental and quasi-governmental bodies that are increasingly affecting operations.

The same list, with some modifications, holds true for multinational corporations.

For Miller, each of these groups has some stake in the actions of a corporation, but the size of each group's stake in any particular action varies depending on the action itself. Whether or not one accepts the concept that each of these groups has a "stake" in the corporation and its action, a stake which imposes specific responsibilities on the corporation, there is no question that, at the very least, these are the groups to which the corporation communicates, actively or passively.

These are also the groups to whom the corporation must listen if it is to respond to their legitimate questions and demands, to take into account their valid interests and concerns, and to make its own communications relevant and effective.

And that is what public relations does—serves as that medium of communications between the institution and its audiences, providing both with the information that each needs to make informed, responsible decisions.

This intermediary position of the public relations function is, on the one hand, essential to the function's success. However, that position is also responsible, in large part, for the difficulties the profession has at times encountered. Many members of management, at least in the past, have tended to look on public relations as superfluous, as not really part of the management team, as too reflective of extraneous concerns. At the same time, many members of the general public have tended to see public relations as manipulative, underhanded extensions of corporate policy.

Neither view was or is true. Public relations works on behalf of a corporation, but it can only do so when it can speak credibly and knowledgeably to the public, and can inform management about public concerns with equal credibility and knowledge.

Outside of the United States, the situation, mission, and purpose of public relations is the same, though at earlier stages of development. In most European countries, the profession has become as sophisticated as it is here, and management is simultaneously coming to realize its value and import-ance. Japan, too, is well on the way to this level. In most countries of the Third World, however, neither the economic nor the political situation is conducive to the growth of sophisticated public relations.

Still, in international public relations the real problems that have to be confronted have less to do with the various stages of public relations' growth than with the historical and cultural differences within and among these countries and the corporations that operate in them. We not only speak languages that are different in alphabet and vocabulary, we speak languages that are different in their very essence. We *mean* very different things. Until public relations addresses this problem, it cannot be truly called an interna-tional discipline.

I am not trying to overassert the case for public relations when I stress the complexity of what we do and the national and international implications of almost all corporate actions. Instead, I am asserting a reality that many would prefer to ignore since it can add yet another burden on already overburdened corporate managers. What this means, in my mind, is that public relations professionals must be ready and able to assist management in understanding and shouldering that burden. The burden is there and will not go away.

This burden has also created a need for more skilled, more professional communicators throughout business who can communicate the relevance of public relations to corporate operations and the significance of corporate performance and action to the outside public. This job may not have changed over the years in its aim, but it has certainly changed in its complexity.

Indeed, that complexity means that public relations must find and foster people who understand its basic functions and mission but who can also manage this function in all its variety. In a corporate setting or in a large agency, this need demands people and modes of organization that can simultaneously meet client needs; provide thoughtful, objective counsel; and create a working environment that stimulates independent thought, creativ-ity, quality of work, and self-motivation. And in both the corporate and agency settings, this means finding and training people who can manage. Public relations has, at its most advanced, outgrown its early entrepreneurial beginnings.

For the future, then, public relations needs better training and different kinds of training for its new professionals, a clear understanding that its real competition is not that bugaboo of advertising agencies, but law and management consulting firms. The future also means a continued emphasis on the kinds of in-depth, quality service that marks a "profession."

The key, here, is education and training. The complexity of the demands being put upon management (and, thereby, upon public relations professionals); the continuing diversification of audiences, concerns, issues, and means of communications; and the increasingly international nature of both business and public relations all mean more kinds of people have to enter the field and more people have to know how to manage these disparate disciplines. We will always need generalists, to be sure, just as we will always need journalists—both print and electronic. But new problems in the pharmaceutical field, for example, will require more people with medical and scientific backgrounds, just as more hostile tender offers will require more people with legal backgrounds. The profession must not only stay open to all kinds of people, it must be able to train them in the discipline itself while taking advantage of their specific knowledge and skills.

If these needs are true for public relations in the United States, they are even more important for anyone working in a public relations field that requires interaction between nations or cultures.

The future, then, will continue to bring changes in the number of areas public relations can be used in and in the ways available to it to communicate. What the future will not bring, however, is any change in what public relations is, what its mission is. As John Hill wrote in 1963, the "roots [of public relations] are fixed in the basic fact that public opinion, confused, obscure, unpredictable as it may often seem, is the ultimate ruling force in the free world. A fundamental function of public relations is to help public opinion reach conclusions by providing it with facts and interpretation of facts.... Only with the understanding and support of public opinion can [business] flourish and grow. To attain this is the main objective of public relations for private enterprise."

CHAPTER

1

GOVERNMENT RELATIONS

William R. Cox

Director, Public Affairs
Gulf Mineral Resources Company and
Western Region, Gulf Oil Corporation

PHILOSOPHICAL OVERVIEW

Public opinion creates public policy—and public relations influences public opinion!

This is the essence of this chapter.

What follows is an amplification of that statement and a description of how public relations is managed to accomplish that task. (Lobbying, a critical element and often the most visible part of government relations, is discussed in Part II, Chapter 14, and will only be mentioned here as it relates to the rest of an effective government relations function.)

We will begin by examining the effect public relations has on elected and appointed government officials, focusing on their most important public, the constituents, those individuals and organizations having a direct interest in and influence with elected officials. Then we will examine the relationship of constituents to business "stakeholders" and public relations organization and techniques to attract, inform, and generate the active support of these publics for political action by government officials. Finally, we will discuss the initiative and referendum process, which is used in some states to exclude representative government and which is the sole arena for public relations in affecting the outcome of initiatives in general elections.

First, let's examine why public relations creates public policy.

William R. Cox joined Gulf in Pittsburgh in 1970 as director of public relations, then served as director of corporate communications until being named to his current position in 1981. Prior to 1970 he was manager of public relations, Celanese Fibers Marketing Company; director of public relations, Frito-Lay, Inc., Dallas; and manager of press relations, IIT Research Institute, Chicago.

CONSTITUENTS AND STAKEHOLDERS

Government is the actual institution that society has created to enact public policy in the form of laws and regulations. While government has the power to enact public policy, it only has that power because the citizens—its constituents—permit or direct government to do so. Whether the political entity is federal, state, county, or one of the many specialized entities created by government—zoning, tax, and utility commissions, school boards, and others—each governmental entity is sensitive to the public opinion of its constituents and provides formal public hearing opportunities for those opinions to be presented.

Government-elected and appointed representatives are sensitive to what they perceive to be public opinion. More precisely, politicians are sensitive to what they perceive is *not* in the public mind as much as they are to what they perceive *is* in the public mind. The exercise of political power is inhibited by pressure from constituents. A politician would much prefer the opportunity to act freely, based upon his or her own agenda, than to be forced to modify that agenda by pressures from constituents.

In a democracy—particularly in the United States—the perceived wants and needs of constituents are the force that drives domestic as well as foreign policy at the federal level. At local and state elective office levels, constituents have even greater power to affect the public policy decisions.

The constituent and the potential power of the constituent are important elements of the political process to understand more completely before we can discuss the effective application of public relations to influence public policy.

Who is the constituent? What do we mean by "perceived constituent wants and needs"? Do constituents permit or do they direct government to enact public policy? Do constituents have the power to direct their elected representatives to do their bidding? Does the politician play any leadership role in resolving public issues? Or does he or she wait to be told by constituents what issues to solve and how?

Answers to these questions are most easily found by examining the political process, starting with the election campaign. As a candidate for elective office, the politician must first be nominated by his or her party, by elected party delegates, and/or (depending upon the process in that state) by registered party voters in a primary election. The candidate also needs money and volunteers to cover the costs of the campaign and wants at least objective news coverage and editorial support. Constituents most important to the politician as a candidate, therefore, are the political party delegates and leadership, the contributors of money and personal time to the campaign, the leaders of special interest groups (which have aligned themselves to one political party at this candidate-selection stage in the campaign), and the political and editorial writers of news media covering the campaign.

These, then, are the people within the candidate's territory who are the most influential constituents to this political candidate. They influence the candidate because they influence the registered party voters to support the candidate. It is at this prenomination stage of the political process when there must be a "meeting of the minds" between the candidate and these most influential constituents on the public issues of highest concern.

How purely democratic this process is may be argued. But it is the beginning stage of the representative form of government and at least provides avenues for all adult and literate citizens to participate if they wish. Party delegates are elected by active party members in local caucus based upon their views on those same issues of highest concern. And these or other constituents can be active in the political arms of special interest groups.

Very few citizens do participate, unfortunately, even on election day. But those who do at least vote qualify themselves, although privately at that moment, also as constituents of the elected candidate. The nominee then must campaign against other nominees to win the general election.

The nominee of the party with the most registered voters in the voting territory may need fewer additional active campaign supporters than nominees of minority parties, but all nominees still work at broadening their base of support. Thus, additional constituents are sought.

Other constituents also surface, whether they are sought or not, motivated by their own self-interest to support the candidate most likely to serve that self-interest. These special interests may be individuals or organizations, but the political candidate cannot afford to ignore any of them. The candidate must knowingly decide whose favor to attract or alienate because these constituents will decide to support one candidate or another.

The attracted special interests, whether they be unaffiliated individuals or leaders of organizations devoted to single issues or specific political philosophies, are added influential constituents to the growing family now supporting the candidate.

How the successful candidate obtains and holds the support of influential constituencies, many of whom may differ on several issues of importance, depends to a great degree on the skill of the politician and his or her campaign advisers. It is important to understand, however, that these differences also must be less important relative to others during the campaign because a diligent news media, used effectively by the opposition, will force those differences into the campaign debate.

Through this cursory examination of the election campaign process, we have identified what we mean by constituents—at least the constituents having the most influence with the elected politician. Will they continue to be most influential after election day? That's the same as asking if a successful politician ever stops being a candidate? Of course, these constituents whose support helped the politician to be elected also continue to be most influential, primarily because they have direct access to that elected official and/or they influence the opinions of important segments of the electorate to whom the politician must be responsive.

The group of influential constituents obviously is quite small relative to the electorate. But out of the electorate—those registered voters served by the elected politician—there is at least the potential for additional constituents to exert influence on their elected official. Those few who are aware of and have an interest in issues being deliberated by their elected representative can and do tell their representative how they want him or her to vote. They may do so by testifying in public hearings or by private and direct contact. Those who represent larger constituencies have more influence than others, of course, but for the astute politician, the weight of influence being exerted must be measured carefully.

Having examined some aspects of the political process, we can now answer some of our earlier questions. "Constituents" we can now define as a relatively small number of politically active people who have influence with the elected official. These constituents have the power to direct their elected representatives to support positions on issues, and they exercise that power in direct proportion to the importance of the issue to their political philosophy and self-interest.

Without exercising their will, constituents permit the elected official to act as he or she wishes, or as influenced by trusted and well-informed lobbyists, or by powerful political colleagues seeking support for a bill in return for a choice committee assignment or as a trade-off for supporting their position on another issue. Obviously, elected officials are never completely free of constituency influence. They know what their most influential constituents "back home" want them to do on many issues because they are of "like mind" with those constituents or they would not have earned their support in the first place. And often, when the issue has inherent conflicts with constituent philosophies, the smart politicians do not wait for an opinion; they ask.

But successful politicians also are leaders in resolving political issues. They are not puppets waiting to have their strings pulled by influential constituents. Successful political leaders identify issues important to their constituents and seek resolutions satisfactory to most of them.

What does all this mean to the public relations practitioner—or more importantly—to the corporate client of the public relations department or agency?

STAKEHOLDERS AND CONSTITUENTS

If we examine the preceding discussion we realize that we can insert the word "corporation" or "business" wherever we identified the "politician" or "candidate." The public relations practitioner has used the word "publics," or more recently, "stakeholders," to describe our client's "constituents." The "campaign" for a corporation is a race for the support of these "constituents" in the marketplace or "electorate" to sell products and services, to attract capital, or generate support for ideas, the latter being the political role of public relations.

Stakeholders are individuals or groups whose support is an important factor in the successful conduct of business or any other social activity. The number and diversity of a corporation's stakeholders has exploded over the past 20 years, primarily due to increasing public and, therefore, government intervention in and regulation of business. A business manager in 1960 was primarily concerned with investors, employees, and customers. Government was little more than a tax collector to the typical manager of 1960. It was difficult enough to balance the interests of these three publics, much less devote daily attention to government too. Lobbyists covered the "government job," virtually alone. But other citizens were being affected by the manager's decisions and demanded to become party to those political decisions, directly and through government regulation. So a multitude of new stakeholders evolved, and today's successful manager—and, therefore, the public relations function—must deal effectively with all of them.

An illustrated stakeholders' analysis of Gulf Oil Corporation (see figures 1.1 and 1.2) comparing 1960 with 1980 is typical of this growth. (Symbols +,

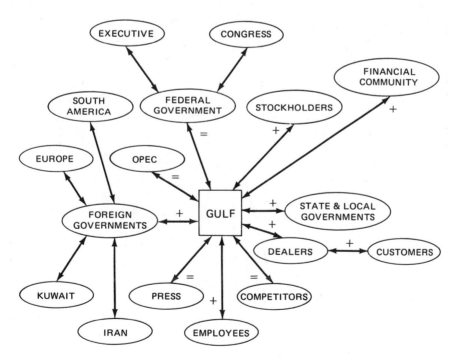

Figure 1.1 1960 Stakeholders analysis of the Gulf Oil Corporation.

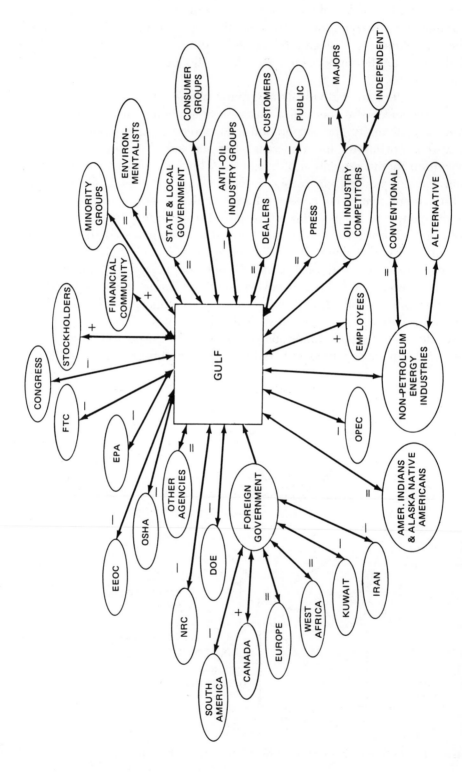

Figure 1.2 1980 Stakeholders analysis of the Gulf Oil Corporation.

⁻, ⁼ represent tendencies to support, oppose, or be neutral on issues affecting Gulf). And this growth is likely to continue for U.S. businesses as new public expectations continue to evolve and citizens organize to achieve these expectations politically.

PUBLIC RELATIONS AND STAKEHOLDERS

Thus, the practice of public relations has had to evolve to help business managers function effectively in the ever-changing political arena.

As a result of the political impact on the oil business, public relations practices of oil companies have not just evolved—they have leaped—as the proverbial cat from the hot stove—and for this very same reason. Until the 1960s, oil companies concentrated their attention, including their public relations efforts, on the "big three"—i.e., investors, employees, and customers. And they served them well, communicating their good return on investment, competitive incomes, and rock-bottom energy prices (plus premium giveaways with every consumer purchase). But government policies in the United States and foreign oil-producing nations changed all that, virtually overnight.

The limited focus of oil industry public relations rarely supported the lobbying effort, leaving large segments of the public uninformed about the industry—and the industry uninformed about the concerns of large segments of the public.

The Santa Barbara oil spill in 1969, with its temporary devastation to that part of the California coastline, vividly televised with its dead birds, fish, and just plain gook, did far more long-lasting damage to the oil industry public reputation, the U.S. energy supply capability, and the U.S. economy than it did to the beaches of Santa Barbara.

Legislation and regulations pressed by environmental groups, and publicly supported, stopped offshore oil and gas exploration and delayed the Alaska pipeline for almost a decade. The United States continued to deplete its low-cost reserves and increased its dependence on imported oil.

Then, as world oil supplies and consumption balanced, the Arab-Israeli War erupted in 1973 and OPEC, the Organization of Petroleum Exporting Countries, suddenly gained political unity. The Arab Oil Embargo in 1973–74 scared U.S. politicians witless. Less than five percent of U.S. imports were affected; but federally legislated allocation systems put fuel in the wrong places at the wrong times, and a minor shortage (which later studies showed the oil industry had reduced further through international oil trading) became a real shortage for consumers. Motorists panicked, shifting gasoline inventories immediately from the limited industry storage and transportation system into full gas tanks of all cars. And guess who was blamed for the long gas station lines? Not since World War II have all

Americans been so united against one "villain"—in this case, *big oil companies*.

Probably the most popular social issues of that decade, other than equal rights and the peace movement, were the consumer and environmental movements. And oil companies became magnets for all of them. Politicians were able to hide their failures to establish a coherent national energy policy by blaming the nation's increasing energy problems on suspected chicanery of the oil companies. Price controls on crude oil, gasoline, and other refined fuels under complex federally-regulated formulas continued long past the inflation-fighting price control era of the Nixon administration. In fact, deregulation of crude oil and gasoline prices was not completely accomplished until President Reagan took office in 1980. Natural gas prices, controlled since 1954, continue to date.

If I have given the impression that oil companies have only recently been involved with government, I need to correct that now. Almost since the day oil was produced, local, state, and federal governments have been involved in the oil business. But for that first hundred years or so, government and the oil business generally have been "partners." Some would say the oil companies were the senior partners in the arrangement; certainly this was the case outside the United States. The reason was simple. Oil produced wealth. In the United States, local and state governments quickly benefited their constituents with legislation giving them a piece of the action—taxes and royalties that for oil-producing states have been the prime source of revenue ever since. It was powerful federal legislators from those states who obtained federal tax incentives (most notably, the oil depletion allowance) that stimulated increased exploration to assure continued growth for the industry and ever-increasing local tax and royalty revenues to benefit their constituents.

But during the 1970s, oil companies discovered they had become, at best, the junior partners with government. In fact, the common perception of oil company managers was that the industry had become a victimized junior partner, being cheated out of its assets almost to the point of unconstitutional usurping of private property. Most foreign oil-producing governments had nationalized oil companies over the decade of the 1970s. (The U.S. Treasury by 1980 was taking some 85 percent of the price of a domestic-produced barrel of crude oil sold by an oil company through a combination of taxes—most notably, through the Carter administration's "windfall profits tax," which actually is an excise tax on the sales price of crude oil.)

Once the oil industry managers discovered they were losing in the public game of politics, they scrambled to recover whatever political influence they could. What these companies have done and how they have done it varies from company to company. They all have lessons to offer to public relations practitioners examining their role in affecting public policy in the field of government relations.

ORGANIZATION STRUCTURE NEEDED

Gulf recognized that some basic facts were necessary to assume before it could provide an organization and program that could function effectively in the new political arena. These basic assumptions were:

1. Public credibility of business was low, particularly for oil companies, which were blamed for energy shortages and price increases.
2. The "profit" system was generally misunderstood, and the public was angered by oil industry profit increases during this period of gasoline shortages.
3. Public understanding of the energy business was so low that any industry critic could misinform the public and discredit the industry easily.
4. Most of these new stakeholders would not be aware, unless they were informed, that their interests were similar to Gulf's and resource development industries generally, due to the complexity of the energy issues.
5. Industry critics—leaders of consumer and environmental movements—were using effective public relations techniques to gain more political support for their positions to keep prices low and prevent oil exploration on federal lands and in offshore federal waters.
6. Mass media advertising by oil companies to generate support for industry positions on energy policy issues was ineffective and even counterproductive due in large measure to the low credibility mentioned above.
7. The industry's old allies—the congressional delegations from oil-producing states of Texas, Oklahoma, and Louisiana—had lost their power due to changes in the congressional seniority system and were overwhelmed by congressional delegations from energy-consuming states, all activated by the effective public relations efforts of consumer and environmental groups, now well funded with highly sophisticated Washington and local community staffs, volunteers, and communications techniques.
8. Gulf had to identify and develop new allies or stakeholders to support its and the industry's positions on political issues. These allies would have to have similar beliefs in the private enterprise and profit system, have a self-interest in the development of adequate U.S. energy resources, and/or a similar self-interest in moderating consumer and environmental regulations. These stakeholders must include moderate forces within the consumer and environmental organizations.

9. Influential constituents of congressional leaders should be a priority target for Gulf's stakeholder program.
10. It would take a long-term commitment of human and financial resources before Gulf would be able to develop a politically effective effort.
11. Public issue management had to be integrated formally with the corporation's business planning system.
12. Gulf had to create a new organization with additional skills to accomplish all of this.
13. Gulf's shareholders, most employees, customers, and consumers were as poorly informed as the general public about energy problems, solutions, and related issues.

Basic structural staff changes were Gulf's first step following a lengthy analysis by a task force made up of representatives of line operations and staffs of public relations, government relations, advertising, human resources, and law.

The new structure was called the Public Affairs Department and centralized all public relations, advertising, government relations, international and U.S. issue analysis, adding a third-party advocacy function, a planning function, and public affairs directors as "account executives" to provide the support of the department for each of the corporation's various divisions or profit centers (called "strategy centers" at Gulf). The vice president of the Public Affairs Department became the account executive for, and reported directly to the Gulf chairman and chief executive officer. A group of senior public affairs directors, reporting to the vice president, are responsible for coordinating the department's policies and programs. (See figure 1.3.)

Senior corporate and strategy center management determines public affairs policy and positions on public issues through a corporate Public Issues Committee, chaired by the public affairs vice president. Committee members are heads of other staff functions—i.e., tax, law, human resources, and strategy center presidents or executive vice presidents.

SENIOR MANAGEMENT INVOLVED

Researched public issues, public and political environmental analysis, and proposed positions on issues are developed by the department's issue analysis and planning staff, with input gathered by strategy center public affairs directors; and drafts are provided to the Public Issues Committee for review and committee recommendations. These are then recommended to the Gulf CEO for decision, which often results in approval, but sometimes modification or, although rarely, rejection.

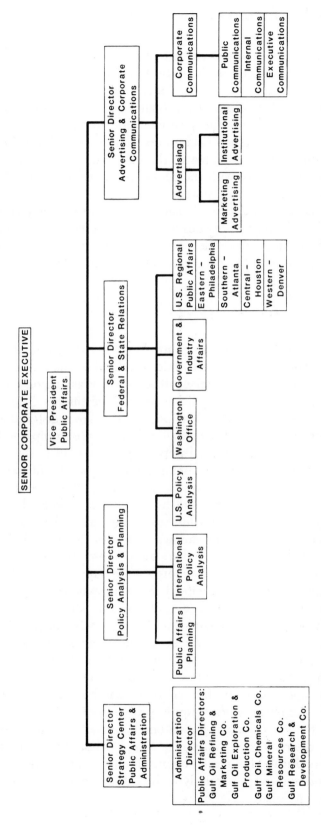

Figure 1.3 Public affairs department organizational chart.

A major benefit of the process is that the top management "buys into" the issue by being involved in the determination of the corporate position. Management then supports and becomes personally active in the public affairs effort involved in affecting the issue's outcome. Also, when strategy center managers differ on issue positions due to the differences in their businesses, the Public Issues Committee can resolve those differences— easily, when they are quantifiable in the corporate interest, or because of their increasing familiarity with the philosophical stance of the CEO when faced with similar conflicting views.

This committee and the issue-management process also enables Gulf to anticipate and track emerging issues well enough to consider them as factors in the formal business planning system and integrates the Public Affairs Department's plans with the corporate and strategy centers' business plans.

PUBLIC AFFAIRS DEPARTMENT UNITS

The *issue analysis and planning* unit also helps determine the impact on Gulf of positions on specific federal, state, and local legislative and regulatory issues at the request of public affairs staff in the Washington office, and in regional offices located where Gulf has major investments. The process for this begins with the Gulf public affairs people, who are registered lobbyists at the federal and state levels. They obtain information on proposed legislation or regulatory issues with potential implications for Gulf businesses; obtain copies of bills as soon as available; obtain analysis from this unit and other staff departments; and then, based upon clear priorities, they "work the issues," as necessary, by direct lobbying and by generating stakeholder support.

Government and industry affairs is a unit created to develop Gulf's stakeholders and coordinate communications with them on priority issues.

Computerized mailing lists of shareholders, employees, royalty owners, and other individuals attracted to energy issue support were developed to enable mailings targeted to specific U.S. congressional districts, or state representative or senate districts, of Gulf's priority states. Gulf can identify automatically in each letter the name and address of the recipient's legislator. Direct mail consultants help improve the effectiveness of the letters.

The Government Advisory Council developed by Gulf is a group of politically influential citizens, most of whom have no direct or indirect business connection to Gulf, but all of whom have a direct interest in resolving U.S. domestic energy supply problems. GAC members all have direct access to one or more legislators because they have been active supporters of their election campaigns, are local leaders of their political parties, head politically influential organizations, or any combination of the above. Gulf communicates regularly with GAC members through meetings, mailgrams, and newsletters.

GAC members are identified by regional public affairs staff and other Gulf employees who are familiar with local and state politics. Active GAC members change more gradually than elections change office holders. GAC members tend to remain equally influential, and their commitment to the issues grows with their knowledge and involvement.

When an important issue is approaching a government point of decision, GAC members are asked to call, write, or visit their legislators (at home or in their offices). Gulf notifies the GAC of the current status of the issue and provides them any information needed to supplement previously provided information. Then regional Gulf public affairs people will conduct phone follow-up to learn how each legislator responded to their contact.

This effort may be directed at legislators or even the "administration" (whether a state governor or the president) to support proenergy legislation or to seek a veto of antienergy legislation. Proenergy legislation may be reform of environmental legislation that, in practice, is stopping energy development without benefit to the environment (some aspects of the Clean Air Act fall in this category); decontrol of natural gas prices; or tax reductions or incentives to increase energy exploration and development. (See figure 1.4.)

The traditional public relations function at Gulf is carried out by the *advertising and corporate communications* unit of the Public Affairs Department. Advertising, publicity, executive correspondence and speech writing, and internal or employee communications are the services provided by this unit. All these activities support the political objectives and programs of the corporation, as well as other public relations and marketing support objectives. I will only concentrate on the political applications because the rest are discussed in other chapters.

Working with the other department's units, advertising and corporate communications provides support for any priority political issue, such as speeches; news releases on those speeches; by-lined editorials and articles for newspapers, magazines, and employee and shareholder publications; videotaped programs primarily for employees and, occasionally, video and audio tape "electronic" news releases for TV and radio news or public affairs programming; special publications, such as one concentrating on environmental issues and company business practices; or a profit explanation insert with credit card invoices.

This unit also arranges most interviews and responds to most news inquiries. Regional public affairs staff is responsible for news in their regions, but coordinates these with corporate communications to assure continuity and consistency.

The *Washington office* is the unit responsible for lobbying federal legislative and regulatory issues. Because the nation's capital is the nation's news center, the Washington office also has news media contact responsibility there.

STUDIES ON THIRD-PARTY ADVOCACY

- A Burson-Marsteller study released in 1982 reported that members of Congress overwhelmingly stated that individually composed letters from constituents are the most effective means of communicating with their elected representatives.

- A Texas A&M survey of shareholders of energy, chemicals, and forest product companies reports:
  - 96% of the shareholders voted in the 1980 presidential election, compared to 53% of the general public.
  - 84% of shareholders think that executives of firms in which they hold stock should speak out on public policy issues (only 8% think executives should *not* speak out).
  - 72% of the shareholders voted for Ronald Reagan and 16% for Jimmy Carter.
  - 65% agreed with corporate positions on public policy issues presented to shareholders.
  - 74% think companies should analyze public policy issues for their shareholders.
  - 90% of shareholders surveyed said they'd like to receive such analyses.

- Business lobbyists report:
  - Legislators tell us, "Yes, I understand your positions, but what do my constituents back home think about it?"
  - Some proindustry legislators have requested grassroots efforts in their districts to help them support a controversial issue.
  - Antibusiness coalitions of organizations have been able to flood federal legislators with as many as several hundred thousand letters on a particularly popular issue.
  - Congressional leaders alone are not able to influence the outcome of legislative issues. Each voting member is important.

Figure 1.4 Third-party advocacy illustration.

The other lobbying offices of the Public Affairs Department are the regional offices, organizationally centralized under the *U.S. public affairs* unit of the department. These public affairs people are responsible for all government and public relations within their geographic assignments. Each person is responsible for one or more states, or for one city or one region of a state where Gulf has major investments. Multistate regions match regions covered by regional trade associations in order to use efficiently the state government affairs coordination provided by those associations.

THIRD-PARTY ADVOCACY (STAKEHOLDER) ORGANIZATIONS

An essential ingredient to an effective centrally organized Public Affairs Department is having all charitable contributions and business, trade, and other nonprofessional organization memberships either centralized within the public affairs budget or, for those contributions and dues budgets managed by strategy centers or the corporate foundation, public affairs is represented on management committees overseeing the use of these budgets. A portion of the charitable contribution budget traditionally is used to benefit community services, the arts, and education where Gulf has business investments. Another portion is membership dues and program support for organizations whose leaders and members are important existing or potential third-party advocates for Gulf positions on political issues, such as specialized trade and business organizations; various industry coalitions, such as the Highway Users Federation; or credible objective sources for political issue information, such as the League of Women Voters. Program support contributions help provide public speaking opportunities before these organizations, either at conventions or before their policy-making groups.

Contributions also can help new organizations in their formative stage— and in the past decade, Gulf has helped several new groups organize because they have been devoted to the political support of public policies needed to foster development of U.S. energy supplies. Membership and support for these organizations has broadened, of course, increasing the influence and the credibility of their efforts.

Most of these organizations' members are business oriented, but in some cases they also represent minority groups, such as black, Hispanic, and Indian business and career interests.

Membership in business and trade associations, such as the Chamber of Commerce, Association of Commerce and Industry, and oil and gas, and mining associations pertinent to Gulf's interests, also is centralized in the public affairs budget, even though line management is actively involved in most of the committees and as officers of these organizations. Public affairs people are active in the government and public relations committees of these associations, to represent Gulf's interests in their development of positions on public issues and programs that affect the political results of these issues as legislation evolves and is acted upon in the state and federal political process.

A HYPOTHETICAL CASE

Public relations is used to support legislative lobbying at the state and federal levels and is used entirely to affect the state initiative and referendum process. First, we will examine a partly hypothetical legislative effort; then we will discuss the initiative and referendum.

We will use a federal legislative example because the federal process provides more time to use most of the public relations tools and techniques. This example is based upon an actual legislative issue. It is modified here to describe more completely than would the actual case history, how public relations can fully support the lobbying effort throughout the legislative process.

During the late 1970s and early 1980s, when antioil industry sentiment was at its peak, many independently owned service station retailers sought federal and state legislation to force oil companies out of the gasoline retailing business. They argued that oil companies could use their profit from oil production and refining to subsidize their retailing operations by using lower retail prices to force competition out of business. Divestiture legislation was passed in Maryland and in weakened amended forms in four other states and the District of Columbia. It was attempted at the federal level, and still returns periodically at the federal and other state levels.

To simplify matters, let's identify our divestiture legislation example as S–10 in the U.S. Senate and HR–101 in the U.S. House of Representatives. A Democrat senator from Ohio introduced S–10. The Democrats control the Senate and the House in this example and, therefore, committee leadership and the majority in committee memberships.

The Senate and House bills have been assigned to the Energy and Natural Resource Committees of both houses. Most of the work and legislative time spent on each bill, the hearings and the markups, will be done by subcommittees of each full committee—the Fossil and Synthetic Fuels Subcommittee of the House Energy and Natural Resources Committee, and the Energy and Mineral Resources Subcommittee of the Senate full committee. The House subcommittee has 13 Democrats and 9 Republicans, and the Senate subcommittee has 5 Democrats and 4 Republicans—and the Senate bill's author is Senate subcommittee chairman.

Through the trade association committee structure of the American Petroleum Institute, a "divestiture steering committee" is formed by the oil company members to establish strategy, plans, and coordinate the industry's efforts to defeat these bills.

Some steering committee members argue that "it's hopeless in the House, so let's concentrate our efforts on the Senate subcommittee." Others prevail with the argument that "writing off the House will produce a terrible bill" that could make the industry's case harder—and that House members are more sensitive to constituency pressures generated by an effective industry campaign effort. So it's decided to direct the industry effort to defeat or amend the legislation in both subcommittees. The steering committee members from API member companies are API staff, and executives and managers of member companies representing law, marketing, lobbying, and public relations. Gulf has named to the steering committee its marketing vice president and its senior director for federal and state relations in the Public Affairs Department.

Gulf, as other oil companies, has also formed its own committee on this issue, chaired by the same public affairs senior director. The Gulf committee also contains the marketing vice president; and from the Public Affairs Department, the director of corporate communications; the policy analyst most familiar with Gulf's marketing issues, the director of legislative relations from the Washington office; the director of U.S. public affairs (who supervises the regional public affairs units); and the director of government and industry affairs (who supervises the staff that has primary responsibility for Gulf's stakeholder program).

The API Steering Committee and the member companies develop compatible positions on both bills (no easy task, but essential before an effective program can be conducted). They also agree on strategy, communications programs, and timing of those programs; and they develop all the communications materials that will be used.

Industry Washington and regional lobbyists help the steering committee analyze each of the 31 members of both House and Senate subcommittees. Lobbyists' consensus is that in the House subcommittee, five members will support the bill, five will likely oppose it (supporting the industry's position), and three members' voting records indicate they might go either way, the "swing votes" on the subcommittee. In the Senate subcommittee, lobbyists agree that four members are likely to agree with the industry position, four will support the bill, and one is the "swing vote."

Industry public relations efforts, therefore, will concentrate on the congressional districts of the three "swing vote" House members, the five House members likely to support the industry's position, and the states of the one "swing vote" senator and the four senators thought to philosophically support the industry's position.

THE LOCAL ANALYSIS AND CAMPAIGN

Companies with major investments, the most employees, and a public affairs representative on site in targeted states and congressional districts are given responsibility for adapting and implementing the campaign in their states or districts.

Gulf volunteers to manage the industry's efforts in New Mexico, represented by the "swing vote" senator and one of the "swing vote" House subcommittee members.

We will now concentrate on the local analysis and campaign as it is conducted in New Mexico. Let's call our politicians Senator Jones and Congressman Smith.

Knowing who they are and the constituencies of both of them, the Gulf public affairs director in New Mexico organizes his own committee, including a Gulf jobber who was a campaign supporter of Congressman Smith and is a board member of the New Mexico Oil Jobbers Association; the chairman of the state Chamber of Commerce, who helped support Senator Jones; other oil company public affairs people located in the state; and the vice president of an industry-labor coalition organization called New Mexicans for Jobs and Energy.

The Gulf public affairs director, as chairman of the New Mexico Divestiture Committee, shares with the committee copies of both bills, the industry analysis of the bills, including arguments against them, background data substantiating industry arguments, examples of proposed constituent letters, newspaper and 60-second broadcast editorials, proposed organization resolutions opposing the bills, speeches of 5-, 10-, and 20-minute duration, and literature for handout or mailings.

It was decided by the industry steering committee that mass media advertising would not be used in this campaign because it would be too costly and would probably backfire as "an example of the advertising power of big business being used against small business." They also know that supporters of the legislation have not used advertising in their previous efforts at the state levels. All materials were prepared under the direction of the steering committee, but are intended to be adapted for use by each company, coordinated by each state committee.

Local committee analysis describes both Senator Jones and Congressman Smith as politically moderate Democrats, likely to support the "little guy," and receiving most of their campaign support from owners of small to middle-sized New Mexico-based businesses (some of them oil company jobbers, who would not be affected directly by this legislation).

Many of New Mexico's businesses sell products and services to energy companies. New Mexico Democrats generally are more conservative politically than, for example, Massachusetts Democrats. Although conservatives generally support private enterprise values, many believe big business "tends to be predatory" and small businesses, therefore, should be protected somehow from big business. It is likely, the committee reasons, that many New Mexicans, without being more informed, may favor the independent service station owners' position supporting both bills. Briefing the business community, therefore, on the oil industry's position on these bills becomes an important step in the New Mexico campaign.

Timing for public relations plans to be implemented is directed by the industry's steering committee, which is tracking the progress of the legislation, preparing and coordinating testimony for industry representatives to present, and recruiting third-party advocates from universities and "think tanks" to testify on studies whose anticonsumer results verify the industry's position against the legislation.

In New Mexico, the following program is conducted.

1. Stakeholders are identified by committee members.
    a. Shareholders, credit card customers, existing and retired employees, oil company branded jobbers and distributors, suppliers, oil and natural gas royalty owners.
    b. People and organizations with no direct interest in oil companies, but a direct interest in the divestiture issue and likely to support a free market philosophy and competition in gasoline retailing, such as retail chain outlets with auto service centers, business and trade associations, influential third parties (such as Gulf's Governmental Advisory Council members in New Mexico, the American Automobile Association, the League of Women Voters), and business-labor coalition organizations (i.e., Highway Users Conference, Americans for Rational Energy Alternatives, and New Mexicans for Jobs and Energy).
    c. Editorial page writers of newspapers, local magazines, and broadcast stations most influential in the state and in Congressman Smith's district.
2. Communications responsibility for each stakeholder individual and group is assigned by the state committee to each member and company and implemented to meet the timetable set by the industry steering committee.
    a. Meetings are held with the identified third-party organizations' boards and public policy committees; and speeches are delivered before their full memberships to generate resolutions and mail to the legislators supporting open competition in the retailing market and opposition to S–10 and HR–101. Organizations send their resolutions to Senator Jones and Congressman Smith. Organizations' leaders are assisted in preparing articles in the organization periodicals to their members and placing by-lined editorials for "Op-Ed" newspaper pages and letters to editors.
    b. Editorial page editors and broadcast station owners and editorial writers are briefed by company experts on the issue and provided background information.
    c. As the subcommittees' votes on S–10 and HR–101 approach, companies send letters and mailgrams to their New Mexico shareholders, advocates influential with Senator Jones and Congressman Smith, existing and retired employees, credit card customers, suppliers, jobbers and distributors, royalty owners—and from previously briefed trade, business, and other organizations and coalitions, to their members—urging all to write to Senator Jones and those in Congressman Smith's district, to him, in opposition of the bills' anticonsumer proposals.

Companies and organizations with computerized mailing lists matching zip codes to congressional districts are able to target mail specifically to Congressman Smith's district. Stakeholders of Gulf and other companies become advocates of the industry position—and merge to become the most active constituents of Senator Jones and Congressman Smith on this issue. Senator Jones and Congressman Smith must weigh these constituents' position against the position of their independent service station dealers' association and examine the facts provided by lobbyists on both sides of this legislation, paying more attention to this than any other issue faced that year.

How they voted, or how the two subcommittees might vote in this hypothetical case, is irrelevant to the point. What is relevant is that the practice of political citizenship is the right and responsibility of all individuals and organizations in this country, and business must wage its campaigns effectively to earn the right to continue functioning efficiently in the competitive marketplace. And public relations plays a vital role in any successful campaign.

STATE GOVERNMENT AFFAIRS

States are becoming increasingly active in regulating and taxing business. Individual state legislatures are meeting longer and considering more bills each year. About 250,000 bills were considered at the state level during the 1981–82 legislative cycle. Some 10,000 of these affected the energy industry specifically and many thousands more had some impact on business generally. Despite the higher speed with which state legislation moves, at least some of all the public relations tools and techniques mentioned in the above federal example can be and are applied by business to support state lobbying efforts.

THE POPULAR INITIATIVE AND REFERENDUM

Public relations, as applied to political campaigns, is used entirely to support positions in the popular initiative and referendum process. (See figure 1.5.)

Twenty-three state constitutions currently provide their state electorate with the power to propose and adopt laws and constitutional amendments by the initiative process. Twenty-four states allow some form of popular referendum, which is a mechanism for the electorate to approve or reject legislation that has already been approved by the legislature and the governor. Of these 24 states, 21 also have the popular initiative process.

There were some 150 initiative campaigns in 23 states in 1982. Five

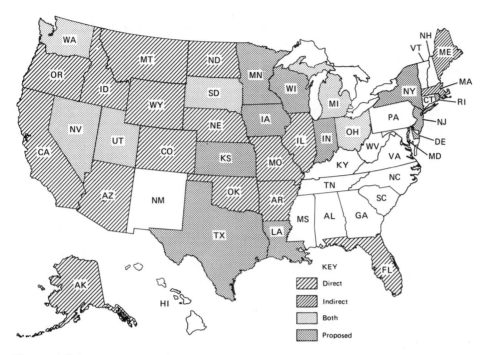

Figure 1.5 Initiatives in the states (1980). The *direct initiative*, currently in 15 states, allows petitioners to present a constitutional amendment or statutory proposal directly to the voters for approval or rejection. The *indirect initiative* enables petitioners to present a similar proposal to the legislature and subsequently to the voters if the legislature fails to enact the measure within a specified period of time. This process is used in eight states, six of which use the direct initiative as well.

states—California, Oregon, Washington, Montana, and Michigan—had 63 percent of all these initiatives and referenda on their ballots. (See figures 1.6 and 1.7.)

A campaign to support or defeat an initiative or referendum is as expensive as any political campaign because the entire electorate is the target. Public relations and advertising agencies specializing in political campaign management are frequently retained by sponsors and opponents of these ballot issues. Sophisticated public attitude measurement and analysis, and tested advertising messages appealing to specific segments of the electorate are keystones of the campaign.

Some important public relations aspects of initiative petitions are:

- need to determine public attitudes
- need to identify various internal and external audiences
- need to develop campaign message
- need to identify communications techniques
- need to monitor and adjust campaign

STATE	1950-59	1960-69	1970-78	TOTAL	APPROVED 1950-78
Arizona	3	5	1	9	6
Arkansas	9	6	3	18	7
California	8	6	7	21	5'
Colorado	8	8	12	28	10
Florida	NA	NA	2	2	1
Illinois	NA	NA	-	-	-
Michigan	3	1	10	14	5
Missouri	-	1	5	6	1
Montana	NA	NA	3	3	1
Nebraska	2	4	1	7	3
Nevada	2	1	1	4	3
North Dakota	16	18	27	61	26
Ohio	1	1	11	13	1
Oklahoma	4	5	2	11	-
Oregon	8	3	7	18	6
South Dakota	-	-	-	-	-
Total	64	59	92	215	75

NA: This form of popular initiative not available during period shown.

Figure 1.6 Number of proposed constitutional amendments as a result of direct initiatives (1950–1978).

The problem, of course, is that complex issues are won or lost on the basis of slogans—images of ideas conveyed in 30- and 60-second commercials. The initiative and referendum process replaces the system of representative government with "bumper sticker" politics. There are signs of the electorate's disenchantment with the initiative process in recent years. Fewer

SUBJECT	NUMBER OF PROPOSED CONSTITUTIONAL AMENDMENTS	NUMBER OF PROPOSED LAWS
• State Government Organization and Administration (deals with civil service, judiciary, departmental organization and official salaries)	62	106
• State and Local Taxes and Tax Limits (dedication of tax receipts, selective tax reductions or exemptions, property tax limits, expenditure ceilings, and tax burden shifting)	39	69
• Legislative Apportionment, Membership, and Compensation (realignment of legislative districts and legislative salaries)	26	32
• Liquor Control, Gambling, and Other Social-Moral Issues (removal of curbs on wagering, liquor sales, drinking age, obscenity, drugs, gun control, and blue laws)	22	56
• Environment, Conservation and Natural Resources (clean air, land use, bottle bills, coastal zone management, petroleum production taxes or restrictions on production of coal, uranium or other natural resources)	6	42

Figure 1.7 Number of ballot questions by major subject area (1950–1978).

STATE	1950-59	1960-69	1970-78	TOTAL	APPROVED 1950-78
Alaska	–	2	6	8	4
Arizona	13	3	3	19	6
Arkansas	2	3	2	7	4
California	8	4	14	26	11
Colorado	1	3	7	11	3
Idaho	2	–	3	5	4
Missouri	1	–	2	3	2
Montana	2	1	6	9	6
Nebraska	1	–	1	2	–
North Dakota	12	20	14	46	27
Oklahoma	2	4	2	8	1
Oregon	6	4	11	21	12
Utah	2	1	2	5	2
Washington	12	11	14	37	18
Wyoming	NA	–	–	–	–
Total	64	56	87	207	100

NA: This form of popular initiative not available during period shown.

Figure 1.8 Number of proposed laws as a result of direct initiative (1950–1978).

initiatives have been able to qualify with enough petition signatures. And of those that qualified, most have been defeated.

It's too soon to predict which way the initiative and referendum process will go. But as long as it continues to be an option for political change, public relations practitioners must be ready to apply their craft to affect the outcome in favor of their clients' interests. (See figures 1.8 and 1.9.)

- The obligatory or compulsory referendum requires the legislature to submit an enacted measure, usually a constitutional amendment, to the voters for their approval;

- the optional or non-binding referendum allows the legislature the option of submitting a measure to the voters for their opinion; and

- the popular referendum gives the electorate the opportunity to vote upon a measure enacted by the legislature, upon petition within a prescribed period of time.

States with referendum available:

Alaska	Idaho	Michigan	New Mexico*	South Dakota
Arizona	Kentucky*	Missouri	North Dakota	Utah
Arkansas	Maine	Montana	Ohio	Washington
California	Maryland*	Nebraska	Oklahoma	Wyoming
Colorado	Massachusetts	Nevada	Oregon	

* These states do not have direct or indirect initiative.

Figure 1.9 The referendum.

LEGAL CONSIDERATIONS

Laws control how citizens, including business, can become involved in politics. The corporation is more limited by law than the private citizen. Public relations practitioners must be familiar with the changing federal laws and the differing state laws affecting every aspect of business involvement in politics—from lobbying to the tax treatment of related business expenses.

CONCLUSION

Yesterday's business practices are no longer acceptable, as measured by today's public yardstick. Public expectations are continuing to change the standards within which business must operate. Stakeholders, the individuals and organizations taking an active interest in how business is conducted, continue to grow in number, strength, and sophistication. It's a healthy trend that can only continue. It's also a natural extension of the democratic process and bodes well for our nation as it attracts involvement of larger numbers of our citizens. For public relations practitioners, it means an increasing challenge to assure our clients an effective voice in government. The corporate executive, frustrated by increasing public intervention in his business plan, may ask, "when will all this end?" Public affairs counsel must answer, "when public expectations stop changing." Business executives who want to function competitively in a dynamic economic climate must function just as competitively in the dynamic political climate. They go hand in hand.

POLICY PLANNING

Marshall C. Lewis

Vice President, Public Information and Communications
U.S. Committee for Energy Awareness (Washington)

Among the difficulties in presenting a coherent explanation of public
affairs planning and management is that no one agrees on what to call it. You
may, for example, prefer "issues management," which implies proactivism in
the management of the public relations function, although some may find it
conceited or manipulative to suggest that public issues can or should be
"managed" in a free society. "Public affairs" is ordinarily taken to mean the
comprehensive task of managing relationships with a corporation's various
external publics, with special emphasis on government. Ditto for "external
relations," "corporate affairs," or even "public relations." So simply put the
words "planning and managing" in front of your favorite title, and we'll
proceed from there.

By whatever name, my purpose is to present a sense of the holistic
process by which communications programs can help corporations deal with
the social, economic, and ultimately political issues which may affect their
success and survival. Perhaps this has always been the definition of "public
relations" in its best and broadest context. As such, I view it more as an art
form than a science, and I ask the reader's patience with my lack of "text
book" specificity, numerous subjective judgments, and a confusing tendency
to use "public relations" and "public affairs" interchangeably. Simply put, our
job is to employ our special communications skills to create a *climate of*

Marshall C. Lewis, formerly director of corporate communications for Union Carbide
Corporation, is vice president of public information and communication for the United States
Committee for Energy Awareness in Washington, D.C. He has been communications officer
of other major corporations, as well as a senior executive of prominent advertising agencies and
a member of industry communications committees.

support for those public policies which are most amenable to the private sector in general and to our own enterprise in particular.[1]

It may be useful to recognize unequivocally that we are being paid to promote the *self-interest* of our client or corporation, no more, no less. Lest anyone feel guilty about that, we should also recognize that we have strong, vocal competitors in this self-interested competition for public support, not only from other interest groups, but also from other corporations who may not see their self-interest the way we do. We'll say more about this later. For now, let it suffice that virtually no matter of economic or social policy goes uncontested in America's political arena: protectionism versus free trade, private capital formation versus government's share of the GNP, regulation versus deregulation, industrial and mineral development versus the wilderness and the environment, and so on ad infinitum. We *are* a contentious, litigious society, and to believe otherwise is at best naive and at worst to be ignorant of what the public relations professional is hired to do.

It is not the purpose of this chapter to deal with the process of conflict resolution or the manner in which disputants can be persuaded to find points on which they are willing to compromise, although these involve skills which one would expect to find in mature public relations professionals. Compromise and concession are the very nature of the democratic process, but I believe that public affairs can best be understood by first thinking about it as a "win-lose" situation for the practitioner. Compromise is what we do when all else fails.

Let me elaborate. One of the best-known definitions of public relations is "the engineering of public consent"—public consent, that is, which permits an institution to pursue its private activities with a minimum of public opposition or governmental intervention. Indeed, in the process of managing a large enterprise and establishing achievable goals, whether short or long range, there is the underlying *assumption* that one's products, processes, or services will pass the test of public consent. Conversely, it would be foolhardy to invest dollars or energy in a product or service which flies in face of one's assumptions about public consent, as it would be equally absurd to ignore cost constraints, market potential, and competition.

For example:

> If, ten or twelve years ago, you had been the public relations officer in a
> major public utility, what counsel would you have given your
> management as it planned the construction of nuclear plants to meet
> future demand for electricity? An extreme case, perhaps; and you might
> be forgiven for your failure to foresee "The China Syndrome," Three

---

1. Corporations are what I know best, but the principles and techniques related in this chapter are generally applicable to other institutions and causes as well. Also, for the sake of simplicity, I use masculine third-person pronouns throughout the text.

Mile Island, and the emergence of what has been called "nuclear phobia" on the part of a large and vocal segment of the public. (Of course, you could also fill a separate auditorium with [utility company] economists who guessed wrong about the nation's economic growth and were, therefore, equally off base on their projections of demand for electricity.)

Similarly, how would you have counseled the management of AT&T ten years ago on the prospects for a 180-degree change in the judicial and legislative policy which had been embedded in the classic definition of a "regulated monopoly"? If you had been clairvoyant, you might have had some inkling of the forthcoming "communications explosion," in which case you might have assumed that other corporations would coalesce into a powerful constituency whose common purpose was to *compete* with AT&T in areas traditionally regarded as the private preserve of the regulated Bell System.

If you had been Johnson & Johnson's or Bristol-Myers' public relations officer two years ago, would you have recognized the potential for lethal mischief in the "conventional" unsealed packages in which you sold your products? Would it have occurred to you that, in a society which every day reveals its capacity for homicidal lunacy, it was just a matter of time before someone thought of putting poison in therapeutic capsules?

Hindsight is wonderful; besides, we are getting ahead of ourselves. The point of these case histories is to sensitize you to the fact that the viability of a corporate business plan depends, at least in the long term, on certain underlying assumptions about the society in which the plan is to be executed. To be more specific, we are concerned about potential *changes* in existing governmental policies which, in a democracy, are presumed at any given time to represent the nature and level of public consent or opposition for our activities. (In less developed parts of the world where we wish to market our products or extract minerals, our underlying assumptions must take into account such "externalities" as the risk of revolution, war, famine, and flood, to say nothing of protectionism, currency devaluation, or freezing of assets.) Nor is this to imply that the risks involved in such changes, domestic or otherwise, are necessarily unacceptable from a business point of view. A public policy-oriented *overview* of the business plan enables management to make deliberate choices:

First, it enables management to consider the externalities and take them into account.

Second, it may suggest that under present circumstances, certain aspects of the plan are sufficiently contrary to good public affairs judgment as to require modification, abandonment, or wholehearted accommodation to a new way of doing business.

Third, it provides the opportunity to assign to public relations the task of moderating the risk or supporting the goals.

At this point, we are back in the business of "engineering" public consent where it may not now exist or maintaining it where it does. Consent for nuclear energy once existed; consent for the Bell System monopoly once existed; consent for unsealed containers once existed. But could the world's most skillful and comprehensive public relations programs have prevented the apparent erosion of public support for nuclear energy, the Bell System's monopoly, or unsealed containers? Or did events and reality simply overtake them? Let us concede that there are limits to the ability of public relations to create the world we and our clients might prefer. Some business practices simply become unacceptable, and the measure of good management is how well it changes its practices to accommodate to this new reality. To put it in the vernacular, "if you can't beat 'em, you'd better join 'em."

HOW THE PROCESS WORKS

In a large corporation (or perhaps any institution which employs more than two MBAs), the annual business plan is virtually certain to be an incredibly complex document that sets out in great and highly quantified detail where the company intends to go, how it intends to get there, and how it proposes to allocate its resources and reward its shareholders. In effect, it represents the collective judgments of senior management, manufacturing, distribution, marketing, sales, R&D, and finance, and it is the basis for establishing the financial goals and budgets of the enterprise. This is to say that at heart it is an *economic* document, not an analysis of the various sorts of social externalities which might affect it. In all candor, for all its apparent quantification, the plan is unavoidably based on a number of assumptions or pure judgment calls about the cost of money, the economic health of various customer segments, access to and price of raw materials, energy, labor, to name only a few. But the business plan also relies implicitly or explicitly on other judgment calls about the society in which the company intends to implement its programs, and the more thoughtful companies delineate these societal assumptions in the plan or in a companion document.

For example, here are two summary statements from a lengthy worldly overview which the planners at a Fortune 500 multinational corporation provided for line management:

> For the next two decades, the world is expected to experience relative
> harmony, lack of major conflict, and an economic and political climate

generally conducive to the expansion of business and trade. No massive discontinuities are anticipated, although tensions in many areas will persist and result in localized, relative short-duration disruptions.
Governments will increasingly regulate business, increased nationalization of industry will occur in some countries, and moderately managed economies will be the norm. In general, the climate for business will be healthy, although competition with non-profit oriented nationalized companies will be increasingly difficult for existing multinational corporations.

The "future assumptions" document may go into considerable detail and extrapolation to explain its anticipation of change or continuity in the worldwide external environment. Regardless of whether the assumptions turn out to be correct, the document has at least spotlighted the issues: "...short-duration disruptions," "... regulate business," "...nationalized companies," etc. Management now has the opportunity to impose a number of "what ifs" on the business plan.

There are, for example, global "what ifs":

- What if there is war in the Middle East and oil supplies are disrupted?
- What if the European Common Market countries form national cartels to produce and market commodities in competition with U.S. companies?

There are national issues of fundamental significance, for example:

- What if governmental regulation of environmentally sensitive chemicals becomes so burdensome that it's uneconomical to produce them in the United States?
- What if natural gas prices are deregulated and lead to a major shortage or run-up in the cost of fuel or petrochemical feedstock?
- What happens to interest rates if the projected federal budget deficit is not shrunk?

And there are local issues as well:

- What will happen to our manufacturing costs in southeastern Pennsylvania if the public utility commission decides to subsidize electricity consumers by raising the prices paid by industrial users?
- What if our access to raw materials is affected by South Dakota voters, who appear willing to support a referendum initiative to ban mineral mining in the Black Hills area?
- Nothwithstanding that the Federal EPA has approved and authorized the use of one of our products in U.S. agriculture, what if environmental activists in California succeed in persuading the governor to ban the product because of alleged danger to public health?

More imaginative corporations may seriously pursue the "what if" line of inquiry into broader social issues: for example, the career implications of working spouses or single parents, the effect on a high tech business of the sorry state of science and math education, the desire for more self-determination on the part of managers and employees, etc. Any of hundreds of such issues, if worst came to worst, will affect our business, some more damaging than others. But what are the odds that they will occur, and how seriously should management consider the threat?[2]

The public relations practitioner has, in addition to his own informed judgment and instincts, a number of tools available to help him judge. Opinion research, analysis of editorial content, "Delphi" surveys, or simply an ear to the ground in Washington or local state capitals or city halls—all of these are useful. A noted pollster once counseled his client: "Marinate yourself in the data before you make any judgments." Good advice; the practitioner can avoid embarrassment by always double-checking his intuitive judgment against more objective data before he offers to distinguish real from perceived threats.

This ability to discriminate between real and perceived threats or perhaps even to see certain threats as *opportunities* (e.g., for an aluminum can manufacturer to set up recycling centers in the interest of conservation and litter prevention) is a critical dimension of planning public affairs–oriented communications. This is simply because *no one has sufficient communications resources to deal adequately with all the prospective ills and political vulnerabilities which may appear threatening to your enterprise.* Nor, as I suggested earlier, are some of them necessarily susceptible to communications or public relations solutions: if you took Hill & Knowlton, Burson-Marsteller, Carl Byoir, and added the resources of AT&T, ITT, GE, and GTE, you wouldn't make a dent in the prospects of war in the Middle East. Nor is it necessarily likely that you will reverse certain domestic trends toward increased taxes, redistribution of wealth, or the growth of environmental activism. Realism as to your capabilities is the watchword here, and priorities must be established.

So this is what we do:

- We identify and describe potentially damaging events of a political or socioeconomic nature, but they have varying likelihoods of actually occurring—let's rank them on that basis.
- Then let's rerank them and put aside those events or issues that are

---

2. I have deliberately chosen my examples of "what if" risks on the basis of purely *external* eventualities. A lengthier chapter could no doubt be written on the subject of risks created *internally* by errors of judgment, inappropriate or unenforced policies, or insensitivity. Even well-intentioned acts of omission or commission by people in positions of high authority run the risk of alienating public opinion. When the public decides no longer to give its consent to certain practices or appearances, lawmakers are not unnoticing.

troublesome but purely beyond our ability to affect or deal with—these
we will happily delegate to futurists and economic and social
philosophers.
- We will end up with a "critical few" issues which cut close to the
corporate bone, have the virtue of being "actionable," and are perceived
by our management to be important enough to warrant attention and
resources.

In a sense, this is not unlike what presumably goes on in the control
room of the USS *Forrestal* in the Libyan Gulf: we see "blips" coming up on
the display screens, we identify them as friendly, unfriendly, or unidentified,
we judge the speed at which they are moving toward our air space. Our
computers calculate and track the order of risk, and finally the captain
systematically dispatches interceptors to turn away or shoot down the
"critical few" which represent a genuine threat. The military metaphor
breaks down only when we recognize that in the case of corporate public
affairs, there are more blips on the screen than we can possibly intercept.

KNOWING WHO YOUR CLIENTS ARE

A strong recognition of "cliency" imposes discipline and direction on the
public relations function. An enthusiastic, supportive client—especially one
whose bottom line is probably more clearly understood by the people who
manage large institutions—provides support, recognition, and collective
purpose to your public affairs programs.

The practitioner has two primary clients. First is the individual or
department within the corporation which has line or staff responsibility for
the function which will be most impacted by potential change in public
policy. These are the in-house experts from whom we take guidance and
direction. For example, the individual who manages transportation and
distribution will be in the best position to evaluate the economic effect of
changes in rail tariffs, barge tolls, trucking deregulation, etc. Similarly, the
tax specialists and accountants will understand the implications of changes in
federal, state, or local tax codes. These specialists or policy experts must be
full-fledged members of the public affairs team, perhaps on ad hoc issue
committees, certainly as participants in the drafting of position papers, and
usually as the expert witnesses who testify at congressional hearings and
represent us in the technical work of our industry associations. In view of the
fact that they *are* bona fide experts on a given issue, it is a great advantage if
they are trained and qualified to handle media interviews and public
presentations.

The second primary client is the lobbyist. An intimate understanding of
how he approaches his job is absolutely essential for the public affairs

communicator, because the lobbyist's role perfectly personifies the opportunities as well as the limitations of any issues-related communications program.

TAKING DIRECTION FROM THE LOBBYIST

Whether at the federal, state, or local level, your colleague lobbyist should be able to give you a realistic ranking of the urgency and immediacy of the various issues on the public affairs agenda. Better than anyone, he should know what's on the minds of staffers of congressional committees, of the administrative agencies as they consider the promulgation of regulations, among the existing or nascent coalitions of special interest groups and adversaries, or among our existing or potential allies on any given issue. In cases where no lobbyist is on the job, the various business associations make it their business to track the rank-order of current issues on the political agenda.

Of even greater importance to the practitioner who may be called on to articulate the corporate position is the fact that lobbyists tend to be the ultimate pragmatists and realists. That is to say, a good lobbyist has a disciplined grasp of the art of the possible; he rarely overpromises or overcommits; he accepts compromise as the nature of politics; he knows that no political victory or defeat is necessarily forever.

Part of his job is to recognize his own limitations and that some political issues represent ideas whose time has come, regardless of how unpopular they may be at corporate headquarters. He lobbies, therefore, not necessarily to achieve an ultimate victory but to see that his client or principal has credible, forceful representation of its interests and that the outcome will tilt as far as possible in his client's favor. Perhaps most significantly, he does not put himself in a position from which he cannot compromise or gracefully retreat.

He lobbies, in other words, in order to be able to lobby another day. His career depends on keeping his options open, notwithstanding that neither he nor his political contacts have the slightest doubt that he first and foremost represents his client's self-interest. Nor does he generally invest a great deal of effort or anguish in featuring himself as primarily devoted to the improvement of the world and the condition of mankind, although that may be a useful context in which to present one's viewpoint to the news media and student audiences.[3]

3. Generally speaking, most media people, liberals, and intellectuals attach a certain nobility to the activities of Ralph Nader or Common Cause, whereas reality suggests that the former are at least as self-interested (and more articulate in making their case) than the typical steel or chemical company.

DON'T BOX HIM IN

Good lobbyists, in my experience, are skeptical about the merits of "communications" as an element of overall public affairs management. The skepticism is not entirely misplaced. Effective lobbying, as I implied earlier, involves negotiation, give-and-take, trade-offs, and a clear recognition that neither we nor our opposition ordinarily gets everything he wants in a given piece of legislation. The lobbyist recognizes that the legislator has his own political obligations and other constituents, his own personal social and economic philosophy, and the potential of being an important force in Washington long after the present issue is forgotten and forgiven. The lobbyist also understands that companies or industry groups which are normally his allies may, in certain cases, object to solutions which best serve his particular client's interests. Lobbying is therefore "the art of the possible" in an unstable, imperfect world.

Accordingly, the lobbyist is customarily chary of being boxed in by pronouncements, position papers, advocacy advertisements, and the like which diminish his ability to negotiate a reasonable compromise on a given piece of legislation. He asks only two things of the communicator. First, consistency. Don't go public with a position which contradicts the one he is taking on the Hill; for example, do not run ads attacking government spending while he is trying to pass a bill which (say) subsidizes barge transportation on the inland waterways. Second, do not "write the bill" in speeches and pamphlets; give him the latitude to negotiate and network the actual language with his own legislative contacts.

Furthermore, recognize that his political agenda is vastly larger than ours. At any given time, he may be following as many as a hundred extremely complicated bills, amendments, and regulations. These may range from social security taxes to groundwater protection, from occupational disease compensation to petitions by foreign manufacturers for duty-free access to U.S. markets. For companies with operations in various states, the list may be so long as to require a computerized on-line filing and retrieval system, a tracking service now being sold by several software companies to enable the lobbyists to stay in touch with local developments.

HOW TO HELP THE LOBBYIST

Notwithstanding these caveats, there are two essential contributions we can make to support the lobbying/public affairs activity. First, we can *legitimate* the corporate cause. That is, by sheer dint of persuasive language, by the manner in which we articulate the corporate position, we can succeed in making our argument appear reasonable, logical, and sensible. Awareness of public attitudes and sensitivity to language is all we have to go on. But the sine qua non of the exercise is credibility: the acid test is whether a relatively uninformed audience will hear or read our argument and say, "Well, that sounds fairly reasonable."

Second, we can motivate and coalesce people into becoming a *constituency* on behalf of our cause; this is the unique property of communications. It is a cliché to say that politicians are influenced by calls or letters from their constituents, or by opinion data which reveal what the folks at home are thinking, or by editorials and stories in the hometown papers. But cliché or not, it still is the way politics works: our job is to get those letters and postcards coming in, as Johnny Carson might say.

Nor can it be done effectively without structure and organization, which exists in varying degrees of formality or informality in most corporations. A relatively formal structure might involve public affairs committees comprised of plant or operating managers within a given state or area, each of whom represents a vested economic interest in his community and therefore a constituency to his elected representatives. Although local managers typically have their hands full with local and state issues such as product liability and business taxes, they must also be responsive to issues at the federal level. It is good public affairs practice to encourage them to make themselves and their views personally known to their elected representatives, an activity which may best be coordinated by the lobbyists or a governmental relations department.

In passing, it is worth asking whether, as a matter of employee relations policy, most rank-and-file employees are offered sufficient encouragement to identify their interests with the corporate interests. There is a good deal of research data, much of it compiled by Opinion Research Corporation, which documents the failure of internal communications to keep employees and even middle managers informed about what's going on in the company. In one particular study, employee attitudes on a variety of critical public affairs issues were largely (and perhaps not surprisingly) at odds with the company viewpoint! The bottom line of this digression is that employee grassroots support for public affairs objectives is integrally linked with the communications and human relations climate within the company.

It is also ironic that corporations are often regarded as being only slightly more autocratic and hierarchical than (say) Czarist Russia, whereas in fact they are generally reluctant to ask even a minimal degree of "constituency activism" on the part of their employees and even managers. In this respect, there is an ethical but perhaps unjustified reluctance on the part of most managements to lean on their employees, even their key managers, lest it be seen as partisan politics or coercion. And it is probably an exceptional case where the local manager's line boss at corporate headquarters ascribes serious importance to any public affairs activity which detracts from the manager's more conventional profit and loss responsibilities.

THE SPECIAL ADVANTAGE OF SPECIAL INTERESTS

Members of voluntary special interest groups, on the other hand, have no such constraints. Being joined in a common and sometimes "holy" cause, they are able to run rings around the corporation as advocates of their viewpoints. If you have any doubt, I recommend that you arrange to get yourself on the mailing lists of the various activist groups—the Sierra Club, Friends of the Earth, Common Cause, Union of Concerned Scientists, etc. You will be astonished at the intensity of their distrust of corporations, the size of their communications budgets, and the professionalism with which they work at building their constituency.

Whether the single-interest groups represent a majority on a given public issue is moot: rarely does even a majority political constituency get everything it wants. But it does appear that activist constituencies are able, with the help of the news media, to *push* society in directions that correspond to their particular biases. Certain legislative and regulatory proposals and approaches, while demonstrably uneconomical from our point of view and perhaps unwarranted from society's, begin to appear to have broad popular support.

Our job, to be blunt about it, is to push back.

PUTTING IT INTO PRACTICE

Let's invent a hypothetical case and work it through. We will pick one that is highly politicized: namely, a "pro-industry" set of amendments to the Clean Water Act. Many of our plants discharge their treated waste into waterways. We have already spent megamillions of dollars to remove 90 percent of the pollutants, and now we face (say) an additional capital cost of $40 million for further (and in our judgment, superfluous) treatment of so-called toxic pollutants under the terms of the act and its 1977 amendments.

Our people in Washington have briefed us throughly on the issue, the mood of the Congress and its committees, the administration position, the industry groups we can count on, and the intensity and effectiveness of opposition by various environmentalist groups. In general, our communications program will be designed according to the following principles:

First, we want to be accorded standing to speak out on the issue—that is, we want it understood that the issue affects us. (As a matter of public relations policy, it almost always makes sense to acknowledge your self-interest openly and candidly.)

Second, we want to demonstrate that our technical competence qualifies us as an expert witness on the subject.

Third, we want to demonstrate that our interest is not incompatible with the public interest.

Fourth, we want other groups to join and support us in the political dialogue—if possible, we want to join ourselves to a larger constituency and coalesce it.

Fifth, in view of the fact (as indicated by our opinion data) that this is a highly emotional issue, we want to solidify the support of those who tend to agree with us and *avoid* solidifying those who disagree. Regarding the people who appear to be uncommitted, we want to persuade them to support us, but under no circumstance do we want to push them over to the other side.

Before we start to "communicate," let us be sure we are in agreement that *public* communications are likely to improve the odds for success. Perhaps it is more instructive to state the converse: *let's be sure that communications will not make the situation worse.* Notwithstanding the public's right to be informed, the First Amendment does not obligate us to pour communications fuel on the coals of inflamed opinion. As one of my mentors was fond of saying, the first principle is to do no harm. Accordingly, we can choose from a wide range of communications options, some more subtle or targeted than others, and it is not mandatory to use skywriting, sound trucks, or even "media relations" to tell our story.[4]

Let's review what we said in principle number five above. Common sense suggests that communications can achieve only three things:

First, communications can impart knowledge where there is ignorance. In other words, we can give our audience new information which may cause them to adopt a certain viewpoint. We can call this the "gee, I never knew that" effect.

Second, communications can correct misinformation. This should result in one of two effects: either "I stand corrected" or "I stand corrected but have not changed my mind." (Short moral: rational information will not necessarily modify emotional conviction.)

Third, communications can affirm and confirm knowledge and attitudes which are now held. In other words, "I already knew that, and now I am more convinced than ever."

---

4. Having come from a journalistic background, inexperienced public relations practitioners may believe that practicing journalists still consider them members of the Fourth Estate. This often leads them to assume that the press will extend the professional courtesy of reporting their client's position in a fair and balanced fashion. There may also be those who still believe in the tooth fairy.

Knowing this, we can design our communications programs and target our audiences more effectively and economically. We may elect, for example, to keep a low profile. Such a strategy would forego advertising and might simply utilize direct mail or telephone calls to our narrow band of dedicated supporters, thereby reducing the risk of energizing our opposition. We would carefully check the editorial positions of the area's newspapers and call only on those which needed affirmation and confirmation. Or we might restrict our communications efforts to our plant communities, where our record of environmental progress (as well as our economic contribution) is well accepted.[5]

Since this chapter did not set out to be a primer on public relations techniques, I do not need to tell you how to organize the overall plan. Obviously, we need a "matrix" which identifies discrete, reachable audiences: employees, neighbors, allied groups, etc. We must decide what needs to be said or done on behalf of each: presentations, appearances on talk shows, mailings to homes, media tours, etc. Presumably we are not strangers to these groups, assuming we've had good "conventional public relations" with them over the years. Our goal now is, at a minimum, to make our audiences *supportive* of our objective to amend the act, and at the maximum, to motivate them to make their views known to their elected officials.

ADVERTISING AS PART OF THE MIX

There are occasions when the importance of an issue may transcend purely "journalistic" public relations techniques. Your client may consider the issue important enough to "take it public" in the most visible sense, beyond the bounds of what is achievable through publicity. To coin a phrase, you often cannot get from here to there without advertising. Only advertising can tell your story exactly as you want it told, and on a certain date. Advertising puts you unequivocally and visibly "on the record." It implies that you feel strongly enough about the issue to put money where your mouth is. It creates a rallying point—a "flagship"—for your supporters. True, it also creates a potential target for your critics, but you may be skillful enough to present your case so constructively as to give even your critics a basis on which they may agree with you.

Association advertising programs can help fill public affairs' communications gaps, although it's a rare association whose members can bring themselves to deal with sensitive issues in other than a lowest-common-denominator manner. Furthermore, association campaigns traditionally are

5. This low-profile tactic in fact was the successful approach used by a prounion group several years ago to defeat a ballot initiative in Missouri. Supporters of the initiative did not know what was happening until the polls closed.

underfunded and do not have much staying power. Perhaps this is because the members correctly recognize that unpredictable events or the less responsible members of the industry will do something to contradict the enlightened premise of the advertising, or because they are so lobbying oriented that they cannot see the need to change underlying public attitudes in order to generate political support. In any event, it is worth the effort to contribute your professionalism to the communications activity of the industry association. If the association does it well, you can concentrate your own limited dollars on more proprietary targets.[6]

An association's pooled advertising dollars may look even better when the individual member faces up to the cost of doing his or her own program. Consider the cost of national advertising for a major consumer-branded product. Using 30-second spot (or shorter) television commercials, you probably need at least $15 million at a minimum to move a *product* on a national basis—think what it would cost to move attitudes! True, we can reach *segments* of the American public, but with only a few notable exceptions (Mobil and AT&T come to mind), most advocacy advertising budgets are insufficient even to make an *impression* on the public, much less change opinions. Even the Mobil program, so familiar to the communications fraternity, is largely unknown to the average American. An amusing paradox here. On the erroneous assumption that "putting it in an ad" is equivalent to erecting a permanent bronze tablet for everyone to see for all time, most corporations have second thoughts about making their position *that* visible. The fact is that it requires more weight and continuity than most corporations are willing to provide for an advertising program to develop public awareness; anything less goes largely unnoticed by the general public and rarely provokes a big fuss.

Parenthetically, if one assumes that communications *can* make a difference—and in marketing and selling it's taken on faith—it is difficult to understand why corporations are so reluctant to put sufficient dollars behind their public affairs objectives, especially when their cause is legitimate and the bottom line regulatory costs are almost as quantifiable as the income from sales. But for the sake of example, assume the resources can be made available.

My rule of thumb is that you cannot buy a "national" program for much less than $10 million, and you cannot pretend to reach the general public

6. Many line executives find it difficult to accept the "cause and effect" connection between changes in public attitudes and eventual bottom line results. Such executives are reluctant, therefore, to judge communications results purely in terms of attitudinal change; they look for more substantive and definitive results. Yet communications per se cannot be held accountable for "results" which go beyond the achievement of measurable changes in public attitudes; in the real world, there are too many other factors and uncertainties which affect the ultimate outcome. The communicator is well advised to have a clear understanding with his management on the criteria, if any, which will be used to evaluate his programs.

without using television. For perhaps $3 to $5 million, you *can* reach the so-called thought-leaders and policy influencers nationally through the news weeklies and key newspapers. For less than a million, you can make several splashes in the *Washington Post,* the *New York Times,* the *Wall Street Journal,* and an almost limitless number of plant-city dailies, and drive-time radio, supported by merchandising of your messages. If you do it extremely well, you may be able to create sufficient word-of-mouth amplification of your program to compensate partially for the budget limitations. In any event, beware of the "blue-serge suit syndrome": unless the program is adequately funded, it may do little more than give the advertiser a warm feeling.

In view of these budgetary realities, it would be correct to say that many such programs are in fact mere *illusions* of public communications. That is, they give the appearance of reaching the masses when in fact they do no such thing, as is confirmed by studies of public awareness of most such programs. I recommend that you not be embarrassed by this reality; if you get the attention of your core group of political activists, if you create even a modest constituency of people who will quote your ads and write letters on your behalf, you may have done all that can be expected. At least the legislators and regulators will know that *somebody* cares, and that is a good part of the battle.

Let us return to the task we had in mind when we came to drain the swamp; namely, to get the Clean Water Act amended. What should be in the communications plan?

HOW TO DO IT

I might work it through like this:

First, I would enlist the support of my plant managers and district sales force in whatever states we do business. I would draft prototype letters for them to use in preparing their own "localized" telegrams and letters to their congressmen and senators. Since we had created a grassroots public affairs awareness in our facilities whereby other managers or workers are reasonably well-informed on the issue and also can therefore be expected to pitch in willingly (we *did* that, didn't we?), we can count on them for support. I would prepare speech drafts to be used by our managers at local business and fraternal meetings, or I would send a corporate expert with a very persuasive dog-and-pony show.

I would encourage our local manager to be professionally trained in presentation and confrontation skills in order that he present our position most persuasively in the local papers and on television. He would also explain our view to the editorial board and if we got reasonably supportive copy from them, I would make sure that it was seen in Washington by his congressman.

Tours would be arranged for local dignitaries to see our waste treatment facilities, and our manager would be the authoritative spokesman on the economic danger of superfluous environmental costs on his plant and on his workers. On the local level, this could be an effective message: elected representatives do not stay in office by consciously wrecking the local economy.

I would then try to provide a flag for potential allies to rally around. Perhaps it would be a scheduled meeting with the mayor and the town council, and we might find that state- and local-level public works officials were on our side. We might run a fairly visible advertisement in the local paper or a message on drive-time radio, and perhaps we could persuade other corporations and industry groups to sign it with us. (An important caveat here: be absolutely certain that the local manager approves the ad. For a variety of reasons, some of them eminently sensible, he may decide that the timing is wrong or that the local situation is too delicate for a high profile.) I would consider "couponing" the ad, asking that the coupon be clipped and mailed to Washington. Although I am open to the criticism that this might be viewed with skepticism by our legislator, my personal bias is that something usually beats nothing. Local publicity would reinforce the information being provided our employees, as would the local plant newsletter and our all-employee corporate publication.

As went the lyric in "Alice's Restaurant," we are trying to start a movement, or at least the illusion of one. So I would consider one or more pieces of advertising at the *national* level, simply to put our well-reasoned argument on the record in Washington, New York, and in the business community at large. Again, a note of caution, be guided by your lobbyist on this judgment call; we are already agreed that national advertising on heated issues can be counterproductive.

In summary, I would always start at the grass roots and, depending on circumstances and the sensitivity of the issue, take my program upward toward national visibility. Of course, our senior people would be prepared to testify at congressional hearings, appear on MacNeil-Lehrer, and personally merchandise our position papers and data to academia and thought-leaders. And when our representatives assemble to take a vote on the issue, they will *know* there is a constituency for our viewpoint. Win, lose, or draw, there was a constituency.

THE CREATIVE DILEMMA

If the foregoing sounds like boiler plate, it is. Therefore, let's move on: we are supposed to be *persuaders*, so let's discuss "forensic strategy." That is, what will be our *message* and *tone* as we present our case in the communications program? Do we want to be perceived as conciliatory or adversarial, subjective or objective, personal or impersonal, self-interested or consensualizing? There is something to be said for each, but it is more realistic to recognize that the choice of communications strategy may be limited and perhaps even ordained by the culture within which the practitioner operates, culture being loosely defined as a collective sense of values, self-interest, and style.

Some corporations and interest groups have a tradition of combativeness when their turf or self-interest is challenged; they compete aggressively, they react aggressively, and they choose their leaders (and rate their communicators) according to that characteristic. Other cultures tend toward the opposite pole (understated, restrained, even aloof), whereas some simply reflect the outlook and attitude of the current chief executive. From the vantage point of an *outsider* to the culture, some public affairs strategies may seem unproductive and inappropriate; from the viewpoint of the insider, there may well be no acceptable or more promising alternative. The following two examples should illustrate my point.

DON'T TREAD ON ME

It is noteworthy that the long-lived Mobil advocacy campaign (see figure 2.1), as distinct from the promotion of their splendid public broadcasting support and other pro bono activities, seems to have fallen into disfavor with many practitioners. When the campaign first appeared, the general reaction within the corporate community was, "It's about time somebody started speaking up." Today, Mobil's approach is more likely to be considered a little "too adversarial," although this notion overlooks the fact that Mobil's messages appear regularly and consistently in the media and the real degree of adversarial intensity varies widely. Notwithstanding that the program is thought to be more contentious that it really is, Mobil's rationale is both intelligent and realistic:

The campaign helps make the record.
Even though Mobil's critics in the public policy area and in the media are overjoyed to use the company's ads for target practice, the fact is that Mobil is able—at least to some degree—*to control the agenda for public discussion.* Whether or not you agree with Mobil's philosophy or with their conclusions, you know where they stand, and you know they will defend their position vigorously and visibly.

The campaign helps keep the record straight.
Do not think for a minute that the media takes its coverage of Mobil lightly. In one respect, the media are just like you and me—they don't like to be proved wrong or to appear unobjective. Admittedly, there may

A tax is a tax is a tax

A recent statement by Senator Robert Dole of Kansas seemed to reflect a prevalent myth that oil companies don't pay their fair share of federal taxes. The statement was made in conjunction with his endorsement of new restrictions on the foreign tax credit.

The Senator said: "We were looking for areas that did not fit with our ideas of equity and fairness, and this stuck out like a sore thumb." Actually, the foreign tax credit is simply protection against double taxation.

Unfair as its curtailment is, the situation illustrates a larger problem: accusations that the oil industry does not pay its fair share of taxes. Another example was a statement by lame-duck Democratic Representative Toby Moffett of Connecticut. During his campaign for the Senate, he offered a pat solution to raising tax revenues: "Start with oil." Similar sentiments have been voiced by Senator Thomas Eagleton, Democrat of Missouri; columnist Jack Anderson, and many others. All lead us to wonder whether they have done their homework.

Without going again into the merits of foreign tax credits or the depletion allowances non-integrated oil companies get, we want to set the record straight on one key point that legislators on both sides of the aisle, and the public, seem to have all wrong. Oil companies do pay taxes. Their fair share. Maybe even more than their fair share. And we're not talking about levies like gasoline taxes and payroll taxes for which the companies are simply collecting agents for Uncle Sam. We're talking about taxes that dig directly into oil company pockets. Consider the picture for last year:

● The 23 leading U.S.-based oil companies paid federal taxes—including the so-called "windfall profits" levy—amounting to 51 percent of their pre-tax net income. By comparison, the 100 leading non-oil industrial companies paid only 26 percent, since they're unburdened by the "windfall profits" tax.

● Even without the so-called "windfall" levy, the oil companies paid an average 33 percent, which is more than the non-oil concerns, according to the annual reports from which these figures were gleaned.

These statistics should make it obvious that foreign tax credits and special extraction industry treatments like depletion allowances and expensing of intangible drilling costs do not reduce oil companies' taxes below the norm for industry generally. The point is that, after such provisions are taken into account, oil companies do pay taxes—income, "windfall," or whatever—more than commensurate with those of other industries. And, of course, we also pay our share of taxes to states and municipalities.

There can be little dispute about the government's need to reduce the federal deficit. But the notion that this should be done with new taxes, rather than politically unpopular cuts in spending, is a prescription for making the recession last longer. If the objective is to revitalize the economy and expand the Gross National Product, making energy more expensive through higher taxes is clearly counterproductive. And the idea that additional revenues should come out of the oil industry's hide, on the grounds that oil companies pay inordinately low taxes, is flawed reasoning at best.

Even so, there have been proposals before the Congress to reduce the foreign tax credit further or even repeal it altogether, withdraw the percentage depletion allowances from those companies entitled to take them, impose an oil-import fee, and disallow the immediate write-off of intangible drilling costs. Any or all of these measures would increase the oil industry's tax burden substantially beyond the fair share the companies already pay.

In view of the current state of the industry, which is feeling the recession like everybody else, additional taxes would be not only unfair and inequitable, they would also reduce the industry's ability to find and develop the energy sources the nation and the world will need in future years.

Mobil®

© 1982 Mobil Corporation

Figure 2.1 A Mobil advertisement. (*Reprinted by permission of Mobil Corporation.*)

be more politic ways of keeping the record straight, but Mobil's willingness to rise forcefully to the occasion unquestionably causes the media to double-check their facts and their interpretation before they publish.

Mobil does have a constituency.

If the prior two arguments are debatable, this one is not: Mobil, like every other large public institution, has a constituency which believes in it, supports it, and wants to be informed about it. By taking its story (or its rebuttals of media reports) public, Mobil admittedly runs the risk of further alienating its adversaries, but there is probably no more effective way to get its side of the story across to its employees, shareholders, suppliers, customers, and others with common interests and a common economic philosophy. There are more of them out there, philosophically speaking, than most liberals are willing to admit, as Ronald Reagan demonstrated in 1980.[7]

BY WAY OF COMPARISON—A LOWER KEY APPROACH

One of the oldest axioms in public relations is "make news, then publicize it." Union Carbide Corporation frequently commissions proprietary opinion research and uses it as the basis of "news," some of it controversial but in no way intended to be adversarial.

The "news" is that there is often greater consensus and public support for certain pro-industry policies than the critics and (frequently) the media would have one believe. For example, in those halcyon times not so long ago when the need for economic growth was being challenged, Carbide's data revealed that a strong majority supported the concept of growth; further, the data indicated public recognition of the private sector's essential role in creating it. Accordingly, Carbide used advocacy advertising (See figure 2.2), understated as it was, to promote this basic support for pro-industry policies on capital formation, exports and foreign trade, and energy self-sufficiency.

In another of its programs, Carbide took on the growing trend for public utility commissions in certain states to subsidize the electricity bills paid by low-income consumers by disproportionately raising the rates paid by industry. Carbide held to the view that when subsidies are justified, they should be provided by social policy, not by discriminating against the industrial user. The company's opinion polls revealed majority public support

7. I often think that public relations people "lag" the societal indicators by as much as ten years. We were late in detecting the intensity of the antiestablishment movement in the 1960s and 1970s, and still tend to believe that America is monolithically "liberal." On the contrary, the potential for economic conservatism and a willingness to hear sensibly conservative arguments is alive and well in our society.

Figure 2.2 An example of a Union Carbide "advocacy" advertisement. (*Reprinted by permission of Union Carbide.*)

for this view, as well as strong recognition of the importance of maintaining the viability of local industry. Accordingly, the company "reported" this consensus through localized advertisements and state-by-state public relations programs.

Technique is less significant than the philosophy behind Carbide's approach. It is, on balance, conciliatory rather than adversarial, temperate rather than contentious, and where appropriate, localized and personalized through the involvement of the company's local managers. Unlike Mobil's approach, it foregoes continuity and deals on a relatively ad hoc basis with a narrow band of issues as they arise. As such, it reflects the Union Carbide "culture," just as Mobil's approach reflects theirs. If the two approaches can be said to represent opposite ends of the creative spectrum, there is probably nothing more than anecdotal evidence to indicate which is the more effective.

SOME ARGUMENTS CANNOT BE WON IN PUBLIC

While we are on the subject of effectiveness, it is important to recognize that some arguments cannot be won in public. This is particularly true when we attempt to deal rationally with emotionally held public attitudes. Environmental regulation will not be substantially lessened; the public is almost fanatical on that subject. Corporate secrecy, even when legitimately claimed in order to protect proprietary data, cuts counter to the openness most Americans ask of their institutions. It can be self-defeating to claim "business confidential" in the midst of public controversy over (say) the health effects of one of your products, notwithstanding that such confidentiality may be justified by the competitive nature of your business and even provided for under the law.

The real mark of public relations statesmanship is to avoid letting an issue escalate to the point where you have to make a choice between "giving away the store" (in your management's opinion) or making your stand on the corporate policy. As in all things in life, you pay a price either way: in the example above, either you *do* reveal valuable competitive information, or you are marked as secretive and disinterested in the public welfare. It is a test of your professionalism to persuade your client that the public relations issue justifies abandonment of confidentiality or even the willingness to accept defeat and get on with the other business of the corporation.

THE BELL CURVE PHENOMENON

Until now, we have discussed public affairs planning and execution in a largely *tactical* sense. It may be unrealistic, in fact, to expect to be able to have an effect on the broad strategic sweep (if such a word can be used) of political and social events. Nonetheless, I think it is instructive and perhaps humbling to step back occasionally from our day-to-day public affairs activities and our relatively narrow constituencies to consider a broader question: namely, what would be involved if one truly set out to change public opinion?

Depending on how the question is stated on any given issue or economic philosophy, opinion polls can give us at least a general sense of how many of the public are for us, how many against us, and how many are undecided. As a rule of thumb in this wondrously perverse society of ours, it is safe to assume that the statistical distribution will look like a bell curve: at one side of the curve, roughly 20 percent of the respondents are opposed to you to the point of irrationality, and at the other side are the 20 percent who support and believe you equally irrationally. The middle 60 percent of the "bell" is where the pay dirt lies; those are the folks whose minds are not made up, although they obviously *tend* to lean in one direction or the other.[8]

Ironically, as professional communicators and alleged persuaders, few of us can claim much success in reaching that silent majority or, more importantly, being *believed* by them. A number of years ago, Bethlehem Steel Company attempted through psychographic research to determine which readers of which publications were more inclined to be open minded on issues like corporate taxes or environmental improvement. The answers, it seems, were not sufficiently definitive to provide much practical guidance. Nor, having done some of my own research on the subject, can I submit definitive data to prove that a company's reputation or "recognition" is accepted by the public as a "credential" for speaking out persuasively on economic or social issues.

My hunch about all this uncertainty is simply that the public tends to believe in *individuals*, not institutions. Lee Iacocca, in my judgment, would be more persuasive debating the arcane merits of (say) the gold standard or floating exchange rates than either the chairman of the Bank of America (who is he?) or the head of the department of economics at Harvard. (This may not fully explain the current spate of television commercials featuring the advertiser's CEO as spokesman, but then again they may know something we do not know.) It is not that Lee Iacocca is necessarily charming, brilliant, or even that television viewers personally identify with him; it is simply that he is real, palpable, and *himself*.

For our purposes here, I offer the hypothesis that *persuasion depends on personification*. If your CEO is personally effective going one-on-one with the chairman of the Senate Banking Committee, but you conclude you need to widen your corporate constituency, you may need to convince him to "go

8. Public relations people tend to spend an inordinate amount of their time trying to reason with people whose minds are completely closed. This approach can teach you a lot of things you never wanted to know about human nature, but it is unlikely to be a productive way to spend your client's resources.

public," as it were. *How* public depends, of course, on your goals and the effectiveness of your man. But if it is true that life has become so complex that the average American does not know *what* to believe, then at least he should have the opportunity to decide *whom* to believe.

THE "BENEFIT OF THE DOUBT" THEORY

Another way of looking at this matter of effective public persuasion is to concentrate your resources and your messages toward a very deliberate and minimal goal: namely, winning the "benefit of the doubt" in whatever public forum you choose to enter. Organizations whose business it is to "train" executives for television interviews agree on one cardinal rule: namely, *be likeable*. A public debate is as likely to be won by strength of personality as by force of logic. Your tone and style will be deliberately understated, you will openly acknowledge that good people hold contrary views. You may acknowledge past mistakes, and you will try to bring new facts and data to the table. You will do your audience the courtesy of treating them as reasonable, thoughtful people. In other words, *you concentrate on the middle of the bell curve*, and your objective is to pursuade the "undecideds" that your position is, on balance, reasoned and reasonable.

Such an approach cannot do any damage to the loyalists already in your camp; it also has the advantage of being unlikely to infuriate your detractors. It's difficult to argue with a logical but good-humored and uncontentious position. True, it runs the risk of being dull, but I am sure you are all creative enough to avoid that. In a word, you may be able to *lead* an audience to a consensus that will give you most of what you want, whereas it is unlikely that you can *force* them there. As far as I can tell, this is the way democracies and responsible institutions are expected to survive.

If I were asked to describe the highest competence and guiding principle of the professional public relations person, I would say that it is the ability to help your client *win the benefit of the doubt* with those folks in the middle of the bell curve—those who are undecided. This unavoidably involves the *substance* of what you are, not what you say you are or how you present yourself, although one hopes the two are connected. "Public relations" is first and foremost a matter of reality. If the reality is that an institution conducts itself responsibly and with deliberate sensitivity to public opinion, if it demonstrates its willingness to strike an enlightened balance between its immediate interests and its obligations to its publics, then the communicator is blessed with a substantive case. If the communicator has, by means of personal stature or tenure, achieved a position where he is able to apply public relations considerations to the design of policy and operating decisions, it makes the task of winning the benefit of the doubt ever so much simpler.

THE CORPORATE CULTURE
VERSUS THE PUBLIC RELATIONS PERSON

Earlier in this chapter I implied that "self-interest" is not necessarily a dirty word. Just as our legal tradition explicitly guarantees the right to counsel in matters of law and alleged criminal conduct, I am content in the view that institutions have the same right to public relations/public affairs representation, regardless of what you or I might personally think of the merits of the case.

That may sound obvious and fatuous, but it relates to a problem one rarely hears discussed. I observe that many public relations people, especially the young ones, possess an individuality or even an idealism which is not altogether comfortable or compatible within the prevailing corporate or institutional culture. Marketing publicity, or perhaps even financial public relations, rarely evokes a conflict between one's personal values and the institutional values: within the limits of honesty and integrity, there is plenty of room to promote products or publicize the financial outlook with confidence and enthusiasm. In other words, in selling it is easy to identify enthusiastically with the culture.

Not quite so simple in public affairs. Public relations people often bear the burden of being the first to observe that the emperor is thinly clad. (Your client or employer may consider this quality either an asset or a liability, depending on the degree of candor and objectivity he expects of you.) There is a skepticism here, perhaps even a vulnerability, which makes it difficult to accept many of the uncertainties and anomalies which bureaucratic systems inevitably represent. How certain is it, for example, that your toxicologists really ran the right tests in determining the long-term health effect of one of your leading products? Or that the corporation is going out of its way to develop and promote women and minorities? Or that management is justified in shutting down a plant without advance notice to the workers and the community? Or that an apparently contentious interest group is not composed largely of rather sensible, well-intentioned people? Yet each of these personal uncertainties may lie at the heart of a public affairs issue on which you will be called to argue the institution's viewpoint without equivocation.

Ah yes, each of us would like to represent a perfect client or an unselfish truth. The practice of public relations rarely offers such an opportunity. This is not to say that it is futile or unworthy of professional effort. If management values the special sensitivity and conciliatory instincts so often found in public relations people, if they credit you with a reputation for professional competence as well as unquestioned loyalty to the interests of the institution, you may derive the personal satisfaction of making a more substantive contribution to policy formation and hands-on conflict resolution. On the other hand, even if you are expected to be nothing more than a communicator, your choice of words for the chairman's speech or for what may seem a perfunctory story in the company publication may move the institution a tiny step closer to the values you care about most personally (which is to say: hang in there, you *can* make a difference!) There is not a bureaucracy in the world which cannot make room for at least one constructive critic.

CONCLUSION

A lobbyist friend of mine proudly asserts that his is the only profession whose freedom of practice is explicitly guaranteed by the Constitution of the United States. It can be argued that the practice of public relations enjoys the same protection. Cherish it, on your behalf and on behalf of the institution you represent; the alternative is infinitely worse. Another friend, a producer of one of the more inquisitorial programs on network television, is reluctantly willing to admit that even corporations are entitled to express their views. And so it goes: we and our adversaries compete for public consent, and each of society's self-interests is entitled to its day in court. The political process is not only unpleasant and messy, it may have become too adversarial to be informative or constructive. But even if it were the worst system in the world, to paraphrase Winston Churchill, it is better than all the others. We can simply leave it at that, unless you are willing to step back for a minute and contemplate public affairs from a broader, more idealistic perspective.

At the outset, I took the view that public affairs is easiest to understand if it is looked on as a win/lose situation. In fact, this may be exactly the problem with our political system: we and our opponents seem to view the political process as a zero-sum game in which no one wins except at the expense of the other. Nor does representative government function very well when the spirit of compromise and moderation is lost, when candidates and constituencies resort to character assassination, when special interest groups hold consensus hostage to their narrow interests.

Fortunately, in my judgment, the vast majority of Americans are better natured and more moderate in their outlook than are most of our political and social institutions. This may be our system's saving grace: notwithstanding a 300-year tradition of populism, few Americans are attracted by either the extremism of single-interest advocacy groups or equally single-interested corporations. Further, I strongly doubt that the public takes Mike Wallace, Robert Redford, or Jane Fonda any more seriously than they take entertainers in other categories of public life.

Nonetheless, anyone with a shred of historical perspective must wonder about the failure of our institutions to *reconcile* the competing claims of other legitimate interests or even to make a visible effort to address them openly. The problem, I think, lies in the failure of leadership in all sectors of our society to transcend the immediate interests of their own narrow constituencies. Statesmanship, compromise, patience, and consensus building are in short supply. Intending no disrespect, where *are* the statesmen in embattled but essential industries like steel, automotive, chemical, energy? What vision do they offer on matters relating to job security and enrichment, minorities' aspirations, structural unemployment, urban disarray, global interdependence, environmental safety? What plan do they have for making their businesses safer, more humane, and (in the deepest sense) more popular?

And if such corporate visionaries existed, whom would they find to reason with among the leaders of the radical and elitist single-interest groups whose own vision relates primarily to the seeking of power and influence in their behalf? Or is this, to coin a phrase, none of our business and properly none of *theirs* either? Do idealism and vision really belong in the executive suite? After all, there is at least a kernel of truth in the view that society would be better off if it sought those attributes in its *elected* officials, while asking its captains of industry to do nothing more than to learn to make better cars and cheaper steel.

Finally, we can ask the same questions as they relate not to *public* affairs but to the private success of the enterprise, of which employees and shareholders are the primary constituencies. Perhaps as a result of the attention being paid to the Japanese art of management, business scholars believe they have now identified a distinctive managing style which is common among "excellent" American companies. In brief, this managing style involves less hierarchy, hands-on involvement in what the business makes rather than how it is managed, a reward system which motivates employees at all levels, openness to dissenting viewpoints, and finally the personal visibility of top management in communicating and reinforcing their vision for the enterprise.

My guess is that companies whose excellence is now reflected in their return on investment and stock multiple will come to be seen as models of excellence in public affairs as well, although I cannot say exactly how. In a competitive market or a contentious society, I take it on faith that it will be leaders, not managers, whose vision and personal values create broader constituencies and a shared sense of public purpose.

In the last analysis if the business of business is really nothing more than business, I doubt that we have much right to complain when others in the news media or in politics or academia represent themselves as America's true visionaries? Personally, I think not, but then I already admitted that the whole subject of public affairs is subjective.

A Postscript: You may ask whether we were successful in our hypothetical effort to have the Clean Water Act amended. As of this date, the answer is no; the Congress is finding the issue too controversial, and our lobbyists tell us that consideration has been indefinitely postponed. However, our lawyers believe they may be able to devise a legal theory on which to sue the EPA for relief. There is a moral in here somewhere.

CRISIS MANAGEMENT

Michael D. Tabris

*Director of Corporate Communications
and Government Affairs
Occidental Chemical Corporation*

Nearly every public relations professional at some point in his or her career faces an emergency—an event or combination of circumstances, usually unexpected, that demands urgent action.

Many emergencies, although serious in the short term, may result in only temporary disruptions to be handled by the public relations department and do little long-term damage to the institution involved. Other emergencies escalate into crises where the success or failure of the public relations effort vitally affects the future of the organization over a long period. Occasionally, an issue emerges—with little or no warning—containing elements of crisis proportions from the outset.

No matter how the crisis evolved and regardless of the cause, a comprehensive public relations program is essential to minimize the damage to the affected institution.

Crises vary in nature, magnitude, and intensity, but they all have in common results that may seriously hamper an organization's ability to function. They can seriously undermine its most valued assets—credibility and reputation. To set the stage for further discussion, following is a brief, arbitrary list of the types of events that could lead to emergency or crisis situations:

Michael D. Tabris's background in public affairs and communications spans more than two decades and includes a wide range of responsibilities that have focused on enhancing corporate reputation and that of its people, products, and services. Prior to joining Occidental in 1979, Mr. Tabris was a member of Celanese Corporation and before that, United Parcel Service. No stranger to sensitive issues and the controversy that goes with the corporate public relations scene, Mr. Tabris acquired a unique perspective on crisis management when the events at Love Canal in Niagara Falls, New York, attracted national attention to the issue of chemical waste disposal.

- Fires, explosions, and major accidents at industrial facilities.
- Product recalls involving allegations of negligence or defects with potential for harm to consumers.
- Any mishap involving nuclear substances, chemicals, or other potentially hazardous materials.
- Charges of wrongdoing by a corporation or its officers, by a regulatory or law enforcement agency.
- A series of plant shutdowns and worker layoffs.
- Broad-based charges of "obscene" profits.
- Inclusion of an institution or its products on "dishonor" lists issued by high-profile activist organizations.
- Charges against a company involving practices that pose threats to the safety and well-being of the public and the environment.
- Transportation disasters, especially those involving allegations of improper design, maintenance, and operation of equipment.
- Fears by certain of its key publics that a company is undergoing divestiture of operations or is the target of takeover attempts by another institution.
- Any hostile third-party actions such as product tampering, extortion threats, kidnapping, and sabotage.
- Perception by the public that an organization is involved in some form of concealment or cover-up of information where there is a public "right to know."
- Allegations of inappropriate business or political activities in a foreign country in which a corporation operates.

The recent emergence of "crisis management" as a recognized specialty field within public relations suggests that crises are occurring more frequently than in the past. There are a number of reasons for this phenomenon, but chiefly responsible are the following developments:

- The technological revolution ushering in the age of instant communications.
- The resulting preeminence of the electronic media as the main source of news for most of the industrialized world.
- Changes in the manner of news coverage, largely related to the electronic media's insatiable demand for drama.
- The rise of citizen activist groups and coalitions which have stimulated public investigation of institutions and government regulation of their activities and operations.
- Greatly increased access to the media by these activist organizations.

The net result of these developments has been an enormous increase in the manipulation of and in turn the power of public opinion, and in the number of "publics" to which an institution must answer for its policies and behavior. Today it is no longer sufficient for a business to be concerned solely with its three primary publics: investors, customers, and employees. External publics with little or no direct relationship to an organization can have profound impact on both the organization and the climate in which it operates. Such effects can be seen most clearly in a time of crisis.

Just as the potential for crisis situations has escalated, so has the potential for disastrous consequences from inadequate crisis management. Some of the potential results of mismanagement of emergencies and crises can be:

- Long-term damage to the organization's reputation with resulting loss of confidence in its management by investors, customers, and employees.
- Continuing deterioration of employee morale, labor relations problems, and recruitment difficulties.
- Adverse impact on stock prices and investor relations.
- Waste of management time and financial resources by prolonged preoccupation with crises issues.
- Political intervention resulting in excessive government regulation, increased scrutiny of other activities and operations, and punitive actions.
- Costly litigation (even if ultimately successful).
- Involuntary bankruptcy or reorganization.
- Community relations problems.

To deal effectively with crises, one must first understand why events that once might have triggered serious yet relatively minor emergencies for the public relations function suddenly have the capacity to provoke crises that can literally endanger the survival of the organization involved.

Let me illustrate by sketching a scenario—totally hypothetical, but unfortunately not implausible—to demonstrate how a crisis might evolve from a rather uncomplicated emergency event.

Suppose an explosion has just occurred in a paint factory operated by the Acme Company, located in Any Town, U.S.A. The plant is in an industrial area, but there are nearby homes. The explosion has destroyed one building, but, miraculously, no one has been killed or injured. At one time this occurrence would no doubt have made the front pages of the next edition of the *Any Town Tribune* and perhaps merited hourly reports on local radio, as well as a minute or two on the metropolitan evening TV news.

Today the Acme fire would likely be given the "instant eye" treatment made possible by the revolution of modern technology. "Chopper 2" (also "4" and "6") will be hovering on site in minutes transmitting the drama live to the public. Radio reporters only need a nearby phone to do the same. Frequently in this type of situation, the only information that can be reported with certainty is the fact of the fire itself. Reporters on the scene are thus faced with the competitive necessity of finding something to go with the drama of the television pictures.

There are many choices available. Reporters might, for example, ask the chief of the firefighting crew whether there are any plans to order an immediate evacuation of the neighborhood, which may in turn cause such an order to be given simply to avoid subsequent criticism. Or reporters may corner any Acme employee (knowledgeable or not) and ask for a description of the materials and operations in the plant. Misinformation and public alarm are the most likely immediate results. If the employee declines to comment, that itself provides a story ("Acme personnel refused to reveal any information of what might have been stored in the building or what activities here might have sparked this explosion and fire..."). Public alarm still results ("What are they trying to hide?").

Meanwhile, the plant official responsible for the facility is explaining to reporters that an emergency communications center is being established, that efforts are being made to pinpoint the cause of the blast, and that information will be released to the media as soon as facts can be confirmed. Such comments might find their way into a lengthy newspaper account of the event; they will most likely not be reported on television.

During the emergency and as long afterwards as facts are in doubt, all opinions are equally valid. As far as news reports are concerned, the views of a hostile neighbor or a disgruntled former employee will be given the same credibility as the comments of the plant manager (possibly more), especially if the latter takes too conservative a position, does not communicate openly, or fails to keep the media sufficiently updated.

In the days following, the Acme fire story will be kept alive as a local television station's investigative reporter launches "an in-depth series" consisting of five three-minute segments featuring interviews of activists or political critics on the danger posed by industrial facilities that handle hazardous materials. This series—each segment replaying scenes of the fire—will almost surely be aired during the next television ratings "sweep" period. Each segment will be introduced with a comment that the issue is a vitally important one in the wake of the Acme fire and the tragic consequences it might have had.

Radio news will interview the same people and call-in shows will lead to further spreading of misinformation. The more drama and controversy, the more likely the entire nation will see the story on network news and read it in stories resulting from wire service reports. Interviewed politicians and regulatory agency heads will promise corrective and punitive action. Hearings will be scheduled. There is a seemingly endless chain of possibilities, all detrimental to Acme's image.

It is at this point that you can begin to determine whether or not your public relations activities have been effective—whether you have achieved any measure of success in containing the emergency and preventing it from escalating to the crisis level.

Although the foregoing is hypothetical, it is certainly feasible. Many events more minor than a plant fire have been given the sensationalized treatment described here. We need to recognize the potential for such events in the organizations we serve and prepare to the extent we can for handling emergencies or crises.

One means of detecting whether an event has the potential for escalation into a long-term crisis is to examine carefully the focus of the media coverage:when the facts are the main area of interest, you are most likely dealing with an emergency that will end when the basic story has run its course. When the facts are unknown, alarming to the public or potentially alarming; or when you are called upon by the news media, politicians, investigating authorities, or activists to account for and defend the organization's behavior and its policies, you may have a crisis that will persist for a long period. It is often difficult to determine in advance whether an emergency will escalate into a crisis with the capacity for long-term damage. As a result, it is essential that management (at all levels in the organization) recognize the possibilities for such situations and be prepared to deal with them.

No single advance preparation is more important than gaining the attention of top management—securing its support and cooperation in advance of problems. It is a basic premise within the public relations profession that those responsible for the public relations function must have this essential access to an institution's leaders.

Ideally, the individual in charge of public relations, by whatever title the position is known, should be a part of the senior management team and be involved in the decision-making process. Just as nearly all forward-looking organizations involve their legal counsel in issues and decisions having legal considerations, they should involve public relations professionals in decisions likely to influence or be influenced by public attitudes. Few issues or policies are immune to such influence. Most line managers and senior executives understandably focus their attention on the operational, technical, and financial aspects of a situation. That is all the more reason for the public relations executive to be involved sufficiently to surface considerations of public impact and include them in the decision-making process. Yet, there remain many institutions where the public relations function is insulated from this management process until an emergency occurs.

The first step therefore is one of identification of the potential for crises and making certain that management has a complete understanding of the stakes involved. The ability to discover crisis potential is, in turn, greatly dependent upon good vertical communication within the organization structure, especially within a large organization with diverse and far-flung operations. Communications must be open and operative in both directions, upward and downward.

Plant managers, for example, must be aware of the potential for crisis and the need for advance planning. They must also communicate with the public relations department, other relevant staff departments (human resources, law, security, etc.) and top management about that potential.

Next in importance is the establishment of a response capability—policies and procedures of open communications between the organization and the news media, political and appropriate governmental authorities, and other interested publics. This must include the assignment of a crisis management team with alternate members to ensure that a decision-making body is available at all times. Creation of good public relations, including a reputation with the news media for openness and candor, is a critical step in planning for emergencies. An operation that conducts itself openly implies that it operates in an ethical manner; an organization with a reputation for reticence or concealment will find it hard to establish credibility when it is most in need of trust from the media.

A part of establishing good media relations is creating management awareness of the realities of the news media. This is not to say that top executives must become public relations experts. Rather, it is to suggest that one of the most difficult problems in a crisis will be the establishment of realistic expectations and objectives for the communications efforts. Unless management understands such realities as deadlines, limited space in the print media and limited time on the air, the need to cater to public appetites for the dramatic and sensational—as well as the growing tendency for the media to view themselves as the protectors of the powerless against the powerful—it will be impossible to obtain agreement on how to respond when you are under fire. Too often the result of failure to understand the role of the media today results in adoption of a "siege mentality" (or to use the term popularized during the Watergate period, "stonewalling") in which the media and management perceive each other as adversaries.

Another important preparation is to encourage persons in management positions to be available as spokespersons on a regular basis and to provide training for such persons to deal with the media. It is not enough to be prepared to deal with the public on an occasional basis and in a controlled situation such as an annual meeting. Managers should be prepared to deal effectively with reporters in situations where those journalists will decide what, if anything, is going to be published or aired.

Additionally, it is most important to inform political and community leaders likely to be part of the story as secondary sources of all known aspects of the emergency. These people are in positions of authority and are more likely to be supportive if they are kept well informed by the institution that is under "siege."

Up to this point, I have stressed many concepts that are basic fundamentals of the public relations profession because those fundamentals are even more critically important when an emergency or crisis occurs. Just as the approach of a hurricane is no time to begin thinking about emergency preparedness, after you find yourself in the middle of a media onslaught is no time to be occupied with creating the structure and internal policies for dealing with a public relations crisis.

Unfortunately, we live in a world where the ideal is most often different from reality. Several of the thoughts and concepts I hope to convey have been brought home to me through hard contact with crisis situations. My own experiences with the unique pressures that come with the emergency and crisis scene—based on happenings in the transportation, textile, and chemical industries, where the potential for crisis is readily apparent—dictate that planning for eventualities is essential in public relations practice. It invariably pays dividends in the form of the most orderly handling of chaos that is possible.

EMERGENCY COMMUNICATIONS GUIDELINES

(Excerpted from Occidental Chemical Corporation's public relations program.)

I. *BEFORE AN EMERGENCY*

A. Designate an emergency communications coordinator (ECC) and an alternate ECC at each Occidental Chemical facility.
B. Select members and alternates for the emergency communications team. Hold organizational and frequent update and review meetings. Alternates, on an as-needed basis, should include representatives from law, human resources, security, medical, and other appropriate staff functions.
C. Prepare contact lists of all area television/radio stations and newspapers, emergency communications team members, and the Occidental Chemical Corporate Public Relations Department.
D. Prepare additional key contact lists, including those of political leaders (federal, state, and local representatives), appropriate regulatory officers, and facility neighbors.
E. ECC should establish contact/relations with members of the local media, political leaders, and governmental authorities.
F. Distribute media contact cards noting 24-hour availability of the public relations staff to appropriate local contacts and news media representatives.
G. Select primary and secondary locations for emergency newsrooms.
H. Arrange for facility photographs (one large photograph for demonstration purposes).
I. Obtain news media identification badges for distribution.
J. Share emergency communications plans with the local news media and governmental authorities.

(cont.)

II.   *DURING AN EMERGENCY*

A.   Contact the Occidental Chemical Corporate Public Relations Department when the type and extent of the emergency is known.
B.   Use preselected backup site location for a newsroom if emergency prevents safe access to the facility.
C.   Answer reporters' questions with facts—do not speculate. Use emergency communications team members to gather necessary facts—who, what, where, when, why, and how.
D.   Depending on nature and time of the emergency, contact employees—spot radio, TV announcements, newspaper advertisements, etc., to establish status of facility operations, resumption of work schedules, etc.
E.   Contact governmental and community leaders/neighbors regarding the extent of the emergency.

III.   *AFTER THE EMERGENCY*

A.   Visits to the emergency area must be approved by the facility manager.
B.   Have a prepared facility photograph available for the news media.
C.   Arrange for other photographs to be taken.
D.   Announce to the news media and local political and community leaders company decisions relating to employee or community relief, plant reconstruction, etc.

IV.   *FOLLOW-UP*

Hold a meeting of the emergency communications team to discuss how the plan operated and ideas for possible improvements. Arrange for copies of all news stories, video tapes, or transcripts of broadcast news to be sent to the Occidental Corporate Public Relations Department. Prepare a concise, candid summary assessing how the emergency communications plan operated and any recommendations for possible improvements or appropriate modifications.

THE LOVE CANAL CRISIS

When I joined Occidental Chemical Corporation (then known as Hooker Chemical) in 1979, my primary assignment was to create a strong public relations capability at corporate headquarters in Houston, Texas. Until then the company had conducted its public relations activities on a decentralized basis with public relations professionals located primarily at divisional or plant community levels.

I had previously heard of Love Canal and was aware that dealing with the issue of chemical waste disposal was to be one of my responsibilities. It was not yet apparent that this issue was becoming a prolonged crisis of national proportions and would be among my first and most pressing projects.

A brief discussion of the Love Canal case will illustrate some of the key concepts of crisis management. The following is a capsule summary of the facts that led to this crisis.

Love Canal, located near Niagara Falls, New York, was originally conceived as a power generation project at the turn of the century. Only about 1,800 feet of the proposed five-mile canal was completed. This portion was not used until 1941, when Hooker Chemical acquired the site as a secure landfill for chemical waste materials. The unfinished canal was ideal as a disposal site for a number of reasons: it was in a remote location; the surrounding area was sparsely settled; the walls of the canal were of impermeable clay that assured that buried chemicals would remain in place indefinitely as long as the site remained undisturbed.

Hooker Chemical used the site from 1942 until 1953. As wastes were placed in the canal, they were covered with a layer of impermeable clay. It is important to note that an environmental protection agency (EPA) officially stated that the disposal methods employed by Hooker at the time would meet today's EPA standards for chemical waste disposal.

In 1952 the growing city of Niagara Falls expressed interest in acquiring the Love Canal site for a neighborhood school. The company was reluctant to agree that the property be used for any type of construction, but school board officials said that they were prepared, if necessary, to resort to condemnation proceedings to acquire the site.

Faced with the threat of condemnation, the company agreed to donate the property to the school board—but with an understanding that the area containing buried wastes be used only as a park, to prevent construction that might penetrate the clay cover over the waste material. The company also insisted upon a detailed restriction in the deed to put the school board on notice as to the nature of the buried wastes. Additionally, the company conducted tests that assured that buried chemicals had remained in place and were essentially unchanged.

On at least two occasions Hooker Chemical officials appeared at public meetings to repeat warnings that the site was unsuitable for development and to oppose plans to build on the site or sell off portions of the property.

Despite warnings by the company, local, state, and federal government agencies later put roads, sewers, and utilities through the site after Hooker Chemical no longer owned or had any control over the property. These and other invasions of the site allowed water to seep into the canal and it gradually filled up, like a bathtub, and overflowed. This finding was subsequently confirmed by a task force of the American Institute of Chemical Engineers.

By 1976 there had been confirmed instances of chemical waste seepage into basements of some homes that had been built on the periphery of the

Love Canal property. In 1978 the EPA issued a report on chemical waste contamination, triggering several other studies by state and federal agencies—reports that were later branded as inconclusive.

In August of 1978 the New York State Health Commissioner ordered temporary closure of a school adjacent to the site and recommended that families with pregnant women and children under two years of age living in the first two rings of homes around the canal property be temporarily relocated during remedial work on the site. His recommendation would have affected approximately twenty families.

One week later New York State Governor Carey visited the site and announced that 236 families would be relocated and their homes would be purchased.

Governor Carey's announcement lit the fire that set Hooker Chemical's switchboards ablaze and led to the issue of chemical waste disposal becoming a subject of national recognition and debate. The full extent of the problem— the fact that the company was faced with a genuine, full-fledged crisis as distinguished from an emergency—was not totally clear by the time I joined the company in 1979.

The first problem encountered by the company's public relations staff was one of merely coping with an unprecedented volume and range of inquiries. Faced with imminent press or broadcast deadlines, media representatives were often demanding in their search for information.

Here are *a few* of the inquiries that typify the thousands received at Niagara Falls, New York, at headquarters in Houston, Texas, and at other Hooker facilities around the nation:

- What chemicals were disposed of at Love Canal?
- What was the volume of each type of material?
- How much of the waste was liquid and how much was solid?
- How much was in drums and how much was in loose form?
- How were wastes transported to the site?
- How were the workers who handled the materials protected?
- How do the various chemicals interact with one another?
- What is the cumulative effect of all the materials there?
- How often were waste deposits made?
- What are the soil conditions at the site?
- What was the use of each chemical?
- How long has each chemical been there?
- What did you know about toxicity at the time of disposal?
- How many homes were in the area when the canal was in use as a disposal site?
- How close were the homes?
- Did the company suspect there were dangers at the time?
- Did the company warn people?

In addition to inquiries regarding factual information, there were countless requests for interviews with company officials and for comments on various company policies.

It should be kept in mind that the disposal site had been closed for 25 years when the controversy erupted. Many of those who might have been able to provide firsthand information were not available. Some had retired or had moved to other companies and could not be located. Much of the information necessary to provide accurate responses simply had to be gathered from stored company files and could not be obtained on short notice.

The company's inability to respond immediately and thoroughly to highly technical and complex questions led to charges of "stonewalling." On the other hand, the company was not about to make statements that could not be firmly supported and that might require later retraction, eroding company credibility. Every effort was being made to uncover the facts and to release confirmed information to the media.

We found it useful to establish some simple ground rules for responding to media inquiries:

- A legitimate inquiry deserves an accurate response. The company will not speculate and will not release information that cannot be documented.
- The company speaks with one voice on matters of corporate policy. No statements will be made that have not been reviewed and approved through the appropriate channels. On the other hand, information that has been previously cleared may be released as needed unless current circumstances make such release inappropriate.
- All inquiries are logged and referred to Corporate Public Relations in Houston with recommended response information. Corporate Public Relations coordinates the process of fact-finding, response preparation, approval, and dissemination of the response.

Aside from establishing the physical capability of dealing with the volume of inquiries, our most urgent priority was to develop a comprehensive plan for managing our response to the ongoing crisis.

CONSIDERATIONS IN DEVELOPING A RESPONSE PLAN

If I were to capsulize in retrospect the basic precepts of developing a response plan (something, I must emphasize, we did not have time to prepare in the midst of the media blitz of the Love Canal crisis), my list of steps to be taken would be as follows:

(1) Recognize that a crisis exists and define as precisely as possible its

parameters. Following is a representative list of the type of questions that require answers in gauging the extent of the problem.

- Has the reputation of the institution's products or services been damaged (consider all publics)?
- Have the national media shown any interest?
- Will the issue cause investors to lose confidence in or question the competence of the management of the company?
- Does the situation affect the health and safety of community members or the environment?
- Have any of the issues in question come to the attention of activist groups?
- Have any questions been raised as to the company's operations (safety, etc.)?
- Does the incident reflect on the overall reputation of the institution?
- Does there appear to be any violation of local, state, or federal statutes?
- Is wrongdoing implied?
- Is there potential for adverse reaction by employees or organized labor?

Tough self-analysis, exemplified by the above-noted checklist (a partial list at best), is a must exercise so that all members of the management team, including public relations, are in agreement as to the nature and magnitude of the crisis they are confronting. This is not nearly as simple as it sounds. The facility manager, for example, may be primarily concerned with restoring normal operations. Legal counsel is justly concerned about possible litigation and avoiding any public statements that might jeopardize the company's legal position. Each area of the business has specific, justifiable concerns that must be reconciled.

In the public relations sense, I believe the issues in the Love Canal crisis were essentially threefold: whether the company had disposed of wastes properly while the disposal site was in use; whether the company had given adequate warnings to the city of Niagara Falls when the latter acquired the property; and whether the company had acted responsibly after the site was disturbed by others once Hooker Chemical no longer owned the property. I believe an objective review of the facts now available supports the company's contention that it acted responsibly at all times. Unfortunately, much of the factual information was omitted from the early coverage of the Love Canal story.

Again, my key point is that the first step is to reach agreement on the definition of the crisis and the issues to be addressed. No effective crisis management plan can be put into effect until this objective has been accomplished.

(2) *The second step is to create realistic objectives that are agreed upon by all members of the management team.*

I stressed earlier that it is important for top management to understand the basic workings of the news media. Given the constraints under which the electronic media must operate, I do not believe that it is actually possible to obtain totally accurate and thorough coverage of truly complex issues such as Love Canal.

For example, I have already alluded to the limited amount of the news air time available to even the most important event. Television reporters must, of necessity, hold the limited attention span of their viewers and focus on visual drama. The corporate response to many issues is usually carefully reasoned, lengthy, and frankly, often dull.

Broadcast and print journalists tend to cover such a broad range of issues that it can be difficult for them to develop an in-depth understanding of the complexities about which they must write. In addition, it is often impossible for the public relations staff to work with the same reporter over an extended period of time (due to shifting media assignments), thus making it very difficult for the media to develop an adequate understanding of the subject matter, especially if it is technical in nature.

An appreciation of these constraints on the news media is essential if management is to be in a position to agree upon realistic objectives. It is the responsibility of the public relations officials to make certain that management has that understanding.

Add to the above difficulties a general antibusiness bias that is ongoing as the media feeds its voracious appetite for exposé and the problems in gaining balanced and accurate coverage become even more difficult.

There are several additional media techniques regarding coverage of crisis stories that deserve mention in this chapter. They are widely used, often with disastrous results for the subject in question:

- Anecdotal reporting: the use by a journalist of personal views of nonexpert, often uninformed third parties.
- Ambush journalism: a journalistic sneak attack involving confrontation of an unsuspecting subject with loaded or biased questions. The end result of the ambush almost invariably leaves the subject looking guilty of some wrongdoing.
- Docu-drama: usually a full-length TV feature which is a combination of fact and fiction with emphasis on the dramatic aspects rather than the documentary.

(3) The third step is to create an issue committee or task force to deal with the crisis, replacing and absorbing the responsibilities of the initial emergency communications team that handled the situation during the early stages.

The issue committee should include the appropriate disciplines and expertise (perhaps one or more of those that managed the initial emergency), including public relations, law, technical, and top management, so that all aspects of the problem can be dealt with concurrently. In a crisis such as Love Canal it is especially important to have available competent technical personnel, detached from their normal responsibilities, to devote adequate attention to the problem. Again, this underscores the necessity of gaining the total cooperation of top management and maintaining their involvement for the duration of the crisis.

(4) *The fourth step is to identify the critical publics involved and to develop plans for communicating with them.*

Although the Love Canal story was receiving sensationalized treatment from the national news media, our own priorities placed company employees and residents of the Niagara Falls community at the top of the list of important publics. Others included our shareholders, the chemical industry, our customers and suppliers, the financial community, government, and the public at large.

It is important to keep in mind that a major crisis will inevitably focus attention on the entire company, including plants far from the place where the original crisis-related events took place. Special attention must be given to keeping local managements and staffs in charge of community relations at these facilities abreast of important issues and developments to avoid embarrassment and unnecessary stories that are out of proportion with reality. These company members must have sufficient support to handle the immediacy of any after-shocks resulting from the primary crisis.

(5) *The fifth step in this process is to identify credible third-party sources who will support your side of the story.*

I have emphasized the absolute necessity of developing good relations with the news media and addressing their requests promptly on a day-to-day basis. If your organization has a reputation for candor and openness, you will find that this perception carries over to a crisis. If the company is regarded as uncooperative, your efforts to cultivate the trust of the media during a crisis—especially when critics are impugning the organization's credibility—will be futile.

In this regard, it is important to avoid adopting a siege mentality—that is, "us versus them"—in which the news media are regarded as adversaries and treated as such.

The media must be regarded as both a target public with an important and legitimate interest in the subject and as a conduit to reach other important publics.

In the Love Canal crisis we achieved a major breakthrough when the *Wall Street Journal* ran an editorial describing the facts of what really happened at Love Canal. The editorial was accompanied by a detailed sidebar piece with a chronological account of the Love Canal history. For the first time, a major third party—one with unquestioned credibility—suggested that not all of the facts had come to light and that some of what were considered to be "facts," simply were not.

(6)   My final point regarding preparation of a response plan is that you must make constant and continuous efforts to correct the record.

Previously reported information, no matter how erroneous, tends to become a "matter of record" and thus self-perpetuating. Misstatements, distortions, and false charges, unless corrected, tend to become part of the background in continuing coverage of the story. Until the record is corrected, you will be forced to live the nightmare over and over again.

Once a crisis has occurred, and even after the turning point has been reached and passed successfully, inevitably new fires will be kindled. Any problems that may exist in other parts of the organization involved will be given microscopic scrutiny and totally disproportionate media coverage.

Consider, for example, the attention devoted by the media to nuclear power facilities since the Three Mile Island accident. Even as minor a problem as a rupture of a sewer line at a nuclear facility may be given headline treatment, inevitably accompanied by references to the Three Mile Island incident. This clearly underscores the longevity of the negative impact of a crisis.

THE "60 MINUTES" SCENARIO

When Occidental Chemical discovered and reported a groundwater problem at our Lathrop, California, facility to environmental officials, we soon found ourselves the target of a "60 Minutes" inquiry.

The Lathrop facility is primarily an agricultural chemical plant, producing fertilizers and pesticides as well as a number of other chemical products. Traces of fertilizer and pesticide residue were found in the groundwater under the company property. There was at no time any contamination of potable water supplies or any real danger to human health or the environment. The company immediately announced its intention to assume total responsibility for any appropriate remedial action stemming from plant operations.

It was somewhat of a surprise, therefore, when I received a telephone call from a producer representing Mike Wallace and "60 Minutes." Actually, I should not have been surprised, since Love Canal had inflated the news value of any story related to our company.

The initial inquiry was tentative in nature, with the producer indicating that "60 Minutes" was "considering" a story on problems related to chemical wastes. He went on to say that the "60 Minutes" approach is one of microcosm, in which one particular case is examined to typify a broader, national problem. The producer requested permission to make a preliminary visit to the facility.

The request presented a difficult choice for our management, but by this time they were experienced in dealing with sensitive issues. The first decision to be made was whether or not to permit the visit. No one at

Occidental had any real doubts that "60 Minutes" had already decided to proceed with a segment on the facility. The real question was whether or not to cooperate in an effort to mitigate the damage. There also was never any doubt that "60 Minutes" could produce a segment without our cooperation. After all, this plant could be filmed from the air and, without doubt, "60 Minutes" could find a hostile neighbor or disgruntled former employee to interview, neither of whom would have access to factual information the company would want to communicate.

We agreed first to permit the preliminary inquiry, but imposed certain conditions. The conditions essentially put the initial inquiry on a background-only basis—a limitation we felt was appropriate inasmuch as the producer had indicated that a story was only being considered.

Once "60 Minutes" informed us that they were proceeding with a segment, our management was again confronted with a question as to whether or not to cooperate. Eventually we agreed to permit their film crew to visit the plant and film virtually anything except proprietary operations. We insisted, however, that the company would speak with one voice, that of our president, Donald Baeder, at corporate headquarters in Houston. No interviews would be permitted at the Lathrop facility.

I have been asked many times why our company would agree to cooperate with "60 Minutes." After all, the show hardly had a reputation for coming up with "not guilty" verdicts on the targets of its investigations. Our decision to cooperate was based on a simple assessment of realities. "60 Minutes" would do the story whether we participated or not. Had we refused to cooperate, our refusal would have been taken as an admission of guilt, while none of the information we wanted to convey would have been included.

The central charge leveled against us was that the company had never informed state water quality officials that we formulated pesticides at the Lathrop facility. That charge was false and Mr. Baeder repeatedly presented evidence of that fact to Mike Wallace during a filmed interview. (Indeed, our company's position was subsequently supported by a federal judge's ruling.) Unfortunately, much of the evidence presented by Mr. Baeder during a two-hour session did not survive the inevitable editing. Only eight-and-a-half minutes of the interview were actually aired. Mr. Baeder defended the company in a very capable manner, winning praise from Mike Wallace on camera regarding his straightforward and courageous answers. This, too, was left on the cutting room floor.

Even in retrospect, I believe we made the proper decision in facing the "60 Minutes" cameras and responding directly to their charges. Incidentally, our own video cameras recorded the entire two-hour interview with Mr. Baeder. We later produced our own fifteen-minute rebuttal tape that also included material not used on the broadcast. This rebuttal was used to communicate with a number of internal and external publics to set the record straight with those audiences of critical importance to the company (i.e., employees, customers, plant neighbors, etc.).

To this point I have emphasized only the problems associated in dealings with a public relations crisis. It may come as a surprise to some to learn that there are benefits from a well-managed crisis that can greatly improve the quality of your organization's communications programs.

First, for some organizations, a crisis is the only way that the public relations function will ever be elevated to its appropriate position in the structure. The costs of poor public relations are often invisible, but those costs are real. A crisis that demands effective communication makes it impossible to continue to ignore the need for a well-managed public relations program.

Second, a crisis provides an opportunity to focus public attention on matters of critical concern and to reach audiences that might otherwise be unavailable. Taking advantage of the opportunities provided by this spotlight of public attention will demand the best you have to offer, but the opportunities are indeed there. In fact, turning the crisis to your organization's advantage by using the media's keen interest in your company's position on the issue is the most effective form of public relations possible in a situation of this nature.

Third, a crisis affords an opportunity to build credibility—trusting relations with the news media—and establish appropriate policies for both internal and external communications for your company that can only be a long-range benefit to the organization involved.

Finally, crisis situations should force an organization to review all of its policies relating to social responsibility in order to assure that it is living up to the constantly evolving social contract that governs our society and its institutions. Social responsibility is, I submit, the cornerstone of good public relations.

CORPORATE IDENTITY

Edward J. Gerrity, Jr.

Senior Vice President
ITT Corporation

Ask 10 public relations practioners what the term "public relations" means and you'll undoubtedly get 10 different answers. Many elements of their responses will be similar, but, depending on the nature of the industry or client they represent, each will list his publics and media according to his individual priorities.

The publics that are important seem to grow and shift each year as market or economic considerations change—employees, shareholders, government officials and agencies, vendors, customers, distributors, plant communities, trade associations, the banking and investment communities, academe, foreign institutions, and the like.

In like manner, the emphasis on media may change according to the situation—general newspapers, magazines, business and financial press, technical and trade journals, employee publications, advertising, motion pictures, trade shows, radio, television, and increasingly, cable television systems.

Corporate identity is the vehicle by which any company shapes its reputation among all those publics who are important to it and whose reaction to corporate activities can mean the continued existence of that company as a viable force.

Edward J. Gerrity, Jr., senior vice president of ITT Corporation, is responsible for all corporate relations, government relations, and advertising for one of the world's largest conglomerates. He reports directly to the chairman and is a member of the Management and Policy Committee.

Mr. Gerrity is a director of the International Economic Policy Association, among other associations, and a director of New York's Bank of Commerce. He has a master's degree from the Columbia University Graduate School of Journalism.

Before joining ITT in 1958, he was a working newsman and columnist. In World War II he was a combat infantryman and won the silver and bronze star with clusters.

In 1971 he was named PR Professional of the Year by *PR News*.

Corporate identity is that factor which sets a company apart from its competitors, gives its publics a sense of its overall makeup and direction, and stimulates a favorable, positive reaction.

There was a time when the consuming public identified the company by the product or products it was best known for, whether it was soup or salad dressing, beer or books, cars or cameras. However, the wave of mergers, acquisitions, and consolidations has blurred the public's focus about who makes what.

The company famed for its tomato and chicken soups now offers vegetable juice, canned pasta, pickles, bread, rolls, and stuffing; and operates several fast-food chains featuring steak, hamburgers, or pizza.

The "Champagne of Bottle Beers" is now made by a major tobacco company, and the old family Chevy has been joined in the General Motors mix by the Opel, Vauxhall, Holden, and Toyota as well as spark plugs, batteries, car radios, and tape players.

Another factor that tends to obscure corporate identity is the alphabetizing phenomenon that has taken place over the last several decades. Names like American Metal Climax, Continental Oil, and Swift & Company have been shortened to AMAX, Conoco, and Esmark, respectively.

Withal, the corporation may also find itself under pressure from environmentalists, consumerists, liberationists, civil rightists, and other activists whose stridency creates a negative impression about the company and dilutes attempts to set the record straight. And the demands of these groups too often translate into government intervention with its threat of crippling legislation.

Thus it becomes readily apparent that the public relations departments in corporate America, and for that matter throughout the global industrial community, must keep reminding their various publics who they are, what they do, and where they are going.

It is important to realize that the publics do react to the identity or character that a corporation takes on. Sometimes a dynamic chief executive becomes the symbol that the public identifies with. Companies should periodically subject themselves to self-analysis in order to review their corporate identities in the light of criticism, unfair or otherwise.

What you are dealing with here is the public's perception of your corporation. Perception is the reality and if it is negative, no matter how unjustified you believe that may be, what really matters is the fact that your company is viewed in a negative manner. You may think you stand for motherhood and apple pie but as far as the public is concerned, you and your corporation or client are bad guys. No amount of chest thumping is going to correct that perception.

You must objectively and honestly assess your position and set out to change the public's biased recognition. You must develop a program to correct those erroneous perceptions.

When restructuring a corporation's identity to alter current public concepts, and at the same time anticipating future challenges and issues that change with time, it is necessary to decide at the outset just how a company desires to be recognized. Should it place emphasis on its high technology, its record as a good employer, or its concern for the communities in which it is located?

The ultimate choice is primarily determined by the CEO, his management, and the board of directors. The corporate public relations executive should lead the decision-making process. Not only does this give the public relations director input, but it also provides him with the insight and thinking of the key officers and directors, and facilitates his job of carrying out the corporate identity program tailored to the various publics.

No corporate identity program can be successful without top management's commitment to the strategies to be implemented.

In this critical process the public relations executive should lead, proposing to management how the corporation should proceed in establishing its identity. This direct reporting relationship is essential. Management's views are not filtered or diffused in any way; the public relations executive is involved in developing management's philosophy firsthand. In the same way, he advises management honestly and factually of the various publics' thoughts and reactions to the corporation.

The public relations function must be creatively active, not passive, proposing programs that will keep the corporation moving and recognized as a dynamic, viable entity in the environments in which it must succeed.

Broadly speaking, the major role of public relations is to generate public awareness of the program itself. This is true whether the program involves raising the level of the corporation's identity or altering an existing one to reflect new directions. In today's rapidly changing corporate scene, many firms are taking on new identities as they acquire unrelated companies and emerge from the old cocoons that once enveloped them.

If a corporate identity program is to achieve its goals, it must also be supported by the company's employees. They must understand the reasons for change, the direction the company is taking, the role they will play, and how the new identity will benefit them.

Given all the aforementioned complexities, pressures, and commitments, how does one go about starting or improving on a corporate identity program?

If one doesn't exist already, a comprehensive how-to manual of policies and procedures should be developed, covering as completely as possible all aspects of the public relations function. Other chapters in this book will discuss these functions in detail. If a systematic program does exist, it should be updated and streamlined constantly to meet current challenges and opportunities. Once the creation or updating of the public relations program has been completed, an objective outside public opinion survey firm should be empowered to audit how your various publics "perceive" your corporation. One basic tenet is to establish a benchmark and at regular intervals resurvey to see how you are moving toward the desired goals.

To provide an example of the structuring of the public relations department, I'll draw from the organization I'm most familiar with—the Corporate Relations and Advertising Department at ITT.

Our CR&A department reports directly to the corporation's chairman and president, Rand Araskog. In this position, we enjoy a dialogue with top management and participate in every key management decision, from price increases to personnel shifts, from litigation to legislation.

Not only do we convey management's views to the assorted publics, but we also recommend policy to management; we help mold its opinion and initiate programs, and we advise on current trends, public opinion, and legislative strategies that have a bearing on the corporation. Thus, the public relations function not only puts out fires but also prevents them.

The public relations function at ITT headquarters is broadly defined. Either alone or in cooperation with others, the headquarters Corporate Relations and Advertising Department is responsible for publicity and advertising; employee and stockholder communications; government relations; information and editorial services; relations with the general, financial, and technical press; public affairs, including community relations; the shareholders' annual meeting; and trade shows and exhibits. The advertising function is responsible for the direction of all advertising and sales promotion activity within ITT, particularly that originating at headquarters.

Responsibility for department activities is line insofar as it involves the performance of tasks directly by public relations personnel at headquarters; it is staff insofar as it involves supervising the performance of tasks carried out by public relations personnel in the field.

We have integrated the advertising function under the public relations umbrella. Most of our institutional ads complement the global program. Advertising is one of the tools of public relations, and since only a portion of the corporation's product mix is sold directly to the consuming public, our advertising people and our agency are charged with developing corporate ads that help position and identify the company and its products in such diverse fields as telecommunications, electronics, pumps, semiconductors, insurance, natural resources, and automotive.

Equally diverse is our geographic presence. We have operations in approximately 100 countries around the world. As a consequence, we maintain a network of offices, staffed by indigenous professionals, who coordinate within and across national boundaries in major news release dissemination, trade show design and manning, tracking legislation that has international implications, and similar matters. This assures a unified corporate identity throughout the world.

Outside of New York headquarters, we maintain a small staff at our

European headquarters in Brussels. Professionals there monitor activities throughout Europe, Africa, and the Middle East.

Until several years ago, we covered the Far East from offices in Hong Kong, but have since combined that operation with our Latin American public relations staff, and the amalgamated group works out of New York. Both this latter group and the staff in Brussels coordinate and assist the public relations departments of our companies operating on those continents.

We also have an office in Toronto that interacts with our many branches in Canada.

Finally, we maintain regional offices in Miami, Chicago, Los Angeles, and Seattle to supervise and lend support to ITT companies in those areas.

We maintain a specialized corporate relations office in Washington, D.C. Our people there maintain personal contact with officials of the relevant branches and agencies of the federal government, members of the press, and the diplomatic corps, so as to obtain and evaluate information of interest to the corporation and to represent our position.

Here again, we recommend policy and initiate programs that are vital to our remaining a competitive force in the many industries in which we operate.

On a regular basis, we bring top management to the nation's capital to meet our legislators, agency heads, the military, and other key people. We testify before various committees to apprise senators and congressmen of our position on developing legislation.

The Washington office operates on the principle that a healthy interrelationship between government and industry is vital to the conduct of business in the modern world. The office provides our marketing staffs with information concerning high-level attitudes and policies affecting their units.

ITT keeps the corporation's needs and capabilities before the eyes of government leaders through a constant interchange of information. Efficient operation of the economy requires that government and business each learn the other's problems and opportunities, and that all parties know all the facts.

In addition, many of the larger ITT companies throughout the world have public relations and advertising departments to promote their products or services and take care of community relations activities. Representing both the staff and line public relations and advertising function requires the efforts of almost 200 professionals worldwide.

Tying this widespread complex of companies and people together is a global telecommunications network. Telephone, high-speed telex, facsimile, and other communications modes link world headquarters practitioners directly to each professional in the field. Not a week goes by that we at headquarters don't initiate a call to, or field one from, each of our men and women scattered around the world. The amount of traffic, both spoken and written, depends of course on the priorities of the situation.

This networking, both in terms of offices around the globe and in the strict sense of high-speed reliable communications, is necessary for instantaneous access to major media markets. If our chief executive announces a technological breakthrough by one of our laboratories or an acquisition of some consequence, this information must flow simultaneously to important media outlets in cities around the world. Similarly, if an event in one country has far-reaching economic implications for other areas of the corporation, we want to know about it right away and develop a cohesive corporate strategy to neutralize any potential negative impact. As mentioned before, we want to present a united corporate position to our many publics.

As the company has grown, so has our headquarters department and field staff. In the same way, growth has generated the need for the flow of more abundant and accurate information to the media, stockholders, the financial community, and government agencies.

What type of people and what level of education are required in a public relations department staffer who works on the team that shapes corporate identity and keeps it fresh in the public's mind?

A college education is, of course, a big help in any business, but it is newspaper or other media or governmental experience that gives the public relations man the real understanding he needs for his job.

In my opinion, press relations are the cornerstone of any well-balanced public relations program. I disagree with the theorists who neglect the general press and aim their primary efforts at the so-called thought-leaders through specialized promotions. Creative thought plays an important role in public relations; but, like everything else, it is the output that comes from plain hard work that pays the biggest dividends.

A number of years ago, *Editor and Publisher* ran a profile on our department's operations. At that time I said that you get the best education for this type of work in a newspaper office and I haven't changed my thinking. In fact, events have proved me correct.

If a man doesn't know what news is, he will not be very effective in dealing with newsmen who are his direct contact with the public.

Our public relations organization is structured like a newspaper.

For example, there is a news services department that handles spot assignments; an editorial services section for longer-term "think pieces" including speeches, annual reports, and related projects; Europe, Latin America, and Far East groups that are like foreign correspondents; a radio-TV section to handle the special needs of these media; and even a library, which performs the function of the newspaper morgue.

We also interface daily with the financial news departments of newspapers and wire services. They are interested in matters that concern the financial community, such as mergers, acquisitions, personnel changes, promotions, new products, technical advances, and the like. These are legitimate news topics, and we send them along to newspapers as they occur, without undue embellishment.

Coordination of a program for getting our corporate story across, in text that can be easily translated into any language, is our broad assignment.

Coordination of what is said is another important element in maintaining a positive corporate identity. Those 200 professionals I mentioned earlier generate an enormous amount of copy. Understandably, each individual has a certain style, and while we at headquarters do not expect to see every piece of copy, we do insist that we be given a chance to review major releases, features, or advertisements.

There are several reasons for this. We want to make sure that our people are making statements that are correct and in line with corporate policy, that the style of writing conforms to the guidelines we have established as part of our department's policies and procedures, and that the release or ad is aimed at the right markets through the right publications; and we want to help in scheduling so as to keep a constant flow of information rather than sporadic placements where one of our units might be competing with another for an editor's attention.

Competition is good, even between units within the overall corporation—but not when it results in confusion that may arise and jeopardize that cohesiveness so necessary to your corporate identity.

Of all the functions we perform, we are probably most interested in attracting the attention of the public through news stories in the press. With more than 280,000 employees in almost 100 countries, we are seldom at a loss for news material, and our press relations alone keep us busy.

Of course, while a comparatively small number of us actually belong to the department bearing the name "corporate relations," we realize that each one of ITT's employees is directly involved in public relations and in maintaining a positive corporate identity. What they say about ITT in their own personal contacts also is important in forming the opinion the publics hold of us. Therefore we also direct a great deal of attention to them.

I mentioned earlier that once the public relations function was established and clear goals set, or if an existing department has been realigned and streamlined to take on the challenge of improving corporate identity, the next obvious step to is conduct a benchmark survey to see what your publics think about your company, its reputation, its management, its products, and services.

In the 1960s and 1970s, when Harold Geneen was engaged in acquiring new businesses and companies under the banner of ITT, the company had little if any clear-cut identity. In 1973 we asked Yankelovich, Skelly, and White to conduct a benchmark study. The results revealed that nearly two-thirds of the American public could not identify ITT's member companies, products, or services. In the absence of a large number of highly visible consumer products, the man or woman on the street failed to relate to the ITT family of companies and their substantial contributions to local communities via employment, tax revenues, and the production of vital goods and services. Many people thought we were the overseas arm of AT&T—but more on this later.

We were not alone, however. Surveys taken at the time showed that most other major corporations were in a similar position, as well as suffering a decline in public respect.

At that time ITT was on its way to becoming the ninth largest industrial company in the Fortune 500. We moved from number 58 in 1957 to number 9 in 1971. Yet research found that the vacuum created by a lack of knowledge about ITT was being filled by news stories making unfavorable allegations.

It wasn't a question of our not having advertised before. Through our corporate advertising agency, we had been running a successful print campaign for a number of years. But we had directed this effort at a narrow, carefully defined target group. We had aimed at people in business, finance, government, and the campus. We believed we were getting through.

What our research told us, unmistakably, was that this wasn't enough. There were too many people out there—prosperous, relatively well-educated people—who didn't know what ITT was or did. They were voters, people who might be potential buyers of our stock, college students who would be the leaders of tomorrow, and so on. The fact was they didn't recognize our name as well as they would the name of the more familiar consumer goods companies. And lacking knowledge, they were ready to believe almost anything said about us.

That is why we decided to shift most of our media dollars into television, taking our message to an audience a good deal larger than the audience we had been talking to. We needed both television's reach and its speed of communication.

There would still be a basic print schedule, directed at that part of the audience that watched little TV. But print's role was considered largely supportive of television's.

Our job was to communicate how we could help improve the quality of life through the quality of our research and development, our products, and our services. Television was a perfect vehicle for this, not only because it could help us demonstrate dramatically our concern and involvement, but because of its speed and efficiency in reaching the large audience we now had in mind.

Also, we knew that many of ITT's products and services—some of them highly complex and unfamiliar to the average consumer—would have to be seen in action to be understood.

We knew that reaching our desired audience and changing minds in a relatively short time would be an expensive proposition. We also knew we had to demonstrate to our management that this expense was justified—that a major corporate advertising campaign, on the scale we projected, could fill the identity vacuum and neutralize the unfavorable publicity we were getting.

In late 1973 we undertook a major research program that had two key objectives. The first was to track changes in awareness, familiarity, and reputation of ITT among people in households with $15,000+ annual incomes. The other was to assess the effectiveness of the campaign in improving attitudes among this target audience.

We developed a questionnaire, carefully pretested it, and administered it before the campaign began in order to get our benchmark. Then we went back six months later, and again six months after that. We are still continuing to chart our progress at six-month intervals. Each sampling has consisted of 1,500 or more telephone interviews.

We started the campaign in early 1974. Television carried the major thrust. The commercials were backed up by print ads in the major news and business magazines, particularly to reach those people at the higher end of the scale who watch very little television.

While our direction has shifted from print to TV, the basic message hasn't changed at all. We were still talking about unusual products and services coming out of our extensive R&D programs that help improve the quality of life. But the subjects of those first commercials—fiber optics and undersea cable—were quite unusual.

Once we started to make progress in creating awareness and improving attitudes, we made another basic decision. Our commercials and our print ads would now have to communicate the fact that ITT has products and services which improve not only the quality of life, but also the company's prospects for future earnings and profits.

Corporate advertising will obviously never market any company as an investment in the same way that consumer advertising sells a product. But corporate advertising can and will play in the future a much larger role in portraying the advertiser as a successful, viable instrument for the making of profits.

From the benchmark research results of late 1973 to the latest research results, ITT's identity has shown improvement in all areas.

Improvement was rapid. Within a year, awareness of ITT rose 65 percent and the company was recognized by nearly three out of every four people, compared with a third before the campaign. ITT was recognized as a "leader in technology." Also increasing were the number of people who felt that ITT was "very profitable," "makes quality products," "a good stock to buy or own," "one of the largest companies," and "cares about the general public." In all, 25 key questions were asked of the survey participants.

The targets of the ads continue to be people commonly known as "movers and shakers," "influentials," or "thought-leaders"—take your pick. They are 25 to 54 years old, today have household incomes of $30,000 and up, and work in professional and/or managerial jobs. We estimate there are 13½ million of them, and we believe they see our ads a little better than 14 times a year.

There's no doubt we've turned the corner and have improved our corporate identity/reputation. But we're not about to rest on our hard-won, expensive results. Keeping your publics aware of your company's who, what, when, why, and where is a constant challenge, and through public relations campaigns and provocative corporate advertising you keep yourself out in front.

These, then, are the elements that comprise a well-developed public relations program aimed at keeping your corporate identity on a positive tack. Key ingredients are top management commitment, advising and recommending to management the course of action in a given situation, surveying current attitudes toward your company, developing a program or programs to correct misconceptions or erroneous perceptions, conducting a benchmark study, integrating all public relations and advertising activity to put your message across to the various publics, and regularly sampling your target audience to assess progress.

Couple this overall approach with a strong, multifaceted media relations campaign, legislative liaison, and a communication network to reach any of your field operations at a moment's notice, and you have the means to continually support your corporate identity as comprehensively as possible.

It takes time to establish and maintain an upbeat reputation, and no matter how complex your corporate structure, your message must be simple, easily understood, and easily interpreted by your publics.

I have stressed that perception is reality—and I want to make that point one more time. You cannot delude yourself by thinking you have done everything to assure your reputation is fail-safe. The public's impression, subject to change at the slightest whim, is the real impression.

However, if you are honest with yourself and recognize the realities, if you are honest in your dealings with the media, if your advertising is reliable and credible, if you are accurate and forthright in your relations with your various publics, then you are on solid ground.

Integrity is at the foundation of any corporate identity program.

At ITT, over 3,800 of our executives and managers throughout the world annually review the corporation's Code of Conduct and sign a document indicating they have read, understood, and will comply fully with each aspect of that code.

Department managers hammer home the importance and significance of the code to their staffs up and down the line. Despite our best efforts, there are slipups from time to time due to the frailty of human nature—something that society has grappled with since the Garden of Eden.

However, when an aberration occurs, we respond to public inquiry in an honest and fair manner.

A reputation for honesty and evenhandedness will help identify your corporation or client in the best possible way. That basic policy, along with the public relations tools mentioned in the preceding pages, will go a long way toward identifying you clearly among the many other companies who compete for the public's attention.

INVESTOR RELATIONS

William E. Chatlos

President
Chatlos & Company, Inc.

THE BEGINNING

The short history of investor relations can be a distinct advantage. We do not have to deal with the convolutions of the ages. We can carefully examine all aspects of a short history with greater intensity than would be possible in a much longer time frame. To this end we can perhaps agree that the beginning of the function of investor relations can be dated to 1950. While some elements of interest can be pinpointed prior to that time, the pre-1950 period can be referred to as IR–BC, Investor Relations before Communications. The green eyeshade was evolving into a new and exciting corporate activity.

The need for investor relations—called stockholder relations at the time—was a by-product of the post-World War II economy. Corporate growth with the resultant need for corporate financing combined with the public interest in equity securities (shares of publicly held companies) to create an interest in Wall Street that was to dominate the American scene for many decades.

The emergence of the security analyst as a professional may be regarded as one of the significant events of that time. Instead of being relegated to the

As president of Chatlos & Company, Inc., William E. Chatlos is a corporate consultant in investor relations planning, corporate ownership direction, and tender offer strategy. He was formerly a principal of Georgeson & Company, specialists in proxy solicitation and investor relations, where he was in charge of management consulting for investor relations. He has also authored articles for *Harvard Business Review, Financial World, Wall Street Transcript*, just to mention a few publications. He is a frequent lecturer at seminars and educational institutions, including Harvard Business School, and is a member of the Investor Relations Association, and a founder and past president of the National Investor Relations Institute. He is on the board of directors of two corporations and has been a consultant to numerous states, appearing as an expert witness before state legislative committees regarding state takeover statutes.

back office to search for undervalued and overlooked situations by browsing through Standard and Poor's, and Moody's, the newly emerging function of the analyst was to create a continuing commentary on individual stock issues. Instead of being regarded as an expensive overhead cost, the security analyst was seen as a means to create public interest in the sale of equity issues. The corporate and consultant investor relations response to the availability of the security analyst was in large measure responsible for the professional stature and growth of security analysis.

In a large sense, investor relations people speeded up the professionalism of security analysts by recognizing the opportunity to make the analyst's job easier. Basic data reports (now called "fact books") were created to provide the analyst with the factual information needed to consider any subsequent recommendation. The trickle of information sponsored by corporations became a torrent. Fortunately, most investor relations practitioners at the time adopted an almost religious fervor regarding the mystical and anticipatory qualities of the "auction market" and disciplined themselves (and, perhaps more importantly, their corporate bosses) to communicating massive and sometime dull doses of "fact," avoiding subjective commentary.

It became the age of "tell the truth, all the truth, all the time." With Securities and Exchange Commission assistance, understanding, and at times leadership, a matrix of factual communications created the basis of the analytical process that has served the public well for decades.

EVOLUTION

By hindsight, perhaps the most astonishing aspect of the investor relations achievement was the education and conversion of tough-minded management to the goal of "effectively communicating and let the auction market dictate the stock price." With some notable exceptions, managements generally followed this rule.

Communications became the chief ingredient in all investor relations activities. Analyst meetings, analyst society meetings, analyst splinter groups, annual meetings, annual reports, interim reports, fact books, even postmeeting reports were factually oriented. Only article placement in the press seemed to run counter to the trend and, consequently, was treated with concern and suspicion by many investor relations people.

The market at this stage of the investor relations evolution was highly reactive. Most of the activity was retail, that is, dealing with the individual investor. Dealing with security analysts and through them to the registered representative and eventually through them to the individual investor was a powerful and successful mechanism. So attuned was the market to new developments that a cover placement on *Time* magazine or a major article in the *Wall Street Journal* was followed by strong response. So a few corporations tried to communicate almost exclusively through press placements, rather than through the more meticulous and relatively unexciting process of dealing with the factual structure favored by security analysts.

There was very little about which to be cynical. The securities market was strong and responsive. Investment funds were largely retail and, through the registered representative system of the brokerage community, dollars were channeled to investment equities based on the track record of the managements. Dollars flowed readily to the universe of stocks without regard to the nature of the industry or the size of the capitalization.

The dream of Benjamin Graham and David L. Dodd in their masterful book *Security Analysis* had been realized. Investment dollars moved to stocks perceived as undervalued, thereby correcting the temporary inequity of market price.

END OF THE RAINBOW

The period of the early and middle 1960s was unreal. Everything worked. The communication function was polished and fine tuned and the responsive marketplace acted in almost perfect counterpoint to the informational flow. Analyst meetings resulted in gradually changing market prices. This was not caused by leaks of inside information, as frequently charged by the financial press, but was a reflection of the market's absorption of marginal information. The pieces of the mosaic, as discussed by the SEC, were filtered and refined in the market analysis, and market prices changed.

Corporations were committed to the disclosure process. Shareholders were important and the market analytical system, while not perfect, constituted an equity screening that kept stock prices relevant to each other.

Every participating element in the system prospered. There was indeed a customer's yacht in the harbor, a reference to the old Wall Street bromide of the customer who, being shown the magnificent view of the harbor and of the broker's yacht asked, "Where are the customers' yachts?" The investor relations function, while an overhead expense, could be regarded as a profit center for its vital role in maintaining full value.

Corporations in the public domain generally recognized the need for full valuation in the marketplace. It was not only a public report card of management's performance, with huge egos at stake, but it was a vital factor in new equity financing, stock option advantages when the tax laws permitted, as well as the "Chinese money" concept of using shares as a medium of exchange in making acquisitions. Sad to say, the self-serving interests of managements and corporations have consistently seemed to be stronger motivation of corporate concern regarding full value in the market price than the corporate interest in servicing shareholders with one of the few benefits of equity ownership—a market price reflecting management's performance.

Whatever the motive, it is fortunate that corporate interest in market price does exist.

CLOUDS OVER CAMELOT

Perhaps the Wall Street love affair was too hot—as the old song goes—not to cool down. In any event, Wall Street proved to be a most ungracious winner. As the trading and brokerage system creaked and strained under the increasing load of activity imposed on it, Wall Street's response was less than prudent. Profitable success after success as "the only game in town" proved to be a harsh taskmaster to the system. When problems emerged because sales activities were extended beyond the back offices' ability to handle the resulting volume, the immediate response was arrogant quick fixes rather than anticipatory long-term business planning.

It took nine months to get a stock certificate through the transfer process. The banking community recognized the problem and a few banks refused to take on any more clients until they cleaned house.

The overheated market became superheated. Success bred a level of expectations that could not be fulfilled. Customers demanded more and Wall Street promised more. New issues were underwritten at a price/earnings ratio of as much as 60. Brokerage back office facilities literally collapsed under the strain, and efforts to correct the mistakes inevitably led to more mistakes. Finally, in a public admission of Wall Street's inability to plan long range, public trading facilities were closed every Wednesday. It was the classic response of the monopolist: "If you can't service customers, control them."

Customers were less than happy and did what might have been expected. They walked away. They didn't sell their shares. They just walked away. For a system geared to the retail trade—and in many respects it remains so today—it was a devastating blow. The system was geared to volume, couldn't plan for high volume, and suddenly had very little volume. Again, as could have been expected, broker failures and bankruptcy-avoiding mergers followed. It was a grim sight and the individual shareholder moved further away from the system. Lack of confidence in Wall Street was reflected in the tidal wave of beneficial holders transferring shares from brokerage name to individual name out of fear that the brokerage house could not survive.

The investor relations professionals were caught in a self-devised trap. We had professed and followed the financial scripture of "God gave us the stock market and God wouldn't cheat!" We believed inherently in the efficiency of the auction market. The market perhaps wasn't always scientifically accurate, but it wasn't that far wrong. We felt strongly about our beliefs because our past history had supported the premises of our beliefs.

Investor relations professionals were service oriented and were conditioned to accept the resulting wisdom of the marketplace. We not only had no answers but were not solution oriented.

The second major storm cloud was almost wholly unanticipated. The geometrical growth of institutional funds was about to burst upon the scene. The institutionalization of the market was not foreseen and the market was not prepared for its impact. A system designed for the retail trade was about to be dominated in volume by institutional activity.

Again, investor relations professionals were unprepared for this second major change. Investor relations programs were geared to individuals as shareholders. In the early days of institutional activity, corporate egos were titillated by large institutional block purchases. But as experience was accumulated, it became obvious that institutional ownership was the epitome of investor self-interest. Shares were bought and sold almost completely without regard to the resulting benefits or harm to the corporation itself. This was a complete reversal of the previous practice of large block holders to gently inquire of the company as to whether the company or another buyer might be interested in purchasing the block. This practice fostered a stable market, and permitted the seller to obtain market price and the buyer to do the same. The new institutions had so much money to invest that there literally was not enough time to observe the prudent ground rules. The new method was to dump the shares when a sell decision was made and to buy as quickly as possible when that decision was made. This had a severe impact on market price volatility.

With individuals out of the market, institutional activity had severe impact on market price, either up or down. While it was corporate fun watching institutions drive prices up, it was agony watching the price drop when institutions decided to follow some other whim. What was particularly devastating was the herd instinct of institutional trading. Institutions are more comfortable acting in concert with other institutions.

The investor relations impact was most unsettling. To have the problem of institutional ownership was bad enough, but not to have the problem perhaps was even worse. With individuals out of the market, the only game in town was the institutions. As sophisticated and informed investors, however, institutions knew that they had to deal with large capitalizations to satisfy the ever-increasing block requirements of the institutional investing strategy. This led to unduly large trading volume in the "Nifty 50" and eventually in the "Shifting Nifty 50."

Large-capitalization companies could attract some institutional trading from time to time, and although managements might not be entirely pleased with ever-increasing institutional ownership, at least there was trading activity. The vast majority of companies, however, had neither individual following nor the capitalization to attract institutional following. The investor relations quandary for most companies was to have no sustained investor, following the result that market price was a happenstance event with very little relationship to underlying value.

EVOLUTION II

The investor relations evolutionary pattern of the 1970s is in direct contrast to the above-described successful evolutionary pattern of the 1950s. Instead of creating and innovating to meet the needs of the times, as was done in the 1950s, investor relations professionals in the 1970s were largely caught by their own definitional trap as communicators. To be a communicator means that we improve the flow of information in the system, rather than change or improve the system itself.

Investor relations professionals, along with most Wall Street observers, consistently failed to recognize that the trading system had undergone a fundamental change that did not permit the return to the long-established ground rules. Market price was no longer self-adjusting to provide fair value. A trading system designed for the retail trade had problems trying to accommodate institutional trading. Indeed, almost every proposed change in the system was resisted mindlessly and vehemently by factions in the Street who perceived the changes as threats to their short-term interests.

The market is currently struggling with the problem of substantial market price swings caused by institutional trading, although such swings were predicted by the author in the early 1970s. In late 1982, the *Wall Street Journal* reported a market price incident and, almost for the first time in the public press, commented on the difficulty of using the old trading system to facilitate institutional trading in the current environment.

Tim Carrington of the *Wall Street Journal* reported on December 13, 1982:

> The criticism comes as the Big Board was reveling in the praise it has generated for its relatively efficient handling of the recent explosion in trading volume.
>
> But the problems in opening Warner [Communications, Inc.] point up broader problems Wall Street executives say the Big Board and its market makers are encountering with the wild price swings in the market. The stock market is increasingly dominated by the large investing institutions, who have tended to move in and out of stocks in droves, causing unprecedented price gyrations. When Warner finally opened, it traded at $38, down $13.88 a share from Tuesday's close.
>
> And where there is a massive buildup in sell orders, officials say an exchange market maker would be hard-pressed to keep prices on a relatively even keel. "They're asking the specialist to absorb 10%" of a company's stock price in one transaction, says one exchange member. "*The system wasn't built for that.*" It is the market makers' function to

stabilize markets, which, under heavy selling, means buying for their own accounts heavy amounts of stock. [Emphasis added.]

"The system wasn't built for that." In that one sentence is the investor relations nightmare. Investor relations limited itself to more effective communications, and the changed system was not susceptible to much improvement by more effective communications.

While investor relations made few major contributions to the changed circumstances in the 1970s, a number of minor experiments were tried. The flight from the market of individual investors began in the late 1960s and continued throughout the 1970s and only recently has shown any slight sign of reversing itself.

A number of laudatory investor relations efforts to service the individual investor met with mixed results. Instead of using the six blocks of Wall Street to attract individual investors through the security analyst system, corporations engaged in road shows throughout the United States to try to get to the individual investor. Meetings were held in cities that would not have warranted a second thought ten years earlier. These efforts are currently continuing although limited success has resulted and the bang for each dollar expended is extremely muted. We have not been successful in bringing the individual investor back to the marketplace.

During this entire period of time the communications function was refined and upgraded. However, if the investor relations professional is to have a high-level future, the job description must be expanded from communicator to strategist and problem solver.

WORTH MORE DEAD THAN ALIVE

A logical outcome of the sequence of events described above would be that market prices would come to bear little relation to underlying value and, indeed, this has proved to be the case. While the famous "capital crunch" in the early 1970s prevented much abuse of the opportunity to acquire underpriced shares, this situation was reversed with a vengence in the mid-1970s as corporations began to accumulate internal cash flow. Literally, well-run corporations were worth more dead than alive.

It is no coincidence that during this period tender offers flourished. One of the first such offers carried an 18 percent premium over market price. Stock market observers were astonished that anyone would be so foolish to pay such a *high* premium over "fair market price." However, the market had long since lost its capacity to reflect corporate performance. Offerers recognized this and bidding contests soon made 100 percent or more premiums commonplace.

In the decade of the 1970s the Dow Jones industrial average did not vary much from 7 p/e (price/earnings ratio). Yet in the latter half of the decade, which saw almost all of the tender offer activity, the prices paid in competitive tender offers ranged from 12.3 p/e to 21.8 p/e. Willing buyers were offering to pay two to three times the value ascribed by the open market! To repeat for emphasis—the changed market circumstances meant that Wall Street had lost the capacity to reflect corporate performance.

A study I made covering that period of time sought to determine stock price values as set by the competitive tender offer bidding process, compared with the open market price structure, and to determine the impact of length of time of the bidding process on the ultimate price offered.

Similar studies were not continued in 1981 and 1982 because substantive SEC rule changes in 1980 made further comparisons difficult. However, in addition to the 12.3 p/e to 21.8 p/e range between 1975 and 1980, the applicable p/e in 1981 and 1982 was close to 20 p/e!

In general, those making tender offers were well aware that stock values were far higher than those reflected in the open market price and the offerers were willing to pay substantial premiums. Also, it would appear that longer time periods for the offer encouraged more competition and therefore higher prices to the shareholders of the target company, which was entirely in keeping and consistent with the congressional intent of the Williams Act enacted in 1968. (See, for a detailed analysis, tables 5.1, 5.2, 5.3, 5.4 and figures 5.1, 5.2, 5.3.)

TABLE 5.1 COMBINED BIDS AND VALUES*

	Days						
	7	10	45	60	90	120	Over 120
11/74–12/76							
Bid	6	4	18	2	2	1	0
Premium	49.8**	22.7	75.3	13.3	13.7	3.9	0
1977							
Bid	4	2	6	0	0	4	7
Premium	44.9**	54.5	212.8	0	0	18.9	331.8
1978							
Bid	0	3	16	10	6	4	1
Premium	0**	79.5	77.3	33.3	81.9	89.2	1.2
1979							
Bid	2	0	20	4	0	0	1
Premium	3.9**	0	228.7	272.0	0	0	16.6
1980							
Bid	0	0	4	2	0	0	0
Premium	0**	0	172.9	4.1	0	0	0
Total bids per period	12	9	64	18	8	9	9
Cumulative bids	12	21	85	103	111	120	129

(cont.)

TABLE 5.1 (cont.)

	Days						
	7	10	45	60	90	120	Over 120
Bid percentage	9.3	16.3	65.9	79.8	86.0	93.0	100.0
Premium per period	98.6**	156.7	767.0	322.7	95.6	112.0	349.6
Cumulative premium	98.6**	255.3	1,022.3	1,345.0	1,440.6	1,552.6	1,902.2
Premium percentage	5	13.4	53.7	70.7	75.7	81.6	100.0
Reciprical percentage (bids)	90.7	83.7	34.1	20.2	14.0	7.0	0.0
Reciprical percentage (premium)	95.0	86.6	46.3	29.3	24.3	18.4	0.0

* This is a historical presentation of all competitive tender offers in the years indicated and by length of time of the offer. Of interest here is the determination of how competition benefits the investor of the target company, compared with the artificial short-term period (7–10 days) mandated by the SEC rules from 1968 to 1980.

Lines 1 through 10 provide the actual history of tender offers under the more liberal state laws then prevailing.

Lines 13 and 16 give percentages of numbers of bids and the dollar premiums attained. *Example*: Under the SEC rule only 16.3% of actual bids took place (line 13), whereas 83.7% of the bids probably would not have taken place (line 17) had it not been for the state laws. Similarly, only 13.4% or $255.3 millions of the actual dollar premiums received (lines 16 and 15) occurred in the SEC 10-day period compared with the $1,902.2 millions actually received under state laws.

The conclusion to be drawn is that if the SEC rules only were applied, to the exclusion of the state laws, the investor would have been deprived of $1,646.9 millions.

** These figures represent dollar values in millions.

TABLE 5.2   COMPETITIVE TENDER OFFERS*

Year	Average Price/ Earnings Ratio of Target	Median Price/ Earnings Ratio of Target	Average Offer as a Multiple of Target's Book Value	Median Offer as a Multiple of Target's Book Value
11/74–1975	12.3	10.4	1.1	1.1
1976	19.0	14.2	1.4	1.2
1977	21.8	18.3	2.2	1.8
1978	16.0	13.6	1.9	1.5
1979	13.5	13.6	1.7	1.6
1980	17.3	15.6	1.7	1.6

* Applicable market price multiples expressed as average and median price/earnings ratios and as average and median book values. These should be compared to DJIA or other averages for the year indicated.

TABLE 5.3   SUMMARY OF COMPETITIVE TENDER OFFERS*

Year	Bids	Average Number of Days from Original Announcement to Final Bid	Median Number of Days from Original Announcement to Final Bid	Average Number of Days to Completed Offer	Median Number of Days to Completed Offer	Total Premium Over Bid**
11/74–12/76	33	30.5	17.5	52.2	46.5	178.7
1977	23	59.8	23.5	110.8	80.0	662.9
1978	40	56.1	48.0	92.8	82.0	362.4
1979	27	48.5	42.0	93.1	67.5	521.2
1980	6	38.5	34.0	69.8	63.5	177.0
					Total	1,902.2

* Competitive bids by year showing average and median numbers of days to final bid, and average and median number of days to completed offer. The premiums shown by year reflect the benefit to investors over the original bid (itself a premium over the existing market price) attained through the competitive bidding process.

** Expressed in millions of dollars.

TABLE 5.4   SUMMARY OF COMPETITIVE TENDER OFFERS*

Year	Cases	Bids	Total Premium Over Bid**	Bids Assuming 1980 SEC Tender Offer Rules	Percentage Change in Reduced Bids	Total Premium over Bid Assuming 1980 SEC Tender Offer Rules**
11/74–1975	9	13	63.5	12	8	51.1
1976	11	20	115.2	11	45	82.3
1977	10	23	662.9	13	44	286.4
1978	19	40	362.4	15	63	143.8
1979	12	27	521.2	9	67	124.7
Subtotal	61	123	1,725.2	60	51	688.3
1980	4	6	177.0			
Total	65	129	1,902.2			

* In January 1980 the SEC 7–10 day rule requirement for the length of tender offers was changed to 20–business days. This table adjusts the previous tables to see what would have happened if the new SEC rule had been applied instead of the previous rule. *Example*: From November 1974 through 1979 a total of 123 bids (subtotal line, column three) occurred. Under the new SEC rule, 60 bids (subtotal line, column five) occurred in the 20–business day time frame compared with 21 bids (Table I, line 12) under the prior 7–10 day rule. The dollar premiums under the 20–business day rule totaled $688.3 millions compared with $255.3 millions (Table I, line 15) under the 7–10 day rule, compared with the $1,725.2 millions that actually was received in the same period.

** Expressed in millions of dollars.

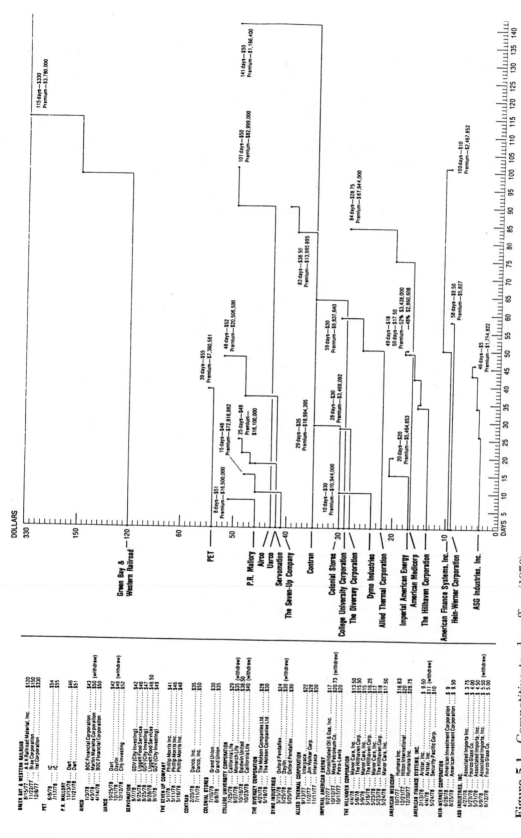

Figure 5.1 Competitive tender offers (1976).

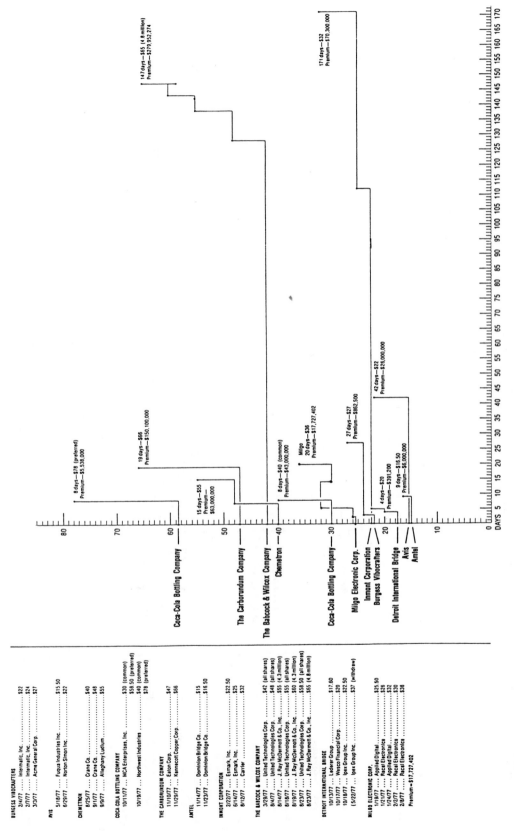

Figure 5.2 Competitive tender offers (1977).

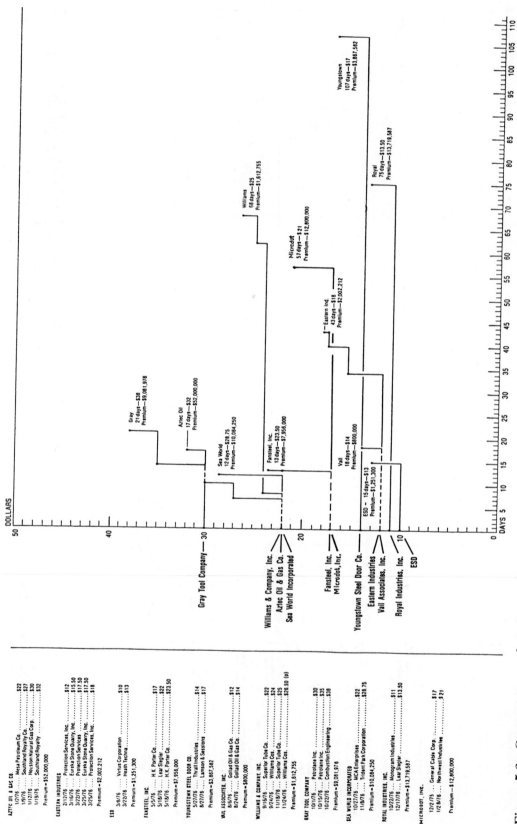

Figure 5.3 Competitive tender offers (1978).

MBO—THE CORPORATE CHALLENGE

These events provide a perspective into both the role and the problem of the investor relations professional. It is clear that the investor relations function is at a crossroads. To continue on the course of the 1960s is to maintain a communications status with no responsibility for results or fairness to investors. Management By Objective (MBO) standards are well established to reward those who plan and achieve. To decline responsibility for results is to limit the function of investor relations professionals and to express a willingness to be a placid participant in a market system whose activities are far removed from the structure of the marketplace.

Suggestions for the restructuring of the marketplace have come from many quarters, but the empirical evidence of over a decade would indicate that change can be anticipated only at an agonizingly slow pace. Those who voluntarily restrict their investor relations activities to "tell the truth, all the truth, all the time" have seen, contrary to the experience of earlier decades, that pure communication is not enough to secure for shareholders true value, or, at least, alternative value.

Shareholders should be entitled to a market system that at all times provides reasonable reflection in market price of the values created by management. To create values on the balance sheet that are not reflected in market price cheats investors and does not serve the self-interest purposes of management. To the contrary, created value not reflected in market price can be management's worst strategic error, in that an undervalued company soon becomes the target of a hostile takeover.

The investor relations function must of historical necessity meld the communications skills with results-oriented strategic planning. This could, and should, be a joint venture with long-range planners and the chief financial officer (CFO). This consortium should investigate the values available to shareholders through a wide variety of economic alternatives. The clear fiduciary responsibility of management is never more evident than in this analysis.

Judging the values available in an objective manner can be stressful to the self-interest of management if only short-term goals are considered. Fortunately, however, the long-term interests of both shareholders and management are totally consistent when the market price consistently reflects true value. Shareholders have access to the value their investment has fostered and management is rewarded with a fair market price that mirrors management's achievements and permits management to plan for the future with a sound financial base and relatively unencumbered with problems of hostile takeover attempts.

The first investor relations challenge is to educate management to accept responsibility for market price. When security market forces are not effective, who else but management should be responsible to shareholders? The problem is more difficult than the solution. Managements are by nature superb problem solvers. The MBO training and track record gives managements a significant head start. It is ironic that managements have applied the problem-solving technique successfully in almost every area of operations *except* the ownership area. Once this hurdle is overcome, managements have all the necessary skills at their command to analyze, evaluate, hypothesize, test alternate proposals, design pilot experiments, and the like. There is no question of the in-house ability of managements to solve problems.

Once a reasonable range of value is determined and supported by the study, an intensive review of the corporation's opportunities should be made. In addition, a detailed study of the corporate trading pattern should be made so that there is a thorough understanding of the supply and demand impact on market price. How much stock is in the supply? What is the velocity of turnover? Given current economic conditions, how many shares are available for trading? At what price levels would additional shares be likely to become available?

Many years of experience convince me that the single most prevalent mistake in investor relations planning is the total concentration on the demand function of selling shares as compared with an analysis of the supply function. A minor adjustment of the supply factor can have the same impact on market price as a geometrically larger increase in the demand. In addition, even if substantial increases in demand were obtainable, the corporation would be faced with the problems of sustaining the demand, determining and adjusting the stockholder mix of the demand, and the ever-increasing difficulty of having any impact on a demand structure that is in effect out of control.

From the rather sad investor relations history of the 1970s, two rather striking exceptions stand out. The unique success of Dividend Reinvestment Plan (DIP) and Kelso Employee Share Ownership Plan (KESOP) should play an important part in corporate strategic investor relations planning. These two plans, in addition to the many other ideas that will emerge from the corporate planning process, have proved their value.

The shareholder response to DIPs in the 1970s, probably the worst investment climate since the 1930s, has been nothing short of astonishing. DIP, an offshoot of the MIP (Monthly Investment Plan) of the New York Stock Exchange, survived and prospered whereas MIP had marginal success in the investment community and was eventually eliminated as a Wall Street product. At this writing over 1,200 DIP plans are in existence with over 5 million participants contributing over $5 billion per year.

It is unfortunate that the terms and conditions of these plans were designed without the help of the corporate marketing department. Many of the terms and conditions are not conducive to encouraging participation. If managements offered products on the same terms and conditions that DIPs are offered, product success would be a rarity. Despite that, shareholders embraced the DIP concept and, further, were willing to accept computer printouts as evidence of ownership in place of the much more expensive certificate. Less than one-half of one percent of DIP participants ever ask for a certificate as evidence of ownership.

At a time when obtaining individual shareholders is difficult and costly, these same individual shareholders have embraced the DIP programs. The shareholders are telling us that they have money, are willing to invest, and that they trust management. The investor relations challenge is to expand this concept and use it to attract the desirable individuals as investors.

The limiting factor of almost all DIPs is that the participants are restricted to shareholders. Most of the better designed plans achieve 20 percent or more participation. The breakthrough is the simple theory of large numbers. Two existing DIPs broke this restriction by permitting participation, through the use of public DIPs by *anybody*, instead of restricting it to shareholders only. The significance here is that a company with an ordinary DIP and 30,000 shareholders has a potential of 30,000 participants. The same company with a public DIP has a potential of more than 200 million participants. Any marketing expert will quickly appreciate the opportunity presented by the public DIP.

A corporate analysis of its constituencies can be a very revealing experience. Instead of selling shares to just anybody, as has been the investor relations practice, corporations should seek out audiences that have more in common with the company, including a full measure of information, making for better informed decision making. The audiences involving KESOPs, TRASOPs, PAYSOPs, bonus plans, customers, suppliers, employees, consultants, and many other groups should be considered as having special interest in a public DIP. This selection may have a response factor that includes a knowledge of the company, an identification with the goals of the company, an interest consistent with the company's future, and an informed participation in an industry in which the company plays an important role.

Those who know the company, understand the company, and participate in some aspect of the company's operations can be logically expected to be more investment oriented than a speculator or other investor motivated solely by a capital gain. To the extent these new audiences will participate in long-term investing, which has been a notable characteristic of DIPs, streams of small but continuous purchasing power can be generated to buy out the marginal seller, remove the shares from the supply, and convert the shares to relatively sterile long-term investments. A thin trickle of continuous buying power seeking shares against an ever-decreasing supply will have a natural tendency to increase market price. Management can and should have some input in monitoring the market price as a reflection of inherent value.

Clearly, a company with highly visible retail product brings to mind discernible groups that could be targeted for the opportunity to participate in public DIPs. But this does not mean that companies without retail products would be noncompetitive. A recent example illustrates the point. A small dental and optical supplier with about 3,000 shareholders and a small capitalization was having a problem with market price reflecting underlying value. Individuals were not active in trading the company's stock, and the company was too small to command much attention from the institutions. In analyzing the company's constituencies it became quickly apparent that the company was highly visible to the country's 120,000 dentists, 80,000 dental technicians, and 100,000 opticians. These professionals knew the company and its products, knew the industry, made their living in the industry, and thus were in an excellent position to be an informed audience to understand what the company communicated. In addition, these groups were independent, were in high income brackets, and were interested in using discretionary income in investing. Without searching for further audiences, the potential involved in increasing the 3,000 shareholders as a potential DIP audience to over 300,000 as a potential public DIP audience would have been a joy to any marketing expert.

Every company has its own set of constituencies. The investor relations challenge is to analyze the situation and develop a strategy to attract individual investors that have a common interest in the company.

The long-range implications are immediately obvious. As the system of investigation results in research input, the company would then be in a position to research a policy as to the appropriate shareholder mix. Rather than accept the happenstance circumstances of an inefficient market, specific efforts can be generated to change the mix of shareholders. The streams of buying power could be a ready attraction for institutions to sell when they wished, at better prices, and to have these speculative holdings converted to long-term investments by individuals.

These means of reaching the individual investor are direct, definitive, and within the control of corporations in exerting some degree of influence as to the audiences to which the campaigns are directed. This should be regarded as a major additional responsibility for the investor relations professional. The economic structure described here requires that the entire existing investor relations program be continued, at least for the short term. As the program begins to create both buying power and more appropriate audiences, the corporate strategy can be fine tuned to more closely align the shareholders with the desired audiences.

Similarly, this program can be easily seen to be a financing opportunity. Most corporations recognized the undervaluation of shares in the 1970s, with a resulting hesitancy to engage in equity financing, even during the few times when it was available, because of the obvious watering of the stock value such financing would create. The net result was that corporate America used debt financing to the point that debt is a large burden on most companies. As this program achieves market prices closer to underlying values, the continuous streams of buying power become available for conversion to selling new shares rather than market shares. This has multiple advantages in that it provides a method for keeping the market price from being pushed to unreasonably high levels. At the same time, it provides management with an opportunity to generate financing at a satisfactory price. Similarly, price increases provide the opportunity for stock splits. Companies that would not have an equity financing at 6 p/e might be more amenable to the needed financing at 16 p/e. This provision should be anticipated while the program is being designed. Such marketing alternatives can be structured into the plan.

The investor relations professional is on the threshold of enormous power and influence in the corporate structure. A problem exists of long duration that desperately needs solving. Those who try to solve problems of the 1980s with solutions of the 1960s can expect to be left behind. Those who have the discipline to understand real value and its importance to both shareholders and management alike bring to management an asset of immense value.

Creative, innovative ideas are needed. Managements well understand that all new products do not succeed and investor relations people must fight for this same understanding in experimenting with new investor relations techniques. A thorough grounding in marketing and MBO procedures will be vital. The relatively safe world of investor relations is about to become very risk oriented, with enormous rewards to those who can isolate the problem, create innovative strategies, and prove capable of achieving sound solutions. The challenge of the risk-reward ratios of the 1980s will far surpass the excitement and opportunities of the 1950s.

6

EMPLOYEE COMMUNICATION

Roger D'Aprix

Senior Consultant
Towers, Perrin, Forster & Crosby

One of the great ironies in the practice of public relations is our tendency to shortchange the employee audience in our organizations. The tendency in most work organizations has been to pay careful attention to public constituencies, but to presume that those who make their living from and in the organization automatically give it their loyalty and their commitment. Nothing could be further from the truth.

Worse, nothing could be more damaging to the functioning of that organization. A leading management thinker and psychologist, Father Thomas A. McGrath, asserts that in the contemporary world of work we must "woo" our people. He chooses that word very deliberately as he emphasizes the need to manage people through relationship rather than by virtue of authority or office.

A crucial part of the wooing process is to provide people with a sense of membership in a work organization. That membership, in turn, depends on the fulfillment of a person's fundamental need to identify with his or her work.

Think of the new employee in any work organization. Or think even of the person assigned to a different job in an organization of which he or she has been a long-term employee.

Roger D'Aprix is worldwide practice leader in human resource communication for the consulting firm of Towers, Perrin, Forster & Crosby. He is also the author of *Communicating for Productivity*, published by Harper & Row in 1982. For thirteen years he was manager of employee communication for Xerox Corporation, and prior to that he spent nine years with General Electric and Bell & Howell in various communication assignments.

Mr. D'Aprix has led scores of communication seminars and workshops for Fortune 500 companies. In 1978 he was named a Fellow of the International Association of Business Communicators, that organization's highest award for distinguished contributions to the profession.

Inevitably, such a person will have some basic questions about his or her relationship to that organization. Not surprisingly, the first of these will be the "I questions."

- What am *I* expected to do on this job?
- (And soon after.) How am I doing? Am *I* performing appropriately?
- (And hard on the heels of that question.) Does anyone care about *me* in this work organization?

If the employee is satisfied with the responses to these "I questions," it is only a matter of time before he or she asks the "we questions."

- What are *we* up to and how are *we* doing?
- What is *our* charter and how does that charter match up to other functions?

Assuming that those questions are satisfactorily addressed, the most important "I question" of all will finally be posed—namely:

- How can *I* help?

That question, when it is asked, signals the beginning of a critical transformation in the psyche of any worker. At that point, he or she is willing to offer freely the talents and skills the work organization is depending on. This moment is really the beginning of worker participation, but it is also only possible as the *culmination* of a careful and intentional process. Those organizations which don't understand this process normally try to begin with a plea or a demand for participation, not understanding that it will only come from a worker who has first addressed the "I and we questions."

Forgetting that employees are well-informed organization members who believe actions and policies far more readily than they do mere words, many such organizations expect that people can be persuaded by glib words. Or they expect—as Father McGrath emphasizes—that they can return to the club of authority and ignore the all-important management-employee relationship.

Practically all research on employee communication shows that when people are asked their best current sources of information, they will usually list the following key sources in this order:

- The grapevine
- Their immediate supervisors
- Company publications and other media
- A variety of company face-to-face communication meetings.

Encouragingly, there have been some recent indications that the immediate supervisor is beating out the grapevine as the employee's primary information source.

A 1982 survey sponsored jointly by the International Association of Business Communicators (IABC) and the consulting firm of Towers, Perrin, Forster & Crosby provides some fascinating findings on the state-of-the-art of organizational communication to and with employees. Based on questionnaires from 32,000 employees in 26 business organizations, it reports that only half of the respondents thought that company communication in their organization was candid and accurate. Two-thirds said that it was incomplete! And more than half said that it was only top-down communication without opportunity for discussion.

The grapevine was cited as a primary source of information—second only to the immediate supervisor and significantly ahead of all company media. When the respondents were asked their preferred information sources, the grapevine came in dead last in a list of 15. Significantly, they said that they preferred to get their information at work from three major sources—their immediate supervisor, senior executives, and small-group meetings where they could discuss what was being told to them. In short, face-to-face communication was far and away the preferred communication source or technique.

In contrast, small-group meetings were ranked fourth at the *current* real information source, and executives were ranked eleventh out of fifteen possible sources. In general, company media were given good marks for credibility and readability. But people expressed the view that significant improvement needed to be made in face-to-face communication when they were asked to match their preferred sources to their real sources. They said that the five sources in greatest need of improvement were the following:

- Senior executives
- My immediate supervisor
- Orientation programs
- Small-group meetings
- Upward communication programs

The preferred topics for company communication were:

- Plans for the future
- Productivity improvement
- Personnel policies and practices

What do such findings imply for the public relations person charged with employee communication responsibility? For one thing, they say loudly and clearly that employee communication is a *process* rather than merely a collection of loosely connected communication programs. Clearly, the people responding to this and similar surveys are saying that they are generally satisfied with the media programs directed at them, but they want a more timely, complete, and two-way communication *process.* Two important implications emerge from that desire. One is the question of how to design and manage that process for this insider public. The other is a key question of functional responsibility, whether this is a public relations or an employee relations (read personnel) responsibility. Both are crucial questions.

Let's take the first one: How do you design and manage the right process? The public in this case is one with a highly vested interest in the organization. It is composed of people who can hold up the organization's words to the light of its actions to test credibility. It has access to a volatile and skeptical grapevine of its own making. And it has the potential to undo any community relations effort if it feels maligned and ill treated, or to make that community relations effort extremely credible if it feels appreciated and informed. This latter power derives from the fact that employees are community residents perceived to have firsthand knowledge of what their organizations are up to. They interact daily within that community and freely pass along their interpretations of the organization's actions. Other publics correctly believe that employees are insiders with firsthand knowledge.

That fact increases the irony that we have often been so cavalier in our communication with employees. Perhaps a good analogy here is the parent who attends faithfully to all obligations outside the home and neglects to cultivate proper family relationships. That person is soon in trouble with the people who should matter most in his universe. So it is with work organizations.

Value changes in the contemporary work force with its greater identification with work, its greater demands for satisfaction from work, and the refusal to accept the kind of alienation seen as natural by our fathers and grandfathers have accentuated the need for management to communicate more effectively. In turn, those value changes have been coupled with another significant work place change. The contemporary worker is much more likely to be engaged in one of the service industries, to be educated, and to labor with an able mind rather than a strong back.

All of these changes mean that organizational communication to the work force must be focused at two different levels: the macro level of programs and publications married to the organization's business and public relations objectives; and the micro level of the line manager, who must be the primary spokesman to and from the organization. Designing and managing the right process means proper attention to *both* the programs and to the manager's role as communicator.

Traditionally, employee communication professionals have had reasonably good success with programmed communication. The employee newspapers, management newsletters, upward communication programs—and more recently—a smattering of electronic communication have been as professional as any other products produced by public relations professionals.

Where the effort has been considerably less effective has been in face-to-face communication by managers. The reasons are complex, but they have to do with the fact that managers have usually been rewarded for two main tasks—meeting bottom line business objectives and staying under budget. In general, we have not seen sensitive management of people as a priority. In fact, the people-sensitive manager has often been looked at with some suspicion as somehow being too soft for the rough and tumble world of business.

Much of that feeling can be traced to a simplistic faith in two management caricatures—the tough but fair exemplar who never takes his eye off measurable results and the dewy-eyed idealist who wants to be loved and admired more than he wants results. In a sense it is a retelling of the myth of Ebenezer Scrooge, who (in this version) wakes up one morning to find that his newfound spirit has led to the demise of his business because he now cares about the people who help him run it.

All of this is palpable nonsense, but its believers are legion. Life is much more complex than that scenario would ever suggest. We find a continuum of management behavior in the real world and a wide variety of management styles to which people react in an even wider variety of ways. Managers can be harsh. They can be sensitive. They can be unreasonable. They can be stupid. They can be just or unjust. They can be wise and reasonable. And people will accommodate any or all of this behavior and adapt as best they can. The question is not whether it is better to be harsh or understanding, the dichotomy we so often try to set up. The question is what works best with a given group of people, what they want and need what is civilized and proper behavior, and what kind of human climate an organization wishes to foster.

The wishes of the work force in regard to communication are clear. They want to know where the organization hopes to go (without any real desire for competitive secrets), how it will get there (without lots of strategic information and detail), and what that means to them (with a clear understanding that these are not promises, but possibilities). And they want it—as the IABC survey quoted earlier emphasizes—in a face-to-face, two-way conversation with their manager and with the leadership of the organization.

All of that says to us that effective communication with employees is no longer an optional activity if we want commitment, understanding, and the nurturing of human productivity.

A good face-to-face communication effort requires the public relations person to work closely with human resource specialists in performing several key tasks:

> First, in making this responsibility a legitimate part of the institutional fabric of the organization—said another way, in influencing communication policy.

Second, in being certain that managers are themselves properly informed so that they can be spokespersons to and from their people.

Third, in advocating that the task become a measure of accountability for all of the organization's managers, either as part of an overall human resource management task or by itself as a communication accountability.

Before we take a brief look at each of these tasks, we need to return to the second question sometimes voiced by the more craft-oriented people in public relations work—namely: Why should any public relations department get mixed up with an activity that looks like the turf of personnel or human resources? The answer tends to separate those who define public relations narrowly as an organizational service activity from those who see it broadly as a task that permeates the whole relationship of an organization with its various internal and external constituencies—and, therefore, as a primary function of good management and good public relations.

If you are a strict interpreter of the function as a service function, then you will probably accept the notion that employee media are appropriate public relations vehicles, but that the manager's communication behavior is "a personnel issue." The trouble with that position is that it ignores the reality that employees don't make that arbitrary division of responsibilities and see communication simply as communication. If it's faulty, they simply blame "management," and they are not appeased that there is still a good employee publication or that they occasionally are shown a good video cassette interview of the president. In fact, such things ironically can worsen their resentment that no one tells them anything face to face. I remember vividly the employee who wrote in a survey of a video cassette interview of the company chairman two telling questions. He asked, "How much did this thing cost? And why couldn't you have bought him a fistful of airline tickets and let him come and talk to us? It would have been cheaper and more satisfying."

Good employee communication practice is necessarily concerned with *both* macro and micro communication tasks. In this connection, how do we persuade the manager that this kind of communication is a vital job task, that it is worth the time and the pain? Some managers do this sort of thing superbly and need little besides support and counsel; others claim they don't have the time or the inclination. In this kind of environment, how do we make good internal communication practice a priority of senior management?

The best answer is to win agreement on a policy level: to persuade senior management that it is positively harmful to the best interests and functioning of the organization to withhold information from its members. And, of course, internal communication must be policy supported by management training and timely information to managers as well as by evaluation.

Accountability is perhaps the crux of the matter. Good communication must be put into the managerial reward system and made a measure of accountability for managers. It also must be inspected, like other management processes, with good performance rewarded and poor performance penalized.

Here again the public relations person interested in effective employee communication finds himself in personnel country. Should he (or she) exit gracefully or should he try to build workable staff alliances and joint plans and proposals that span such organizational fiefdoms? Practically speaking— unless public relations wants to relegate itself only to communication craftsmanship—there is no choice.

CEOs and their senior staffs cannot divide an enterprise into walled kingdoms and succeed in today's complex competitive environment. And the CEOs certainly know it and are frustrated too often by the parochial and narrow-gauge functional specialists who can't see beyond their own job descriptions.

A successful employee communication effort, then, must inform every area of an organization's business. It must be a global effort that matches effective communication process with the business objectives and issues management needs to discuss with the work force.

Given this broader view of employee communication, what kind of person makes a good employee communicator? What sort of talents and interests are necessary? In my mind, the basic public relations skills of writing and good planning are essentials. You can't do this job well if your own communication skills are deficient. Beyond that given, the employee communication specialist should have a solid appreciation for management's problems and perspectives. He should understand management both as science and art, and he should be comfortable with ambiguity because, by definition, the management task is often an uncertain one. Communicating those uncertainties so that they are understood, but in such a way that they don't create excess anxiety is sometimes a tall order. It requires intellect, good planning, and the ability to share both management and employee perspective.

Good employee communication costs money. Print media or audio visual media all have a direct price tag. Face-to-face communication requires staff support from the public relations professionals. It also takes people away from the work routine, and therefore, there is a cost in lost production. Such costs are highly visible and sometimes are the justification for cutting employee programs or for funding them at a marginal level.

On the other hand, an uninformed (and thus probably an uncommitted) employee public offers a staggering obstacle to the effective achievement of business objectives. In the United States we have traditionally seen the work force as a cost of doing business, as one more overhead item that tends to be a drag on profit levels. Contrast that view with the more progressive attitude of the Japanese, who see labor as the essential means of accomplishing work. In

Japan, the mindless tasks are assigned to automated assembly lines "manned" by robots. The creative tasks which require human ingenuity and persistence are performed by skilled workers who see themselves as part of a team process. An important, though not the only, factor in their commitment is good communication between worker and management, with little of the strong adversarial overtones that handicap the management-employee relationship in the United States.

The cost of poor communication—though rarely, if ever, measured—is a lost opportunity cost. We don't know that cost because we have never really isolated its effect on our efficiency or our productivity. If we could demonstrate a relationship between effective communication and bottom line results, no management would neglect this process. In the absence of that demonstrated relationship, we have tended to cover our bets by sponsoring and funding employee communication programs. The result has been a program rather than a process approach, with employee newspapers, newsletters, and other media as our program solutions to employee communication.

Because they are so visible and because they cost money, media programs are often vulnerable when an organization becomes uneasy about its overhead cost. On the other hand, those organizations which make programs part of a clearly articulated communication *process* strategy are much less likely to make arbitrary cuts in employee communication budgets. The reason is that the communication process has been carefully planned and institutionalized, and the programs are well-thought-out tools for achieving an effective process.

In recent years many organizations have begun to search for better ways to evaluate their communication efforts. Audits, focused interviews with small groups of employees, attitude surveys, readership studies, questionnaires of all types have become commonplace in the sophisticated organization that wishes to gauge the success of its communication initiatives. The results of these evaluation techniques are the basis then for informed planning and for the establishment of organizational benchmarks against which improvement or deterioration can be measured.

Planning, careful budgeting of resources, and evaluation are all indications of an attempt to upgrade employee communication activities and public relations in general in institutional organizations. They are hopeful signs that organizational communication is coming of age as an institutional process.

With employees, this welcome change is being driven by the changes in the values and needs of the contemporary worker, the changing nature of work itself, and an economy that has been beset by stagnation and low growth. All of these things plus the necessity to increase human productivity and compete more effectively in the international marketplace are causing managements to look more introspectively at work cultures and to ask how we can change from our adversarial tradition between managers and workers and to foster a healthier work climate.

Many managements are seeing improved human resource management and improved communication as a key part of the strategy to make our organizations better adapted to the realities of the 1980s and 1990s. In this more sophisticated environment, the public relations professional will have to be more counselor than craftsperson, more oriented to management tasks, planning, and goal setting than to the late-breaking news. For many, it won't be an easy transition.

The alternative, of course, is to try to carry on business as usual—to continue a craft orientation in public relations and to treat the employee constituency as just one more constituency with an interest in the organization. If we do, I will make a glum prediction. That strategy will leave the process need I have been describing to be met by the data and information-processing specialists anxious to solve human communication problems with more convenient and more accessible computers and other paraphernalia of the office of the future.

That *could* be the final and (sad-to-say) logical outcome of a long countervailing trend toward the dehumanized work place. It would also be one of the great lost opportunities of all time for public relations. The people who work for our institutional organizations and who take so much of their identity from those organizations deserve much better from us.

COMMUNITY RELATIONS

Alvin Golin

Chairman and Chief Executive Officer
Golin/Harris Communications

COMMUNITY RELATIONS: AN OVERVIEW

Community relations has many faces. To the local politician, it may be appearing and speaking at a neighborhood charitable event. For the social worker, it is helping direct the activities of the phenomenon known as "street gangs" into productive channels. To the PTA and the police department, it is helping keep school traffic crossings as safe as possible. For "Keep America Beautiful," it is enhancing the local environment. To the YMCA and the YWCA, it is swimming safety and perhaps summer camps.

But for American business, community relations is both an opportunity and an obligation. The opportunity is to establish a partnership and build trust among those who utilize the products and services of a particular business. The obligation is to be a "responsible" corporate citizen—with the understanding that there in fact exists a moral obligation for American business to give something back to the society from which it derives profit.

This chapter represents one case history in the corporate community relations spectrum, that of McDonald's Corporation.

Alvin Golin is founder and chief executive officer of Golin/Harris Communications. In the first film ever produced on the public relations industry, *Opinion of the Public*, he was featured for his agency's work on the McDonald's account.

As consultant to the U.S. Department of Commerce, his work centered on a major public relations awareness program for U.S. companies on the benefits of exporting to help our economy, increase employment, and reduce the balance-of-trade deficit.

He is a member of the advisory board of the School of Communications at the University of Tennessee; the advisory board of the Easter Seals Telethon; and public relations adviser to the National Multiple Sclerosis Society.

McDONALD'S: A MODEL FOR COMMUNITY RELATIONS

McDonald's has always believed in putting something back into the communities where it does business because the essence of McDonald's is the individual, locally operated restaurant. Each restaurant's management and employees have an important stake in the community or neighborhood where they are located. They owe their success and their jobs to the patronage of their neighbors and those who pass through their area.

Therefore, it makes sense that McDonald's has an unusually strong commitment to being a leader in community citizenship in each restaurant's trading area. There is a tradition of personal local involvement in community service that extends throughout the McDonald's organization. From crew-people to McDonald's independent franchisees, you will find a strong dedication of skills and resources to helping meet community needs—whether in a project as ambitious as a Ronald McDonald House serving families of seriously ill children, or simply sending off a local high school musician to march in the Macy's or Tournament of Roses Parade as a member of McDonald's All-American High School Band. But no matter what the project, it will always deliver a tangible benefit to the community, for that must come before any publicity can be generated.

Positive community involvement is basic to McDonald's way of doing business. It is a reinvestment in the future of the community—and therefore a reinvestment in the business. It's been that way at McDonald's since Ray Kroc started out in 1955, and it hasn't changed.

McDONALD'S COMMUNITY RELATIONS COMMITMENT

We had principles when we were poor. We
certainly have those same principles today.

RAY A. KROC
Founder and Senior Chairman
McDonald's Corporation

The principles referred to by Ray Kroc not only refer to QSC&V—the McDonald's motto of Quality, Service, Cleanliness, and Value—but to another guiding principle of the company, one which is part and parcel of its business philosophy, the role of community relations. That principle is to put something back into the communities where McDonald's does business.

For a franchise organization, in which 74 percent of the restaurants are owned and operated by, or are joint ventures with, independent businesspeople, community relations represents more than just one facet of the public relations spectrum—it forms the basis for McDonald's public relations programming.

In 1957, Ray Kroc hired our firm, then Cooper & Golin, for a retainer of $500 per month. The move infuriated Harry Sonneborn, then president of the company, because as Ray Kroc admitted, he didn't know what Cooper & Golin was going to do for McDonald's. And, furthermore, Kroc and Sonneborn couldn't even afford to draw salaries at that time.

In those early years, our role was based on delivering two audiences: (1) customers and (2) potential franchisees. Our efforts were linked to new restaurant openings and to building awareness of the McDonald's concept in the local community. In those days, McDonald's couldn't afford advertising, and public relations had to build both awareness and credibility.

At the same time, we had to live up to the company's commitment to "put something back" into the community. Our vehicle was the restaurant's grand opening, which of course was accompanied by balloons, hoopla, local dignitaries, and always a donation to a local charity or nonprofit community organization. The franchisees were asked to become "Mr. or Ms. McDonald's" in their communities—making frequent presentations to local community groups and putting dollars back into the community through proceeds days for charitable organizations, the high school band, civic and service group projects.

As McDonald's grew and prospered, the role of public relations changed. On the national level, that "cute little hamburger company" was becoming the "darling of Wall Street," and when McDonald's was listed on the New York Stock Exchange in 1966 we even served hamburgers to the traders on the floor. In 1965, Ronald McDonald was introduced to a nationwide television audience through the Macy's Thanksgiving Day Parade. And internationally, we had a lot of fun with the Hamburg, Germany, opening by recreating the "history of the hamburger."

But while the demands for national awareness and more sophisticated public relations programming increased, the realization that the local restaurant was the focal point of our efforts never faltered. It is amazing to think that a company which grew from one to more than 7,000 restaurants in 28 years has not changed its attitude toward community relations. From McDonald's viewpoint, the 1,500 independent franchisees still share that commitment to be "Mr. and Ms. McDonald's" in the local community. In fact, Fred Turner, McDonald's chairman, refers to those 1,500 "presidents" as one of the great strengths of McDonald's.

With growth came significant change. Our role as national public relations counsel for McDonald's took on new perspective. We could no longer be the "arms and legs" servicing the local media for every new grand opening. But we could provide the input—the plans—and the materials for the local McDonald's franchisee to fill the essential community spokesperson role. A breakthrough in this area came in the early 1970s, with the introduction of the community relations representative program into the McDonald's system.

Employed by local McDonald's restaurants, the community relations representatives were charged with the responsibility of delivering local programs which evidenced McDonald's community commitment—from safety to school programs, from entertaining at senior citizen homes to arranging hospital visits for Ronald McDonald. As national public relations counsel, our job was to prepare the guidelines for involvement; to provide the training materials for the CRRs; to create the new ideas (although it is important to note that many of the best new ideas for national programs continue to come from the local marketplace); and of course, to deliver the media materials, and in some cases, the media coverage.

Evidencing the continuing commitment to community relations today is the fact that McDonald's co-ops in larger markets employ local public relations agencies, and that many of the local advertising agencies working for local co-op groups also provide public and community relations services.

The evolution of community relations at McDonald's is best illustrated by the criteria applied to the development of national public relations programs. Each must (1) deliver a tangible social benefit to the target audience; (2) generate positive national media exposure; and (3) provide an opportunity for local extensions into the community by the local restaurant.

A tangible example of how this works is the McDonald's All-American High School Band (see figure 7.1), which made its first appearance in the

Figure 7.1 McDonald's All-American high school band performs in the Macy's Thanksgiving Day parade in New York City and in the Tournament of Roses parade in Pasadena, California on New Year's Day. Both parades are extensively covered on both national and local television.

Macy's Thanksgiving Day Parade in 1967 and in the Tournament of Roses Parade in Pasadena in 1969, and has been a McDonald's tradition ever since.

The social benefit delivered through the band program is that it provides outstanding young high school musicians with the same all-American status and recognition traditionally accorded only to athletes. By sending nomination forms to every high school band director in the United States, Puerto Rico, and the U.S. Virgin Islands, young people have a chance to be recognized for their accomplishments. The local publicity is generated by sending every nominee a hand-lettered certificate, which is then presented at the high school or in the restaurant by local McDonald's representatives.

National publicity is generated in stages. First, through a "search is on" release which accompanies the mailing of the nomination form. Next, when the 104 band members are selected (two from each state and the District of Columbia, one each from Puerto Rico and the U.S. Virgin Islands). Not only are the band members honored in their local communities, but through airport send-offs, at halftime of football games, and as "local celebrities" upon their return from the parade appearances.

Of course, the nationally televised appearances of the band provide significant national exposure, as has a traditional appearance on the "Today Show" on the morning of Thanksgiving Eve. But even in New York City, the local aspect of the band is emphasized. When the band performed in a special Carnegie Hall Concert on Thanksgiving Eve with Lionel Hampton in 1977, tickets were not sold. The McDonald's New York Co-op offered the tickets to local band directors on a "first come, first served" basis to give local band members the chance to see their all-American compatriots in action.

The band is but one example of how McDonald's meshes community and public relations. And while the band's appearance might have changed, and its music and our publicity strategies have become more sophisticated, the underlying commitment to deliver a benefit into the community is the foundation for the program.

COMMUNITY RELATIONS: ANALYSIS AND FUNCTION

The basic community relations "catalog components" utilized by McDonald's are a community relations manual and field guidelines packages for the individual programs. Understanding that not every franchisee, restaurant manager, or community relations representative will be a sophisticated public relations practitioner, these materials are prepared in a simple, concise format and updated yearly.

Generic media alerts for local events are contained in the guidelines, as are suggestions for events which will generate local media coverage.

The community relations manual is designed to help generate local publicity from the preopening period through the restaurant's grand opening. In special situations, such as those in which a McDonald's restaurant is in a unique location (e.g., a riverboat in St. Louis, in Children's Hospital in Philadelphia, Water Tower Place in Chicago) we will either work directly with the local agency or be directly involved in the opening.

Another basic community relations component is a slide-script-VTR presentation entitled "This is McDonald's." Once more designed to be adaptable to the local marketplace, this presentation becomes the primary vehicle through which the local franchisee or restaurant manager introduces McDonald's to local community and civic groups.

As mentioned, McDonald's provides its system with a number of guidelines packages for the implementation of local community relations programs. But the basis for the success of those programs is the commitment of the local restaurant management to get involved in the community.

MANAGEMENT OBJECTIVES

Obviously, community relations must provide a return on investment. However, it is to the credit of McDonald's, operating in a highly competitive business environment, that it does not measure community relations success based on individual or collective restaurant sales.

The first key management objective for community relations is to establish the restaurant as a partner in the community, in the same manner that the franchisee becomes a partner in the corporation. There is no question that McDonald's believes in community relations as a reinvestment program—in the same sense that adding a McDonald's Playland or redecorating the restaurant is a reinvestment. Given the McDonald's record of success, this objective has remained firm over the years.

Another essential management objective is to build consumer trust in McDonald's. The premise is simple: we'd all rather do business, or give our business, to someone we trust. Community relations enhances that trust and, given the fact that McDonald's will open some 500 restaurants per year, that trust must extend beyond customers to zoning boards and the potential work force in a community.

From management's perspective, community relations also has strong global ramifications. Because most McDonald's restaurants internationally are operated as joint ventures or partnerships with citizens of the specific country, it is essential to position the restaurant as a locally owned and operated business—not the property of an American multinational. McDonald's overseas is a highly visible symbol of America and the "American way of eating," which in some cases can be perceived as a threat to local tradition and culture.

Therefore, the role of the international licensee in the community is essential to the success of the venture, and McDonald's continuing international growth has proven the "translatability" of community relations into international markets.

McDonald's made the decision to enter the European market with the same site selection process used in the United States. This proved to be a wrong decision. McDonald's executives selected suburban locations as they did in the United States some 27 years ago, with the thought that families, particularly those with children, would be critical to their success. Instead they found that the restaurants had to be in very heavy-traffic areas with high visibility, so that McDonald's could establish its identity before making the move to suburban locations. One of the major problems was that eating out on a regular basis was not in the European life style, especially when children were concerned. An educational program—with emphasis directed to children—had to be established. This is being accomplished through community relations activities as well as promotion and advertising.

AUDIENCES

Because McDonald's serves some 50-million customers per week, it is difficult to choose a target audience that is not relevant. Our approach to developing audiences is not traditional. Since the commitment and objective is to put something back into the community, the first step is to identify a real need. Once the need has been established, the audiences are evident. Two major McDonald's programs illustrate the validity of this approach.

The idea for Ronald McDonald Houses evolved when Fred Hill, a tight end for the Philadelphia Eagles football team asked his teammates and owner for support in fund raising to fight leukemia, an afflication that affected his daughter Kim. Dr. Audrey Evans, head of pediatric oncology at the Children's Hospital of Philadelphia, was contacted for advice on where money was needed. She suggested that families of these seriously ill children had heavy emotional and financial problems and discussed the need for a place to stay near the hospital which might have a homelike atmosphere. Jim Murray, the general manager of the Eagles, was in touch with the local McDonald's co-op group in Philadelphia and the idea was born. The first fund-raising idea was to donate sales of McDonald's Shamrock Shakes. Other McDonald's co-ops throughout the country were made aware of the program, and many adopted the idea for their towns.

At the end of 1982, there were 44 Ronald McDonald Houses (see figure 7.2) open in the United States, Canada, and Australia. These homes provide lodging for families of seriously ill children being treated as outpatients at nearby hospitals and served more than 100,000 family members in 1982.

The Ronald McDonald House is perhaps one of the most meaningful and tangible examples of good community relations and of how business can serve as a catalyst to help meet a very real social need.

Figure 7.2   Ronald McDonald has become more than just a television spokesperson. He now has his name on the doors of some 50 Ronald McDonald houses throughout the country. Ronald McDonald houses are homes for seriously-ill children and their parents. The houses are usually situated adjacent to children's hospitals in major cities.

Community partnership is the key to the Ronald McDonald House program. It entails the active cooperation of the local medical community, a volunteer parent group, and the local McDonald's co-op members. The local McDonald's restaurants provide the funds to build, buy, or renovate an appropriate home near a children's hospital. The medical community identifies the hospital, which treats a large number of children coming from distances too far to return to on a daily basis. And the volunteer parent group takes on the responsibility for ongoing Ronald McDonald House operations, once the facility has opened.

Families stay at Ronald McDonald House for a minimal price, or if they cannot afford it, for free. A local not-for-profit organization is established to administer every house, and a national not-for-profit organization exists to provide "seed money" for local houses and direction in terms of establishing the house through a national advisory board.

A full-time Ronald McDonald House coordinator has been on the Golin/Harris staff since 1978, helping local communities determine the feasibility of a Ronald McDonald House, as well as with fund-raising activities and ongoing counsel relating to administration and operations.

Who is the audience for Ronald McDonald House? It is comprised of the public in general, of government leaders, of the medical community, of every parent. What has resulted from the program is an ongoing, tangible commitment by McDonald's to help meet a real social need. The fact that President Reagan publicly cited the Ronald McDonald House in 1981 as a classic example of volunteerism; that *Reader's Digest* devoted a feature article to the house; that it has earned a PRSA Silver Anvil Award; and most importantly, that it provides a real community service through the local McDonald's franchisees, makes it clear that community relations starts with the identification of a need—not necessarily with an audience.

However, it is important that once a need is identified, specific audiences be targeted. Once more by example, McDonald's commitment to the 1984 Olympics illustrates the point.

When McDonald's negotiated with the Los Angeles Olympic Organizing Committee to become the official fast-service restaurant sponsor of the 1984 Summer Olympic Games, it was the company's intention to do something more than merely paying a rights fee. During those negotiations, it became apparent that there was a need for new facilities to host some of the Olympic events.

Therefore, McDonald's committed itself to build the McDonald's Olympic Swim Stadium on the campus of the University of Southern California, with the agreement that the pool would be made available to both students and the surrounding community following the 1984 Summer Olympic Games.

Following that commitment, and in order to extend its Olympic involvement into communities across the country, McDonald's became the sponsor of Age Group and Junior Olympic swimming in the United States. In its first year of sponsorship, 1982, local McDonald's restaurants were involved in more than 180 swim meets across the country—helping to develop future Olympians—and helping to show parents that McDonald's would not only build an Olympic site, it would extend that commitment into the communities where it does business.

And once more, although the identification of the need came first, the audiences became readily apparent once the project unfolded.

COMMUNITY PARTNERS

Both the Ronald McDonald House program, and McDonald's 1984 Olympic program, are good examples of community partnerships. In the former case, the partnership is with both the medical community and volunteer parent groups, although it is important also to credit the National Football League, which has been an active partner in the Ronald McDonald House from its inception. This came about when the Philadelphia Eagles football team and the local McDonald's co-op banded together to fund the first house.

In the case of swimming, on the national level McDonald's works with both the Los Angeles Olympic Organizing Committee and with U.S. Swimming, Inc., the governing body for amateur swimming in this country— and on the local level, McDonald's is involved with virtually hundreds of local swim clubs in the community.

Partnerships are essential to community relations. A safety program, not only to carry credibility but to ensure that it meets a real need, would call for a partnership with the National Safety Council. McDonald's educational programs, ranging from grade school "action packs" for teachers to instructional films, are developed in conjunction with professional educators.

As one of the first corporate sponsors of the Muscular Dystrophy Association, McDonald's has worked for years with both the national association and its local representatives to raise funds to help fight this crippling childhood disease.

But partners must be chosen carefully and must bring a tangible commitment to the specific community relations effort. Over the years, we have learned that those who merely want dollars, or use of the McDonald's name, must also be willing to contribute of their time and skills in order for a successful partnership to result. Because McDonald's believes in committing itself to those same hours, it is essential that the partner be actively involved—not in name only.

It is also essential that responsibilities be clearly defined up front in developing partnerships. Amounts of dollars and time to be expended should also be determined up front and a limit set. Good partnerships are based on good business practices.

TOOLS AND TECHNIQUES

From an advertising viewpoint, McDonald's is a television-oriented company. Over the years, our efforts have evolved into the electronic media as well. Today, with a virtual electronic media explosion in cable, pay, and public access television, there is a tremendous need for programming, especially in the "features" area. Television news is one of the most credible media in existence today, and expanded local news programming offers significantly more opportunities to tell positive community stories than in previous years.

With the introduction of commercial satellites, the television news film clip has become a more timely vehicle with which to tell a business story than in previous years. Obviously, the first step in generating positive media exposure is to secure actual local or network news coverage—but the production of a television news clip also ensures that the story is told the way you want it told, which has significant benefit.

Public service announcements also provide broad opportunity for a business to evidence their community commitment. However, public service announcements should always entail a partnership with a viable nonprofit or public service organization and generate significantly more success when a well-known spokesperson is involved.

From our perspective, it's not so much the specific tool used as it is the ability to put yourself in the media's role. Whatever we submit is tailored to the audience of the media—for that is the best way to assure the media's and therefore the public's attention.

BUDGETING

Because McDonald's is a franchise organization, each co-op will normally have a local public relations budget. Therefore, we will budget only for those programs which generate national exposure and for national media materials.

However, because McDonald's is committed to community relations, a budget will be developed for local program opportunities, on the basis that such dollars represent a public relations research and development investment.

McDonald's also believes in testing—in terms of new products, promotions, and public relations programs. The existence of a public relations testing budget is somewhat unique, but does enable us to measure the viability of a given program before extending it throughout the McDonald's system.

As a guideline, we would recommend basing a community relations budget on the return it will deliver. That return can normally not be measured in terms of increased sales or profits, but can be measured in terms of comparable advertising space or time bought. However, it is essential to emphasize the *quality* of the exposure generated through a community relations program, and not just the quantity. You don't embark on a community relations program to "get your name spelled right, no matter what they say," you do it to build a reputation, to evidence a commitment, to favorably influence targeted public attitudes—and if you just budget quantity and not quality, it will be a short-term pro-position.

One of the real pitfalls of establishing a community relations program has often been a lack of understanding of most communities. It's easy to sit in an ivory tower setting in New York or Chicago and create a program that you think will play in Peoria—but without thorough research and experience this approach can prove to be extremely embarrassing for the public relations agency or communications department of a corporation. Some of our worst failures have been due to lack of thorough research and understanding of local communities. The best idea or concept in the world doesn't have a chance unless the myriad of details necessary for the success of a program are executed at the local level. Our best successes have been those ideas and programs that have been thoroughly tested on an individual basis in small markets as well as large.

It is also important in the budgeting process to have a sense of what clients spend in advertising and promotion, and what they have spent in past years. Many large companies look at 4–5 percent of the advertising budget as being a figure to spend on public relations, and community relations would have to fit within that framework.

EVALUATION

For years, the public relations profession has wrestled with formulas for evaluation. From McDonald's viewpoint, evaluation is based on meeting the program objectives. And one of those objectives that has not changed throughout the years is to generate positive recognition for what McDonald's has done.

We do compile numbers—that is a maxim of our business. But quality is in fact more important than quantity to McDonald's. It is not an image we seek to project through community relations; it is a reputation we have helped the company build. Ray Kroc once said, "If someone does anything just for the money, it will seldom ever happen." If you get involved in community relations activities for a quick return in sales, forget it. You can't measure community relations this way—if it's a long-term involvement.

It is our belief that there must be a corporate commitment to community relations as an investment. That is not a short-term process. As business people, we realize there is also an agency commitment to produce results, and to do it continuously if you want a long and satisfying relationship.

Today, McDonald's annually spends more than $300 million worldwide on advertising and promotion. The Golden Arches have become a recognizable symbol of quality and dependability to a major portion of the American public, and now, throughout the world. When a company has reached that position, you don't continue to put something into the communities where you do business just for the sake of exposure. You do it to extend and reinforce your leadership—and the trust of your publics.

I'm prejudiced, but I believe Ray Kroc said it best in his book, *Grinding It Out*: "In our business there are two kinds of attitudes toward advertising and public relations. One is the outlook of the begrudger who treats every cent paid for ad programs or publicity campaigns as if they were strictly expenditures. . . . I never hesitate to spend money in this area because I can see it coming back to me with interest. Of course, it comes back in different forms. . . ."

CHAPTER

8

MARKETING SUPPORT

Kenneth Lightcap

Vice President Public Affairs and Investor Relations
Chesebrough-Pond's Inc.

If you agree that a company's reputation or position with the public is vital to its success in the marketplace, and if you agree that people first pick up a magazine and newspaper, then listen to radio or watch television for the editorial content and not to gain exposure to the advertising, then I think you can appreciate why the public relations function can be and sometimes is vital to today's marketing efforts.

I want to make that statement right up front in this discussion of marketing public relations because it is too easily lost on today's marketers, whose first orientation toward public relations is as a support mechanism for advertising (i.e., the basket of clippings philosophy).

I suppose it's fair to say that marketing public relations got its start gaining attention for products. And there are those who say that antics like those used by P. T. Barnum were heavily employed in the early days to grab attention. The old adage "there's a sucker born every minute" would help explain why the trickery of the past and the slick maneuvers of yesteryear's press agents provide an all too frequent reminder to us today of some of the heritage associated with marketing public relations.

But if yesterday's public relations man has become today's marketing publicist, he/she has done so with some adherence to things past; that is, that the special event—like the circus hype—draws attention. That fact is still very relevant to public relations today.

Kenneth Lightcap serves as vice president of public affairs and investor relations at Chesebrough-Pond's Inc. He began his career as a newspaper reporter, has represented a variety of companies as a communications counselor, and has held key corporate positions in this field.

He is a member of the National Investor Relations Institute and the Public Relations Society of America, and is a member of the board of trustees of the National Association of Investment Clubs, Inc.

124

Today's marketing public relations is, by design, attention getting, but through adherence to a marketing plan that calls for publicity directed to specific audiences, at specific times, with specific messages. No longer is it appropriate to just get attention, because the "mention my product to anyone at anytime" philosophy becomes confusing and obfuscates the overall marketing plan. In short, it's just not effective communication.

Today's sophisticated marketing corporations have well-thought-out and precisely scheduled marketing plans for products. These plans outline two key points:

- The overall objectives for the marketing plan—what is to be achieved?
- The strategies to be employed—how is the objective to be reached?

That seems simple enough, and indeed it is, but lots of new products don't make it in the marketplace. Obviously, there must be a substantial art to the marketing function to go along with the science of selecting the right objectives and strategies, and properly executing a marketing program to meet them.

Let's assume we've got a good product; we've developed the proper objectives and strategies to introduce the product; and now we're in need of some effective communication. Typically the marketing managers at today's marketing corporations will turn to the advertising community to come up with a creative advertising campaign and media schedule to carry out the strategies. The enlightened marketing manager might even have asked the ad agency to be part of the objective and strategy-designating decision, but this doesn't always happen. And as far as the marketing public relations man is concerned, it almost never happens.

Why isn't marketing public relations considered up front in the discussion of objectives and strategies? For a lot of reasons having to do with the visibility and understanding of what public relations is and does, but probably more likely because public relations doesn't command big marketing dollars and therefore, in the eyes of the marketing manager, can't be very important.

Typically, and this is a best case scenario, today's marketing manager looks at the proposed advertising budget and takes an automatic 10 percent for public relations without understanding what that 10 percent is going to achieve. In most cases, the promotional needs (couponing, trade deals, etc.) come before public relations, and the public relations budget is left with the "if we have any dollars left we'll put them in PR" consequence.

How can public relations then gain entrance to the thought processes that are part of the big decisions? It certainly must overcome the "how good or valuable can PR be if it doesn't cost very much" thinking. Or the singular view that public relations will produce lots of clippings—and that's good enough.

Maybe those of us in the public relations profession have failed to make our point (and now go back to my opening paragraph) that people buy magazines, for example, to read the editorial, not the ads. "Well, if that's true," you say, "why isn't that fact obvious to astute marketing managers?" And that's easily answered too—because the editorial content that contains the marketing information on a particular product does not carry sufficient regular exposure to get the product message across. Thus marketing public relations must play a support role for advertising messages—right? Yes, if you only view marketing public relations as a product publicity tool. But if you think about marketing public relations as a positioning tool, then the whole ball game changes.

MARKETING PUBLIC RELATIONS—THE POSITIONING TOOL

Over the years there have been many outstanding positioning programs, if you will, that utilize public relations techniques and practices to position or gain a "share of mind" with a particular public or publics. And when I suggest share of mind, I'm not just talking about what you might have read in yesterday's newspaper that changed your mind on a particular topic, but rather a general perception that you have about what a certain company stands for, or a well-known personality represents, or a city has as a reputation. Each of these shares of mind, for good or bad, exists out of general impressions gathered over a period of time. You don't necessarily make an instant decision about people, places, or things from having read one or several articles, and you certainly don't form lasting impressions from any single product advertising campaign.

Marketing managers talk about positioning all the time, but they tend to want to buy their way in over a very short period of time with big exposure via big advertising dollars. This doesn't work, because meaningful impressions are formed gradually over a period of time and that's not something that big dollars alone can achieve.

POSITIONING—HOW IT'S ACHIEVED

Let's consider what a major baking products company did over a period of time to gain a position or share of mind with consumers who did a lot of baking. It's no secret that the structuring of an event called "A National Bake Off" gathered a share of mind and an accurate perception that this particular company was center stage in the theater of baking.

Let's do a little role playing here. Think of yourself as a consumer interested in baking things in your own kitchen. You're now someone who spends a good number of hours in your kitchen; you have invested in the best stoves, refrigerator, freezer, mixer, blender, etc. You can afford the best and you read media that speak to your interests.

Now suppose you receive meaningful information on a regular basis from a particular company in the baking field. And suppose this information was not about this company's particular baking products, but instead gave you information on how to bake better and how to use new products available for baking (over pans, new gadgets that made mixing easier, etc.), charts which explained the nutritional value of various baking flours, articles on the uses of spices and seasonings, and so on. Keep in mind that this information reaches you in the magazines you read, the cooking and baking shows you watch (especially on cable TV), the mailings you receive, and even from your children, who bring wall charts and work assignments home from home economics classes—all dealing with the subject of baking.

The gradual buildup of impressions about this particular company is beginning to form a lasting impression with you to the extent that you begin to recognize and maybe even look for this company's name on the baking products shelves at your supermarket. Now let's assume that you receive information from this company on how to organize a baking club where receipes can be developed and exchanged and let's assume at this point a company representative visits your club to present a program on the latest in baking technology.

You have now been involved in the world of baking for a couple of years, working with material supplied by this particular company, and you have an opportunity to participate in a local baking contest sponsored by this company which, if you win, will entitle you to compete in a statewide contest—and if you win that, will entitle you to go on to a national bake off, with publicity surrounding your achievements every step of the way.

When you get to the national bake off, you will find yourself competing with 50 other state winners in the development of the best receipes for 1984—for distribution by the sponsoring company to as wide an audience as possible.

Now let's ask some questions:

- Has this company gained a meaningful position or share of your mind as being center stage in the world of baking?
- Do you respect what this company has to say about things to do with baking?
- When you think of things to do with baking, do you think of this company?
- And this is the big one—when you think of products you need to bake with (flour, pans, other things this company makes for baking) would you buy the products of this company?

If you're bright, alert, and not an advertising agency account executive, you'll answer yes to all of the above. And even if your ad agency background clouds your vision, you'll be delighted with the response to your agency's product advertising for this company, for it will succeed as never before.

To review all of this, what I'm saying in an oversimplified way is that marketing public relations has established a solid reputation for this company in its particular field of expertise—and now it's up to advertising to sell this company's specific products. Put another way, public relations positions the concept of baking and advertising sells the specific baking products.

This scenario can be repeated in lots of places, for example, in the world of sewing. It would be quite promising for a major national sewing machine manufacturer to use the same marketing public relations positioning techniques in the world of sewing. By developing information and materials on the subject of sewing (sewing techniques, how to use patterns, understanding materials, etc.—all supplied by a particular manufacturer) a sewing machine manufacturer could begin to establish a position for itself in the minds of people who sew. The development of sewing clubs established with help and direction from this company would be an obvious technique, and ultimately a national or even international forum for "things sewing" would pin down a reputation for this company.

In the world of sewing then, the use of marketing public relations is to position the concept of sewing in the minds of consumers. Once the consumer is into sewing in a meaningful way, she/he will sooner or later be looking for the best equipment with which to sew. That's where advertising comes in and extols the benefits of this particular company's sewing machines.

PROPER POSITIONING IS UNASSAILABLE

Most people will agree that reputations gained over a period of time tend to be solid and well earned. So it is with the reputations or positions earned by our baking and sewing company examples via the use of marketing public relations. Once you have achieved a share of mind that sticks, it's not going to be taken away or preempted by some clever stunt or even a massive advertising campaign.

A company cannot effectively achieve a solid positive reputation for itself in a short period of time—and if it tries to, it must be willing to risk the opportunist label or worse as a result. If a company does not appear on the horizon of consumer awareness and perception on day one, it cannot expect to be positively positioned there on day two. I say positively positioned because public disaster or calamity will, of course, put it there overnight.

POSITIVE POSITIONING FIGHTS CALAMITY

If bad reputations can be gained overnight, what does that say about all the effort it takes to establish a good reputation in the first place? It says a lot, because solid, well-earned reputations will help immeasurably to hold the line of positive public opinion when catastrophe or calamity does occur. No one who has grown up with today's solid consumer product companies, for example, is going to immediately change his/her mind about the quality of what those companies do (i.e., their products).

POSITIONING VERSUS PRODUCT PUBLICITY

It is important for this discussion not to view positioning public relations in opposition to product publicity. The two are distinctly different functions within the public relations practice and serve the marketing function in different ways.

Marketing public relations—the positioning tool—sets up the market-place for product publicity and allows the publicity message to be that much more effective. If, for example, you read about a particular sewing machine in a general interest magazine, you will be much more receptive to the editorial message if you have a positive impression of that company to begin with.

To be sure, this discussion of the use of public relations as a marketing tool is not new. But it's amazing how few public relations programs employ the position factor in any meaningful way. The one-two punch of public relations in the marketing sense is to position first, followed closely by or in some case simultaneously with product publicity—then advertising. This sequence is important, because to move first with advertising is to pay dearly for stealing your own thunder.

CONSUMER AFFAIRS

Joanna Maitland

President
Joanna Maitland Associates

Today, consumer affairs can be identified as a specific function in an organization. However, fairness and honesty in dealing with the consumer have always been the basis of a successful buyer/seller relationship.

In the mid-1800s, the Chicago *Daily Democratic Press* had some good advice for new Chicago businessmen: "Have good articles to sell, deal honestly and honorably, be courteous to all; and what is, if possible more important than all these, study the right use of 'printers' ink.'"[1]

The early Chicago firm of Field, Palmer, and Leiter offered a daring goods-on-approval promise: "If, when you get your goods home, and Do not find them Entirely Satisfactory, Please return them and your Money will be Refunded."[2]

Later as Marshall Field & Company grew and prospered, its executives concentrated on implanting this philosophy in the minds of all employees. Instructions, proverbs, exhortations, and rules posted on bulletin boards throughout the store read: "To do the right thing, at the right time, in the right way; to do some things better than they were ever done before; to

Joanna Maitland has been one of the leading consumer affairs professionals in the business community for twenty years. As director of consumer affairs for the Sperry and Hutchinson Company, she formulated policy and managed internal and external consumer relations for the corporation. Her efforts have had decided impact on the formation of cooperative coalitions of government and business.

She serves on the Government and Regulatory Affairs Committee of the U.S. Chamber of Commerce. She is a charter member of the Society of Consumer Affairs Professionals and received their award for "Extraordinary Achievements on Behalf of Consumers."

1. Lloyd Wendt and Herman Kogan, *Give the Lady What She Wants* (Chicago: Rand McNally, 1952), pp. 1–2.

2. Ibid.

eliminate errors; to know both sides of the question; to be courteous; to be an example; to work for the love of work; to anticipate requirements; to develop resources; to recognize no impediments; to master circumstances; to act from reason rather than from rule; to be satisfied with nothing short of perfection."[3]

As Field strolled through his store one day, he saw an assistant retail manager speaking heatedly with a woman customer. "What are you doing here?" asked Field. "I am settling a complaint," replied the manager. "No, you're not," snapped Field. "Give the lady what she wants."[4]

Marshall Field's set of rules in the 1870s formed the basis of the code for service and elaborate courtesy which created the unofficial maxim, "The Customer is Always Right."

THE CONSUMER MOVEMENT

During the past two decades, consumers have attained status as a specialized public group. A variety of explanations for this development have been offered: the tremendous growth in technology, the proliferation of products flooding the marketplace, and the newfound mobility of Americans.

Customers were finding it difficult to adjust to shopping in large environments, to making value judgments with limited information at the point of purchase, to caring for products manufactured from unknown materials, and to resolving complaints when they were no longer in the vicinity of the original seller.

During this same period, the pressures of rising inflation brought a reduction in purchasing power. In an attempt to keep prices in line, some companies lowered product quality and customer service.

The foundation of consumerism was not concern over price alone, but disenchantment arising from expectations that fell short of reality. This disenchantment centered more on the quality of goods offered and services rendered than on the prices they commanded.

Out of frustration, consumers crystallized and verbalized their demands. Consumer groups formed around specific issues and became increasingly vocal and demonstrative. Their actions paralleled other political and social movements of the 1960s. A shift in consumer attitudes produced a "psychology of entitlement." The progression in attitude moved from desire to demands to rights.

In the 1970s, the consumer movement became part of the marketplace and the word "consumerism" a part of our vocabulary. Consumer activist and advocate groups received new life through increased membership and the

3. Ibid.
4. Ibid.

infusion of funding from private, government, and labor sources. Acceptance by the middle class gave the movement a real power center.

Consumerism today is increasingly diverse and has gained permanent acceptance in virtually all public and private sector organizations. The focus of consumer activist groups has shifted to grassroots organization.

If it seemed hard to categorize consumers in the past, it is going to be even more difficult in the future. The group that represents the largest market in the next decade is impossible to label. The 74 million 22- to 39-year-olds are America's largest, best educated, most affluent adult generation ever.

The question for the business community is this: Who are these people and what do they want? Companies who want to market to this group, which now represents many billions of dollars in annual buying power, will have to earn their trust by giving them quality products—"good stuff" and good service. These consumers know what that is, and shopping is their favorite indoor sport.

CORPORATE RESPONSE TO CONSUMERISM

The enlightened management of corporate America responded to the consumer movement in the early 1970s with the creation of consumer affairs professionals and departments charged with representing this new public segment labeled "consumers."

They were given the dual assignment of telling the story of the company and its products to the consumer and of representing the consumer's interests within the company. In our struggle to establish consumer affairs as a viable addition to business, we've learned several good lessons.

If the consumer affairs function is to be given any credence inside or outside the company, there must be intense top management interest. This function cannot be successfully applied in a wholly bottom-up way. No matter how well a consumer affairs department is managed, without a top management mandate for consumer satisfaction, it is doubtful that companywide cooperation can be achieved.

It is also essential that management commit itself to economic and political status for consumer affairs equal to other operating units. Within any organization a substantial appropriation of resources will signal management priority. If a department or function is to be seriously considered, it must be assigned equal value.

Assigning the title of vice president of consumer affairs to a "Peter Principle" employee can end up costing more in customer trust than a well-run program would cost. An honest consumer program involves a deep concern for customer satisfaction from top management to the sales clerk or

delivery person. It is an attitude that must be in place all day...
everyday...with every employee.

So for the 1980s, the enlightened corporate response to consumers is a
dedication to quality in products and service with a renewed emphasis on
"value." The basics for achieving this goal of consumer satisfaction start with
management objectives for the consumer affairs department:

- To build a consumer affairs program that will earn for the company a
  reputation of concern for the consumer.
- To achieve a corporate reputation for consumer responsiveness that will
  permit operation with minimal interference from consumer, legislative,
  regulatory, political, or other outside organizations.
- To operate a consumer affairs function that will contribute to the
  operation and profit of the company.

A written company policy on consumer satisfaction can be very simple
and straightforward. One company policy is stated: "The Sperry and Hutchinson Company's objective is consumer satisfaction. We seek to eliminate any
basis for valid customer complaints swiftly, courteously, and fairly."

Publicizing the policy

Once the policy is finalized, it should go out to all employees over the
signature of the president so they will be aware of the commitment to
consumer satisfaction. Publicize it in stores, employee handbooks, catalogs,
brochures, and in advertising (see figure 9.1, for example).

The company believes in the right of consumers to be fully informed about its
products and services. It strives to provide sufficient facts to enable
consumers to make knowledgeable and confident buying decisions. Further,
it encourages its customers to contact the company if the company's products
or services do not meet customer expectations.

Figure 9.1 An example of a written company policy statement.

If you are a manufacturing company, retail customers should receive
copies of your policy so they know you stand behind your products. This is a
good opportunity to solicit their swift help and feedback on *all* product or
service problems.

American manufacturers and retailers are finding it to their mutual
advantage to work together to serve consumers. Bob Elliot, chairman of
Levitz Furniture Corporation, the largest furniture merchant in the country,

believes good business/consumer practices are essential if the United States is to compete with imports and not go the way of those industries which seem to have forgotten the consumer. Levitz management feels that being number one carries an obligation to set a good example in customer satisfaction, much as an older child does in a family.

Eleanor Pari Eckardt, Levitz vice president of consumer relations, who works closely with Elliot, says: "We are relentless in our search to find ways to improve product quality, packaging, shipping schedules, care labeling, and product warranties for our customers. We expect the furniture manufacturers who supply our products to share our commitment to meeting consumer needs, and in return, we pinpoint for them defect and quality problems by product and by plant."

THE CONSUMER AFFAIRS DEPARTMENT

The excellent companies in the United States are really close to their customers. Having a consumer affairs function in a company helps develop and sustain that closeness. It creates a centralized location where corporate executives can tap into expertise on consumer acceptance or products and monitor emerging consumer issues and regulations.

In the past it has taken approximately ten years for a consumer issue to grow from an activist cause or government agency predilection to the point of government legislation or regulation (see figure 9.2).

Many of the regulations we have today have gone through the cycle: seat belt installation, unit pricing on food products, freshness dating on dairy and meat products, automobile exhaust standards, warning and ingredient labeling, safety bottle closures, credit terms and interest rate restrictions, children's sleepwear, carpet and mattress flammability standards.

Upholstered furniture flammability standards, air bag installation, and nutrition labeling are still in the cycle.

Usually the consumer has had no explanation of the costs or trade-offs they will be required to make in order to receive the extra protection or service, such as increased taxes to administer, increased taxes and product costs to cover industry compliance with the regulation, as well as restriction of marketplace choices.

In the early 1960s the businesses involved in the regulation of a product may have ignored the early warning signals. However, they soon discovered that consumer group communication and lobbying fueled by the press at each step of the cycle had created consumer acceptance of the need.

Most aware companies today realize that the best time to address any issue is at the beginning of the cycle. With adequate information on long- and short-term implications provided to the consumer, the affected industry may end the cycle.

Consumer Activist Leader
Introduces thought, cause, or idea for consumer protection in a public forum.
↓
Media Coverage
↓
Consumer advocate groups add to program of work.
↓
Media Coverage
↓
Issue moves to state consumer groups and grass roots.
↓
Media Coverage
↓
Adopted by thought- and opinion-leaders for debate.
↓
Media Coverage
↓
Moves to congressional committees concerned with consumer protection, usually through their staffs. Briefing comes from consumer lobbyists and/or government protection agency with jurisdiction over the product or service: Federal Trade Commission, Department of Transportation, Consumer Product Safety Commission, U.S. Department of Agriculture.

Figure 9.2 Consumer issue cycle.

Industry should, however, approach collecting and studying the consumer concern with an open mind as to its resolution. If the concern is legitimate, every effort should be made to find a cost-effective method to address it.

The new consumer service may be converted into a marketing tool by a forward-thinking company. When the Food and Drug Administration asked manufacturers of sun-care products to grade label their products as to efficacy, one leading company decided to cooperate and to turn the potential problem into a marketing opportunity. Their "tan by the numbers" publicity has paid off in sales and in increased consumer protection from skin cancer and sunburn.

The consumer affairs department provides a central location for the collection of data that may have been scattered throughout the company. This data can be compiled and analyzed for patterns, trends, and early detection of consumer displeasure. Consumer affairs personnel bring an understanding of consumer needs and expectations to the decision-making process that will help all units and departments. These internal consumer affairs professionals have been of great assistance in diffusing public opinion or confrontation.

Placement of the consumer affairs function within the corporation strongly affects the degree of cooperation and acceptance regarding consumer affairs in the corporation, in the community, and with consumer advocate groups.

Placement possibilities include: an independent department reporting directly to the president; a department located within the public relations or corporate communications area reporting to the top communications officer; or a department in the marketing area.

Because the placement level of the consumer affairs department signals to the world what its role will be, let's explore the options:

Top management: Perceived as having clout within, the ear of management, and freedom from pressure from operating departments. Strong dotted line relationships to department heads prevent isolation from operating units.

Public relations: Assures coordinated program in communications and community. However, may be perceived as "window dressing" by the media, consumer activists, and government.

Marketing: Can be perceived as a marketing tool, rather than an independent effort on behalf of the consumer. Pluses include valuable input on product labeling, point-of-sale materials, and consumer suggestions for product changes.

It is not recommended that the department report to sales, legal, or government relations. These departments have a strong focus and bias in one direction. In many instances, their direction may be in opposition to the concerns of the consumer.

Whatever the placement, it is desirable that steady working relationships with other divisions and departments be mandated. If corporate reporting channels do not formalize these relationships, informal opportunities should be created. Progressive companies are more and more maximizing resources by basing their plans and strategies on the organized use of all departments working in concert on each project.

Personnel choices for management and employees of this department will be a major factor in the success of both internal and external efforts. Dealing with the consumer requires a very special combination of experience, sensitivity, creativity, talent, and training. The department head should have experience working with the consumer and education in one or more of the following disciplines: consumer affairs, public relations, business, journalism, home economics, consumer economics, government relations, and consumer law. The individual skills, education, and experience of department employees should represent the various department functions, so that the whole is greater than the sum of its parts. Salary and other benefits should be high enough to attract top people and in line with those of other departments.

CONSUMER AFFAIRS DEPARTMENT PROGRAM OF WORK

To be effective in the dual role of representing the company to the consumer and the consumer to the company—and to be cost effective at the same time—requires thought, planning, and a dash of ingenuity. Each program and project must service the company in several different ways, inside and outside the company.

Let's look at an example of how one consumer affairs program might work on behalf of a company. Bigelow-Sanford, Inc., a producer of carpeting for well over 150 years, has consistently provided quality print and film materials explaining fiber characteristics, carpet use and care, and basic decorating principles. In addition they now label each carpet to reflect the wear potential so that consumers can purchase the carpet best suited to the different traffic areas of their homes.

These informational and educational materials are used in a variety of ways. By adding teacher and leader guides, they reach thousands of classrooms and women's clubs. Generous media coverage for these community efforts translates to goodwill for the company.

The marketing and sales departments of the company work with the retail stores which handle Bigelow carpets to set up decorating clinics using these materials. In addition to helping the stores increase their in-store traffic, the materials are used to train their salesmen concerning the products.

Proper targeting and planning of consumer projects will build brand identity both short and long term, encourage preferred treatment by retail accounts, and provide opportunities for increased sales and profits.

Possibilities for internal functions include counseling management in areas involving consumer affairs; assisting and counseling other departments and units; developing and maintaining a system for handling consumer complaints and inquiries; setting up a mechanism for converting complaint data and consumer feedback into improved performance; and establishing a consumer feedback system using consumer advisory boards, focus groups, consumer surveys, product questionnaires, and community events.

External programs could encompass developing a consumer contact plan in the private sector; producing and distributing consumer education materials; establishing contacts in government offices of consumer affairs; working with consumer activists, where possible, to detect emerging issues, diffuse adverse opinion, and explain company positions; publicizing and promoting company consumer affairs programs and materials; and becoming familiar with the consumer press, "action line" columnists, media associations, and organizations.

INTERNAL FUNCTIONS

Communications

Public relations, financial relations, government relations, and consumer affairs should be a cohesive working group. This is particularly important to the consumer affairs area, where many activities overlap with other functions. Public relations cooperation can multiply the effectiveness of the positive programs operated by consumer affairs.

As publics change and multiply, public relations is faced with an open-ended search for new techniques and approaches. Consumer affairs offers an approach that is as new as today. A well-managed, well-financed consumer affairs program is a 100 percent positive public relations effort.

Campbell Soup Company, for example, is combining several of their corporate resources in a public relations effort to develop and distribute educational materials on nutrition. The community sector is reached through the General Federation of Women's Clubs, National 4–H Council, and senior citizens groups. Campbell Soup is also supplying materials produced especially for professionals: doctors, nutritionists, dieticians, and public health workers. The feedback from this consumer communication is reported to all corporate departments.

Campbell Soup's community efforts in supplying nutritional information to all demographic sectors is establishing them as a company which is concerned over public health in general and their customers in particular.

Press coverage of these programs has been prolific, reaching millions of consumers. The company received the Home Economics Vocational Education Association Public Service Award in 1982. They were the only company so honored.

Government Relations

As government activity shifts to the states, as consumers become more actively involved with local issues, and as constituency support groups become more essential, contacts made in the community by consumer affairs are becoming increasingly more important. These grassroots contacts are an invaluable communications link, as well as a source of identifiable support.

Back in the early 1960s, the Sperry and Hutchinson Company realized that the consumer was a friend indeed. They were one of the very first companies to form a consumer relations department, some fifteen years before SOCAP, the Society of Consumer Affairs Professionals, was formed.

The company developed substantive consumer education materials with teacher's guides for the classroom and leader's guides for clubs. One program, "What Every Woman Should Know About Trading Stamps," explained the economic advantages to the retailer and consumer of using and collecting trading stamps. This effort proved to be right on target as consumers consistently rejected legislation to regulate trading stamps when it was introduced in various states.

Marketing

Consumer affairs professionals can be of invaluable assistance in the field of consumer information, providing labeling, use and care information, point-of-sale materials, safety warning, product features, and components or ingredients.

To be effective, this information must be in accordance with government regulations, but be written in easily understood language—not laboratory terminology or lawyer-ese.

Advertising

Ads are being much more closely scrutinized by the public, as well as consumer, government, and women's advocates. It is wise to ask consumer experts to review all advertising for their perceptions of content, clarity of product information, and proof of claims.

Recently, consumer advocates have been pushing for comparative advertising. That is the presentation of information that will enlighten the consumer in the advantages of one product over another.

Most consumers who are careful shoppers are interested in information on product features and use. They resent advertising claims that are exaggerated and in some cases blatantly untrue.

Some other frequently heard objections to advertising include the use of sex to sell products; unfair portrayal of youth, elderly, women, and minorities; lack of taste used in presenting certain products; and selling products that are harmful to health.

The American Association of Advertising Agencies has for several years had a voluntary screening group of industry leaders that monitor advertising claims. Many major companies have been forced to cease unfair or deceptive ad campaigns.

The Federal Trade Commission has in practice an ad substantiation policy that requires the advertiser to have proof of substantiation before making a claim for its product. The FTC policy is now being challenged by some in Congress on a cost/benefit basis.

Manufacturing, Quality Control, Research, and Design

All can benefit from current and regular information feedback from customer service, advisory boards, and consumer complaints and suggestions on product safety, packaging, product modification, suggestions for new products, the need for more care and use information, and complaints in product quality.

LADD, a furniture conglomerate, attaches a consumer questionnaire to each furniture suite. The questionnaires, structured for ease of answering and a minimum investment of time, have produced a high percentage of return. The answers are computerized for quick access to the information.

As a result of the customer feedback, LADD has been able to spot defects in construction, finish, and packaging and to move swiftly to correct the problems. Tightening of quality control, manufacturing changes, and new efforts by R&D have stemmed consumer dissatisfaction and subsequent loss of future sales.

Furthermore, by analyzing the contents of the returned questionnaires, LADD has been able to design new products to fill gaps identified in their product line.

Customer profiles were created from the demographic information on the buyers of each of their furniture suites. These customer profiles are utilized by the sales representatives who sell LADD furniture to retail stores. In turn, the retail stores use the profiles to identify families which are potential customers for specific LADD furniture designs.

Legal

Consumer affairs should work closely with legal departments in the areas of warranties, product liability, and recalls.

Consumer Complaints and Inquiries

In some organizations, this is the only specified area of consumer activity. Whatever the size of your company, establish a system that will assure complete customer satisfaction.

The up-front investment in this function, even if it includes the latest in computer equipment, word processing, and sophisticated communications systems, will pay for itself many times over in increased sales, improved products, customer retention, and operational efficiency.

Studies show that it costs much more to get a new customer than it does to keep the ones you have. Companies which are responsive to complaints are rewarded with the greatest degree of brand loyalty. A loyal customer is worth $70,000 in repeat business to an automobile manufacturer, according to Ford Motor Company. A national study for the Coca-Cola Company shows that sales and brand loyalty can be reinforced by good complaint handling. When a customer has a good experience with a product, he tells 3 people. When he has a bad experience, he tells from 10 to 20 people.

By handling company transactions properly in-house, the possibility of losing control to a third-party complaint handler is eliminated. The number of third-party mechanisms is growing and includes community mediation boards, press reporters, industry consumer action panels, Better Business Bureaus, consumer advocacy organizations, district attorneys, and government agencies at all levels.

Your method of handling complaints should be well organized and as simple as possible. It should be designed to cause minimum disruption and inconvenience to other operating personnel. Yet, at the same time, it should satisfy the customer as promptly as possible.

Communicating with the customer in a swift, intelligent manner will prevent a growing sense of frustration. The more unhappy the customer becomes, the more difficulty you may have in settling the complaint. There are many examples where customers have instituted lawsuits of a serious nature which could have been prevented with considerate attention to the original problem.

Staffing the complaint handling department is a number-one consideration. Remember, these employees are handling your customer at a time when he is most disturbed. Staff members should be sensitive to the needs of others, friendly, and able to exercise good judgment. They should be able to balance both company and customer interests. They should have knowledge of the company, its products, services, and policies. Training in written and verbal communication skills, human relations, and the art of interviewing should be a basic requirement.

Presented here is one example of a good, simple complaint handling method:

1. The complaint is received and acknowledged.
2. The complaint is recorded.
3. The complaint is reviewed and sent to the appropriate location for handling.
4. The complaint is resolved.
5. Complaints are analyzed periodically and recommendations for corrective action made to the appropriate location.
6. Audits are conducted periodically to check the effectiveness of the system.
7. Procedures are reviewed frequently and updated.

Many companies have established "800" numbers to answer their customers' questions and to give a swift response to complaints. A very valuable by-product is the wealth of information they get from their customers.

The Whirlpool Corporation was one of the first to use this new communications tool. The company achieved, in a remarkably short time, a nationwide image of concern for the consumer.

Proctor and Gamble was the first consumer goods company to put its toll-free number on all of its packaging. More than 200,000 calls are handled each year and summarized for monthly board meetings. Proctor and Gamble credits their 800-number information as being a major source of ideas for improving the quality of their products and services. The key is listening!

Consumer Feedback

Many consumer affairs activities can be used to gather information on the company, its products, and services. Some of the techniques include surveys, consumer advisory boards, focus groups, conventions, exhibits, seminars, and consumer questionnaires.

Consumer advisory boards have members selected on the basis of the demographics of the country, area, or customer base.

Consumer advisory boards are composed primarily of consumers who meet on a regularly scheduled basis to discuss the quality of goods and services being offered by a particular business. They provide the opportunity to learn firsthand what customers need and want. At the same time, boards help business and customers bring their expectations in line with economic realities.

Luncheon and dinner meetings permit almost all types of people to participate.

It is not recommended that you pay even a token fee to participants, since this can influence their objectivity. However, any legitimate expense they may incur, such as carfare or baby-sitting costs, should be reimbursed. You may provide sample merchandise if you want participants to evaluate products. Your appreciation for their help can be shown with a gift when they leave the board. Periodic rotation of advisory board members provides fresh opinions and attitudes.

Focus groups are formed to deal with a specific subject on a one-time basis. If a new consumer service or major policy change is contemplated, the group would probably be the same kind of cross section as for a consumer advisory board. However, if the issues pertain to a particular group—such as low income, ethnic, senior citizens, or youth—members would be drawn from that segment. To get a valid consensus, at least two separate focus groups should be convened on each subject. Members from one group should not serve on the other.

EXTERNAL PROGRAMS

Personal Relationships

A consumer affairs department runs on contacts and personal relationships. They are its fuel. Whatever the need—consumer input, access to resources, publicity, consumers to testify at a regulatory hearing, help with a third-party complaint handling mechanism, speakers—contacts will help get the job accomplished.

The key is to decide where the contacts will be needed and to plan activities so the contacts you need will be cultivated in advance. Generally, friends that are in place when the need arises are of much greater value than those made out of desperation.

A solid basis for developing a working relationship requires involvement in some form of mutually beneficial public relations program: sponsorship of awards programs, training seminars, educational exhibits, or distribution of generic consumer education materials.

Clubs and organizations, especially the General Federation of Women's Clubs, are representative of real consumers. GFWC is the largest women's organization in the country, with one million members. Junior Clubs (age 20–24) and Senior Clubs are located in almost every town throughout the United States. This is a highly regarded organization because of its community-building and improvement projects. Its publication, *The Clubwoman*, outlines these projects, many of them sponsored by business. Members are a good source for advisory boards, focus groups, and for constituency-building activity.

Civic and community groups include the Lions, Jaycees, Kiwanis, and Rotary. They are good sources of help with projects, audiences for programs, advisory board or focus group members. Also check out the local Chamber of Commerce, hospital guilds, Junior League, and churchwomen.

Senior citizens are targeted by the AARP, the American Association of Retired Persons (11 million members), which recently merged with the National Retired Teachers Association (1 million members). Their *Modern Maturity* publication reaches these 12 million older Americans, many of whom have time to become involved in consumer and community affairs. Politically and economically, they have emerged as a power group in this country.

Professional associations can provide guidance in the counseling role and in maintaining the "state of the art" in consumer affairs program content. They include SOCAP, the Society of Consumer Affairs Professionals in Business; PRSA, the Public Relations Society of America Consumer Affairs Section; and the Public Affairs Council.

Industry trade associations provide an opportunity to monitor the industry level of consumer affairs performance; sources for marketing and product information; a chance to contribute to industry decisions and cooperate on actions that will improve the reputation of business; and an opportunity for you to meet leaders in your field and share methods and practices.

Minority groups can be reached through the Organization of Negro Business and Professional Women, National Council of Negro Women, many Hispanic organizations, minority journalists, minority educators, and the like. As you work with these various community groups, your corporate staff will begin to identify the opinion- and thought-leaders among their officers and members. These leaders will form your connecting link with the various organizations.

And what is the bottom line of all this effort? Let me give you an example. When the furniture industry was faced with the possibility of having the Consumer Product Safety Commission impose a mandatory furniture flammability standard in 1976, they went into action.

Informational materials and study kits were developed for the industry, CPSC, and consumers. These materials included CPSC, industry, and consumer positions on the issue. Economic costs, short and long term, were projected for the CPSC standard and an alternative voluntary industry effort. Charts were developed picturing the steady increase in furniture safety under the voluntary program.

Consumers were encouraged to weigh the extent of the hazard, its causes, increased costs of upholstered furniture, the impact on small businesses, and the fact that 65 percent of Americans do not smoke. The public overwhelmingly supported a voluntary industry program to improve furniture safety in a cost-effective manner as technology improved. The CPSC agreed, and no mandatory government regulation was imposed.

Consumer Education Materials

Producing and distributing consumer education materials is beneficial to the organization both short and long term. Generic materials equip consumers to make good buying decisions, long range and at point of sale. Your efforts should not be seen as self-serving and must use solid educational concepts as their basis. Company identification is important, but it should be tasteful and unobtrusive.

Using leaders in the field of study and top educators on a development advisory committee will assure credibility and broaden use of the materials. SOCAP, the Society of Consumer Affairs Professionals in Business, has prepared a brochure on this subject, *Guidelines for Business Sponsored Consumer Educational Materials*.

In addition to providing materials to classrooms and adult clubs and organizations, you might also consider contacting youth organizations and the education community.

Youth organizations offer a rewarding way to build long-term business friends. Establishing brand identity with youth as they are embarking on a life of purchasing can have great value. While working with youth, you are reaching other adults involved in the program, as well as parents, brothers, and sisters. Some of the groups which encourage business sponsors are:

- 4–H
- DECA, Distributive Education Clubs of America (career-related programs)
- Boys Clubs
- Girls Clubs of America
- Future Homemakers of America
- Future Farmers of America

The education community includes three bodies (listed in italics below) which have organized information distribution systems that include print, radio, TV, and personal presentations to classes and community organizations:

- The *American Home Economics Association* includes 35,000 professionals whose purpose is to improve the quality and standards of individual and family life.

- The *University Extension Network* reaches 20 million people daily through:
  - *National Association of Extension Home Economists*
  - University extension specialists at land grant colleges
  - Extension homemakers
  - County extension agents
  - National Association of Agricultural Agents
  - State departments of education

Government consumer affairs representatives should be cultivated to develop working relationships with your government peers. Contact:

- Office of Consumer Affairs, Washington, D.C.
- U.S. Department of Commerce, Consumer Affairs Division
- National Association of Consumer Agency Administrators
- State consumer affairs or prosecuting attorneys offices
- Federal and regional Federal Trade Commission representatives
- Federal and regional Consumer Product Safety Commission representatives

Consumer activist organizations are influential advocacy leaders. Monitor their activities to spot emerging issues and action trends. Cooperate with their movement when philosophy permits, in some educational efforts, for example. These groups include:

- CFA, Consumer Federation of America
- NCL, National Consumer League
- ACCI, American Council on Consumer Interests (education oriented)
- COCO, Conference of Consumer Organizations

Media groups should be kept informed of positive company programs and company positions on issues. Back in 1909 when Pendleton Dudley left the *Wall Street Journal* to start his public relations business, he described his view of appropriate corporate behavior like this: "Do good things, and tell the world about it."

Because most consumer affairs programs are not self-serving, publicity concerning these services are relevant to educators, consumers, and the community. In addition to regular media contacts, you should also stay in touch with:

- Action Line Journalists Association (500 journalists resolving 2 million complaints a year)
- State press associations
- National Association of Broadcasters
- American Women in Radio and Television
- National Federation of Press Women
- Women in Communications

Company employees and customers are a part of their communities, many of them active in local organizations. Keep them informed and proud of your efforts. Use company advertising, store facilities, company communications, and publications.

CONCLUSION

Whatever organization you serve—large or small, in industry, government, or the not-for-profit sector—lead, inspire, and cooperate with your fellow workers in a "quest for the best."

Many American companies are currently implementing major quality improvement programs. Top management is committed to error-free work in every department, not just the production areas. To restore economic health and consumer confidence in American products will take all our combined efforts.

Feel free to review and apply any of Marshall Field's mottos!

ASSOCIATION PUBLIC RELATIONS

James N. Sites

President
James N. Sites & Associates

Every association is in the communications business. Communications forms the web that ties an association together with its members. It serves as a unifying force, a catalyst for action. No association could operate without sound communications links.

Despite this intimate interrelationship, however, the state of communications within most associations is, in general, poorly developed. Most association executives recognize the need to create an effective *internal* information flow and gear up to act in this area, with varying degrees of success. But all too few are utilizing public relations skills and mechanisms effectively in meeting *external* communications challenges—in informing the public of the association, its industry, and the merits of its positions, or in shaping singular identities and attracting membership and revenues.

One reason is that among associations, no less than elsewhere, executives skilled in general management often see public relations as an ephemeral area that defies easy definition and measurement. These managers will thus often set up solid systems in technical, legal, administrative, and government relations areas while treating communications as a routine function or even a necessary nuisance. A great deal obviously needs to be done to get across the organization-building, role that public relations can

James N. Sites is president of a Washington-based communications management counseling service, James N. Sites & Associates, and senior consultant to a nationwide public relations firm, John Adams Associates.

His former positions include vice president for communications for the Chemical Manufacturers Association; director of public affairs at the U.S. Treasury Department; and vice president in charge of the Carl Byoir & Associates Washington office.

In 1961 he was chosen U.S. Eisenhower Exchange Fellow.

play within association management. It is important to address these fundamentals, with particular reference to meeting Washington communications challenges.

One of the biggest, hardest-hitting public relations campaigns in association history was mounted a few years ago against "featherbedding" work practices on the nation's railroads. The Association of American Railroads was the leader of that campaign. And even though the effort eventually enveloped the entire country, Washington, D.C., was its focal point.

The choice of focus was based not only on the fact that Washington is home base for the AAR, but also:

- The capitol figured in the strategic planning as the crucial battleground · on which the final national decisions on the issues would be made.
- And, most important from the viewpoint of professional public relations campaigning, Washington is probably the most sophisticated communications center on earth, with press and other information channels reaching out to every nook and cranny in America.

In short, here is the ideal base from which to communicate in a big way—assuming you know intimately both its nature and the ever-shifting rules of the Washington communications game, particularly how to deal with this renowned wonderworld of government officials, diplomats, lobbyists, and news representatives.

As every association executive who has ever worked along the Washington communications beat knows, it can truly be said that the practice of public relations in the nation's capitol is unlike that anywhere else in the world.

The obvious reason is the immense presence of the federal government, a colossus whose size and influence in tax and spending terms has been multiplying inexorably—and which, despite repeated efforts to rein it in, appears likely to grow further in the next decade and beyond.

Government's influence over the ways we live and work has become so pervasive that a government presence is now felt in almost every aspect of life. During 50 years of depression, war, rising free-world burdens, and growing national affluence, business has had to learn to live with expanding government taxation, regulation, monetary and credit controls, and other programs affecting the economy, our health, survival itself.

We have also had to learn to deal with government as a major purchaser of goods and services; as a large-scale employer and wage pattern-setter; as a subsidizer; and, at times, a rough competitor.

It is precisely because of this penetrating impact that Washington is becoming headquarters for more and more associations, as well as for the widest range of other interests. Clustering around the federal government are not only trade and professional groups of every description, but also corporate, labor, and farm representatives; foreign agencies; law and public relations firms; and the biggest and best-trained press corps on earth.

These groups represent the public, or key segments of the public, just as government itself does. They influence the scope, direction, and tone of government activities and, in turn, provide channels for helping government implement decisions and operate effectively.

Washington can best be viewed as a giant communications center. Here originates much of a TV or radio show's network news content and the daily newspaper's front-page copy. Washington is also the operations base for political and economic analysts of every persuasion.

Washington reporting and public relations are made doubly difficult because this fair city must surely be the one place on earth where sound travels faster than light. Here is a circus of curved mirrors and distorted images, of lights and shadows, of smokescreens and red herrings—where it daily becomes more difficult to separate fact from fiction.

Here indeed is the place where the special interest has come to be favored over the public interest, where personalities and politics are emphasized over policies and positions, where problem symptoms and results are feverishly attacked rather than causes, where short-run gains are the reigning goal and the long term is interpreted as the next election.

Providing grist for the Washington communications mill, government itself continually churns out mountains of reports and a multitude of publications. For instance, Capitol Hill's *Congressional Record* offers prestigious circulation for speeches or statements important enough to warrant insertion by sympathetic members of Congress.

Washington can further be viewed as an international liaison center. Here are well over a hundred embassies, virtually all of which have press and commercial counselors and others who can be helpful on projects involving their homelands. The world's leading newspapers also have staffs here.

The giant U.S. Information Agency is still another highly competent group ready to cooperate on carefully adapted news and features, with its services reaching people around the world.

Washington-based trade and professional organizations themselves offer an endless variety of opportunities for public relations tie-ins. Trade groups often have unbeatable experts who can provide valuable intelligence and other help in relating to government. It often is possible to arrange for particular executives to speak on subjects of mutual interest at another organization's meetings and other activities. Such appearances can both guarantee wide internal distribution of materials and serve as attractive publicity platforms.

The National Press Club perennially provides one of the most influential of Washington platforms. However, as a long-term member of the club, this writer has learned that an executive must be deeply involved in a significant public interest issue to obtain an NPC appearance or heavy news coverage.

Finally, one could not hope to function effectively in the national capital without a good feel for opportunities to cooperate with this town's huge law corps, as well as with other public relations professionals. Washington is said to have more lawyers relative to its population than any other city, a point affirmed by their massive attendance at congressional hearings and regulatory agency proceedings.

The Washington Chapter of the Public Relations Society of America has 500 members, but this represents only a fraction of the people handling communications and similar functions here. Government agencies and congressmen employ thousands of information directors, speech writers, and press secretaries. And virtually every association of any size has a public relations staff, with many using professional outside firms to provide counseling and supporting services.

And now, how? Given this setting, how do you operate effectively on the Washington public relations scene?

Answers to this central question vary as widely as the nature of associations themselves. It's axiomatic that no two public relations programs or Washington operations can be alike. Each must be as carefully tailored and fitted to an organization as an airplane's skin is molded to its frame.

For instance, every association is born out of some fundamental membership decisions as to what it will be doing, in what areas how big a budget and staff it will have, how public it will go in its activities and how much public support it will endeavor to mobilize for its policy objectives. Obviously, the size and nature of its public relations program will vary accordingly— as will the balance it strikes between carrying out programs with internal staff or utilizing public relations consultants.

Why consider outside public relations counsel? Precisely because they are on the outside. Public relations counsel can provide an often priceless objective viewpoint and policy guidance. A long-established national firm can also bring to bear on both public relations planning and day-to-day emergencies the invaluable experience gained from working on similar problems over many years.

At the same time, the internal communications job must not be neglected. As the organization gets larger and more dispersed, the vital job of internal communicating and base building becomes proportionately more urgent.

Early in its development a Washington association must go through its own unique "positioning" discipline and continually keep this updated if it is to operate effectively. One begins by listing contacts of basic importance to objectives: key congressional committees and congressmen, government offices and regulators, other associations and corporate representatives, trade reporters and general newsmen.

Such a list easily can get so long that it becomes unmanageable. So priorities must be assigned. All this is forerunner to coming up with a long-range plan of informing these people on your positions—and to the never-ending, crucial job of developing personal contacts, without which nothing can be done in Washington.

Assuming you have set up realistic policy goals and defined approaches, the association public relations program is then ready to roll, its Washington activities falling into these major categories:

- Reporting basic information on government developments and analyzing public policy trends of concern to the association and its members.
- Setting up meetings and handling other essential contacts with government and private leaders.
- Working closely with the Washington press and other communications channels to promote favorable publicity on behalf of the association, the industry it represents, and member companies.
- Counseling management on the public implications of and the means of coping with breaking Washington developments, such as agency investigations and congressional hearings—as well as implementing long-range programs of building goodwill and support among capital thought-leaders and influence centers.

Some examples from the writer's own experience will illustrate these services and show how complexities can be handled.

When the Consumer Product Safety Commission asked a major group of retailers to pay for large-scale advertising to alert the nation to the first "imminent hazard" in the commission's history, an alternative approach was recommended utilizing national news channels and grassroots point-of-sale action. Implemented through a public relations firm and the involved businesses, this "total communications" program resulted in hundreds of newspaper stories and television and radio broadcasts across the nation. When the commission persisted in its demands for advertising, the author argued the superior effectiveness of the industry's voluntary action as chief witness before the commission and, eventually, before the U.S. District Court. In a precedent-setting decision Chief Judge George L. Hart, Jr., rejected the CPSC demand and upheld the industry's approach, setting the stage for a more rational approach to such safety problems in future cases.

Or take another tough case: manufacturers who had joined together to promote the sale of a certain housing product were suddenly attacked by a congressman who represented the producers of a competing product. His charge was that the product was unsafe and not durable, and he demanded that FHA cancel its approval until a product investigation was held.

Public relations forces encouraged the association to make a public demonstration to refute the charges. They enlisted support from the member companies' congressmen, and a press conference was arranged at which a demonstration was held for a roomful of reporters and TV cameras. The result: FHA cleared the product, the congressman dropped his charges, and the national publicity generated by the press conference helped double the sales of the product over the next year.

Another association rose to a much broader challenge when it sought to pioneer fundamental action to improve news reporting on business—and, in the process, to improve its own image with the press. Working with news organizations, journalism educators, and business leaders, the author developed a nationwide program of economic workshops for both university students and reporters, with a special series on current issues designed for the Washington press. A team of 12 top editors was assembled to write a book titled *Reporting on Business and the Economy.* And a university-level center was set up as the plan's enduring action centerpiece.

Since the association budget could not finance these "outside" activities, an educational foundation was established and in two years raised a striking amount of money. Program implementation proceeded apace. In time, however, the programs ran into a number of internal problems, headed by a question of "germaneness": that is, they were seen by many members as too remote from the association's normally defined mission. Termination eventually resulted. Even so, the textbook and university center continue to work their impact, providing continuing evidence of one of the more far-reaching association action efforts.

These examples are necessarily limited in that they are fragments of widely varying public relations action plans. Nor do they get into the area of direct lobbying, which public relations personnel often leave to general executives and lawyers.

On major public issues, nevertheless, lobbying must be realistically viewed as only the tip of a very long spear that stretches back to 50 states and 435 congressional districts. Public opinion support is the indispensable power needed to drive the spear's point home.

This underlines a key point of operating technique: The Washington public relations person never forgets that the shortest route to a government official often runs through a congressman—while the shortest route to a congressman may circle all the way back through his constituency; that the best approach to a wire service reporter may be through a member newspaper; that the most effective way to get an association to move may be through its key members.

All these details add up to the real payoff for public relations, as distinct from such individual arms as publicity, advertising, and membership communications. Success lies in a carefully researched, cross-analyzed, purposeful plan for building up public support for an organization's public policy objectives over the long term.

Even with all the unique characteristics that are present in every public relations program, some common methods can often be applied on behalf of associations in helping the public understand and take action on issues clouded by misinformation, political rhetoric, self-interest, and public apathy. This three-part strategy was followed in the rail featherbedding fight and other campaigns:

1. *Make the issue public.* Get the facts out and understood. If the issue is one truly involving the public interest, rather than a cloakroom fight between lobbies, public officials will thereby be encouraged to stand up and support you—or else will have to justify their opposition before the voters.
2. *Enlist the help of experts.* There are many people—well known and respected for their accomplishments in other fields—who, if they knew and understood the issue, might be induced to rally to your cause. Their testimony, based on fact and presented in the public interest, heightens the believability of the issue, adding a scope and depth far beyond that which can be accomplished by industry spokesmen alone.
3. *Recruit allies.* An association's goals affect more than just its members. They affect suppliers, manufacturers, consumers, workers, financial interests—all of whom may already be represented by still other trade, business, or social organizations. Many of these can be counted on to be vocal and persuasive once they are brought to understand the problem and its effects on their own interests.

As a postscript to the railroads' anti-featherbedding campaign, it is noteworthy that public opinion came to support management's side so heavily that when a crucial vote on the issue came up in Congress, only a handful of votes were cast against the industry's position—despite all-out union efforts to achieve this end.

The chemical industry is a striking recent example of the application of the foregoing three-part strategy. Faced with increasingly negative public attitudes over environmental impact, coupled with mounting governmental controls, its leaders decided that their association should be restructured from a low-profile reactive group (like so many, unfortunately) into a hard-hitting *advocate* of chemical industry policies. In less than two years, this brought about a change of name, a doubling of staff (one addition being the author), and a tripling of revenues—including a *sixfold increase* in the public relations budget.

Most important, the action plan behind this greatly expanded communications effort was painstakingly developed in coordination with the members—who, after all, were the real experts on both the problems and their solutions. They were, therefore, that much more receptive to financing the program and helping in its grassroots implementation. And even though the 1982 recession brought a cutback in the advertising portion of the overall public relations budget, the basic public support campaign remains in place.

On the other side of the ledger is another industry I know that has terrible public relations problems, with politically damaging perceptions of its being a hazardous place to work and a source of grave environmental damage, yet is doing nothing—absolutely nothing—about either the problem or its communication needs.

This gets to perhaps the biggest single challenge facing associations in this field: creating close teamwork between government relations and public relations. Washington-based associations typically revolve around the government relations function. With notable exceptions, however, this does not assure a commensurate development of communications expertise—despite the fact that most association executives now realize that the public opinion of today is the public statute of tomorrow. And despite the fact that the first thing a congressman or public official thinks of in taking a position on an issue is the state of public opinion on the matter—and how to relate to it or take advantage of it.

Paradoxically, this all too often seems to be almost the *last* thing business and its myriad associations think of or act on. Year after year, public support action gets the short end of funding and attention. And each new year sees the private enterprise system a little closer to total governmental control than the year before. One could hardly blame people for feeling there ought to be a better way to run a public affairs program. And there *is*!

In conclusion, here are some guidelines that can be drawn from this sketch of the art of practicing public relations in Washington:

- First of all, the foregoing examples indicate this is no place for amateurs. You need a solid grasp of press skills and public relations approaches to work effectively on the expert-loaded capital scene.
- Nor could you bring off really important projects without wide, intensively developed contacts—and the kind of personal integrity and spirit of helpfulness needed to retain and expand these through the years.
- Also underscored is the basic need for intimate knowledge of government functions and the diverse policy issues which public officials and the nation are continually struggling with.
- But most important of all is the need pointed up by Washington experience for adherence to a simple but crucial concept—that of serving the public interest.

While all public relations practice must be concerned with this last guideline, it is an absolute essential in dealing with government policy issues. Nowhere in Washington can you achieve public respect and support unless you earn it. And you earn it by positive performance and by taking the kind of constructive positions that can be demonstrated to be in the public interest.

Just as congressmen and government officials at all levels forever seek to justify their programs, proposals, and decisions in terms of contributions to the public interest, so must private parties.

In fact a general rule might be formed on this basis: if you can't build a convincing case that what you want is in the public interest, *forget it.*

And now to conclude with another general rule of deep significance to all association executives: This is the reality all Washington insiders recognize— that government issues are seldom decided on their objective merits but, rather, on the basis of their political implications and their interplay with public opinion.

Here, indeed, is the ultimate clarification of the crucial impact of astute public relations on political decisions—now, certainly, and even more in the years ahead.

HOW PUBLIC RELATIONS OPERATES— ITS TOOLS AND TECHNIQUES

An Overview

Harold Burson

Chairman of the Board
Burson-Marsteller, Inc.

Within the lifetime of many of us, the principal requisites for a successful public relations practitioner consisted of a typewriter, a mimeograph machine, a mailing list, and an abundant supply of postage stamps, plus a working knowledge of a newspaper, magazine, or wire service. Public relations, in terms of its tools and techniques (as differentiated from the counseling function, which then, as now, depended on intellect, analytical ability, persuasive communications on a personal level, and credibility), was essentially press relations, and pre–1960, was limited almost exclusively to the print media.

But no more. The practice of public relations, no less than other human endeavors over the past two decades, has responded to change—technolo-

---

Harold Burson has headed Burson-Marsteller, Inc., now one of the world's two largest public relations firms, since its founding in 1953. He has been recognized as a leading public relations practitioner with the 1980 Gold Anvil Award by the Public Relations Society of America and as Public Relations Professional of the Year (1977) by the readers of *Public Relations News*. He has taken an active role in such organizations as the Kennedy Center, the Joint Council on Economic Education, Catalyst, and the World Wildlife Fund. He is a presidential appointee to the U.S. Fine Arts Commission.

gical change, to be sure. But even more important, it has responded to an increasingly complex society—made up of private sector and public sector, for-profit and not-for-profit alike—that has placed demands on the public relations practitioner once barely dreamed of.

In the area of technology, we as public relations people find ourselves dealing with the reality of television as a major disseminator of news. We accept the premise that two-thirds of all the people in the United States obtain two-thirds of the news they receive by sitting in front of a television tube. Nor is the response as simple as developing an acquaintanceship among television news directors. Instead, we find ourselves producing television news clips, employing satellites to disseminate our messages or to facilitate our news conferences to distant points, and developing tapes that accord with the special interests of cable outlets.

Our news releases are in typefaces that can be optically scanned by the newspapers to which they are addressed, to facilitate electronic typesetting. Our word processors communicate with our client's word processors, and with the word processors of some news outlets.

Corporations and public relations firms alike have their in-house television studios. Increasingly, closed circuit television and video cassettes are supplementing, even replacing, the company magazine. Overhead slides have given way to computer-controlled multimedia.

The rate of changes on the human side has been equally dramatic. The former newspaper reporter stereotype of the public relations practitioner has been replaced by a variety of specialists educated and trained in a broad spectrum of disciplines that affect our business and professional lives. Men and women who know politics, the law, economics, marketing, finance, corporate management, engineering, medicine, nutrition, and, of course, communications, electronic as well as print.

These changes have had a profound impact on the practice of public relations. They have enhanced the relevancy of public relations. They are contributing to make it a more meaningful, a more measurable activity in the eyes of those who require our services.

Nor are we nearing an end to the changes that have permeated our field for twenty years or more. As technology continues to expand the reach of communications, and the variety, so will we in public relations adapt. And as social needs change, skilled public relations practitioners will draw on the specialized talents required to fulfill our mission.

CORPORATE ADVERTISING

Thomas J. Fay

Vice President, Communications
TRW Inc.

One morning recently three magazines arrived on my desk: *Business Week, Forbes,* and *U.S. News & World Report.* Leafing through them I found no fewer than 21 examples of advertising that had either no product to sell, products that could be sold to only one customer (the government), or products that were apparently being advertised not so much to sell them as the companies that made them. Those 21 messages were all examples of corporate advertising, which we'll loosely define here as *any advertising a company does for purposes other than solely to sell its products or services.*[1]

And what a diverse collection it was, ranging from single-page; black-and-white ads with snapshot-quality photos to four-color extravaganzas spread across two pages, a couple with silver-tinted backgrounds (at an additional cost of about $3,000).

On that same day, the page opposite the editorials in the *New York Times,* carried a 75-word message from the "principal subcontractor" for a new Navy jet.

A day earlier three such ads appeared in the "Outlook" section of the *Washington Post* (which sells its op-ed space to no one).

Thomas J. Fay joined TRW Inc., in 1979 to head the company's worldwide communications function, which includes government relations, public relations, and advertising, as well as community affairs and international public affairs. He also has coordinating responsibility for investor relations and employee communications.

Prior to joining TRW, Mr. Fay ended his 17 years with Mobil Oil Corporation as general manager of public relations, the position he attained in 1975.

Mr. Fay is president of the TRW Foundation, which provides support for nonprofit organizations for educational, health, welfare, youth, civic, and cultural purposes. He also serves as a trustee of the Educational Television Association of Metropolitan Cleveland and is vice chairman of the Great Lakes Shakespeare Festival.

1. Trade and professional associations and unions also make use of such advertising, but in this chapter we'll refer only to companies.

By very rough calculation the total cost, just for space, of those 25 ads was close to three-quarters of a million dollars. Not only that, but at least one advertiser (and there may have been more) appeared to be in desperate financial condition.

Why did they do it?

THE PURPOSE OF CORPORATE ADVERTISING

Using the examples in this random handful of publications, a careful reading reveals at least two distinct purposes behind corporate advertising:

- To call attention to the company, or to separate it from its competitors in the eyes of the financial community, shareholders, customers, employees, and other important audiences. This, the most common type of corporate advertising, used to be called "institutional advertising," but that term has gone out of vogue.
- To help solve a problem or ward off a threat by offering the company's views on an issue. This is a more recent type of corporate advertising, and it has a variety of forms and names: issue advertising, idea advertising, or advocacy advertising.

Of the 25 ads mentioned, only three dealt directly with issues: the importance of America's railroads, the economic significance of the self-employed, and the survivability of the advertiser.[2] That ratio, about eight to one, is instructive. Only a very small portion of all corporate advertising, probably less than in our rough sample, can truly be called issue advertising (see figure 11.1).

Of the remaining messages, it was frequently difficult to determine exactly what audiences were being appealed to. For example, one ad pictured three applications of an oil company's chemical products that would be familiar to consumers. One could easily infer that the target audiences included not just the manufacturers of the kinds of products illustrated (in other words, potential customers), but perhaps the financial community, which might be interested in the diversity of consumer markets the company served.

Further, the headline used the words "consumers," "benefit," and "quality," which could be construed as an effort at even broader appeal to consumers themselves or government agencies charged with regulation; in other words, as a broad attempt to show the company in a favorable light (see figure 11.2).

It should be acknowledged that this kind of analysis of corporate

2. In terms of issue advertising, these are fairly "soft" (i.e., noncontroversial) messages.

North American Van Lines, Inc. bet 16 million dollars that we'll keep pulling through.

They just bought a fleet of 275 International® Trucks. They're showing their confidence in the leading truck-builder in America. And we think it's a sure bet.

Why?

Because we build the best truck for their money. A truck that costs less to run. We've proven it with fuel-efficiency tests. Fleet owners have come to expect thousands of dollars in fuel savings over the long haul. Because we can build trucks lighter, with better aerodynamics, and the most efficient componentry. And with operating costs increasing every day, it's more important than ever to keep a close watch on the bottom line. That's why more truck buyers are standing by International than any other truck manufacturer.

And we've got the figures to prove it.

Over three consecutive years, International has sold more medium and heavy trucks than anyone else in the business. More people believe in International trucks. And not just because of their performance. But because they know we'll also back them up with the largest dealer network and parts inventory in the country. To get them running sooner. And rolling longer. Now, and in the future.

That's why we're planning for the future right now. We've already invested over $200 million in new product development. We're continually working to make our trucks even better. By making them more cost-efficient. And more dependable. So today's truck buyer can be assured that with an International truck, he's getting nothing less than the state-of-the-art in truck-building technology.

So it's easy to see why more people are putting their faith in International. We've proven our performance in the past. And we plan to keep proving it in the future. You can bet on it.

We're not giving in. We're going on.

International Harvester

Figure 11.1 An International Harvester "issue" advertisement. (*Reprinted by permission of International Harvester.*)

advertising runs the risk of literary criticism, which often finds meanings far beyond what the author intended (or, at least, is willing to admit). The point is that many corporate messages are meant to appeal, directly or indirectly, to several audiences at once.

How consumers benefit from Shell quality.

Consumers can rely on plumbing pipe made of DURAFLEX™ poly-butylene resin. This dependable and quiet pipe resists corrosion, freeze-breakage, and water hammer.

Clear, strong sealants based on KRATON® rubber make home owners comfortable by keeping cold wind, hot air, and moisture where they belong—outside.

Safety-capped pill bottles made of Shell polypropylene protect children, while vials made of this moisture-resistant material protect the medicine.

Shell Chemical Company

One Shell Plaza, Houston, Texas 77002

Media No. X01289
MDR No. X02188

Figure 11.2   A Shell advertisement showing the company in a "favorable" light. (*Reprinted by permission of Shell Chemical Company.*)

Perhaps the most frequent target is the financial community, the security analysts, portfolio managers, and others who can influence the value placed on a company's stock.

One example among several was headlined: "What do you call a company with a 22-year record of increases in earnings per share?" The answer, of course, was the name of the company. In a brief but statistic-filled block of copy, the ad documented the company's strengths in assets, revenues, and dividends. It offered readers more information, including the annual report. And it appeared in *Forbes*, considered a prime medium for reaching the financial community (see figure 11.3).

In the same issue of *Forbes* was a two-page message from "a world leader in electronics." On the left-hand page, in large white letters on a black background, was the headline: "KEY THINGS TO REMEMBER IF YOU'RE TRYING TO SELL THE JAPANESE." Above it, in smaller type, were the lines: "Meeting Japan's Challenge. Eleventh in a Series." On the facing page, the company outlined its "strategy" for selling to the Japanese.

Since companies are not charitable organizations, it's safe to conclude that this manufacturer intended to do more than instruct its brethren.

In fact, in the context of beating the Japanese commercially, a crusade that has caught the enthusiasm of so many companies, here was a firm that was claiming victory, at least in one battle. The company was positioning itself as one that had found the way, that had actually beaten the Japanese at their own commercial game—electronics.

How did they do it? By having "a strong enough commitment to get through the tough initial stages." What's more: "We committed ourselves to exceeding the quality standards they set for us." The ad goes on to note that "as a result, orders for 50,000 units are expected this year alone." It declares that its "participative management attitude" (a mark of the Japanese themselves) was also a basic factor in its success. Finally, the ad suggests that the same techniques which enabled the company to "sell the Japanese" would benefit other potential customers.

This message (see figure 11.4) illustrates corporate advertising in its most developed form. The depth and extent of the appeal are nothing short of astounding. Let's take a closer look (keeping in mind the possibility of finding things the author never intended).

First, the overall look of the ad: the reversed white-on-black of the left-hand page fairly shouts at the reader. It is hard to overlook. The small headline above, "Eleventh in a Series," shows that the advertiser is seriously committed to this theme: ten other messages have been written about it. The right-hand page is chock-full of copy, but in somewhat larger than normal type that is easy to read. The copy is relieved by a photo of the product itself, on which are stamped Japanese characters. The caption under the photo reads: "Made in America."

The copy is straightforward and, by advertising standards, modest. It

What do you call a company with a 22-year record of increases in earnings per share?

SØNAT

When looking for a leader in energy, energy services and resources, it's often advisable to check beyond a company's recent performance.

For example, has the company shown strong, consistent growth over 20, 10 or even 5 years?

Sonat has. We're a company with assets and revenues of over $2.6 billion. Sonat's earnings increased 18% in 1981. During the most recent 5- and 10-year periods, earnings per share grew at 16% and 15% respectively. From 1959-1981, earnings per share grew at a compound annual rate of 14%.

We've paid a dividend every year for the past 45 years. Over the past 5 years, the dividend rate has grown at a compound annual rate of 19%, outpacing inflation by over 9%.

Today, Sonat Inc. operations across the U.S. and overseas include: Southern Natural Gas, Sonat Exploration, Sonat Offshore Drilling, Sonat Marine and Southern Forest Products.

To learn still more about us, write: Sonat Inc., Corporate Communications, P.O. Box 2563, Birmingham, Alabama 35202. Telephone: 205/325-3800 or 212/344-7955. Ask for our annual report.

Figure 11.3 A Sonat advertisement aimed at the financial community. (*Reprinted by permission of Sonat Inc.*)

takes the form of an essay, saying, in effect, here's how we beat the Japanese.

What is the net result? This is a company, the ad says, which is seriously dedicated to the greatest commercial crusade of our time: competing with the Japanese. Only these folks have actually *won*. At a time when practically every American company is talking about the *need* to compete with the Japanese, these folks have *done* it. And they're willing to share their "strategy" with the rest of us (in wartime, selfless sharing is de rigueur). The "Made in America" caption has bumper-sticker simplicity; it appeals to our hearts more than our heads.

The question "To whom does this ad appeal?" is almost irrelevant. It *ought* to appeal to every red-blooded American in business. These folks are winners. And the world of business loves winners.

And, like too few good corporate ads, this one has another important strength. Its message can be absorbed even without a careful reading of the text. One has only to glance at the left-hand page, the photo on the right, and the logo at the bottom to get the message.

The "message" of that message, however, may need some further explanation. Corporate advertising, at least effective corporate advertising, has a gestalt of its own. The whole is greater than the sum of its parts. An advertisement may never use the word "quality," for example, yet the reader, through the layout, the art, and the choice of words, may receive a clear impression of quality. And corporate advertising may convey other important "messages" to the reader: candor, for example, the endearing admission that "our company isn't always right"; responsibility, "our company is worth listening to; we know and are concerned about this subject," etc.

In other words, corporate advertising often tries to exhibit a *personality* as well as an explicit message. Frequently, the charge to the writer goes something like: "We want our audience to feel they are listening to an intelligent, interesting, sometimes amusing person."

RADIO AND TELEVISION

The gap between the amount of corporate and product advertising in the electronic media is even wider than in print. For one thing, television production is a formidable obstacle, arcane and expensive. Radio is less intimidating but still "different."

Most corporate advertisers are more comfortable with the printed word, which can be seen in close-to-final form in advance of publication at very little cost. Radio and television require the advertiser to trust not only the company's own communications people, but agencies, production houses, and other outsiders at considerable expense. Further, the conventional wisdom is that messages designed to make people reflect on them *belong* in

Meeting Japan's Challenge
Eleventh in a Series

KEY THINGS TO REMEMBER IF YOU'RE TRYING TO SELL THE JAPANESE.

One of the most difficult challenges facing American business has been to find a way to sell to the Japanese. We think we have a solution.

It's a simple strategy and involves only a few basic steps. But it has worked for us.

Instead of just talking about building quality products, years ago we committed our entire company to doing it. And in living up to that commitment we've proven that with the right approach American manufacturers can meet the Japanese on their own home grounds.

A big key to success is having a strong enough commitment to get through the tough initial stages. We learned this in 1978 when, with the encouragement of the U.S. government, Motorola decided to compete for some of the electronics business traditionally awarded only to Japanese companies by Japan's giant Nippon Telegraph and Telephone Public Corporation.

It was a bold undertaking that required substantial investments of time and money. In fact, just to enter the competition it was necessary to complete an exhaustive survey of competitive products and to translate and study all the pertinent Japanese specifications.

But if you want to sell to the Japanese you have to make the effort. So we did it.

Then we did something even tougher. We committed ourselves to exceeding the quality standards they set for us.

And succeeded. In early 1982, after competing with a number of Japanese electronics manufacturers, Motorola demonstrated in rigorous testing that our pagers exceeded NTT's reliability standards, while complying with their strictest price and delivery requirements.

As a result, Motorola was officially qualified by NTT as a supplier of pocket pagers. The first and only non-Japanese firm ever admitted to this heretofore closed group.

Made in America.

Orders for over 50,000 Motorola pocket pagers are expected this year alone.

In striving to exceed quality and reliability standards, though, it is equally important to maintain high standards of customer service.

We are convinced that this success in the Japanese market is due largely to the way we approach every one we serve.

It's a simple common sense way of doing business that says we pay as much attention to the wants and needs of our customers as we do to the quality of the products we make for them.

We think there's one other basic factor that's also responsible for Motorola's success in selling to the Japanese. Our participative management attitude.

One of our goals is to make every Motorola employee in every Motorola plant an effective part of the management team of our company. And because employees are motivated by this chance to participate and are rewarded for their efforts, we've found we're able to bring to bear on every product we make the enthusiasm, the dedication, and the attention to detail that result in the highest kind of quality.

The kind of quality that has allowed an electronics company like Motorola to sell in a country where they make some fine electronics themselves.

(M) MOTOROLA A World Leader in Electronics

Quality and productivity through employee participation in management.

Figure 11.4   A corporate advertisement in its most developed form.

print, because that's where the thoughtful audience is and because print is a more leisurely medium, there to be read and reread more or less permanently.

There is some validity to the first of those ideas. The so-called upscale audience does read more than the average person. And selected audiences, such as the financial community, can only be reached in a cost-effective way through publications that amount to "required reading" for them.

But depending on the message to be conveyed, radio and television can be even more effective than print, given their capacity for drama and immediacy. (Politicians have learned this, which accounts for the proliferation of political announcements on radio and television in the weeks before an election.)

But television and, to a lesser degree, radio are complex media, and the corporate advertiser is well advised to approach them cautiously. The world of $100,000-plus commercials, intricate media "buys," and endless residuals is not for everyone.[3]

THE PROCESS

The best way to approach a corporate campaign is to consider whether the attainment of a company's goals *requires* it. Advertising that does not sell products directly is always suspect (and in lean times is usually among the first programs to be cut). To lessen the tenuous nature of the program, it should be tied firmly to corporate business objectives.

This is sometimes difficult, because a judgment about whether the attainment of some goal will be aided by corporate advertising is usually subjective. For this reason, the judgment should be a collective one. Top management and senior operating people should share in the decision to begin a program. Without strong management support, a campaign begins with two strikes against it. Equally important, since a corporate advertising campaign should reflect the thinking of "the company" (i.e., the management), the company's public relations people need to learn what it is that management wants to say, how it wants the company to be seen.

The data gathered in this process should be reduced to a few simple goals for the campaign. They should be stated clearly and unequivocally, so that the creative people who develop the messages have a very accurate picture of what they are supposed to do.

A hypothetical first-draft statement of the campaign's goals might read:

3. There are any number of books available on radio and television advertising. One of the most interesting is *The Responsive Chord* by Tony Schwartz (Anchor Books, 1973). Don't be put off by the cover blurb: "How radio and TV manipulate you...who you vote for...what you buy...and how you think." Tony Schwartz is probably the most profound and certainly one of the most effective practitioners around.

1. We want potential investors, especially institutional investors, to
    see us as a particularly good buy, to understand all the things we
    have going for us:
    - A practically unblemished record of year-to-year earnings
      increases;
    - A patent position that's stronger than any of our competitors;
    - Increasing diversification into businesses that are not only
      attractive in themselves, but help smooth out the cycles of our
      basic business.
2. We want prospective employees, particularly engineers and MBAs,
    to think of our company as a good place to work, a place where
    individual performance is rewarded, where they won't be part of a
    herd.
    (N.B.: nine of our top fifteen executives have engineering degrees,
    seven of them are under 50, and four of them have MBA degrees.)
3. We need to be better known generally, so that prospective
    customers will understand they'd be dealing with a company that
    has an outstanding reputation for quality products.
4. Etc.

Naturally, the goals above should be sharpened and amplified as the
statement is developed. Most important, priorities should be established,
because a given campaign can convey only a limited number of messages.
And as the process of shaping the campaign's goals proceeds, another list of
key priorities will become evident: the audiences which are most important
to the company.

When the goals have been stated as clearly as is practical and the
priorities determined, it is time to consider who will produce the campaign.
For many companies the answer is automatic: our advertising agency, the one
which does our product advertising. That may be the wrong answer.

As corporate advertising has increased, some agencies have taken to
claiming a special expertise in the form. They see corporate advertising as a
new business area in which their product advertising experience gives them a
head start. But the fact is, some of the better corporate campaigns are
produced inhouse or by public relations firms.

There are a number of reasons why the decision to use a firm's regular
advertising agency should not be automatic. First, corporate advertising, as
we have seen, should grow from within the company. An outside firm will
have more difficulty catching the real spirit of what the company wants, with
all its subtleties and shifts, than people who are part of the company.

Second, corporate advertising deals in ideas that are frequently not
rooted in anything tangible. The copywriter who is used to extolling beer or
cosmetics or motor oil sometimes has difficulty getting at the heart of an idea.

Third, the corporate advertising message should be written plainly, not enmeshed in verbal tricks or too slick a presentation. It may be more like an editorial than a product ad. The very artfulness of some agency approaches can defeat straightforward communication.

This is not to say that advertising agencies cannot produce good corporate messages—some have for years—only that the advertiser should look carefully at the options before deciding.

An approach followed by a number of companies, including TRW, is to work jointly with an outside agency. Some of TRW's advertising is researched and written in-house; some, by the company's corporate advertising agency, which also places the messages.

Sometimes a careful blending of internal and outside skills yields the best program. The point is that the company usually has to stay deeply involved with the campaign, more closely than with product advertising.

PRODUCING THE CAMPAIGN

Once the statement of objectives has been finished and the creative people selected, a media plan should be developed. While the selection of media is a separate task, it is wise to have a fairly firm plan in place before the creative work is too far along. Obviously, the kind of campaign to be produced depends in part on media selection, which is governed by the priority audiences and the budget available.

The selection of media is an art in itself. Here the experience of an advertising agency can be very helpful. The typical corporate advertising budget will be much less than that of a product campaign. Choice of media is therefore more limited and more important.

It is at this point, too, that media and creative decisions begin to impinge on each other. Is it better to have six color spreads, or ten black-and-white ads? Is the production portion of the budget sufficient, or do we have to run one less ad to save some money? What about repetition? Shall each message be different, or shall we repeat fewer messages in the same publications?

There is, of course, no one answer, except to say, "it depends." Now is the time to examine the whole project, both creative and media issues. If the budget is rigidly fixed, start with that number and consider several different combinations of media, frequency, size, copy and design approach, etc. How many messages really need to be delivered? Can we deliver them in a page—or less—or do they require spreads? Will the art or photos take more than a reasonable share of the budget? Do we need lots of copy, like LTV, or do we want the stylishness of a United Technologies color spread, where a photo occupies nearly all the space?

Again, the only answer is, it depends on the messages—and the budget. There are a few guidelines the advertiser can cling to. First, a corporate campaign is generally best run more or less evenly over a year. You may choose to skip the summer[4] or holiday periods, but seasonality is usually irrelevant in corporate advertising.

Second, a corporate campaign is almost always a multiyear effort. It's just not feasible, ordinarily, to expect to reach the audience and effect a significant change in attitude in less than three to five years.

Third, it's usually best to start a corporate campaign with a "burst." That is, you should try for a heavy impact with the campaign's kickoff, perhaps running a single message in *all* the publications you will ultimately use.

A new campaign, a fresh message, will get the same kind of attention as new neighbors. There is a natural curiosity about the campaign at its beginning. You should capitalize on that crucial period by running a really stunning ad as heavily as the budget allows. (One technique is to start with two-page spreads and then drop to single-page ads for the bulk of the campaign, or, in newspapers, to start with a full page and drop back to smaller ads.)

Fourth, while a corporate campaign is not bound by the conventions of product advertising when it comes to repeating messages, it is usually a good idea to run a message more than once in the same publication. Research shows that, in addition to reinforcing your message with readers who have already seen it, a repeated ad can pick up a whole crop of *first-time* readers.

An advertising agency can provide statistical background to help make the decision on how often to repeat a message, but that judgment should be moderated by the advertiser's sense of when the particular message will become stale or tiresome.

RESEARCH

There are two kinds of research to consider: pretesting your ads (through copy tests, focus groups, etc.), and opinion research to see whether your messages are having the desired effect on your target audiences. Pretesting is desirable, but it is often difficult to pretest individual corporate ads or even the whole campaign (in the unlikely event all your ads are completed before the campaign begins).

However, it can be particularly useful in certain circumstances: when you plan a radically "different" campaign, for example, and simply have no idea of the reaction; when you are uncertain about what "side effects" an ad may have (negatively, when the subject is controversial, or positively, when you want to create a particular impression, such as stylishness or candor, beyond the main message); or when your competition is already in the field and you want to compare the impact of your ads with theirs.

---

4. Although that may be a good time to reach all those opinion-leaders in the Hamptons, Nantucket, etc.

When a campaign is intended to support business objectives, when a multiyear commitment has been made, when the objectives have been clearly defined, there is almost no excuse for not doing opinion research to see if you are accomplishing what you started out to do.

The best procedure is to do a benchmark study—before any advertising runs—to determine the state of the target audiences' knowledge and attitudes. Subsequent testing, perhaps once a year, will then show changes.

A number of advertising agencies offer this kind of research capability along with pretesting services. While there is no objection to an agency handling pretesting (in fact, if they are involved in creative aspects of the campaign, they *should* handle it), it may be preferable to deal directly with a survey organization for opinion research. The reason is that any research should be carefully tailored to the audiences and the company's business goals, and should reflect consideration of activities beyond advertising that could affect audience attitudes.

Further, it can be cheaper and more efficient in some cases to take part in a multicompany opinion survey which tracks attitudes from year to year, a service offered by at least one opinion research firm.

Don't overlook another source of "research"—the letters, phone calls, and casual remarks you'll get from your audience. Collect them as the campaign proceeds. Learn from them. Use them appropriately in reporting progress to management. (One veteran practitioner says: "The right comment to my chairman on the 5:39 to Stamford is worth ten opinion polls." Cynical, but too often true.)

A final word of caution on research: it doesn't work very well for issue advertising. I have seen numerous claims that issue advertising adds little or nothing to a company's reputation and may even alienate people. I have also seen research that shows exactly the opposite—that issue advertising, even when deliberately aggressive and controversial, actually increases so-called favorability ratings.

The best, and perhaps the only, effective measure of issue advertising is whether the legislation that was feared actually passed or whether the mass protest that was brewing actually developed. Like television advertising, issue advertising is no place for the beginner. If you are faced with a situation that seems to demand it, my advice would be: hire or retain someone who has a proven track record—and start small.

DO'S AND DON'TS

There are scores of "rules" that could apply to any corporate advertising campaign, each with its adherents and opponents. The trouble is, almost every successful campaign violates one or more of the rules—because every campaign is different in its objectives, its concepts, and the company culture behind it. So what follow seem to me to be the most important and most general tips. Even so, a few of them require qualification. In the "do" category:

1. Ground your campaign firmly in the company's most cherished objectives—to be sure it is designed to help the company reach them.
2. Get top management's input and unqualified support for the campaign as a multiyear commitment.
3. Put your campaign's objectives in priority order. A single ad can carry only one or two primary messages; a whole campaign probably no more than five or six.
4. Before you begin advertising, weave the campaign objectives and any ancillary messages into a clear, cohesive statement, as if you were describing a person your audience had never met. In other words, create a complete package that embodies all your messages. Refine it to the point where you can state, in a sentence or two, exactly what you want the audience to believe about the company (this is what advertising people call "positioning").
5. Do opinion research before and during your campaign, unless you are doing issue advertising.
6. Begin with a burst. Make your audience aware of your campaign right at the start.
7. Spread the word to key groups directly, using reprints and publicity: employees, customers, shareholders, the business press, and anyone else who should know about your new campaign. (The chairman of a top corporation once told me, only half in jest, after a potentially sticky but successful board meeting: "Mother always said, never surprise your directors." That applies to all *your* constituents.)
8. Find the best thinking, writing, and design for your campaign. Nickels and dimes saved on development and production may warm your heart, but they probably won't add up to enough to pay for an extra insertion.
9. After your writers, photographers, and designers have given you their "best," send it back with editing and criticism. Get their *very best*. Advertising that "reads well" in typescript, that merely "looks good" in mechanical form, is probably just adequate. All ads look good on boards; on the printed page, crowded in among everyone else's best and the editorial content, your ad won't seem the same. Unless you are genuinely excited by the campaign, it's probably not good enough.

And here are a few don'ts:

1. Don't underbudget. If you haven't got the money (and a long-term agreement for more), don't advertise. There's no magic formula, but I'd be skeptical about beginning a major campaign with less than $1 million a year.
2. Don't try to fabricate a corporate personality. There is nothing worse than a campaign which tries to present a dull company as exciting, or a hierarchical one as the fast-track MBAs nirvana.
3. Unless you know exactly what you're doing—or know someone who knows—don't get into television. And think twice before you start using radio. It sounds easy. It's not. The same for issue advertising.
4. Don't let casual comments sway you. Many lawyers, accountants, engineers, or whatever, are magically transformed into "experts" in the presence of corporate advertising. Practically all of them will favor you with their opinions, unasked, or give you their "great idea" for a "perfect ad." Be polite but firm. To these people, communicating is simple. (It's just putting one word after another, right?) Remind them of Sheridan's dictum: "Easy writing is curst hard reading."
    On the other hand, be alert to the possibility that a grain or two of wheat may be buried in the chaff.
    A related point: don't let even genuine experts fill your copy with technical niceties. Your message is not a legal brief or a scientific paper. Your job is to communicate persuasively.
5. Don't be a slave to anyone's dogma in advertising. For example, David Ogilvy and his followers seem to love long copy. If you write as well as David Ogilvy, you may be able to gain the reader's support; if not, your ad will be boring and go unread. On the other hand, one of the most striking communications I have ever seen contained only four words. It was an antiwar poster, vintage 1970. It consisted of a color photograph of perhaps a dozen dead Vietnamese women and children strewn along a dirt road. Superimposed across the top of the photo were the words: "Q. And babies?" and at the bottom: "A. And babies." Regardless of one's feelings about the war, that message had to make the reader think, and perhaps begin to shift his or her attitude. Short, of course, isn't always good. Probably most corporate advertising copy is on the long side, and properly so. But don't let that dictate a choice. It is almost always the exception, rather than the rule, which captures attention.

PUBLICITY

Media Usage

Fred Clay

Director of Public Relations
Norton Simon, Inc.

Perhaps the most visible and vital of the public relations functions is media relations. Visible because through its media relations capability, the corporation discloses information to the target groups of all the public relations disciplines—shareholders, consumers, investors, government officials, communities in which the organization operates, suppliers, and the general public. Vital because through this post, the organization interfaces with one of the most powerful manipulators of public opinion in our society.

The media relations manager is the corporate spokesperson next, of course, to the chief executive officer. They broker a much-sought-after commodity which serves as the nucleus of a multibillion dollar industry—news. The media is our consumer, our customer, if you will, and our product or service is news. Like the consumer goods company, our objectives is to identify information which will be of interest to the press and furthers the goals of the corporation; to package it; and to sell or transmit it for world consumption.

Ours is a dual obligation—making as complete a disclosure as management judges appropriate and the press deems necessary. The two are not always in harmony. Take, for example, the purchase by XYZ company of a small North Carolina apparel manufacturer with annual sales in excess of $70 million. The press release noted that the terms of the acquisition were undisclosed. To management, this was full and complete disclosure. The

Fred Clay is currently director of public relations for Norton Simon, Inc. Prior to joining Norton Simon in 1977, he served as manager of media relations at International Paper Company, financial press relations specialist at American Telephone & Telegraph Company, and assistant editor at Merrill Lynch Financial Newswire. He holds a B.S. degree in economics from Fordham University and an M.S. degree in journalism from Columbia University's Graduate School of Journalism.

media felt otherwise. Our job is to satisfy the needs of the press and management at the expense of neither. If you are not at liberty to disclose the terms, tell the press so as tactfully as possible. If you have leveled with them in the past, you'll have their trust and understanding. That's not going to get them the answer they would like to have to complete their story, but it will go a long way in your future encounters.

Trust on the part of the media and management is that all-essential ingredient which will further your dealings with both constituents. With it, the doors to the newsroom and the executive suite are open to us. Without it, we are virtually ineffective.

I can't stress enough the importance of credibility and trust in establishing and maintaining a good working relationship with the press. Periodic contacts with the press can cement relationships, and reserve for you and your organization a spot in the recesses of the reporter's mind. Take the case of a short roundup feature on the forest products industry. The reporter can't possibly feature each company in the field. He is going to solicit comments from a representative sampling of companies comprising that industry. You may have a great story to relate, but if you have been less than cooperative in your dealings with the reporter, if your relationship with the reporter has been less than amicable, if your credibility rating on a scale of one to ten is five, it stands to reason that the reporter will probably exclude your company from the roundup.

ON POSTURING

With the advent of advocacy journalism, investigative and interpretative reporting, we've witnessed the power of the press. Look at Watergate. That power has, in some circles, given rise to fear and paranoia. I won't say that such fear doesn't exist in the business community because I know it does. How we perceive the media's use of this power and our past experiences with the media generally shape our perception of and, consequently, our attitude toward the press. Has the media been fair in its coverage of your organization's activities? is what it all comes down to. Hence, our posture with the media is reflected in our response to this question, a response which in the end determines how willingly we accept the media's right to exist and our attitude toward the freedoms with which they have been bestowed. Our posture, too, hinges on the corporation's perception of itself. Like people, corporations are unique. They have different personalities and modes of behavior. Some are secure, open, and outgoing. Others are insecure, paranoid, and reactive; while there are yet others who are islands unto themselves—the "don't bother me, I won't cope" types. Personalities aside, they have varying degrees of news appeal. Take an AT&T versus General Telephone & Electronics, for example.

The public corporation is the domain of the public. Yet some organizations choose not to court the press, but operate as though they were private, particularly when the going gets rough. They recoil at any advances made on them by the press, likening themselves to a family or privately held company which shrouds itself in secrecy. Unlike the family, the corporation cannot, without some form of backlash, slam the door in a reporter's face just because the company has fallen on difficult times, though I'm sure you know quite a few corporations that would like to or wish they could have done so at one point or another.

Those accepting media scrutiny as a fact of life either take a more active and aggressive posture in their dealings with the press, or as Franklin D. Roosevelt once advised in reference to fear, "convert retreat into advance," or they simply tolerate the media, choosing a reactive course of action.

There are three major corporation "personality types" I'd like to bring to your attention. One is the idealist, which actively seeks all the publicity it can get, usually with the aid of a publicist or newsmaker. This type is interested primarily in statistics—number of press clippings and the like. There is the reclusive type, or isolationist, which is content to be left alone and enlists the aid of someone with a goalie or watchdog media relations mentality to keep the media at bay. Then there is the realist, which accepts the ground rules and opts to "play to win, rather than play not to lose," to use a much-used phrase by my board chairman, David Mahoney of Norton Simon, Inc. To their credit, the realists employ the services and talents of media relations professionals.

The newsmaker, honoring the mandate set forth by the organization he or she is representing, is a publicity seeker, and his public relations program is programmed accordingly. It will consist of heavy news placement activity, with heightened visibility for the corporate chief, gaining for him speaking engagements before prestigious business forums, security analysts, congressmen, and senators on the vital issue or issues of the day, interviews for the company head with major business publications, and the same for division heads with the trade press. The program will include editorial briefings with selected company officers and key newspaper, magazine, and broadcast people, and placement of op-ed articles on a pressing issue of the times authored by the company president. In other words, it will contain the standard ingredients of the boiler-plate public relations program.

There are tremendous benefits to such a campaign or blitz. The company gets the word out to its target audiences and shapes public opinion in the process. If effective, such a campaign could conceivably impact on product market share, earnings, improved relations in the company's host community, and the public's general recognition and awareness level of the company.

The downside risk is that such a posture is all but impossible to reverse overnight without some fallout, particularly when the tides of fortune take a turn for the worse. So, timing and a well-thought-out strategy should not be overlooked.

Take, for example, Company A, which embraced such a program. For nearly a decade it was posting record earnings results and, consequently, was the apple of the financial community's eye. It was a dream machine. Dividends skyrocketed during the period along with the market price of the company's common shares. After ten of the most prosperous years in its history, the economy pitched downward and with it went the healthy earnings picture at Company A, which was more susceptible to the side effects produced by recessionary times than the vast majority of other companies in its league.

This Cinderella story was not glossed over by the press. A barrage of interviews were requested by the same reporters whom the company befriended during the glory days. Previously open and aggressive, Company A suddenly silenced its media relations staff, which either failed to return the reporters' calls or summarily rejected all requests received. This was wrong. The company should have maintained its policy of openness and honesty toward the press. The company should have turned the negative into a positive. If the bottom has fallen out, tell about the constructive, corrective measures you're taking to get the organization back on sound footing. That, in and of itself, is newsworthy. But Company A chose to retreat and hide behind the media relations man's shield of armor, which in time was worn so thin it couldn't protect even him. The stories appeared, nevertheless. Damaging ones. In an effort to placate unhappy shareholders, corrective measures were taken. Several division heads resigned. Round two with the press was rung in with these sudden dismissals, and the press was in there jabbing. Predictably, the media relations manager/publicist was no longer viewed in his earlier light by either the corporate hierarchy or the media. He was persona non grata as Company A slipped into the reclusive mode, and all the press clippings or souvenirs he had acquired during his honeymoon with the press couldn't change that.

Company B, a long-time believer in reclusivity, reaped neither the rewards of the prerecessionary media relations campaign conducted by Company A, nor did it find it necessary to alter its tactics when the financial wealth of its company declined.

I'd like to believe that the great majority of our institutions fall into the category of the realist, employing the services of the true media relations professional, for professionals are in the arena playing to win no matter if they're leading in the first quarter by 20 points or down 10 in the last minute of the game. The media relations practitioner, unlike most team players, must be a generalist in his specialty. He has to be a real communicator who is a team player, but a complete player. By that I mean you're not effective if you're ranked the team's top scorer but have racked up those impressive statistics by being "shot happy," shooting when you shouldn't and, as a result, causing costly turnovers one after the other. You're not of optimum value to your organization if you are a guard or goalie who doesn't know how to react with the ball or puck after successfully defending an offensive play by the opposition. You're of little service to your company if you're content to just sit on the bench and allow yourself to be called into action only in case of an emergency or as a last resort.

Skill, timing, strategy, and fair and reasonable expectations of your efforts and abilities by management are essential to a good media relations effort just as they are in team sports. By possessing the necessary skills, by timing your activities, by having a well-thought-out strategy, you can counsel and guide your organization from the opponent's goal to your own territory. The good media relations practitioner is neither "shot happy" nor solely a "defensive player." He or she is a complete player, a team player. He has a strategy and works in unison with his teammates. He knows the opposition's moves, knows what to expect and when to expect it, and has a well-thought-out game plan to counteract the opposition's strategy. He has the backing of his coach and the team owners, whose expectations of him are fair ones. He senses all that's happening around him and, at the right moment, takes his shot.

THE MEDIA

Underneath that receptive spirit of cooperation and responsiveness to the media, corporations, for the most part, would prefer a "don't call us, we'll call you" arrangement with the media. This is virtually true of all three personality types because, let's face it, how often if at all has an unsolicited inquiry enhanced your company's bottom line results? As far as top management is concerned, these are but unnecessary intrusions, distractions that only help the media sell its product.

If there is news, a company would much prefer to announce it according to its own timetable rather than be forced to divulge this information in response to an inquiry from a reporter who has been tipped off by some "unidentified source."

There is always uncertainty as to the outcome of any story—hence, the reluctant, cautious attitude of most companies in their dealings with the press. Many a day has ended with the media relations manager heaving a sigh of relief because nary a press inquiry was received. So, too, would there be relief if press inquiries were received and handled to the satisfaction of all concerned.

To work successfully with the media, one must first recognize not only their right to exist, but the partnership that exists between the media relations manager and the press in the news-making process. Stereotyping the media is a faux pas, for the media comes in all sizes and shapes. As Robert

L. Woodrum, vice president of corporate communications at Norton Simon, Inc. has duly noted, even some forms of pornography have been classified by the Supreme Court as belonging to the media. Incorporate the media into the international arena and the list multiplies tenfold.

Each branch of the media has different criteria, audiences, approaches to covering the news, and reporters who have their own personal differences in attitude, knowledge, interests, and ambitions with varied means of achieving them.

The reporter's responsibility lies not in merely rewriting your press release and filing it for publication, but also in going after the story your management is not telling as well. Where the press is concerned, there are two sides to most stories, and your disclosure is not a story until both sides have been addressed. There are very few secrets in the world of business, perhaps due to its interrelatedness. The undisclosed, unfavorable, or negative aspects of a development have a way of surfacing. For each company or individual who chooses not to divulge information, there are a half-dozen who want to talk: for example, your counterpart at the competition who's trying to make brownie points with the press. The reporter can just as easily do the story without you.

By refusing to discuss a sensitive issue, the company is, in a sense, telling the reporter that it may be hiding something; and the sheer energy and effort expended to shield the facts may force the reporter to conclude that the story you are not revealing is more significant than the story you are reporting. Return the call; speak to the reporter. In responding, be honest. Be credible. The most mortal of all sins from a reporter's vantage point is to be told a lie. It destroys not only the media relations manager's credibility but the company's as well and, equally important, can negatively affect the article's outcome. Tell the reporter you can't comment when you can't. It won't guarantee a story of which you are likely to order 5,000 reprints, but you will have been honest. If the story is unfair or inaccurate, you have recourse. Sit down with the editor and discuss your differences or, if you have no qualms about resurrecting the story in the minds of the reader, write a letter to the editor.

IDENTIFYING THE NEWS

The word "news," some say, is derived from the first letters of the four main directional points on the compass: north, east, west, and south. But news simply is not anything and everything that happens everywhere. The role of the media relations specialist is to determine what is and isn't news.

Occasionally, the media relations man or woman is called upon by management to issue information or promote an event that is void of news value. Shortly after I joined one company I've had the good fortune to be employed by, I had to respond to my CEO as to why his annual stockholder meeting remarks weren't picked up in the press. I incurred his wrath when I told him that there was not one bit of news in the text. The following year, I got myself involved in the preparation of those remarks and convinced the CEO to work into his upcoming remarks before shareholders details of planned plant expansions. Most of the business pages carried the story and even picked up some of the non-news in the remarks to round out their stories.

Peddling news that's no news serves neither the interest of the organization nor that of the journalist, and certainly not yours. Quite the contrary, it discredits the media relations representative and the corporation in the eyes of the journalist. What you should keep in mind is that competition for the relatively small amount of space allotted by the print media and for time on the air waves for news is keen. There is a preponderance of news that never even reaches the public. If you are forced to promote non-news, develop a salable angle and go to it. I don't want to bore you with annual meeting stories, but this one makes my point. The Norton Simon, Inc., annual meeting a few years back had all the elements of a non-news event. But, happening as it did the day after election day, it turned out to be a media relations manager's dream. The newly elected governor of the state of New York, who was making brief appearances throughout the city, made an unscheduled, unexpected appearance at our meeting. When he walked in and joined my CEO David Mahoney at the podium, I immediately saw headlines. Thanks to the speedy photo processing by the photographer covering the meeting and the quick turnaround by the transcription service recording the meeting and a lot of legwork, photographs, excerpts of the governor-elect's remarks, complete text of the chairman's remarks, and a short piece listing the celebrities in attendance— the company's founder, two widely acclaimed movie stars, a world-renowned fashion designer, and one of the foremost authorities on wines in the world—were in the hands of the press in a matter of hours. Those headlines which had raced across my mind the day before were no longer fantasy but reality. One writer noted later in a story entitled, "How to Make News When There Isn't Any," that a forecast of earnings for the following year, which led off the financial part of the story, was not reported until halfway down the column.

PACKAGING THE NEWS

There are numerous procedures for releasing information to the public. News is disseminated routinely through responses to press inquiries, press releases, media interviews with the chairman of the board or other top spokespersons, as well as through press conferences and briefings.

The nature of the news, its timeliness, and the audience are prime considerations in determining the most appropriate method. Corporate earnings are generally issued in a press release, whereas announcements relating to a major plant closing involving hundreds of workers and the economic health of the community might more effectively be handled through a press conference. A broad-based story on a corporation is usually the result of a personal interview with the chairman of the board and other officers of the company, as well as with external, "unidentified," "knowledge-able" sources. Disseminating information in the aftermath of a plane crash or natural disaster, for example, is generally best handled by a press briefing.

SELLING THE NEWS

Before releasing a story, determine the target audience. There are countless numbers of publications, and each has a clearly defined audience. Virtually every news item has its own media receptacle. Find out what publications would most likely be receptive to the news you are about to disclose. The routine press inquiry is a reporter's cry for help. The manner in which the media relations director responds will be reflected in how well you are received by that same reporter when management has a story to report. General corporate information, confirmation or denial of rumors, and state-ments relating to a particular development are typical.

The press release is one of the most commonly used public relations tools. Before issuing a release, in addition to addressing the developments at hand, address the questions the announcement is likely to generate. If your quarterly earnings are up only because of a substantial drop in the number of shares outstanding, make note of the fact in your press release. Not only will it make the reporter's job easier, but it will reduce the number of press inquiries. Undoubtedly, it won't be possible to incorporate every bit of information each and every reporter is likely to ask as each reporter possesses a different degree of knowledge about the company and the subject area in question. In any event, be prepared to respond immediately. Seek out the answers to anticipated questions before releasing the document.

The larger and more visible corporations are frequent targets for media coverage. They have news appeal. If a company has a good story to tell, in most cases it is advantageous to grant a media interview. Most corporate decisions are made with the shareholders' interests in mind. Before submit-ting the CEO to an interview session, ask yourself, "Will the resulting article serve the interests of the shareholder, the CEO, and the company or is it purely an exercise for the benefit of the media?" If there is no upside benefit or downside risk, a company might be best advised to agree to the interview for no other purpose than to maintain good relations with the news organization in question. Careful preparation is required. The chairman should be just as prepared as the reporter with whom he will be sparring. Obtain the reporter's biography. The chairman should be as familiar with the reporter's background as he or she will be with his. Acquaint your company with major articles he or she has written recently. Surely the reporter will be abreast of the management decisions the chairman has made in recent months. Alert the chairman to the thrust the reporter is likely to take and map your strategy as to how to best present the story *you* wish to report. Then, prepare a backgrounder for the chairman and one on the company for the reporter. The fruits of your labor may in the end be bittersweet at best, but laudatory or devastating results are conceivable as well.

The broadcast media generally is limited both in time and information concerning most corporate activities, for their viewers and listeners, who are great in number, run the gamut of all segments of the population. They are more interested in the big picture—the economy versus International Paper Company's year-end earnings results. Very few corporate developments find their way onto the six o'clock or national evening news programs. Those programs, like their audiences, are preoccupied with world news, national news, sports, weather, and an occasional feature that has widespread appeal. If the news fails to appeal to the public in general, don't waste your time. If it does, bear in mind that broadcast time is a fraction of the time needed to relate fully the facts that the *Wall Street Journal* or *Los Angeles Times* would consider sufficient coverage of the news. Prioritize the information.

News conferences are rare in most organizations and fairly common in others. Government agencies, for example, use press conferences as often as most companies issue press releases. They're probably the exception. A news conference should be called only when there is hard news—news that impacts on the world around us. Invariably, though, news conferences will be called to relate information that would be more appropriately disclosed in a press release and, in some cases, not at all. In these instances, management's time as well as the reporter's time is being wasted. It is a costly proposition to send a camera crew, reporters, and photographers to a news conference when they could be covering bona fide news events. The media are also being alienated in the process. You'll find out just how much they are being alienated the next time one is called. Fortunate will the media relations manager be if even your management agrees to hold another one. If you're unsure whether you have a real story, call a few reporter friends and ask their view.

We have discussed the significance of the major news publications and the broadcast media in the news reporting process. Too often, media specialists have a tendency to overlook another important media outlet—the trade press, or special interest publications. *Time*, the *Wall Street Journal*, the CBS Evening News, and the five-minute radio news broadcasts can accommodate only so much news. As ours has become a much more educated society, the public thirst for information has become almost insatiable. As competition for space and air time has become keener, the trade press and special interest publications have become even more valuable in filling the void. Research these publications, prepare a mailing list, and establish contact with the editors. You will increasingly find that with the exception of hard news, their news pages will comprise most of the clips your firm will receive on any given announcement.

In selling anything, be it a product, a service, or news, the success of any sales executive is tied directly to the existence of a market for the product, knowledge of the market and the product, and his or her marketing skills. Selling news is no different. News is news if there is a ready market for it. The media relations practitioner's success in selling it depends on how well he understands that market and knows his product.

13

WHITE HOUSE NEWS CONFERENCE

Ronald Nessen

Executive Vice President and Managing Director
Marston and Rothenberg Public Affairs, Inc.

The president of the United States has available to him a unique tool for implementing his public relations objectives—the White House news conference. There is nothing else like it available to any other public figure or institution. Perhaps the nearest comparable public relations event is the corporate chairman's appearance before the annual stockholders' meeting. But that is, indeed, a pale and distant similarity.

In some ways, the presidential news conference ought to make the White House director of communications and the press secretary the objects of envy by their colleagues in the public relations profession. After all, by merely announcing the time and place of a presidential news conference, the White House communications staff is assured of a huge turnout of reporters and usually live television coverage. No need to unleash the media relations specialists to persuade the press to attend!

By delivering an opening statement on an issue for which he is seeking support and understanding, the president often can channel the reporters' interest for the rest of the news conference. And, because of the traditional respect for his office and the ground rules, which allow each reporter only one question and sometimes a follow-up, the president usually is in control of the sessions. (Since Vietnam and Watergate, and the rise of a younger, more

---

Ron Nessen is executive vice president and managing director of Marston and Rothenberg Public Affairs, Inc., in Washington, D.C., and senior associate of the parent company, Robert Marston and Associates in New York.

He was White House press secretary to President Gerald R. Ford from 1974 to 1977. He was a writer-editor in the Washington bureau of United Press International from 1956 to 1962 and a news correspondent for NBC from 1962 to 1974.

He is the author of an informal history of the Ford administration, *It Sure Looks Different from the Inside*, and two novels, *The First Lady* and *The Hour*.

skeptical generation of reporters, however, presidents are no longer immune from rough treatment. Certainly no president will ever again be able to get away, as Herbert Hoover once did, with telling reporters that he was going to skip most of their questions because he was late for a golf game.)

Having commandeered heavy press and broadcast coverage by simply appearing, the president then is in a position to reap a public relations jackpot by delivering his messages directly to all his many publics: the voters, Congress, his own political party, the opposition, rivals for his job, special interest groups of every kind, allies and adversaries overseas, members of his administration, the bureaucracy, etc. He can be sure they're tuned in.

But, while the presidential news conference offers public relations advantages which cannot be matched by any other person or organization, there are also incomparable dangers. A slip of the tongue, an error of fact, an unfortunate choice of words, a misconceived strategy, a flare of temper, even a momentary look of fatigue or noncomprehension—any of these lapses by a president at a news conference can set off a political firestorm, defeat a piece of legislation, endanger an election, or precipitate an international crisis.

The way a president maximizes his chances for a public relations triumph and minimizes his chances for a public relations disaster at a news conference is to follow the bedrock rule for any encounter with the media—decide ahead of time how *you* would like the story to come out and then take infinite pains with preparations to try to make it come out that way.

HISTORY

Teddy Roosevelt was the first president to submit to periodic questioning by reporters at the White House. However, his successor, William Howard Taft, abandoned the practice. Woodrow Wilson, though, revived it and established a regular schedule for meeting reporters. Warren Harding, Calvin Coolidge, and Herbert Hoover continued regular question-and-answer sessions with the White House press corps. But their meetings with reporters bore only a faint resemblance to the modern presidential news conference. For one thing, all questions had to be submitted in advance in writing. The number of reporters who attended the sessions in the president's office was tiny compared to the hundreds who now throng to televised news conferences in the East Room or the Executive Office Building. And a reading of the transcripts of those long-ago news conferences reveals that presidents were allowed by the reporters to decline to respond to those questions they did not wish to answer.

Franklin D. Roosevelt was the first "media president," using the print press and the infant radio as public relations vehicles to rally a depression-crushed nation and later a war-mobilized nation, to generate support for his programs, and to advance his own and his party's election prospects. Roosevelt was an enormously successful public relations practioner for himself and his policies, partly because of his charming personality, his wit and knowledge, and his sure sense of how to use the press. By then the White House press corps which crowded around his desk had grown to a hundred, and the web of radio reached to every corner of America, greatly magnifying his messages.

After Roosevelt, the evolution of the presidential news conference was guided by three factors: (1) the growth in the number of reporters covering the White House; (2) technological advances in communications; and (3) increased sophistication by the president and his staff in using the news conference as a public relations tool to promote policies and political objectives.

Harry Truman was forced to move his news conferences out of the Oval Office into an auditorium because so many reporters showed up, destroying some of the intimacy and informality, and thereby, perhaps, diminishing some of the president's persuasive powers with the White House press corps regulars.

Dwight Eisenhower permitted his news conferences to be filmed for later broadcast on television. For the first time, a president could be seen nationwide by his many publics advocating his views, a giant step toward making the presidential news conference the supreme public relations vehicle it is today. At the same time, though, television made presidents more guarded, lest they be caught making a damaging remark. The practice of speaking off the record or for background obviously was no longer possible with television present, consequently reducing the flow of useful information.

John F. Kennedy—youthful, handsome, bubbling with humor and intelligence—was a natural on television. He and his communications advisers felt so comfortable with the medium that Kennedy permitted live television broadcasts of his news conferences. This raised the risk of a damaging slip and ruled out the possibility of a president saying "no comment" or begging for time to obtain additional information. Despite these risks, Kennedy used television with great effectiveness as a tool of persuasion and communication, most memorably during the Cuban missile crisis with the Soviet Union.

All the subsequent presidents—Lyndon Johnson, Richard Nixon, Gerald Ford, Jimmy Carter, and Ronald Reagan—maintained the ritual of the televised news conference. Each attempted to use television as a public relations tool to rally support from the voters and other publics, and each was less than successful: Johnson could not sell the Vietnam War; Nixon could not cover up Watergate; Ford could not overcome public displeasure with his pardon of Nixon, nor could he escape his image as an amiable bumbler; Carter could not reverse a perception of ineffectualness, particularly in the

Iranian hostage crisis; and Reagan had difficulty living down his reputation as president of the rich, uncaring about the troubles of the poor.

The difficulties experienced by recent presidents in communicating convincingly through their news conferences can be blamed, to some extent, on a growing skepticism—even hostility—by the White House press corps toward the presidency. Much of the questioning is adversarial, bordering on the prosecutorial, with some of the "questions" amounting to little speeches in opposition to the president's policies. Additionally, much of the press coverage of the White House in recent years has tended to attribute many presidential statements and actions to raw politics, to a blatant effort to appease voters and voting blocs. This approach portrays presidents as lacking conviction or an overall philosophy guiding their decisions, and has undermined their credibility.

Nevertheless, a good deal of the responsibility for the difficulties recent presidents have had in using their news conferences as effective vehicles of persuasion and image building must rest with the presidents themselves and their staffs.

In some cases, they have not planned and implemented a media strategy to explain complex or controversial decisions with the objective of generating support and undercutting criticism. (Ford and the pardon is an example.) In other cases, they have fuzzed their image by failing to adopt and articulate a coherent, consistent policy. (Reagan first fighting for tax cuts, then advocating a tax increase, is an example.)

But the most important reason some presidents have not been able to use the incomparable vehicle of the White House news conference to sell their programs and themselves is that they have ignored a first rule of public relations—no amount of careful planning, no communications stategy, however skillfully carried out, can succeed unless the substance of what is being communicated represents beneficial public policy. (That's why Vietnam, Watergate, and the Iranian hostage crisis were public relations disasters for the presidents involved.)

ORGANIZATION

Prior to the Nixon presidency there was no formalized public relations organization within the White House worthy of the name.

Until then, each president's press secretary (Franklin Roosevelt's Steve Early was the first) and a small press office staff looked after the day-to-day needs of the reporters covering the White House.

The White House public relations operation would have been shamed by a medium-size agency or a moderately enlightened corporation. That changed in the Nixon administration when the well-respected Herbert Klein established the White House Office of Communications.

At last, all the public relations functions that any large organization needs came to the most powerful organization in the nation: a daily news summary; a speakers bureau; research facilities; coordination of public affairs activities in departments and agencies; media plans and background materials for announcing and explaining presidential proposals; contact with publications that do not normally cover Washington; contact with journalistic organizations; an office for booking administration officials on TV interview programs and for arranging editorial board meetings and background briefings; an elaborate mechanism for handling the media during presidential travel; a system for devising communications strategy, both reactive and proactive, including crisis management; etc.

Each subsequent president has modified the communications office to suit his own notion of public relations and in accordance with the needs of the times.

President Ford initially reduced the communications office nearly out of existence because it had been tainted, and its original purpose distorted, during Watergate. Later, however, Ford restored the office.

Jody Powell tried to serve as both the day-to-day press secretary and as the long-range strategist director of communications in President Carter's White House. But the demands on his time and energies were too great, and he gave up the communications post. However, because of his long and close relationship with the president, Powell continued to advise Carter on public relations as well as other matters.

The importance of the White House director of communications was further strengthened when President Reagan assigned that position to the experienced and savvy strategist David Gergen. The unfortunate incapacitation of well-liked press secretary James Brady and his replacement by yeoman Larry Speakes, who was given only limited information to pass on to reporters, further downgraded the position of press secretary in the public relations hierarchy of the Reagan White House.

As was stated earlier, no public relations activity in the White House is more important than a presidential news conference, and a great deal of time and effort is spent preparing the president for it.

PREPARATION

Before any encounter with the media, the three most vital instructions for a public relations professional are: "prepare"...."prepare"...and "prepare." Given the possibilities for either slipup or success, this rule is particularly important before a presidential news conference.

Each president has his own favorite method of preparation with which he is most comfortable. For instance, Kennedy and Nixon staged rehearsals in which aides took turns firing questions at them and judging their answers.

By contrast, Ford preferred to prepare alone by reading lists of anticipated questions and plowing through loose-leaf volumes of background information to frame his answers.

All the methods of preparation for a presidential news conference have one thing in common: the president and his aides try to guess ahead of time what questions the reporters will ask. Usually they are successful, and a president is almost never taken totally by surprise. In fact, some White House staff members have gloated smugly that they have asked tougher questions during the rehearsals than the reporters did during the actual news conference.

Once having compiled a list of anticipated questions, a president and his advisers set about devising the answers. The full resources of the government are at their command. The call often goes out to the Pentagon or the Treasury or some other department or agency to provide background material from which the president can draw.

Far more difficult than memorizing factual responses is fashioning the tone, the strategy, the approach for answers to sensitive questions. This is where public relations planning is most important. Shall the president, in an answer, strike a conciliatory or a threatening note toward Congress or foreign nations? Shall he signal adoption or abandonment of a policy? Shall he embrace or exile a controversial figure? The proper choices properly enunciated, can create a public relations success.

Sometimes an impending news conference will force a president to make a decision before he really wants to. Knowing that he will be asked about an unresolved situation may cause him to resolve it so he can answer the question without appearing to duck or procrastinate.

There is a myth that presidents seek easy questions at their news conferences and try to avoid the tough ones. Experience suggests otherwise. Most presidents respond forcefully and articulately to tough questions, delivering their previously rehearsed copy points, while softball questions invite rambling, unfocused—and unhelpful—answers.

Another myth depicts presidents as trying to ignore hectoring or accusatory questioners at their news conferences. In fact, presidents traditionally have called on abusive reporters with their own ax to grind, knowing they will usually change the subject and divert attention from a bothersome line of questioning.

CONCLUSION

Of course, most reporters understand that the White House press conference is a magnificent public relations tool for a president, and they gripe about that, about being "used," about the president "controlling" the sessions.

Well, certainly he does. But short of kidnapping and torture, there is no way a reporter can force a president (or anyone else) to say anything he doesn't want to say.

A president has the right to speak directly to the people, to explain himself and his programs in his own words. And the people have the need to watch and listen to the president speaking directly to them, making his case. This is the way the people, in a democracy, decide whether to follow the president's leadership or reject it.

So, while the White House news conference can be beneficial to a president's public relations efforts, it also is beneficial—indeed, vital—to the public.

LOBBYING

Robert Keith Gray

Chairman
Gray and Company

Lobbying in the 1980s is a much different profession than it was even a decade ago. Washington has changed, the number of interest groups has multiplied, the issues that confront a legislator have become more complex, and Congress itself has fractionalized into scores of power bases. Yet most of the lobbyist's time is spent negotiating one-on-one with government officials, and, therefore, the lobbyist must employ certain courtesies that are as old as the handshake.

Lobbying owes much of its vitality to the intricate and very often confusing process by which a bill becomes law under the U.S. system of government. Lobbyists are involved in every phase of this process. Their mission is to have an impact on legislation as it proceeds on its intricate course, either by encouraging or discouraging passage of the bill and amendments.

THE INFORMATION GAP

As the federal government has grown as a factor in every American's life, legislation has proliferated. Senators and representatives, and their staffs, spend most of their time studying legislation, a mountainous task in itself. In

Robert Keith Gray is the founder and chairman of Gray and Company, the first major national public affairs/public relations firm based in Washington, D.C. He was cochairman of the 1981 Presidential Inaugural Committee and director for communications during the 1980 Reagan-Bush campaign. He also served in the Eisenhower administration as secretary of the cabinet and appointments secretary.

He is former vice chairman of Hill & Knowlton's Washington operations, holds the rank of commander in the Naval Reserve, and has been decorated a Knight Commander by the Italian government.

He holds an M.B.A. degree from Harvard University, an honorary Doctor of Business degree from Marymount College, and an honorary Doctor of Letters degree from Hastings College. Profiles of his career have appeared in *Forbes Magazine*, the *New York Times*, and the *Wall Street Journal*, and he has appeared on NBC's "Today Show."

one recent congressional session, 10,442 measures pertaining to virtually every issue under the sun were introduced. The members' duty is to keep abreast of these issues as best they can. It is fair to say that the task at many times proves elusive.

One of the lobbyist's functions is to bridge the member's information gap, offering refined material about how a given issue will affect a certain group of people. For example, a representative may be reviewing a bill for a new national park. The member, particularly if he or she is from the concerned state, will want to know the ramifications of this bill: Will local jobs be sacrificed or created? What is organized labor's stand on the issue? Will the consumer be protected? These are details the lobbyist can supply.

The bill will stand a much greater chance of eventually becoming law if these elected officials are made aware of how various groups will fare under the legislation.

ENGAGING A LOBBYING FIRM

There are a number of reasons private institutions either base their own staff of lobbyists in Washington or hire Washington-based lobbying firms. Absolutely nothing will be accomplished in a group's favor until the governing body in Washington becomes familiar with its cause. Personal contact with a member is the most direct method of promoting awareness of a given issue and is usually the most effective.

Business also has become ever more entwined with government. On the positive side, we are seeing more and more instances where business and government are working together, and where each feels less threatened by the other. But given the weighty infrastructure of the regulatory process—a complex web of rules and requirements to which businesses must adhere—lobbyists are needed to monitor the latest regulatory developments and act quickly to advocate the interests of the group they represent.

The lobbyists' strength is their familiarity with Capitol Hill and the executive branch. Their ability to run through the maze of the legislative process is particularly important. Washington-based lobbying firms and trade organizations can provide the resources required for an all-out lobbying effort. Both have established a network of contacts, and both have the capacity within their organizations to push efficiently for a cause and at a time when it would do the most good.

ACCESS

Washington is a city that runs at full throttle whenever Congress is in session. Time limitations on a senator or representative are tremendous;

members' schedules are tight, which means they must be quite selective about the people they choose to see and the ones they choose to avoid.

Contacts are employed by the lobbyist to provide clients with access to government officials. The term "contact" seems lifeless, as if it is merely a tool the lobbyist uses to pick his or her way to a member's office. This is a misconception. In many cases, a contact is a close friend, another lobbyist who has a good angle on an issue, or perhaps a staff member who has been cordial to the lobbyist over a long period. The best contacts are individuals on whom the lobbyist can trust and depend; likewise, they are people who have a good, trusting relationship with the lobbyist. A good lobbyist develops contacts and learns to keep them. The art is in maintaining a productive relationship with a given contact year in and year out.

Lobbying has grown more complicated in the last decade due primarily to changes in Washington. Senators and representatives increasingly are independent. Many are extremely perceptive and capable of quick study on a variety of issues. More than ever before, they weigh the issues and vote their minds, which, from the lobbyists' standpoint, puts more weight on the arguments they present than on the contacts they acquire.

Likewise, there have been significant changes in congressional staffs, which have multiplied as Congress has reasserted its equality with the executive branch. Because of the amount of information a member must digest and given the complexities of most issues, more and more responsibility is transferred to key staff members. Today's lobbyist must be able to work with both the member and his or her staff.

PREPARING THE CASE

The following sequence of events will shed some light on how a lobbying effort is coordinated in a large Washington-based lobbying firm.

A firm usually is approached by a client who feels outside assistance is needed to accomplish a specific legislative task. The account is then managed by the lobbying firm and assigned to an individual or team within the firm. In most cases, the organization seeking lobbying assistance has prepared an argument or has people within the organization who understand every aspect of the issue. It now becomes the lobbyist's responsibility to know the issue thoroughly, since he or she ultimately will be presenting in some form the client's case to Congress, whether it be in a subcommittee hearing or a private meeting with a member and his or her staff.

The lobbyist's most important assignment is to package the argument. Here are some tips if you are presenting a case to a member of the House or Senate.

1. *Rehearse Your Argument.* The argument itself should be concise, carefully worded, and adroitly prepared. You are dealing with members whose schedules are planned to the minute, which leaves little time for anything but direct talk about the issue in question.
2. *Know Your Opposition.* Very often a member will ask the lobbyist to outline the cons as well as the pros of the issue in question. A good lobbyist should be prepared to do so and should manage it in such a way as not to detract from his or her argument. Be straightforward with the member. Once he or she gets the impression you are not being candid, your credibility may be irreparably damaged.
3. *Know Your Member's Politics.* Find out how a certain proposition will affect a member's district. You do not want to place a member in the awkward position of requesting him or her to support something that runs contrary to overwhelming constituent opinion or previously publicized positions. By the same token, if a bill will have positive ramifications on a member's district, these should be brought out. As Speaker "Tip" O'Neill says, "All politics is local."
4. *Leave Taking.* If the member agrees with your position, leave as soon as possible.
5. *Leave a Written Statement Behind.* Do not expect a member to remember your position; provide a copy of your arguments so they can be reviewed later by the member and his or her staff. One page is best.
6. *Follow Up on Your Interview.* In the basic sense this means keeping an eye on your proposal after it has been placed in the member's hands. If a senator or representative decides to push for your cause, remain in close contact with him or her. And keep them up to date by sending articles or other new and pertinent documents.

In any event, the lobbyist follows a timeless code of etiquette. If a member or staffer has granted you an audience, a written thank-you is in order after the meeting. Mention should be made to the member of anyone on the member's staff who was helpful.

Congresswoman Lindy Boggs put it best: "Always say 'please' and always say 'thank you.'"

CHAPTER
15

EDITORIAL SERVICES

Jan Van Meter

Senior Vice President
Hill & Knowlton

As a term, "editorial services" resembles "public relations." It means nothing and everything. Seemingly, everyone has one, but none resembles another. And what each does differs radically.

Yet, there is one important common trait to successful editorial services departments in companies or in public relations agencies. Properly staffed and managed, they are an active *resource* to the organization. And they are seen as a resource by other staff and line managers, a resource which responds to their needs on time with high quality work. They are managed entrepreneurially and that atmosphere of entrepreneurship pervades the department. And it is managements which encourage, or even demand, that kind of entrepreneurial activity which find themselves with a department of endless usefulness and real value.

For the purposes of discussing what editorial services should accomplish for any organization which has such a department or is considering setting one up, and for the purposes of describing how such a department is best managed, then, I will discuss a kind of ideal department. That it is an ideal, however, should not be taken to mean that such departments do not exist. They do.

Jan Van Meter joined Hill & Knowlton in 1976 as a member of the editorial services department. Since then he has become senior vice president of Hill & Knowlton and director of its communications task force. In 1978 Mr. Van Meter helped form Hill & Knowlton's public issues/public policy group.

Receiving his B.A. degree in politics, economics, and philosophy from Wesleyan University, he joined the Central Intelligence Agency as an intelligence analyst in 1963. After four years with the CIA he completed his Ph.D. degree in English and taught at the University of Texas.

He is on the board of advisers of the Women's Equity Action League.

THE FUNCTIONS OF AN EDITORIAL SERVICES DEPARTMENT

At their most complete, editorial services departments are capable of delivering high-quality work in the following areas:

1. Speeches
2. Internal communications, including newspapers, newsletters, magazines, and employee annual reports
3. Issue analyses and backgrounders
4. Position papers
5. Feature articles
6. News releases
7. Benefit booklets and other personnel documents
8. Annual reports and quarterlies
9. Presentation scripts, including sales presentations and financial analyst presentations
10. By-lined articles for op-ed pages and letters for letters-to-the-editor columns
11. Issue, corporate, and other nonproduct advertising copy
12. Shareholder letters
13. Sales and corporate brochures
14. Corporate histories
15. Scripts for audiovisual presentations

In other words, an editorial services department should be able to turn out quickly any kind of written material needed by an organization and turn it out in comprehensive, readable, interesting fashion.

STAFFING THE DEPARTMENT

People who best fit in editorial services departments are not necessarily, or even often, the same kinds of people who inhabit the other parts of the public relations department. A often-made mistake in staffing an editorial services department is to look only for people who have extensive experience in public relations or in journalism. An experienced manager is important, but an experienced staff is not. While public relations or journalism experience can be useful for some of the editorial work, like writing news releases or feature articles, it is almost useless for other equally vital editorial services work such as speech writing and backgrounders.

Indeed, experience is not nearly as essential in staffing an editorial services department as are three specific qualities: an ability to learn very quickly, a good, lively and critical mind, and an ability to write well. These are qualities which are hard to find, especially if one confines oneself to those with the more traditional, and more comforting, kinds of experience. Indeed, success is often easier found by looking elsewhere. The two best people I have ever hired came from places one doesn't usually look: one, a Ph.D. in philosophy from a CETA program in suburban Boston where he was teaching community relations to a police department, and the other from the office of an independent movie producer where he was managing the distribution of an independent film.

In fact, when looked for with an open mind, these people are not as hard to find as they are to keep, since they are stolen quickly by those who do hire on the basis of experience.

Why not experience? First, good editorial services people with experience are hard to find and are usually expensive, especially if their primary skill is speechwriting. Second, if you find people with the ability to learn rapidly, with lively minds, and with the ability to write well, you can teach them the other, ancillary skills far more easily than you can teach someone with experience how to learn, think, and write in the way that fits your organization's style and needs. These kinds of people are usually far less expensive to hire, as well.

But, having such people does not necessarily make your life easier. Bright, creative people are hard to manage, if you insist on the traditional management methods. And, too often, their work is managed and structured to ensure that they produce pedestrian, or worse, unreadable, work.

MANAGING AN EDITORIAL SERVICES DEPARTMENT

First, whenever possible, allow the creative staff enough time for each assignment. Certainly, allowing enough time for assignments is not always possible, and people must be able to create and write under a great deal of time pressure. However, far too often, the extreme time pressure that characterizes many organizations is a result of the military mentality of hurry up and wait, or the bureaucratic mentality of avoiding any action in the hopes that the need for it will go away. Such pressure, if it is induced often enough, creates in the editorial services staff a tired cynicism and frustration that erodes quality and efficiency at the same time.

But what is enough time? Obviously, what is "enough," depends on the nature of the assignment, the individual, and the extent of clearance needed. However, any competent writer can, with a fair amount of accuracy, estimate the time he or she will need. What is important is that a time estimate be discussed ahead of time and a deadline set.

Second, give your writers the information they need to do the job. At best, this means that the writer assigned will meet with the person who needs the speech or the backgrounder or the annual report. A face-to-face discussion where questions can be asked and answered in their complexity is far more likely to produce the desired result the first time than second-hand information which withholds vital facts.

I and many of my colleagues still shudder when we remember a speech assignment from a client CEO who refused to meet with anyone. All the information that was ever given was the subject: "The Free Enterprise System." The fact that the subject was hardly novel was not disturbing; new things can always be said about old subjects. What was—and still is—disturbing was the fact that we never have managed to find out what he wanted to say. And that's after five speech drafts, five different writers, five different approaches—and five different bills. All he'd say is, "That's not what I want." It is an expensive game of "Pin the Tail on the Donkey."

Third, be open to new solutions. Creative people like to be creative, and that's why you hired them in the first place. To use as your reference point the way the employee magazine has always been written merely ensures a result that looks like the way that it always looked.

Fourth, avoid group editing. It is hardly news that committees only function through compromise, and compromise editing is uniformly dull. It is far better to send out as many copies to as many people necessary to review a document and have the writer do the mediating with his or her own solutions.

Fifth, keep clearance on any document—speech, quarterly report, or sales brochure—to as few people as possible. (See above for comments on group editing.)

Sixth, keep your writers busy and challenged. Hiring bright, quick people means that the worst thing you can do to them is bore them. Of course, some part of their work will be repetitive and even dull. Some part of all work is. But there is no reason that it should all be. If necessary, switch people from assignment to assignment, from kind of writing to kind of writing. Specialization, even in such naturally specialized work as speech-writing, leads to boredom. The twentieth speech on the energy crisis by the same writer is just not going to be as good as the first five, not because the writer is burned out, but because he or she is likely to be bored with the subject.

Seventh, provide feedback. No one can improve without knowing how an assignment was received. Specific criticism allows people to make specific changes. Generalized criticism only makes people frustrated. And don't be afraid to tell the writer that a job was good. The number of people who will only tell you if something is not what they want, but never praise good work is a source of never-ending astonishment. That style may fit a macho, taciturn company, but it hardly encourages more quality work from most creative people.

Eighth, manage differently. The kinds of people needed to staff a first-rate editorial services department are not the kinds of people who adapt well to command-control management. Certainly, they must be able to fit into the organization and its style. Certainly, they must be able to complete assignments on time. Certainly, they must be able to find solutions to difficult writing problems. But you cannot expect them to respond enthusiastically to arbitrary orders, to time clocks, to corporate game playing. Indeed, the two major jobs of the manager of an editorial services department are (1) to provide a physical and psychological environment that is conducive to high-quality work, and (2) to protect the creative staff, when necessary, from the excesses of the rest of the company.

The management style that works best is peer group management, in which all are equal when faced with a specific task. The task itself becomes the boss. This open style of management encourages creativity and contributions from the group, and makes individual success far less important than group success. Not only does this kind of peer group management tend to produce work of higher quality, it also produces a group-centered high morale that sustains its members during their inevitable dry periods and their most difficult assignments.

Such peer group management also acts to discourage overspecialization since an individual can rely on the assistance of every member of the department when he is called on to do an unfamiliar assignment. The group skills are broadened, and the individuals are given the kinds of variety and challenges that bring out the best in creative, bright people.

THE INTERNAL ORGANIZATION OF THE DEPARTMENT

No matter what the size of the staff, the manager (and the deputy manager, if the staff is large enough) should be the focal point for all assignments. This will allow one person to ensure an even flow and a high quality of work. There are two important qualities that the manager should have: an ability to "work" the organization and thereby get assignments for the department, and an ability to act as conceptual and textual editor. The first ability is important since successfully run editorial services departments are entrepreneurially managed.

By "entrepreneurial management," I mean that the manager does not wait for work to arrive, but runs the department like a small business, like a profit (rather than a cost) center. He or she actively seeks assignments, searching out ways to assist the other staff and line departments which give assignments and seeking to create new products to meet the needs of the organization as a whole or of any of its parts.

The second ability is important since quality control is crucial if assignments are to keep coming and if new writers are to be trained in new skills and new ways of writing.

However, the fact of the manager as departmental focal point should never mean that he or she acts as buffer between the writer and the individual needing an assignment. Secondhand instructions and assignments rarely produce as good results as personal discussions. The manager must always resist the temptation to run everything and to be a part of everything if the creative staff are to develop their own internal followings and grow in their professional skills and corporate acumen.

Given the manager as focal point, the internal organization of the department is far less important and depends more on size than anything else. Very large departments often compartmentalize into such specialties as internal communications, speechwriting, and external communications. Smaller departments have no formal organization, but delegate some specific responsibilities such as publications editor or speechwriter, though these responsibilities are rotated on some regular basis.

There is no rule about whether assigning writers specific specialties is better than having a number of writers who can tackle a wide range of tasks. However, a good department should have people who can do a range of tasks. This makes life a great deal easier for the manager and for the company or agency. It also gives the writers themselves variety in their work, and variety always improves the quality of a creative person's work.

RELATIONSHIP TO THE REST OF THE ORGANIZATION

Externally, the department's organization generally reflects the kinds of work most often asked of it. If top management relies on the department for a large number of speeches and uses it only for editing the internal publication, then assigning specific speechwriters to specific members of top management makes sense. The internal publication editing can be done by those who are free at the time the job needs to be done. If there is little attention paid to issues but a great demand for sales brochures and presentations for a number of divisions, then writers can be assigned to each division as "their" writer.

It should be repeated, however, that some form of assignment switching or rotating is important, both to maintain freshness of approach and creativity, and to develop a department which is fully capable of handling any assignment. If you have hired bright, quick people, their learning curves will be very steep and short so there is little risk involved.

While the editorial services department manager should act as the primary "business getter" in the department, each staff member should be encouraged to seek out work and to suggest new ideas for projects on his own. This groupwide entrepreneurial style not only acts as to create future new managers, it also forces the staff to become closely involved with the business itself, thereby ensuring the relevance of its activities and avoiding the threat of becoming yet another ivory tower staff operation.

EQUIPPING AN EDITORIAL SERVICES DEPARTMENT

While it is possible—and traditional—to set up an editorial services department in the traditional staff department manner, that organization no longer makes any human or economic sense. One secretary to two or three writers was certainly standard and even effective before the advent of word processors, but it is not so now.

One word processor for each writer will not only save the salary, benefits, and overhead of a secretary, it will also allow each writer to be far more productive than ever before. The time of drafting, typing, editing, retyping, proofing, and retyping again is cut by at least half. (One warning: a body of evidence is developing that the very existence of word processors has now created the opportunity for endless editing and rewriting. At least one company I know of went through 157 drafts of its annual report, just because everyone who had clearance felt that a new draft was no real work. This search for a nonexistent, impossible perfection is only abetted by word processing.)

The existence of word processors also determines the internal structure and organization of an editorial services department. Certainly, one secretary can be assigned to as many as six or eight writers if they are all equipped with word processors. Someone is needed to answer the telephone, file, keep appointments, and do other important, if routine, jobs; but each writer or pair of writers have no need for an individually assigned secretary. Both the money saved on support staff and the increased efficiency and productivity will make the editorial services department far more cost effective as a staff function.

TO HAVE OR HAVE NOT

All the work of a editorial services department can be free-lanced out or assigned to a public relations agency. The question of whether to have an internal department thus becomes one of need and cost, two closely related factors. If the organization rarely requires speeches or brochures and has no internal publication, then free-lancers or the public relations firm can save the organization money. If the organization only needs one major speech a year, then that should be sent out to be written.

However, the use of free-lancers means that the individuals hired will not know the organization, its people, or its needs very well, certainly not as well as the public relations agency and its account executive. Nor will the public relations agency know the organization as well as internal staff does. But the agency can have highly qualified, highly paid specialists on staff for use by an organization only when needed. Their cost is spread out among all the agency's clients, and they have to be adept at quickly picking up knowledge of the organization and the subject, however arcane.

There is no firm rule about creating an internal department or using outside help. Most companies that have editorial services departments staff them with generalists, but turn to their public relations agency or to free-lancers when highly specialized projects arise. All the managers can do is to reassess continually the respective costs, keeping in mind the cost of internal overhead and benefits as well as the more obvious cost of salaries.

CHAPTER

16

SPEECH
WRITING

John B. McDonald

President
John B. McDonald & Associates

The economic turmoil since 1973 has made most corporations more "practical," including a de-emphasis on "frills." Most companies now expect their communications efforts, including speeches, to support corporate goals directly, rather than be any sort of optional luxury.

The suggestions in this chapter are based on my own experience—a decade of concentration on speechwriting at high levels in business and government; over a decade prior to that in writing, general public relations, and Washington wire service news. First, my bottom lines:

- Corporate speeches to key audiences can help advance corporate policy—not by themselves but as a supplement to and dramatization of legal, legislative, R&D, regulatory, and industry initiatives by the company.
- CEO speeches, particularly, also can be used as a live catalyst to fix corporate policy, where none exists, or to modify or clarify existing policy.
- Corporate speakers are most effective when they are logical authorities on their subject and when their speeches include as much personal experience and personal opinion as so-called facts.
- To have a decent chance at the desired cumulative impact, corporate speakers basically should address the same corporate repertoire of policy themes each and every time they speak.
- Corporate speeches probably will *not* have any direct effect on general

John B. McDonald is a New York consultant on corporate speeches and annual reports. In his corporate career, he has written for, among others, CEOs Irving S. Shapiro of Du Pont and Dr. Edwin A. Gee of International Paper Company. In government, he served as director of editorial operations for HEW Secretary Casper W. Weinberger and was a member of President Nixon's writing staff in 1972. He also served for five years on the Washington staff of the Associated Press.

public opinion, or on governments in Washington and state capitals. They can have plenty of indirect effect, however.

- Communities, employees, stockholders, customers, suppliers, competitors, industry groups, related businesses, local and trade news media, consumer organizations, academic centers, private enterprise groups—these are the targets that Washington and state governments heed. Without support or nonopposition here, few corporate policy goals are going to be achieved.

That's where I come out. Now I'll take a lot more words to tell how I got there.

Years ago, when I was a Washington newsman without corporate experience, I was interviewed by a major CEO looking for a new speech-writer. He stressed that each of his speeches required heavy research and that each dealt with a different subject. When I suggested one possible subject, he smiled, saying: "Oh, I covered that two years ago at the Conference Board."

I didn't get the job. The interview left me with mixed feelings, both impressed and puzzled. I was impressed because he was so caring that each speech required heavy research. But why would a major CEO need such heavy research—didn't he *know* what he was talking about?

I had ghosted speeches for Washington politicians. In these, research was window dressing. Research was glancing at that morning's headlines. Heavy research was actually reading the stories and making a few notes. *What the speaker thought and advocated*—right or wrong, documented or not—was the heart of the speech and the news it produced.

I was impressed by the CEO's intellectual range, willing to tackle a new subject each time. But wasn't he dissipating his potential impact by jumping here and there? Why wouldn't he specialize in some subject area, become an expert and be so recognized by peers and the news media, as most prominent politicians did?

(And as some news organizations did. My wire service mentor told me: "Jack, if we've got a good story we run it every day for at least a month—especially if it's been officially denied.")

Come to think of it, why would the CEO believe that anyone would remember his two-year-old speech to the Conference Board—or that it was still pertinent? In our fast-changing world, two years ago is Dead Sea Scrolls stuff—few issues worthy of discussion today are what they were two years ago.

Unbeknownst to me at the time, I had stumbled into the suite of one the handful of top CEOs I now think of as the "superstars" of business rhetoric. They are the intellectual statesmen of the corporate world. They've earned their spurs by impressive deeds, probably served a stint in government. They've won the right to talk about issues beyond their corporate interests, putting a badly needed sheen of objective thought on the corporate world. It is to be hoped that they encourage other businessmen to think of business not as an all-important end, but as one part of a dynamic society of adversarial forces.

Superstar corporate leaders normally devote some of their time to pressing their individual corporate causes. In addition, they hold the credentials, the "weight," to speak out on issues affecting all of business and society. Sometimes these two intersect, when national policy is viewed as the answer to individual corporate or industry problems.

Even on issues where they've had no (personal) experience, the opinion of the superstars counts—because they've proved by deeds that their judgment, leadership, and strategic thought is equal to any in the land.

Sometimes the multiroles of the superstars gives them a problem with public focus. This was wryly captured by Chrysler's Lee Iacocca—clearly a leading business superstar of the 1980s—in his March 21, 1983, cover feature in *Time*. "If you only talk cars, people say you're a provincial son of bitch," Iacocca said. "If you're outspoken, then they say you're running for office."

Whatever people may say, they pay attention to what the corporate superstars are advocating, as the Iacocca spread indicated. These CEOs are watched because they chart the forward edge of corporate thought— projecting the business viewpoint into the media/political melting pot of ideas which forges national policy decisions.

But the pattern of the superstars shouldn't be copied by anyone who isn't a superstar. Each superstar is a world unto himself who doesn't really offer any guidance for corporate speakers in general. They have clout with the movers and shakers in other spheres, and unique ways of delivering messages through many influential private channels.

I think it's wrong for an average corporate speaker to read a speech that represents only staff research and not any of his own personal experience. I think it's wasteful for the average corporate speaker to seek out a new topic each time.

Most corporations want to *change* something that is adversely affecting their business, or they want to *preserve* something that is under attack from others. These are the things that most corporate speeches should hit— *repetitively and in targeted places.*

That is the kind of speech this article addresses. However, there are other recurring types of corporate speeches that any topflight speechwriter or department must be able to turn out with literate ease:

- When a corporate executive must address some general topic, such as "Does a Liberal Arts Education Have Anything to Offer Business?" or "The Future Role of Business in Society." Those are two actual titles of speeches I have written. I think of them as quasi-superstar outings that are fun to work on, while outside the corporation's gut agenda.

- When the speaker is personally involved because of some tribute or award (I call this speech the Irish Wake: The speaker is like the corpse—the event couldn't be arranged without him, but he isn't expected to have much to say).
- When the speaker is explaining the latest corporate strategy philosophy to inside audiences (I call this the Analysand: the speaker wants to make sure that everyone, including himself, understands the latest strategic reasoning).

This last type of speech is rising in importance in these days of cutbacks, divestifications, acquisitions, and other redeployments of capital and assets. Speechwriters, or departments, must be particularly well tuned on the strategy speech. All effective outside presentations should be based on clear understandings of the corporation's strategy, business operations, and inside directions—even if these are not the direct subject.

Can a corporate speech program, based on recurring policy themes and targeted at opinion-intensive audiences, really be effective? Evidence is mixed.

Some corporations, including some industry leaders, do just fine without ever making a major policy speech in public. Some corporations have their people speaking anywhere and everywhere, without making a noticeable dent in public or news media opinion, sometimes even stirring up backlash. Other corporations score big with their speech campaign—becoming known as the authority in their area.

Some years ago, one CEO reported that his public relations staff had told him that polls showed his personal recognition was not what it should be. On their advice, he hit the road for 18 months, breaking his and many staff backs to cover the countryside with corporate rhetoric. Afterward a new poll was taken. You guessed it: he polled even lower than before.

With all of the implied caveat emptors in place, let's examine how a corporate speech program can be organized with the specific purpose of trying to use it to advance corporate goals, or to protect corporate practices against unwanted change.

The first thing to do is to look realistically at the potential impact of a corporate speech program. This can avoid a lot of unpleasant delusions.

The speech program won't have any major impact on general public opinion. Even the president has problems making a dent here. Most of the public will never hear the corporate points and wouldn't remember them if it did.

The speech program probably won't have any direct impact in Washington or state government, both of which make too many of their own speeches to be impressed by anyone else's. Government doesn't run on rhetoric: it runs on *influence*, as moderated by "evidence" and by political, public opinion, interest-group, and news media pressures. (I was there some years ago when a major corporate official tried to open a chat with Senate committee staffers with a conversational version of his "business must serve the public interest" speech. ("Cut the crap, Mr. XYZ," said a young woman lawyer, pleasantly, "what do you think of the new draft of Toxic Substances?") Corporate executives, particularly CEOs, probably can be more effective with governments through such private meetings than with speech forums.

Corporations *can* look for speech program impact in a number of crucial areas:

In their own front and back yards. Corporate speeches can be effective in welding support—or at least nonopposition—from all those many groups with connections to the company, its products, its locations, its employees, its customers, its suppliers, its stockholders, its industry group—and with groups interested in private enterprise itself.

A solid lineup of management, unions, communities, and customers on a particular issue—such as is occurring in some of the domestic companies and industries hard hit by foreign competition—is difficult for any official, legislator, or regulator to oppose. "Is anybody opposed to what you're asking?" always is an early question by politically sensitive people.

In the news media. Particularly look for impact in the news media with a basic editorial interest in the company, its products or services, or its industry group. All news media—even the national—are always looking for odd facts of public interest, rhetoric that enlivens concepts, headline angles, and, above all, controversy. All good speeches should contain these elements.

Inside the company. The support of employees can no longer be taken for granted, if it ever could. Speeches pointing out employee stakes in corporate policy issues can be very effective. In addition, the outside corporate speech can be effectively used to create and communicate corporate policy inside. Policy surely comes through more clearly as a speech—given life by its delivery—than as tab-indexed paper in those corporate-color ring binders that no one ever opens.

With their customer base. Speeches on policy changes or retentions needed to assure future supplies of products or services can deliver customer support. In addition, corporate evidence that it understands the business needs of its customers as well as its own business can attract new customers—vital in these days of savage competition at home and abroad.

None of the above groups probably has the clout to deliver a corporate victory on some policy issue—*but any one making a big negative fuss certainly can deny such victory.*

In one example that most corporations could duplicate, a Du Pont plant in Mississippi was delayed for years, at great cost, because of the opposition of a small recreational organization whose members didn't even live in the area full time. One obscure academic set into motion the events that ended most consumer applications of fluorocarbons. In the 1980s, corporations are facing stiff opposition to their decisions to close down plants—perhaps even legal restrictions. A lot of this can be avoided if the corporation is out front early and often with the reasons for its decision, including special plans to cushion the inevitable impact.

Most members of government, administrative and legislative, are inclined to listen sympathetically to business proposals. They know the general public (voters) doesn't care about most of the technical policies business seeks.

But one mayor, one local newspaper, one union, one customer, one consumer group, one politically connected academic can convert a business goal into a headline controversy—and that's when the politicians turn into statesmen. An effective corporate speech program can diffuse a lot of potential flak before it can build, through ignorance or resentment, into what all politicians hate: a decision on something that is news and, therefore, noticed by the general public (voters).

Who should speak for corporations, and where? The spokesman (male or female) business is, by its nature, a very personal activity. Much—almost everything—depends on the inherent credibility of the individual. This doesn't have a lot to do with speaking skill—in fact, a very polished speaker can come across as a glib phony.

Speaker credibility can't be programmed, though I guess it can be improved by training and practice. Credibility is something an executive usually earns with professional credentials and through a *sustained* performance of demonstrated candor; willingness to discuss weaknesses as well as strengths; a balanced rather than a zealot's view of things; and a natural sincerity that makes itself felt.

Over the years, Du Pont has earned a reputation for candor. As a result, it is believed when it has something dramatically good to announce. I was impressed by the way the company made no attempt to disguise the dismal results of 1975, commenting that "we can hardly wait for 1976." Among other things, the company said the textile fibers business would not recapture its economic health until the 1980s—quite a corporate admission, one that reflected about a third of the company's business.

Booking the right speaker into the right meetings is important, as is having him make the right speech. A CEO, for example, won't ring true at an engineers' meeting if he tries to make an engineers' speech. If he makes a CEO speech, okay. An engineer won't ring true at a CEO meeting if he tries to make a CEO speech. If he makes an engineers' speech, fine.

Abraham Lincoln summed up all successful precinct politics in a letter before he became president. Abe's advice, paraphrased: Make a perfect list of the voters, then ascertain who favors our position by sending *lawyers to talk to lawyers, farmers to talk to farmers, etc.* Then get our voters to the polls on

Election Day. The same ingredients should be involved in programming an effective corporate speech program.

Corporate communications planners also would be well advised to take an objective measure of speakers before firing them out as corporate rhetoric missiles—some of these can self-destruct, carrying the corporate banner with them.

I've know corporate executives who could sell the proverbial icebox to the proverbial Eskimos. Irving S. Shapiro of Du Pont was one of these. Irv—as he was called by all who worked with him—was a basically candid and forthcoming person, secure enough about his own views and Du Pont's inherent strengths to talk about any facet of business or society, good or bad. A former trial attorney, Shapiro knew that Du Pont and the rest of U.S. business lived not in some imperial cocoon, but in a world of adversaries, sincere and duplicitous, and that sound business advocacy should recognize this. As one result, he could always get balanced press coverage for Du Pont's reports.

"This son of a bitch is one smart cookie!" I was once told by a consumer activist who came to a seminar to rattle Shapiro but who left empty handed. This was an ultimate tribute.

On the other hand, I remember another executive of similar corporate rank. This poor guy, probably because of inner uncertainties that resulted in a bullheaded "I know it all" attitude, couldn't sell a lifesaver to an almost completely drowned person. Newsmen delighted in focusing on the negatives in his company's reports.

I remember one SEC proceeding. This executive, who fancied himself a communications expert, rejected all sound advice and prepared a fancy and confusing chart talk for the quasi-judicial SEC. The chart show, delivered with the executive's usual bluster, brought a collection of frowns and bemused smiles to the faces of the SEC commissioners.

The next speaker provided a good model for corporate speech programs. He was the head of a wildcat oil company in Texas (oil company accounting was the subject). This guy had no staff, no prepared text, and obviously was very nervous about addressing the SEC. Nevertheless, he so obviously knew what he was talking about, from actual experience that he described, and he spoke (from a page of scrawled notes) so obviously from the heart, that he carried the day. Fortunately for us, he supported the same position as we did.

Having set the scene, the potential, and some pitfalls, let's move to some specific ingredients of a corporate speech program, primarily the generic content of the speeches. First, some anecdotes to foreshadow the points to be made:

- A Maine farmer arrives late at a political rally. As the speaker continues to assault the audience, the farmer asks a nearby spectator: "What's he talking about?" The reply: "Don't rightly know. He ain't said yet."

- A senator criticizes his speechwriters: "What's the matter, boys? This draft contains nothing but facts—haven't we got any issues?"
- At the victorious end of the 1972 presidential campaign, our White House director, Raymond K. Price, Jr., compliments his 10 speechwriters, telling us his notes show we wrote some 2,000 speeches for the campaign. "Wrong," I interject, "we did the same speech 2,000 times." Smiling, Price agrees this is close to the truth.

On March 6, 1983, the *New York Times Magazine* made this point with regard to Ronald Reagan. The *Times* claimed that when Reagan made his second State of the Union address in 1983, he in effect made only the second speech of his 20-year political career. All of the thousands of earlier speeches were all variations on the same themes. In the second State of the Union, the *Times* judged, Reagan switched to something different for the very first time.

Impact—issues—repetition—these are obvious ingredients of any successful speech program. What else? Some years ago, Ray Price—one of the best speechwriters and issue strategists—took a look at corporate speeches.

"As a citizen," Price wrote, "I don't really give a damn what the chairman of Consolidated Widget has to say about the future of remedial reading. I don't need his rehashed funny stories, or his quotes from Aristophanes. But I would like to hear, from him, some blunt talk about what Naderism is costing the consumers of his company's products. I'd like to hear his account of his harassment by a headline-hunting Senate subcommittee.

"In short, I'd like to see him take off the gloves and fight back—from his unique personal perspective that only he can bring. Audiences do have a sense of reality, and I'd like to see him reach out and try to touch that sense."

Making a professional recommendation, Price said that corporate executives should "tell their writers to toss those speech formulas into the ashcan, along with their textbooks from communications schools, and listen while they—the executives—tell the writers what it is really like."

Price saw little sign that was happening. "Too few executives today really have anything they want to say," Price reported, "and therefore they turn to their technicians—their wordsmiths—to come up with something appropriate to an unavoidable occasion."

He suspected corporate executives feared their real viewpoints in public would be too controversial, that they'd be dismissed as "old fuddy-duddies or economic royalists." Price speculated: "It's much easier to peddle a few silken soporifics about corporate responsibility or the new dimensions of citizenship."

I think things have improved since Price's evaluation was made back in the 1970s. By being more aggressive and by targeting more speeches to things business knows about, the corporate viewpoint has won a new place in national decision making. In addition, the long spell of hyperinflation and recession has brought the public's attention back to basics—jobs, the health of local companies and plants, the economic price involved in many quality-of-life improvement programs.

I have included Price's comments, however, because his analysis still hits at the heart of potential weaknesses in corporate speech efforts: The lure of "safe" or irrelevant topics; the odd tendency to shun one's own credentials and expertise; the misjudgment that a speech is a set of facts rather than a set of opinions—supported here and there by "lump sum" facts of real impact. And, the crucial matter of personal input by the speaker.

I'm going to make a few comparisons between speeches for government and speeches for business, drawn from my own personal background.

In government, most officials (politicians in mufti) can tell writers in some detail how to "put the hay down where the goats can get at it"—to use George Wallace's pithy summation of the objective of public speaking. They've made a lot of speeches; they know how audiences react to their particular repertoire; they've debated a lot of opponents; they've gossiped with a lot of news reporters, finding out what "plays" in the media.

In business, most executives (with many brilliant exceptions) seem to regard speeches as an appropriations proposal to the board of directors, a set of facts and statistics arranged in dull copybook outline style. They all too often fail to see that what they happen to know personally, believe, or advocate—whether it's true or not—is the real stuff of speeches. Facts are to speeches what the guy with the green flag is to the Indianapolis 500—a starting point, nothing more.

In my opinion, nothing can really be "proved" and there are no real "facts"—at least, I've never seen one that couldn't be debated.

But how many corporate speeches have you heard or read which are nothing but a set of alleged facts and statistics indicating there are a lot of problems to be solved—whereupon the corporate speaker says, "thank you," and leaves the rostrum? Too many.

You'll seldom hear a government speaker discuss problems without plugging the hell out of his particular nostrums—and that's what the audience will remember.

Drawing up a list of specifications for effective corporate (or any other) speechmaking, I come out with these:

- The speaker should have something mind-catching to say, including some proposals for or against change.
- He should be a logical authority on his subject.
- He should enliven facts with his personal experience, impressions, and opinions, even though these are not subject to proof.
- He should organize things in a way that keeps audience attention (basically a rifle, not a shotgun, approach—and as brief as possible) and attract news media interest.
- He should keep making his repertoire of policy points over and over again.

Government officials (politicians) seem to understand these things instinctively. Many corporate executives don't—and they probably won't so long as they regard a speech date as a chore rather than a medium-range opportunity to make their business life easier, and more profitable.

Government officials, for another example, seldom if ever make speeches to each other. They seek warm bodies of uncommitted people who perhaps can be persuaded to vote the right way. Too many business speeches are delivered to audiences comprised largely of philosophical clones of the speaker.

Government speakers relish press conferences and debates with adversaries, because they know these attract attention and they feel confident of their skills and position. Many business speakers shy from spontaneous settings—is this because they know their sure knowledge of the subject ends when the staff-written draft ends?

Government speakers wouldn't waste time talking about anything but their pet plans. Business speakers all too often address exotic subjects they don't know anything about and which, even if well presented, won't do much for their business goals.

In government, staff people and lesser executives fight like tigers to get personally involved, with due recognition, in preparation of the leader's speeches. In business, the attitude often is that helping with the leader's speeches is an intrusion not vital to careers—could this attitude often be right?

I know that these comparisons are inherently unfair, since rhetoric is a main business of government but only a sideline—if an important one—of business. The differences in the government and business environments perhaps are one cause of this—the pace and the agenda, particularly, are startlingly different from the speechwriter's viewpoint.

"You might start thinking about XYZ," Tom Stephenson told me one day shortly after my arrival at Du Pont, "Irv's booked in there next spring."

It was then October. Why was the director of public affairs thinking about a spring speech now, I wondered? By next spring, all those Szechuan Chinese restaurants in New York could disgorge guerrilla troops who could take over the Eastern seaboard, only to be confronted with a Southern invasion from Mexico sparked by Castro. Why not wait until next spring to see what might really be worth talking about? At the White House, or HEW, "What's he going to say on TV tomorrow night, and what's our answer to the XYZ attack this morning?" is the reality—even next week is a distant eternity.

The agenda is quite a bit trimmer in business. The average top-level executive will limit his speaking to maybe a half-dozen speeches a year, though these are (and should be) bolstered by related appearances by lesser executives and company technical experts. When I headed Cap Weinberger's writing staff at HEW (staff of 20, including 6 other writers), we did more than 365 major items the first year. And, to forestall management productivity objections, Weinberger at the same time effectively ran an operation bigger and more complex than any business corporation—the Fortune 500 included.

All of this may sound unglamorous to speechwriters because I haven't talked about soaring phrases, clever anecdotes, quotable quotes, or how to develop lines that draw spirited audience reaction—and I don't intend to.

The plain fact is that the day of the orator is over, even in politics (with a few exceptions). Speakers reaching for immediate emotions—rather than lasting impressions of policy views—probably always were a rarity in business (sales booster meetings excepted).

Sure, an accomplished speechwriter should help a business speaker's effectiveness with parables that thumbnail difficult concepts; with anecdotes that illuminate issues; with rhythms that emphasize serial points; with "cheer lines" that reasonably can be expected to provoke audience reaction.

But let's face it. The business speaker is there primarily to convince the audience of the correctness and the sincerity of his policy views. The oratory is secondary. He's there *not* because of his speaking abilities—but because of what he knows and believes, from his particular position of responsibility.

If this can be accepted, it reinforces my basic views: if the executive is speaking about anything but his policy views and beliefs, on which he is a reasonable authority, then he's probably wasting his time. If he's reading some staff-generated gobbledegook he personally knows nothing about, he's surely wasting his time. And if he is not repeating some basic message or messages each time he takes to the microphone, he's certainly wasting his time.

It's always been very telling to me that corporations, when big bucks are on the line with multimillion dollar advertising campaigns, do the communicating right.

They wouldn't think of varying a carefully prepared ad campaign. They wouldn't think of talking about anything but the product. They wouldn't consider limiting the advertising to existing customers. They wouldn't consider advertising that wasn't hard hitting and simple. They wouldn't think of basing advertising entirely on facts, as opposed to reasonable opinions and claims. Yet all too often those are precisely what corporations do in their executive speech communication programs.

Years ago, I was chairman of a major political party in a densely populated urban county. To cut down the calls on me, I wrote a one-page guide to help our novice candidates prepare their speeches. Looking it over now, I think some of its precepts might be helpful in this chapter:

- Always propose something, even if it's a negative proposal. That's what people remember and what the news media covers.
- When you're finished preparing a speech, try to write a punchy eight-word imaginary newspaper headline about its basic thrust. "XYZ

SAYS. . . ." What did XYZ say? If you can't get it into eight words, you probably haven't got a speech worth delivering.

- Focus your campaign as narrowly as possible. The best campaign is one issue. The second best is two issues. The third best is three issues . . . etc.

Now, talking about business speeches, I'd add a few points:

- Don't let the character of the audience or the nature of the event (within reason) prevent you from hitting your policy points, or at least some of them. Try making them an example of whatever it is that you're supposed to be talking about—this usually works.
- Don't try to cover the waterfront on each speech. Corporations love photographs showing montages of all their products. This format makes for a weak speech. The laundry list approach leaves the audience with a fuzzy image or no image. A speech isn't supposed to be a compendium of everything the speaker knows on the subject, just a focus on several of the more timely things he knows about it.
- Think of a delivered speech as the beginning of something, not the conclusion of something. You now have, or should have, a verified and delivered policy paper. What else can the communications department do with this in various recycled forms?

I am now at the point when I should bring the focus down to "how you go about writing a speech." I shy from this because my real response would echo Mark Twain when he reported: "I was gratified to be able to answer promptly and did. I said I didn't know."

What I do is write the speech in my head, in some vague subconscious manner. Only when I "feel" it is ready do I sit down at the typewriter and type it out. By doing a rough draft, in which I keep going and don't stop to play around with parts, I "teach myself" how to organize and present this particular speech. Then I do that—usually, that second draft is what I present for openers. Occasionally, I'll take a third pass at some sections. A playwright once told a New York critic that he had finished his next play: "all I have to do is type it out." I knew exactly what he meant.

Getting off to a good start is vital. Doing my second draft, I'll tear up the first page 50 times until it feels right. Remember, you are not talking to yourself—you have to develop a "hook" of some kind that pulls the audience along with some vital logic.

Take it slow. Assume the audience is made up of dummies from outer space. "Our language is based on a series of letters called an alphabet. This includes 26 letters. Today, because talking about all 26 letters would take too much time, I'm going to discuss just 3 letters. They are G, P, and S"—that's the approach.

Structure is more important than rhetoric. Before you start writing, the skeleton must be clear in your own mind. Three to five clear segments are about tops for an effective speech—and the order in which they come is vital to audience understanding. The transition lines or phrases leading from one segment to another are a vital test. If the transitions are difficult to write, the order is probably wrong.

Headlines and cheer lines come last. With a draft of flowing structure before you, look it over for places to convert words and concepts into "purple prose" that helps audience understanding and attracts media coverage. Don't be afraid to use clichés—they are clichés because everyone knows what you mean when you use one.

Review the draft as a news reporter would. Where's the "lead" and the headline? What, in a few words, does this thing say? If you can't find a theme, as I advised earlier, do more work until it does contain a single thought which is more important than all the others, but which flows logically from all of the others. (This also is a good test for policy responsibility: Would it be all right if this made the front pages of the *New York Times* and the *Wall Street Journal*, and thus provoked other coverage and maybe some TV time for the speaker?)

The ending of the speech usually begins about three-quarters down page 9 of a double-spaced speech. (It begins on page 10 at the outside.) Don't present speeches that are more than 11 or 11½ pages double spaced—10 is best. Think of the pages involved as you form your basic three-, four-, or five-point structure—together they must total no more than 10–11 pages at the most, so how much room is there for each point? I found out early that a 20–page rough draft doesn't advance the cause very much. *Each draft, beginning with the rough, should be the length of the final.*

Pick up sections that have worked before. This is writing smart, not lazy, particularly if you're doing speeches for a corporate program in which cumulative impact is the target. If you've said it right once, say it that way again—this also avoids unnecessary policy review clearances. "If it ain't broke, don't fix it" is a good policy to follow, particularly on corporate theme, corporate goal, corporate history and performance segments. Also repeat jokes and anecdotes that have worked before. If they've worked once, they'll work again—knowing this will give the speaker more confidence. (I remember a victorious national political chairman telling his writers: "When the press corps throws up when they hear our basic campaign speech, we just might be starting to get somewhere with it.")

Another thing I learned early the hard way is *not* to begin serious writing or research until you're sure of what your client wants to talk about and the angles he wishes to pursue. If he's leaving it all up to you, then it's important to know *that* prior to writing.

I've been on some staffs where we wasted a lot of time developing full-length drafts, debating among ourselves, rewriting them—all before meeting with the speaker. As I once said in an internal memo: "Let's make sure he wants to talk about Angola *at all*; and, if he does, then which of the three dominant factions there he wants to support and why—*before* we start writing and researching seriously." *You should research to develop evidence supporting a point of view—not to discover a point of view.*

Going through the whole speech process on a staff level is tiring yourself out before you climb into the ring. In my experience, few final drafts follow detailed preliminary drafts or outlines—because preliminary points are canceled or modified by the speaker, by the comment of informed experts, or by the findings of research.

Unless you have worked with him a long time, don't send a speaker a full draft or developed outline as a speech suggestion. Send a short memo outlining possible alternate topics and angles in a few paragraphs. The reaction to this will be your guidance. Outlines, particularly, can be very misleading. It looks to the speaker as if all points in the outline are equal, when the writer actually intends to leave one point as a single sentence and blow another point out into four full pages of text.

It's impossible to do too much research on the speech event, its sponsor, and prospective audience. The more you talk to people arranging the event—and to corporate sources familiar with it—the more "ties" you can find between its goals and yours. I don't favor including a lot of puffery about the speech sponsor, but the more I know about the event the more telling I can make the speech—and the more pointed I can make its essential touches of humor. Humor that flows naturally out of the speech setting itself usually is better than unrelated jokes, no matter how funny.

After you've been writing for someone for some time, of course, you should be able to "think like he does." As this relationship grows, you can more surely forecast and recommend speech themes, submitting full drafts on which the speaker is asked to concur with new topical touches.

The basic trick to good corporate policy speechwriting, in my view, is *to become creative in how to dress gut themes in new rhetoric and link them to the self-interest of each new audience.* That way, you hit each audience while making your policy position once again.

With his tongue only partly in cheek, the late Dean Acheson once commented that "most government policy is made because an official is invited to a speech forum for which no topic has been assigned."

What Acheson meant can be a valuable guide for more effective use of top-level executive speeches—viewing each speech as an opportunity to establish or to clarify corporate policy.

A corporation should set policy on public and business issues by looking inside at its own operations. What's getting in our way? What threatens our business? What changes are needed to open up new opportunities? The answers to such questions are the grist of corporate policy.

Maybe I'm old fashioned (I type with two fingers on a 1964 IBM), but I'm leery of the recent wave of "public issues analysis" and "trend-tracking" and "futurism," particularly if they are limited to the public relations or any other single department. No one corporate department by itself can make corporate policy. Policy has to be set by the seasoned judgment of top management, after hearing the case from the company's various specialists.

Public and business policy responsibility really cuts across the corporate horizon—part of it is business operations, part is marketing, part is corporate image, part is legal, part is environmental, part is technology, part is public opinion, part is financial, etc. Normally there is no corporate unit that embraces all these functions (if there is, that's the place to analyze issues and develop policy).

The CEO speechwriter—when he is developing a speech on behalf of his CEO—can serve as a practical catalyst. His work can bring together, on a particular subject, all of the various corporate voices that have to be reflected in corporate policy. What is the CEO going to say about XYZ? Well, whatever he says, that's going to be the corporate policy on XYZ—so everyone should make damn sure what he says is right.

Such a mission imposes heavy responsibilities on the speechwriter that go beyond writing skills to his personal integrity and the trust he must win from associates throughout the company:

- He must be able authoritatively to report the views of the CEO to others, uncolored by his own.
- He must faithfully report the precise views of others to the CEO.
- He must not use his access to override suggestions on his own whim; that is the job of the CEO.
- He must make certain that all affected units and departments get their shot at the speech, and that all language and policy disagreements are negotiated to a "sign-off" by all concerned.
- He must make certain that all facts and concepts in the speech, particularly those of his own organization, will stand up to close scrutiny by competitors and adversaries, and the news media.
- He must make certain the speech, well in advance, becomes a planning, recycling, and distribution project for the corporate communications department.
- Finally, he must think how this new speech can be dressed up in new rhetorical clothing for the CEO's next appearance, and for the CEO's senior associates and *their* speech dates.

In my business, a major financial services company is probably my most canny client when it comes to using speech forums effectively. First, I've found all of the top executives of this company candid, with specific ideas of their own for most forums, and open to suggestions for additional ideas. Perhaps this attitude prevails because this company has the greatest "retail" outreach in its industry, by a wide margin, and thus knows the importance of what people think and believe.

This company makes no bones about policy repetition. We have all of the current policy statements in the word processor and one or more of these terse, clear statements is triggered into every speech—no matter what the rest of the substance might be—in the same identical words.

Perhaps the speaker is "gratified to address this major consumer convention," or bar association, or university, or civic organization or whatever. He then tells the corporation's story from whichever vantage point is most appropriate, leaning heavily on his own experience and convictions as well as facts and statistics. Somewhere in each and every speech, the same policy message or messages is delivered, such as: "We think several things must be done to assure fair play for everyone, particularly individual investors, as the boundaries of the financial services industry continues to evolve. Here are our ideas."

As I've indicated in several places, no measurable results can be assumed. But when the cumulative effect of all these "identical yet different" speeches to opinion-intensive groups in and around financial services is considered, this company just has to have strengthened its prospects for getting what it wants in Washington and elsewhere—and that's one basic job description of a corporate speech program.

The executives of this company are not afraid to hammer repetitively on what they believe to be the real issues, as opposed to peddling vague mishmash. They believe they know more about their business, and the needs and interests of their clients, than any headline hog in Congress, any consumerist fanatic, or any academic theorist—and they sound like it. This is "the right stuff" that's needed to win and hold significant opinion to corporate objectives.

17

AUDIO-VISUAL TECHNIQUES

Joseph Feurey

Director of Marketing Communications
Cone Mills Marketing Company

The huge world of audio visuals and the many complex techniques it encompasses can be more fully understood if you follow this one rule: Don't use them unless you have to.

That may seem a strange premise for a chapter on audio-visual techniques. But it's so important that it has to be restated: When in doubt—don't.

If you can get your messages across by simply talking to people, then go ahead and do it. You've learned an awful lot that way. So has the rest of humanity.

Moses set down a code of laws for human behavior that much of the world follows 4,000 years later. And he didn't even have a blackboard. He did of course have two stone tablets. But, as you recall, he only used those to get the attention of his audience—by smashing them to pieces.

And Jesus spoke in parables. He told people stories. He answered their questions. And he loved his audience.

Granted, both Moses and Jesus used some spectacular special effects. But we'll get to that later.

Their messages were clear and simple. Their sentences were short and they always made sense. Honor thy father and mother...love thy neighbor.

Joseph Feurey, director of marketing communications for Cone Mills Marketing Company, directs the company's advertising, publicity, public relations, and audio-visual sales support programs.

At the public relations firm of Burson-Marsteller, he established and managed the television news release program. He is a communications consultant to Mobil Oil, the American Medical Society, the Metropolitan Museum of Art, and the Public Relations Society of America.

He was an editor at both WABC-TV and WCBS-TV, and his news programs and special features have won 45 Emmy Awards. As a former writer and as director of editorials at WCBS Radio, he won the Radio and Television News Directors Association Award for best broadcast editorials in the United States.

They changed their worlds with messages that were clear, direct, loving, and simple. As did Jefferson and Lincoln, Gandhi, and King.

Now, unfortunately few of us have the verbal skills and the charisma of these dynamic leaders. But fortunately modern technology can help us along.

When you can speak face to face with your audience, using something as elementary as a flip chart or a blackboard may be enough to get your message across. And even if your writing isn't pretty, your spelling perfect, or your drawings accurate—you're still there to answer questions, clarify points, and keep your audience happy.

A good public speaker who is confident, knowledgeable, friendly, and entertaining is far more effective than all of the wizardry and audio-visual aces can come up with.

Something as simple as an overhead projector can be marvelously effective if the presenter keeps his delivery simple. Overhead projectors are best used when the presenter is doing something to whatever is in the projector.

In other words, the projector should be used like a blackboard. Its advantage over a blackboard is that prepared text can be placed on it. Then that text can be, say, edited with a marking pen. Relationships between figures can be shown, and charts and graphs can also be explained and perhaps altered for the audience.

Talking directly to people is a wonderful way to get information across to an audience. So if the speakers are good, their examples are clear, and their rapport with the audience is pleasant, there probably isn't a better way to communicate ideas.

Most people who have to communicate ideas today are not professional communicators. They don't spend the majority of their time practicing the communications arts. And even some professional communicators—like teachers, writers, and the clergy—don't have all the qualities of great communicators.

In fact 95 percent of the people who give speeches should not be giving them without strong audio-visual support.

How many speeches have you suffered through?

If you can't count that high, try and come up with the number of speakers you have witnessed who—on their own—can capture and move an audience? Is it 5 percent? You're lucky.

Most of the people who give speeches start off with bad jokes, follow up with long-winded rhetoric, stay on the podium too long, and bore their audience to pain.

But their failings aren't their fault.

The speech as an effective means of mass communications really belongs in another, previous century.

Then, everyone was used to public speeches. Then, those who were successful were sublime. They trained for their presentations, they polished them, they gave them again and again to different groups of people. They learned their craft in the medium of the day and perfected it through practice, competition, emulation, and reflection.

But the medium of today is not the speech.

And because giving an effective one is an arcane, though valuable skill, audio and visual techniques can enhance the skills of any speaker. And why not use, say, television techniques to improve a presentation?

The presence of television in our homes has been blamed for our inability to communicate. Television has been accused of being the enemy of the educator. But it can very easily become the friend of the communicator.

Where audio-visual techniques really begin to become effective is when speakers lack the ability, personality, rapport, patience, experience, or courage to do an outstanding job of communicating their ideas.

That does not mean speakers who use audio-visual techniques have essential character flaws. It is just an admission that they need help.

Through the proper use of audio-visual techniques, anyone can become a great communicator.

Those who fear audiences can record their messages in a room alone.

Those who flub lines can have those flubs removed before anyone hears what they have to say.

The humorless can be made funny.

The boring, exciting.

The bland, colorful.

The confusing, lucid.

The plain, fancy.

Good audio-visual work is a medium where language, time, and space are compressed into valuable capsules of easily assimilated information. These capsules are decorated with pictures, enlivened by music, and colored with a variety of voices and sound.

And those capsules are so technologically sophisticated that when they are well prepared, the technology vanishes and the information remains in the minds and the emotions of the viewer.

SEEK AN EMOTIONAL RESPONSE

The purpose of audio-visual techniques is to convey information and emotion.

Emotion?

That's right, emotion. Without it you don't have effective communications.

If you really want to teach people something, to change the way they think about something, to motivate them to change, you must do more than present them with the truth as you see it. You must touch their emotions.

To be truly effective you must move your audience to laughter or tears, pride or fear, love or hate.

Great speakers have always been able to do it.

And although you may want to merely nudge the emotions of your audience, not shatter them, you must share your emotions and your facts with your audience.'

That also means that audio-visual techniques must be entertaining—unless you want to get your message across to your audience by scaring the hell out of them or getting them mad at you.

So if you are going to use the audio-visual medium effectively, you must be willing to entertain your audience.

Now there is an army of audio-visual experts out there. . .and many of them have great power and are firmly established in the AV world. . .who go crazy with outrage and indignation at the mere suggestion that AV must entertain.

"You have to understand," one of them told me recently, "that there is a difference between the real world and the business world. In the real world when people look at a screen they expect to be entertained. But in the business world they know they're getting paid to watch that screen. It's their *job* to assimilate what you show them.

"Besides," he continued in the condescending tone only mastered by the truly incompetent who have reached positions of power, "it's much too expensive for companies to provide the kind of audio-visual experience one might watch on, say, prime time TV."

Having spent a great portion of my adult life either writing, editing, producing, or hiding from prime time television I knew what he was saying was nonsense.

And having had the opportunities to write, edit, produce, and consult for a lot of industrial audio-visual presentations, I know corporate AV can be better than network TV.

And it certainly is a lot less expensive. If you know what you're doing you can produce a better product at one-tenth the cost. No kidding, you can produce something better at a 90 percent saving.

Of course there was no telling this AV expert that. What with all his experience! After all, he had been president of the AV Club in his high school. There, his ability to thread projectors and change bulbs in overhead projectors got him out of a lot of those boring English classes.

And during his college training in communications, he had managed the studio. There he learned every single technical detail about equipment that has been outdated and unused for a decade.

"Now if you want quality work," the expert said as he handed me a folder," it's expensive. And while we aren't cheap, we're good." Then he laid out a budget for a half-hour program that totaled $250,000.

A careful , knowledgeable look at those figures showed the actual cost of the production to be about $20,000.

I never did do any business with the man, although his budget proposal contained the essence of good AV production: It was informative, entertaining, and produced an emotional response.

CRUEL PUNISHMENT

As an instructor for a joint project sponsored by New York University and the Public Relations Society of America, I've had the opportunity to review hundreds of industrial television productions. Most of them are unwatchable. Many of them should be declared unconstitutional because they represent cruel and unusual punishment for the employees who must watch them.

The programs fail not because of the lack of time, money, energy, or talent put into them. They fail because most of the people involved with their production didn't know enough about the skills of television production.

They were video illiterates. They thought because they could watch television, they could produce it. They believed if they could turn the camera equipment on, they could operate it. They believed if they could get an image on a video screen, they were finished with their jobs.

Good television production, while not difficult, does involve the mastery of three disciplines. Lack one and you're destined for failure. Ignore one and your audience will ignore or despise what you're trying to tell it.

DON'T GET TRAPPED IN THE PAST

For years 35-millimeter slides have been the mainstay of the audio-visual industry. And although many people have rational, mortal fears of being trapped in a darkened room with someone else operating a slide projector, slides have survived as the principal AV medium.

Simple slides are fine for simple presentations. Slides that illustrate what you're talking about through pictures, charts, or graphs can help get your meaning across in two ways:

1. They show people things that they may not be able to visualize, or understand, just from hearing about them.
2. They are an aid to the speaker because they can be used in place of, or in addition to, a prepared script. They encourage the speaker to look at what he's talking about. And they involve the speaker in the process of showing and telling. They help stop him from just reading or talking at an audience.

But the slides, like the writing of any AV presentation should be kept simple. Try to convey only one idea with one slide. And three words per slide are enough. The picture or the graphs should tell most of the story. Make sure the few words you do put on the slides are large enough to be read—easily—by someone sitting in the back row of wherever you're presenting them.

Remember, slides are used to create variety, illustrate points, help the speaker, and aid the viewer in remembering and understanding. That's a large mission, so keep each slide simple and focused on one point.

Although slides are simple, they are not inexpensive. Historically the artwork for charts and the like had to be prepared; then they had to be photographed and developed. But now there are a growing number of very inexpensive programs that can generate slides through the use of simple, inexpensive personal computers.

There are several personal and small business computers that can generate their own charts and graphs on a television screen. These computers work with real, up-to-the-minute data and give the user an infinite variety of visual support.

They can easily, inexpensively, and dramatically turn rows of figures into easy-to-understand pictures.

They will probably replace the huge, expensive industry of producing slides from artwork.

There are different programs for different personal computers. And there are more on the way. By the time this book is published there will be at least one program available for every computer from Apple to Zenith. They'll cost somewhere between $100 and $500.

These computers could be brought into a presentation area and hooked up to a television screen. The charts and graphs you want can be called up or erased with a touch of the computer keyboard.

For under $5,000 you could buy a personal computer, television screen, and program to handle the charts and graphs you'd like to present. And there are connections that can enable you to take the charts and put them onto videotape as well as the computer screen.

Laying one chart over another on videotape will give the appearance of movement. So, using computer-generated slide graphics can now produce animated presentations which, just a year ago, cost hundreds of times more.

There are other computer-generated slide makers that produce 35-millimeter slides from your data. These machines, which range from $25,000 to $350,000, may pay for themselves eventually. They produce slides on a television screen, then photograph and develop them.

But before committing yourself to that kind of outlay, you may want to ask yourself: Why do we need so many slides?

Slides won't do everything.

Although they will help the viewer grasp concepts that may be buried under numbers, they will not insure that the viewer will remember those numbers.

People's ability to remember a large amount of data is limited. Just try remembering that number you got from the information operator long enough to dial it.

When people watch slides, they'll take away an impression of what you're presenting.

They'll remember whether the charts go up or down, or stay at the same level. They'll know whether business is predicted to be good or bad, better or worse than last year. They're not going to remember all your numbers, no matter how good your slides.

If you want viewers to retain specific facts from slide presentations, make sure you hand out those facts and figures printed on paper in good old black and white letters.

Audiences can't really study AV presentations. The information goes by too quickly. Audiences want those presentations to inform and entertain, to set a mood. But if you want people to study what you have to say, to learn it, to memorize it—provide printed backup.

TALKING TO THE TELEVISION GENERATION

Originally slides were often used to jazz up presentations because producing moving pictures was too expensive.

But videotape has changed all that. Now, for what it costs to produce one half-hour, multimedia slide show ($30,000 to $50,000), you can buy enough videotape camera and editing equipment to produce quality television programming.

There are all kinds of debates in the audio-visual community about the relative qualities of film and videotape. People who own or are familiar with only film will insist on a variety of advantages it has over videotape. But there is only one.

Film and slides can be projected onto a very large screen. Videotape projections are limited to screens about six feet high.

But a large television projection screen or several smaller screens placed throughout the room are just as effective for virtually all audio-visual presentations.

The advantages and popularity of television for today's audiences hardly has to be documented. The average American watches at least 25 hours of it a week. It's from television that most Americans get most of their news, information about the world around them, and entertainment.

And people tend to believe and like what they see on television. To many of them, especially those born after 1950, television is an old, trusted friend and entertainer.

It's taught millions of them the alphabet, how to read, and how to count. Programs like "Sesame Street" and "The Electric Company" entertained them day after day while it taught them word skills they could rely on for the rest of their lives. And television showed them the four corners of the world, the distant reaches of the universe, and the limits of their imagination. All this before they were old enough to take a bus ride alone.

But even though television is a popular and very affordable medium for audio-visual presentations, it's not being used extensively or well outside of the television industry.

That's because too many people tried their hands at television production without the essential skills to produce good television.

And everyone—especially those who were raised with television as an omnipresent entertainer and educator—is an expert television critic.

These critics know good production from bad. And you can't fool them. If the report from the chairman of the board isn't as professional as Big Bird's spelling tips on "Sesame Street," the television generation will tune off.

They won't say so. They won't boo or shut the machine off. But they won't really listen. And some influential part of their psyche will remind them that the chairman of the board doesn't even have the finesse of the Cookie Monster.

LEARNING FROM HISTORY

Unfortunately, AV has grown up in a three-tiered system. Historically there have been these three general categories:

- Visual—artists, photographers, form cameramen, videotape cameramen.
- Technical—AV equipment operators, film editors, darkroom specialists, videotape editors, audio technicians, lighting technicians, and studio managers.
- Creative—writers, directors, producers, on-camera talent, voice-over talent.

Almost all of the above may for some reason object to the category they are placed in.

They all consider themselves absolutely essential for the successful completion of an Audio-Visual Production.

And each one will blame the other when something goes wrong.

The modern AV production doesn't need those hordes of specialists. The technology has changed so that one person should be able to do any AV job.

And certainly one person should assume total responsibility for any particular production.

Those huge, unwieldy production groups grew up alongside of unions in Hollywood and the broadcasting industry. The unions controlled the industry and in many cases encouraged featherbedding.

In television, cameramen weren't allowed to touch sound equipment—

even when it was attached to the camera—and they could get in trouble if they moved a light. If they wanted to move a plant out of the way, they'd have to get a stagehand to move it. And in some studios, you'd have to call for a "green" man. Only he could move plants.

As industry began to produce its own work, the class system of work segregation accompanied it. The system affected not only the work that was done, but even the way people dressed.

In some shops writers, producers, and managers wear ties and suits. Techies wear jeans, even though their work and working environs are cleaner than any newspaper city room in the country.

Their need to wear work clothes has long since passed.

And so has the need for such ridiculous divisions of labor and responsibility.

Insisting that people in AV departments be competent in all areas of production will do more than just shrink the staff and cut costs enormously.

It will insure that one person is personally responsible for the success of a project.

It will end forever the following, or variations thereof:

- The writer doesn't understand video.
- The cameraman didn't show any imagination.
- The lighting tech screwed up.
- The sound man wasn't listening.
- The producer lost control.
- The director didn't shoot the right footage.
- The editor doesn't understand cinematography.

There are thousands of other similar remarks that you will hear, but that's only because the system allows such things. And because human nature is what it is, there are few who will take responsibility for failure.

The present system of segregating production and responsibility has an even greater inherent flaw. It allows warring factions of production teams to sabotage each other's work. And because present productions setups are so fragmented, you won't really be able to hold people accountable. But you will know something is wrong.

When someone watches television they know what's good, professional, and entertaining. And they certainly know what's bad.

An audience will react to bad television by turning the channel to another station. But in a corporate setting they can't do that. So they will just turn their minds to another channel. And depending on how bad and how long their incarceration with a bad television program is, they will develop emotions, from distrust to hatred and revenge, which they may or may not ever exercise.

WRITING: THE ESSENTIAL SKILL

To avoid the manifold pitfalls that have grown up with the video world, a revolutionary but simple change is essential: Anyone involved in television production must be able to write.

Writing for television doesn't demand any great intellect. But it does require the writer to put his words together in a clear, simple, straightforward manner.

The viewers are only going to hear the message once. It's going to pass by their eyes and minds and be gone forever...unless the writing is so clear and simple that they just can't forget it.

One of the main problems with the poor quality of much of the audio-visual programming is that it has been left in the hands of the "artists" and the "techies," people who have valuable skills, but may not be good writers.

And until one masters the ability to write simply and clearly, audio-visual support becomes video support without understandable audio.

If something isn't written for television, it has no chance of pleasing its audience. And writing for television is different from most kinds of writing in the business world. A television producer who can't write, cannot produce television, regardless of his technical expertise.

Writing is the track on which all the movement in television must run. If people can't write, they have no business near any audio-visual production.

Now this writing talent we're looking for should not be hard to find. We're not looking for great novelists. We're looking for people who can write simply.

Short sentences and easy to understand words.

They should be able to express complex ideas in simple prose. They must remember always that the viewer will only hear the information once. And if the audience doesn't understand it while they're watching it, two things will happen:

- They'll tune out.
- They'll think the producer is dense.

AV professionals who can write should also be able to type. Once they've mastered those skills, the rest should be easy.

Anyone who can type can operate a videotape editing console...and a video camera.

If AV professionals have learned the myriad rules of the English language, they can learn the elemental concepts of cinematography.

They can turn on a microphone or a light and adjust it. They can certainly take a photograph with any one of the superb automatic cameras available.

Modern video cameras are lightweight and easy to operate. With a monitor, you can see what picture you're getting while you're taking it. They work well in normal room lighting and they look spectacular out of doors.

CINEMATOGRAPHY: IT'S MORE THAN TAKING A PICTURE

The availability of lightweight, inexpensive, easy-to-operate video equipment has created a huge group of producers and cameramen whose efforts are not unlike those of people in the early days of Punk Rock.

In those days, a lot of poor musicians got ahold of instruments, synthesizers, and amplifiers and made a lot of bad music. Because they had the instruments. They were of course musicians, artists if you will.

In time, some learned the fundamentals of music and improved their ability to play. And a whole new, exciting world of music emerged. It was similar in force to the early days of Rock and Roll, when a small band needed a knowledge of only a few chords and a singer who could stay on key.

In today's world there are legions of people working in the video industry who shoot and make money as camera people. But have no idea of cinematography.

The art of cinematography is too vast to explore in great detail here. But there are some basic principles which, if followed, can easily drastically improve the content of videotape presentations.

These principles are used predominantly in major market television news programs. And although relatively simple to carry out, they can produce very sophisticated information modules.

Here they are.

Write a rough treatment of the story you want to tell before you do anything else.

This treatment enables you to visualize how the finished project will look. And it will help you when you go on location to shoot the visual elements necessary to tell your story. And if you don't see any potential for video, rewrite the treatment.

If your audio-visual presentation is only going to be one person talking, it will be frightfully boring. And since few people have the ability to hold the audience's attention, your project is doomed to failure before it starts.

Any scene should start off with an establishing shot—a picture wide enough to show the viewers where the story is. This not only sets viewers' minds on the story, it also helps get them involved in your presentation. And viewer involvement is essential to viewer understanding.

The worst possible way to start a presentation is to focus the camera on someone's face and have that person start talking. Very few people have the desire or patience to stare at someone's face for more than a few seconds.

Even nightly newscasts which focus heavily on anchor people start the program with graphics and pictures which tell the audience: "Just wait a few seconds and we'll show you some of the most interesting stories in the world today."

Television stations quickly sweep the viewers away from the anchor person to other things and places. And that's what the viewers expect from any program they're watching: to be taken away from the humdrum world of here and now and be transported to a world of entertainment or easily understandable news and information.

GET OUT OF THE STUDIO

The majority of corporate television producers do most of their work in studios.

But studios are really the weak point of television production.

The single most effective means of improving corporate television would be to turn the studio into a storeroom and forbid anyone ever to use it.

Studios help propagate all of the weak points of bad television.

They make people sit down and sit still. And that's the last thing you should be doing in the television medium.

Television is a medium of movement and studios prohibit this.

But why, you may ask, do television news shows use studios?

In broadcast television the studio is only a transitory focal point. The anchor uses it to introduce a story. Then the audience is taken through videotape to another location where the story actually happened.

In a good network news show, an anchor person is only on the air for about two minutes of a half-hour show. And generally his face isn't on camera for any more than 15 seconds at a time.

The only regular use of studios in television news are those many boring Sunday morning, meet-the-newsmaker type shows.

Modern lightweight, light-sensitive portable equipment eliminates the need for expensive studios.

Without studios, people would be videotaped where they work or play. At their desks, in their offices, at the plant.

Money and space used for studios would be better spent for a good portable camera and editing equipment.

Corporate television, all too often, traps the viewer in a studio, where he is forced to stare at executives who are staring back at him.

The person being televised may be uncomfortable in such a strange setting and the viewer is getting bored silly. Remember, the part of his experience that knows what professional broadcasters do is comparing the corporate effort against it. And the corporate effort doesn't measure up.

Professional broadcasters read stories in 15 seconds. They show film stories in 90 seconds.

The broadcasters know that this is the way people like to get their information. They keep their shows moving. They keep the action and the viewers' attention out of the studio as much as possible.

Studios, of course, grew up in Hollywood, where there was a need to control the environment to make pictures. They spilled over into television, where they were a stage for performers. They were necessary for the special lighting conditions and the weight of the cameras that were used then.

They are still fine for situation comedies. But people are used to getting their news and information from a medium in which the whole world is a stage.

COMPRESSING TIME, SPACE, SOUND, AND IDEAS

A television program becomes enriched in proportion to the amount of information that's compressed into it.

Each second, 30 frames flash by the viewer's mind. And in just 10 of those frames—one-third of a second—a viewer can recognize and remember an image.

There is, of course, sound: natural sound on tape. It could be the chirp of a bird or the cry of baby. Then there is the narrator's voice, conveying its own emotion, or sense of urgency. And all these can be mixed with music selected and played to create its own evocative effect.

The medium is not limited to the here and now. It shouldn't be. You can assemble pictures and people and scenes from all over the world. In the blink of an eye you can bring the viewer from earth to the moon, from the past to the future.

The medium is at its best at its richest. It's at its worst as a recorder of the here and now—especially when the here and now is boring and poorly done.

Corporate producers may not be able to bring their viewers to the far corners of the world. But they can illustrate their programs with pictures of what the story is about.

If the program is about new machinery, show the machinery running. If it's about employee morale, show employees at work or play. If the program is about finance, show what that finance is financing.

But never keep one face on camera for more than 15 seconds. The audience will get bored, then restless, then hostile. You've probably taken them out of an office with a window and put them in a darkened room with a talking head. They'll hate it.

Remember, the eye seeks motion as the brain seeks information. There should be a new picture on the screen every 10 seconds. And those pictures should move.

If it's necessary to have this cover footage stand still, the camera can pan/zoom in or pull back on stationary pictures.

But in good television production there is always some movement.

Slides that illustrate numbers, trends, etc., should only be in view long enough to give the viewers the information. If they're supposed to memorize the information, include written handouts to take home later.

TRAINING THE PERFORMERS

No one would step up on a stage to speak before hundreds, if not thousands of people, without preparation and training. Yet in the corporate world, executives routinely sit in front of cameras and perform with little or no preparation for tapes that will be shown to large audiences.

And what makes it even worse is that their winces, flubs, nervousness, lack of sleep, and excess of anxiety can be watched under close scrutiny over and over again.

Few producers take the time or the trouble to rehearse these people so they will look good. Techniques for training people to look good on television are simple.

But producers often through fear of someone higher up in the company, through incompetence, or through a secret wish to let the boss look like a jerk, let the person on camera give a bad performance.

The producer may say to himself, "I can't help it if the president of the company doesn't look warm, trusting, and generous. You couldn't prove it by what he's paying me anyway."

Before people appear in front of camera they should be well briefed about what they are to talk about.

If they are going to read from a script, the script should be on a teleprompter screen. This is basically a system that projects the script onto a lens in front of the camera. That way the speaker can look directly at the camera and read the script at the same time.

And the speech should be written in the kind of language people speak: short sentences, easy-to-understand words, conversational style.

The speaker should be reminded that about 40 percent of his personality is going to get lost somewhere in the electronics that make television work. And if the speaker is to be effective he or she is going to have to put a lot of energy into his/her delivery.

Once the producer is happy with the performance, he has a wide range of techniques to use to improve it. Make no mistake—any action in front of a camera is a performance, and the better the performance, the better the delivery.

A producer can edit out all the flubs, twitches, "uhms" and "ahs." He can layer over the initial performance with scenes, pictures, illustrations, charts, and graphs. He can add music or other interviews that will highlight the points.

Videotape cries out for the perfection of a product *after* it is produced. And there is always something that can be done to improve an initial performance.

It is in this postproduction period that flubs can be taken out; that nervous faces can disappear under strong, interesting cover shots; that boring statistics can turn into lively graphics; and that pictures can be mixed with music and sound effects, and lovely fantasy can erase boring reality.

There are thousands of ways to improve an initial performance. And it is just a matter of time and technique that limit the improvement of a production.

And with video, you can improve your technique just by paying attention to the television programs you enjoy, to the movies that entertain you.

Cinematography may be an art. But it is one that is easily copied. The electronics handle the recreation of reality. And the perfection of your production is limited only by your imagination and your desire to share your creativity with your audience.

GOING PUBLIC

Once a corporation has mastered the techniques of professional development, it's a short step to using television as a publicity medium. There is a huge market in America for television news releases. They're similar to the old press releases, but they're geared for television news.

Few of these releases are used by networks of the top 10 television markets. But thousands of stations in smaller markets welcome them. Their chances for getting on the air improve with the degree of professionalism with which they're produced.

The television news releases should be short—about 90 seconds is maximum. And they should be produced so that they can be aired any time within 60 days after they are released.

Television producers are not out there, even in the smallest markets, waiting for any kind of public relations programming to put on the air. But there are times when they can really use professionally produced news stories about business, industry, and consumer products.

These tapes should be sent out on five-minute, three-quarter-inch cassettes to producers who have expressed an interest in getting them. They should not be distributed via satellite services. If no one is running a recorder at the receiving end, the story will be lost. And if something is sent to a producer's desk in a clearly marked package, it's easier to find and get on the air than screening a tape machine that's been monitoring a wide assortment of programming for hours.

Audio cassettes for radio news release can serve as a valuable public relations tool. But, as in television, they should be sent only to producers or editors who have expressed an interest in getting them. They should be short too. Thirty seconds is fine. A minute is the maximum.

Instead of sending out cassettes, some organizations provide a toll-free number to radio stations. When the calls come in, they're answered by a tape machine that plays the prerecorded release.

The American Medical Association headquarters in Chicago has some of the best such programs in the country. Medical editors are provided with a monthly calendar which tells them what medical topics will be covered on what days.

Despite the availability and viability of these outlets, many companies ignore their potential. And because they don't reach out into the electronic media, American business complains that news leans towards the sensational rather than the practical.

But there is a hunger in the electronic media for stories from and about the business and industries that make America work. But business has got to establish programs that continually reach out to the electronic media and the people it serves.

The investment in learning and technology is small. The rewards in terms of public understanding and support are great.

SPECIAL EVENTS

William J. Corbett

Director of Public Relations
Avon Products, Inc.

PURPOSE OF SPECIAL EVENTS

A special event is usually produced to gain favorable attention in the media for your client, your company, or your product. It may also be designed to convey a specific message about your company: for example, the fact that your company provides equal employment opportunity, is a good place to work, is a socially responsible corporate citizen, is a good neighbor, is interested in progress for women, manufactures fine products, or is a substantial taxpayer in the community. A special event might also be a product launch or a product publicity event.

Before you determine the event, you have to define very clearly your objectives and come up with an event that will help you reach your promotional or public relations goals.

Many people who have been successful in public relations insist that the long-term progress and continuation of any specific special-events program must be directly related to increasing the profits of your company or client. While a favorable impact on the bottom line can be a factor, this does not mean that in bullish economic times you should not consider events that may

---

William J. Corbett is director of public relations for Avon Products, Inc. During his 15 years at Avon he has had responsibilities in the areas of state, local, federal, and international government relations; product publicity; consumer affairs; media affairs; special promotions; and international public relations.

Mr. Corbett holds a bachelor of arts degree from Hobart College and a law degree from Fordham Law School, and has served as an assistant district attorney in Nassau County, New York.

He is a member of the International Committee of the Public Relations Society of America, the board of directors of the Forum for Corporate Social Responsibility, and the advisory board of the Center for the Study of the Presidency.

have marginal impact on the corporate profit picture but are socially responsible projects to undertake. An example of such a project would be throwing your support and expertise into sponsorship of an event for a charity or a minority organization. Such groups are normally in need of your financial support, but equally important is the expertise that can be provided by a public relations professional. There is no doubt though, a sound business reason will make a program easier to "sell" to your client or your senior management.

At Avon, in the mid-70s, we expanded our program of special events to supplement and, at the same time, complement our already existing programs, which included employee communications, financial and shareholder relations, community affairs, branch and field publicity, consumer affairs, international public relations, government and public affairs, and media relations. Our senior management believed that new, external, exciting events would enhance our reputation as the world's leading manufacturer and distributor of cosmetics, fragrances, and costume jewelry.

Looking back over the past eight years of the program, we can see that the resources we devoted to the development of a wide variety of special-events programs was money well spent in further improving an already excellent corporate reputation. The events in which we have participated have, for the most past, been upscale and have resulted in an expanded market, in addition to the many other benefits that have inured to our company.

In selecting an event of any type in my company, the tone was set by our former chairman of the board and chief executive officer, David W. Mitchell, and his team in senior management. Their direction is that we should only sponsor an activity if it is a "great event, one of which we can be very proud," and one which the 1.2 million Avon representatives around the world will greet with enthusiasm. Just to give you an example of the types of activities that we consider to be special events, I want to outline for you some of our projects here at Avon during the past year or so.

In one year we produced or sponsored 40 women's long-distance running events in 17 countries, a 22-city tennis tour, a grand-prize-winning float in the Tournament of Roses Parade, the Women's International Bowling Congress' Avon Queens Bowling Tournament, the World Figure Skating Championships for the Avon Cup, and the Avon/Women's Sports Foundation Women's Sports Hall of Fame (see figure 18.1).

We also had a plant dedication in Northampton, England, with a member of the royal family, Princess Anne, in attendance, and a plant dedication in Japan with a Shinto priest and government officials participating, as well as a plant dedication in Thailand with His Supreme Patriarch, highest Buddhist priest in Thailand, attending. We sponsored the National Commission on Working Women Broadcast Awards; the Avon/Girl Scouts of America Leadership Conference in Washington, D.C.; the Avon Awards to

Figure 18.1   Avon Chairman of the Board, David W. Mitchell, presents the sterling silver Avon championship trophy to Tracy Austin. This particular tournament took place in New York's Madison Square Garden before a record-breaking crowd of nearly 15,000 people and an international television audience of millions.

Women program in Japan and Europe; the Women's Forum Conference on women's perspectives on world issues; a conference on women in midlife crisis; a conference on fund raising for not-for-profit groups; and a press conference announcing a scholarship program in France for housewives returning to the work force.

In Germany, we held a series of "sundowner" meetings with influential community, government, and business leaders, and held international "consumer leader dialogues" involving Japan, the United Kingdom, Germany, and the United States. We also had press tours of our facilities; product launches; sports clinics in inner-city areas for underprivileged youth; a press tour of the Sloan-Kettering Cancer Research Center after announcing a $500,000 grant to endow an Avon chair in gynecological research; a reception, tour, and makeup demonstration at our corporate headquarters for wives of United Nations' delegates; and a minority leadership conference in Detroit; a tour of our manufacturing facilities by officials from the People's Republic of China; an exhibit booth at various conferences; and our corporate annual meeting combined with a luncheon and tour of one of our manufacturing and distribution facilities.

As you can see, each of these activities in one way or another supports one or more corporate objectives. It is up to you to shape and mold your program to fit your specific needs.

The possibilities for a special event are absolutely unlimited. Currently the commercial sponsorship of special events, especially sports and the arts, involve billions of dollars annually. In spite of this proliferation of corporate sponsorships, there are still numerous opportunities that could involve a unique special event or promotion for any corporate entity. With a sluggish economy and less government support for education at all levels, there is a crying need for business to assist in sponsoring amateur athletics at the high school and college level. While this would gain promotional benefits for sponsors, it would also free the dwindling pool of public monies for filling other educational needs.

Corporate special events in support of the arts are also vitally needed now more than ever due to the rising costs of maintaining exhibits and museums. Once again, the potential is enormous so long as the arts group is willing to permit the proper degree of corporate exposure. Corporate patronage must certainly not be exploitative, must be in good taste, and must be a proper "fit" for all parties.

An example of such a tie-in was an opening in October of 1982 in Dallas of a Tiffany & Company store (Tiffany is an Avon subsidiary). A party was held for the benefit of a local Dallas cultural organization, which drew a crowd to Tiffany and money for the local organization.

It appears that commercial sponsorship of sports events, cultural events, and art exhibits is most common in the United States and United Kingdom, but there is an increasing trend toward further business sponsorship in Europe and in the Orient. Many Japanese firms are jumping into the sponsorship of special sports events, including the Olympics, not only in Japan, but abroad as well. I think the Third World nations also need the infusion of corporate funds, innovative techniques, and professional skill in producing special events.

Special events have become so prolific that the publishers of *Advertising Age* are producing a twice-monthly international newsletter called *Crain's Special Events Report*. In their promotional flyer they say, "Special events is the brand new public relations technique for the 80's." There are other specialized newsletters for those involved in sports promotions and sports marketing. There is even a relatively new association of sports promoters.

THE DAY-TO-DAY FUNCTION

On a daily, routine basis much of your time is spent researching concepts, defining objectives, and preparing budgets for these special events. In presenting these programs to your client or to your management, extensive preparation is necessary so you are ready to answer any questions that might be asked. The fact that a program will not receive approval the first time you propose it is no reason to give up your efforts to gain approval. After several years of rejection we have often had programs approved when the timing was "just right" for that particular event. It is important to always be exploring new events, new concepts, and improving and changing the old. Newness and change are essential for excitement, freshness, vitality, and success in a special promotion.

In overseeing a large department or even working with just a few people, it is essential that good management techniques be employed to insure that tasks are properly assigned. It is impossible to produce a major special event without delegating some of the responsibility to others.

The most important day-to-day function is attention to detail and follow-up to insure that everyone is performing his or her assigned task. You will probably never get into difficulty with items you are directly handling, but it is the little items that have been left to others which can cause you the greatest trouble when they are not properly executed. While you must delegate, it is still essential that you keep your "hands on" the project through frequent meetings and reports.

With regard to little details, I recall one snafu some years ago at Palmetto Dunes Resort at Hilton Head Island, South Carolina, during my first year in organizing professional women's tennis events. Avon's chief executive officer, David W. Mitchell, was ready to go on the court in front of an audience of several thousand people and the press to present a professional woman tennis player with her prize check. I asked the local coordinator for the check and it was not there. Between us we did not even have a blank envelope to "fake it." After a mad dash to a nearby tennis shop, we secured an envelope, and the event proceeded without any noticeable interruption. Since that time, I always personally follow up to be sure the check, flowers, and trophy are in hand before the match begins. We became so efficient over the course of 100 tournaments that we actually had a check made out for the proper amount to present in an envelope to the winner seconds after the match. The players had been accustomed to receiving empty envelopes, and one top player actually threw away an envelope containing a $100,000 check thinking it was empty. We now tell the player in advance if there is something in the envelope. In many situations, the top tennis players prefer that you send the check directly to their agent or business manager. A final note on check presentations—have your sponsor's name appear in large letters or have a large logo on the prize envelope (see figure 18.2) so it will show up in the photos. In this way, you get your sponsor's name in the

Figure 18.2 William J. Corbett, Avon's Director of Public Relations, presents the champion's tray and the $15,000 winner's check to two-time Avon bowling champion, Katsuko Sugimoto of Japan. This event is televised both in the United States and abroad. The winner's check is presented in an Avon envelope, ensuring corporate identification.

newspapers even if the press leaves the name out of the caption or the TV commentator omits the sponsor's name. The gimmick of using a huge oversized check has really been overdone, and I suggest that most people consider it now to be corny, unless, of course, your client is a bank and is promoting its checking service.

After the event, it is important to go through a very critical evaluation to see whether the project met its goals and whether any aspect should be modified if the program is to be repeated or continued.

You must have the courage to go back to your senior management or client and admit that a project was less than successful, even if it was your own idea. Provided you have an enlightened and reasonable management or client, the admission that you have made a mistake should, if anything, increase your credibility when you go back the following year for the approval of your program.

PROMOTING SPECIAL EVENTS INTERNALLY

To insure the continuation of the special-events program by your company or client, you must actively communicate the success of the program to the rank-and-file employees in the company. This is important because with a weak economy and zero-based budgeting, you have to justify each year the continuation of any special promotional series you may be producing. In any company, there is always some degree of competition for promotional funds from advertising, sales promotion, and other groups. Those programs which have proven their worth in the past and have broad corporate support will have the best likelihood of continued funding. Others will be constantly calling on your client with new, fresh, and exciting ideas. If a better idea is proposed you should adopt it, but you may still want to continue with your existing special events.

It is important to get your senior management out to observe and participate in the special event so they can see firsthand the value the company is getting from the event. A skeptic can often be converted into a staunch supporter, which will be helpful when the programs are reviewed. Some corporations conduct market research studies on the attitudes of their sales force concerning the value of continuing specific programs. It is difficult for your employees or sales force to make an informed assessment of their feelings unless they have been exposed to the program or event. Through employee publications, you can promote the event, and at the same time, let a sales force know the value of such positive support through specific special events. Each year as you seek new funding, it is essential that you review the benefits gained in the past year.

SKILLS NECESSARY

When discussing the skills necessary to create and administer special events, I can almost recite the "Boy Scout law" enumerating all of those good and noble attributes. First, you must have a knowledge of public relations and a knowledge of your particular business. Administrative skill is essential. You have to be innovative and creative or know how to instill these qualities in others working with you, or have the ability to help shape, mold, and modify the ideas of others. You can always hire individuals with "creativity," but you must possess the management skills. Once again, attention to detail is absolutely essential. Hopefully, people dealing with the public and producing special events will have an even disposition and not become rattled in accomplishing the exhausting work that goes into producing a special event. Those entering this field must realize that it is not all glamour and that weeks of hard work is the price you pay for those few minutes of glory in the spotlight.

Several years ago, this came home to me when a member of our senior management commented, partly in jest, that the last four times he saw me that week was at parties or receptions. It is essential that you keep your management informed as your projects progress. In this way, they are kept fully aware of the work that goes into producing an outstanding special event. They will then realize it goes far beyond attending parties.

The ability to plan, create a budget, institute cost controls, and double-check financial projections is also an important quality. Knowledge of public relations agency practices and ability to deal effectively with consultants are important.

While the ability to get along with all types of people is required, you must also be able to get very tough when necessary. When you are in a highly visible business and have had successes in special promotions, you will find hundreds of people pursuing you with all sorts of flattery and inducements in an effort to get your corporation or client's money for their own pet project or production.

Stamina is also essential, since many special events are held on weekends and during the evening. During one recent year, I found that these special events required that I be away on the road 12 weekends in a row, in addition to my normal weekday work at the office. A supportive and stable home life can help make such a workload bearable. The bottom line is that there is no substitute for hard work, determination, and dedication.

PRACTICAL TIPS ON STAFFING

After you have clarified your objectives and selected a specific event that is suitable for meeting your goals, the first decision to be reached is whether to conduct the event with in-house staff or go to an outside agency or consultant. In many cases, it is more efficient and cost effective to set up an internal group if the project is designed to continue over a long period of time. With a one-time event, an outside group might be preferable. A corporate public relations department or a public relations agency can normally handle this type of assignment.

When a competitive sport is involved, it is essential to hire or retain someone with expert knowledge of the particular sport, its problems, personalities, and the special media which cover the sport. Prominent sportswriters are often available on a part-time consulting basis. As part of your consideration as to which event to sponsor, you should conduct research on the types of retainers and consulting fees paid in the particular sport, since they vary widely and will always be negotiable. There are great variations, in which some so-called experts command an enormous fee and are grossly overpaid, while some of the most competent and dependable people are woefully underpaid. Many companies needlessly waste their money by failing to negotiate on the matter of fees and retainers. For example, many public relations and advertising agencies, if you insist, will waive the 17.65 percent commission which several try to add on to the expenses. Such fees and add-ons have no legitimate basis or justification in public relations and are just a holdover for those with advertising agency backgrounds.

THE SPORTS STAFF TEMPERAMENT

The people who are attracted to sports public relations projects are unique. Many are very dedicated and are fans of the particular sport. This can be both good and bad. It is good in the sense that they enjoy their work and will put in long hours, nights, and weekends because they love the sport and are excited by just being involved in sports with all its glamour. It is bad in that they can be so enthusiastic that they can lose their objectivity and place their prime concern with the welfare of the athletes and the perpetuation of the sport, and before the promotional advantage that you are seeking from the project.

Special-events staff members deserve special consideration. It is not fair to expect the sports group to be in the office from 9:00 A.M. to 6:00 P.M. all the time, since at peak periods of the year they may work as much as 15 hours a day, 7 days straight, as many sports events are at night or on weekends. Within limits, they should be given flexibility on their working hours.

Even the smallest decision on a sport-related matter should not be made without consulting the sports staff since there are hard-learned nuances and details that may well be overlooked and mistakes made. With all sports, keep in touch with the specialists; they should have the knowledge and expertise to guide you through the sports politics, obtaining the approval of the various local and international sanctioning bodies, and the day-to-day sports gossip that might have a great bearing on the success of your event.

TELEVISION

For your event to really make its mark, you have to arrange for TV coverage. Just having TV cameras present makes your event seem more important. There are companies you can work with if you decide to seek outside help. Some might well put together a TV package for you without any charge since they may work out a deal with the station or network to sell off commercial time instead of a fee. If your event is unique or important enough, you might even demand rights fees from the TV outlets. Personal connections are important in this area, and a novice can waste a great deal of time and money through ignorance. If a network is not interested in your event, you might work with a firm which can pull together an independent syndication of the event.

Public broadcasting is another outlet for consideration. Public broadcasting companies have to cover their production charges from some source since they have little or no budget for special events. Most sports events are subsidized by a grant. The old rule was that a company could not underwrite through a grant its own event on television, but the restrictions have been loosened and varied arrangements are now possible.

Cable TV is also an alternative. While it may seem that viewership is limited, you may well be surprised by the coverage you can achieve for a very low cost. One bowling event that we sponsored on cable TV was shown at least three times last year, and recently I received calls from several parts of the country saying that the event has been seen again even though it had originally been shown over a year ago.

In making a TV deal you must specify the percentage of major markets you expect to reach and the time slot you want to achieve. Several years ago in one of the key markets for Avon our sports event was aired starting at midnight, which had very little value to us. If your contractual goals are not met, you should receive a reduction in the cost. You should insist on receiving a list of the stations which ran the event, and the time it was shown. You should impose penalties if this statement is not received within a reasonable time after the event. Problems arise with follow-up since many of the producers move on to other shows the minute that your show is "in the can." Included in the contract should be the provision permitting you to withhold part of the fee if the follow-up is not completed. Withholding part of the fee should give you the leverage to insure that all the conditions are met.

You should retain for yourself the right to sell your event to TV stations and networks in other countries if your company does, or plans to do, business in international markets. There are several firms which specialize in making such overseas sales through a regular network of outlets which they maintain. While it is to your advantage to have your event shown on TV in as many countries as possible, and you might possibly be willing to pay something to achieve that end, you may be pleasantly surprised to discover that some of these stations are willing to pay rights fees for the use of your videotape. These international marketers will work with you on a contingency basis in which you and they apportion the income after deducting their expenses. It is important to consult one of these firms well in advance of the event, so the appropriate videotapes, narration, and other adaptations needed for international broadcasts are completed at the time of the actual event. As we have done for the Avon International Marathon, which is often shown on television in many countries around the world, we conduct foreign language interviews of the runners from the countries most likely to show the videotape, and we edit in these segments, which then become an integral part of the tape which is sent to a station or network in that runner's country.

As you get into the matter of TV rights, both domestically and internationally, you may find that the athletes, the player associations, a sports federation, and the arena may claim those rights for themselves, thereby depriving you of both coverage and revenue. Do not give up, since all of these items are negotiable; remember, you hold the "trump card," which is your money and your sponsorship. Promoters need sponsors and you always have the option of finding another event to sponsor. Compromises can and usually are reached to substantially satisfy all of the concerned parties.

All of these items should be raised during the earliest stage of your negotiations. It is understandable that when the operators of the arena are participating in the profits of the event, they would like to have the event "blacked out" in the local area so that television will not compete with the paying spectators at the gate. Beyond the local area, the arena operator should have no interest in or claim to these rights. On the other hand, there are some arena operators and promoters who claim that having the event on TV in the local area heightens the importance and attraction of the event, and improves gate sales in both the current year and in future years. This has proven to be true in Madison Square Garden with the Avon Women's Tennis Championships, which year after year set new all-time world attendance records for women's tennis.

It is not unusual in situations where the event is not newsworthy enough for you to receive rights fees that you can arrange to get the event on TV by paying the production costs. Often a sleeper here is the added cost of installing extra lighting to bring the facility up to TV standards. The lost revenue from the seats that will be eliminated or blocked out due to the TV equipment is another minor factor.

You should also specify in advance in your contract that competitive products may not be advertised during your telecast. The placement of banners and signs to give the event your identity on TV is extremely important (see figure 18.3). Opening and closing billboards, station breaks, interviews with your client on the air, and plugs by the announcer or commentator are also negotiable. So long as you exercise good taste and don't

Figure 18.3 Tennis pro, Bonnie Gadusek, competing in an Avon-sponsored tournament. The Avon logo encircles the court ensuring recognition in any photograph.

try to overreach in achieving corporate identity, the TV executives will generally be reasonable and a pleasure to work with. Unfortunately some major networks will try to deny you your legitimate requests for identity unless you purchase a substantial number of commercials. You should reserve to yourself the right to select or approve the on-the-air TV talent, and you should attend the production meeting held in advance of the event to insure that your requests have not been overlooked and have been communicated to those who have a need to know. The selection of a prominent and knowledgeable commentator will help you produce a "classy" event. The familiarity that such a person gains in working on your event may well pay dividends during other events throughout the year.

LAWYERS AND AGENTS

In drafting an agreement for a specific event, be it a one-night show or a multimillion dollar contract spanning several years, it is essential that you have legal assistance. Chances are that the people you will deal with across the table will have been involved in other events before and know all of the negotiating techniques or tricks of the trade. In some of the sports in which you may become involved, you will find lawyers who are criticized for wearing several hats. One might be an event owner, a TV producer, a sports announcer, players' agent, player association official, and attorney all in one. Some may construe these various involvements to be a conflict of interest. I do not feel that there is a conflict of interest so long as all the relationships are known and out on the table. I have never found in the seven years of promoting professional sports that these relationships were a hindrance in dealing with such individuals. Their expertise can often be helpful to you in achieving your objectives. In analyzing contracts prepared by attorneys who specialize in sports, player agents, and player association representatives, it is important to pay particular attention to the items which are not included in the contract and which have been left out. Such items pop up later and cause you trouble, surprises, and unanticipated expense. Be sure that everything you expect from the other party is clearly spelled out. There are several very large sports marketing firms which are very powerful in tennis and other sports and do an excellent job for their clients. There are many lesser known companies and attorneys in the business who represent players; they are equally well versed in the nuances of sports negotiations and serve their clients extremely well.

The lawyers and agents often get a percentage of the earnings of their player-client so it is in their best interest to drive hard bargains. While most prominent sports figures have agents, some still handle their own affairs or have a member of their family running their business. Often in negotiating with the larger firms you can work out a package arrangement including players, an event, and a TV broadcast. It is important that you talk with as many people as possible to gain knowledge of the particular sport you are considering, and always seek out a number of options. It boils down to doing your homework.

If you intend to become deeply involved in a sports promotion program on a continuing basis, it is important that you remain personally visible throughout the year and attend some of the industry fund-raising dinners and social events. For example, a lot of business concerning tennis is conducted during the U.S. Open and Wimbledon. That is why many people in the tennis business can be seen at these two events; and, generally, except for the semifinals and finals, many of them rarely watch the tennis matches. They are too busy socializing, politicking, gossiping, cutting deals, forming alliances, and seeking new business.

As you plan a sports event where prize money is involved, be sure to consult your corporate tax department or an outside tax attorney or CPA since there are tax ramifications in everything you do. There are requirements that a portion of the prize money be withheld for income tax purposes, especially in the case of non–U.S. players. There are complicated forms, and the amounts to be withheld may vary. In your contract you should state who is specifically responsible for these matters. If you use an outside firm to manage or produce the event, you must insist on a signed statement covering the sums of money withheld, where it was sent, and signed copies of the forms which were submitted to the government. Retain these documents for several years because such matters have been known to come back and haunt corporate sponsors years later, when the promoter may be unavailable and your client or corporation could face an unexpected financial liability. The same guidelines should apply to state and local taxes on the ticket sales, concession sales, and any other financial obligations.

STARS AND ATHLETES

Do not be fooled or misled into believing that merely sponsoring an event with large prize money will guarantee the appearance of top athletes and gain press exposure for your event. Money is often not enough, even when you are contributing hundreds of thousands of dollars to a prize money pool. It is a fact of life that some athletes do not like to visit certain cities or certain parts of the country. Others prefer not to perform in cold weather, and others who are wealthy only work a few weeks a year. In tennis, some top players fear that they do not do well indoors or on a particular surface, such as clay or grass. Some sports have so much money available, with events held 52 weeks a year, that the players can be very selective in deciding where they will perform. That is one reason why you must go out and get to know the players and their agents to gain their participation in your events. While we have never done this at Avon, I am aware that some athletes will demand appearance fees which may, or may not, be deductible from the prize purse, depending on your negotiations.

Placing all your hopes for a successful promotion on one or two superstar athletes can also be disastrous. Illness and injuries frequently occur. I have experienced this in both women's long-distance running and tennis. While Jerry Diamond and his staff at the Women's Tennis Association do a commendable job in meeting their contractual obligations, they cannot control illness or injuries to specific players. When our Avon Tennis Circuit was plagued with this problem, Martina Navratilova proved to be a true champion by filling in for others time and time again, as did Billie Jean King. They did not do this for money, but out of a sense of responsibility to the sponsor, their player association, and the tennis fans.

Some sports, unlike tennis, are starved for commercial support. Women's bowling, for one, is a very fertile area for corporate sponsorship.

The interest in many sports surged in 1984 with the Olympics in Los Angeles. An Olympic involvement can be a very special event. Many corporations wanted to get on the bandwagon in one way or another. Olympic involvement cost millions of dollars, and many who committed these large sums think it was a very worthwhile endeavor. Some corporations were in it, I am sure, to gain exposure, and others just to keep their competitors out. Women's sports in particular, according to the Women's Sports Foundation, are expected to experience a substantial growth in public popularity because of the 1984 Olympics. There are many nuances and legal considerations involved in Olympic sponsorship, and it is advisable to consult someone who has been involved in Olympic negotiations for advice. There are numerous committees, federations, agents, and associations with which you may have to deal.

PLANNING FOR ADVERSE PUBLICITY

Nothing can detract more from your event than serious injury to a participant or spectator. In spite of the fact that you might have a contract covering liability for injuries within a specific sports arena, theater, or other facility, you must be sure yourself that every possible safety precaution has been taken. I cannot describe the agony I experienced in 1974 during the first Avon Marathon, when we received a police radio report that one of our runners had been hit by a car and the extent of the injuries was unknown. As it later turned out, a spectator had stepped in front of a vehicle near the race course and suffered a broken leg. You can never be too careful in trying to prevent injuries or being prepared in advance to cope with a medical emergency. At the opening session of Avon's very first of over 100 successful tennis tournaments, there was a mixed professional-amateur team match. The dean of the local sportswriters participated and suffered a heart attack during the match. Luckily, as at all of our events, we had adequate medical staff standing by to provide lifesaving assistance. Whatever the special event, you must give adequate forethought to everything that might go wrong and be prepared to act quickly to minimize the effects of an unfortunate occurrence. Insurance is very important so be sure to consult someone who is an expert in such matters.

INNOVATION AND DETERMINATION

If you have a great idea, develop it to its fullest and never become discouraged or take "no" for an answer. Several years ago we decided it would be great to hold an international women's marathon through the downtown streets of London. Time and time again we were told it could not be done, and each time I told the staff to go back and make it happen. Finally, after several tries, we were able to get the cooperation of all the necessary parties and had an outstanding sporting event that garnered TV coverage throughout Europe and on TV networks in Canada and the United States. This was a bold idea at the time, but with persistence we broke the barrier and reaped the publicity and acclaim for being the first company to ever close the downtown streets of London for a sporting event. With enough determination and drive you will be amazed at what can be achieved in a special event and in a very cost-effective manner.

Creativity is important. Great ideas may come from anywhere within your company or agency, and you will be surprised at the creative genius or at least the germ of a great idea that might come from people at every level in your company. During a recent sales promotion event, we asked all our public relations staffers to come up with new promotional ideas. One of our new, young secretaries came up with several ideas which we used, including a special poem which she wrote that was printed and distributed to promote the event. She also wrote a song which we recorded and distributed on a cassette to enhance the event.

When seeking the "great idea," do not limit yourself to just the public relations people in your own group. Reach out to your friends in advertising, sales promotion, and marketing for creative ideas. Not only will this help you to have a better event, but it will make them feel a part of it as well. Let them feel they share in the success, and you will have gained a friend and a supporter. Since your prime goal is an overall success for your company or client, be sure to give credit where credit is due and make sure appropriate recognition is given to the individual who came up with the innovative idea. In this way, people will be more receptive to your suggestions in their area of responsibility, and you will avoid internal battles over "turf" or jurisdictional responsibility.

CORPORATE CLUTTER

There are some promoters of special events who encourage a proliferation of corporate sponsors or subsponsors of the same event to enable them to sell off part of the event for added revenue. Some corporations might not object to what we term "corporate clutter," but at Avon, the hallmark of all of our special events over the past 10 years has been exclusivity and continuity.

Where we have a choice we do not like to share the limelight with any other commercial sponsor. There are some situations where other corporate identity is unavoidable. For example, some athletes are locked into endorsement contracts requiring them to wear and advertise certain products. Some arenas, theaters, and stadiums have year-round contracts in which they have sold off the scoreboard, the clock, the programs, or other advertising space. It is important to determine well in advance any other preexisting contracts or arrangements. We have always sought a clean, cosmetic look for all of our banners, posters, backdrops, and other promotional materials. Being in the beauty business, this clean look helps to reinforce with the public our reputation for quality and style in our special events as well as with our products.

SPECIAL EVENTS IN THE INTERNATIONAL ARENA

Doing business in 32 countries, we have learned that almost all well-conceived special promotional events can be duplicated and adapted to overseas areas. This has been true of our women's awards program and our women's running program, which boasted 40 races in 17 countries in 1983. While there may be some need on occasion for slight modification in a program, our experience has been that if it works well in the United States, it probably will go well in the overseas markets. We also know of successful programs in other markets which have been brought back here to the United States with great success. When a program is new, there may be a reluctance on the part of local management to be the first in their country to back an event. The answer is to bring the skeptics to another country to view a successful event, which will normally make them converts. All the doubts and difficulties can be overcome with a proper orientation.

One of the major objections from overseas business associates is that obtaining favorable press for a special event is difficult in their country. In some cases they have said that commercial identity is never permitted on TV or in the press and is impossible without purchasing advertising or making some other financial arrangement with the press. We have found this not to be the case. Where you produce a monumental event, there is no way in the world they can ignore you. It is impossible for the press to ignore thousands of women, ages 7 to 80, running through the main streets of a city of any size, especially when they are wearing bright red Avon T-shirts. It is front-page news or will at least appear in the sports pages.

Unfortunately, throughout the world, most multinational corporations continue to suffer a negative press for being "aggressive," "insensitive," and "ethnocentric." This situation calls for sensitivity in presenting ideas, recommendations, and suggestions. I must stress the need to be diplomatic in communicating corporate programs, especially to your own subsidiaries.

We have to keep in mind that American attitudes, values, and business style do not necessarily apply in other countries. The whole concept of time is important to note. The concept of a deadline is nonexistent in some countries. Attitudes towards work or the work ethic also differ.

In whatever you do, seek local assistance. Where you do not have public relations professionals on your local in-house staff, hire a local or international public relations firm with a local affiliate or a local public relations person.

SPECIALIZED PRESS FOR SPECIAL EVENTS

To achieve the publicity goals surrounding your special event, you must allocate a substantial portion of your resources to developing the proper relationship with the press that is expected to cover your event. Their needs must be met to insure outstanding coverage. Where a sports event is involved, it is wise to consult with several newsmen who cover that particular sport to determine their specific needs. The needs of TV, radio, newspapers, and magazines are quite different, and you must insure that they are all satisfied. On numerous occasions we have used specialized local public relations agencies for most of the initial legwork in dealing with the local press since it is more efficient if the event will tour many cities. Although an on-the-road public relations expert is needed to travel with the event, there is a strong need to retain someone with local press contacts.

Mailing List Preparation

Months before the event is announced, mailing lists must be prepared and should not be limited to just sportswriters, since there are always other publicity opportunities of a nonsports nature. There are human interest angles; business angles; fashion, health, and food news pegs; and many others. If a large city is involved, the suburban dailies, weeklies, and free shopping news or penny savers should not be overlooked. At radio stations, the sports broadcasters and news desks are a must, but the hosts of the phone-in talk shows are also a fertile area for coverage to publicize your event. Once, some years ago, we appeared on a talk show in a small southern Florida city and had to fill in for two hours since only one call came in. This was fine since we were able to work in dozens of "plugs" publicizing the event, but it would have been better to have had some friends at home listening to the show and prepared to call in if calls were slow in coming. Then the event would have appeared to have a more exciting following and would have elicited more local interest and support. Television sportscasters, women's feature shows, and talk shows should also get the releases.

Local and regional magazines, and magazines that are placed in hotel rooms often give you months of exposure in their listing of coming events.

With attractive artwork, you can often arrange to get your event featured on the cover of such magazines. The magazine of the airlines serving the city where the event is to be held often has a calendar of events also.

Do not overlook the wire services, since they can help to create national and international recognition for your event. If there is no local bureau, file with the local wire service stringer.

News Releases

To promote your special event, a well-structured series of news releases is one of the most effective and efficient ways to reach the largest number of people in the shortest time. A master schedule of releases should be prepared months in advance. Releases should be sent out on a regular basis to establish continuity and build excitement. Such a schedule requires careful thought, and you have to know the deadlines of the various media since local magazines need much more lead time than other media outlets. In every release, regardless of the subject, always be sure to repeat the name of the event, the site, the date, and where tickets may be purchased. Action photos of the participants should be sent with the release—one with the athlete player in front of your logo would be even better. Most local TV stations will use a slide of the athlete if one is available, so have color slides prepared of both the player and your logo. You will often find it on the screen behind the newscaster during the newscasts.

Personal Contact

Close personal contact with each news media representative builds upon the foundation created by the news releases. You must have someone establishing him or herself with the media as a dependable, helpful, and honest source of information. Writers from magazines should be supplied regularly with feature ideas and angles, and key columnists should receive notes and features. Even if the athletes are not in the city yet, advance interviews can be set up by phone to help "hype" the event. Visits to television news directors should be used as an opportunity to provide them with slides of each athlete. Your event can often be the focus of a local or regional magazine or newspaper special supplement. A special supplement is possible no matter how large or how small a community. This is often attractive to the newspaper since it gives it an opportunity to go out and solicit ads from others involved in your event. Often, it looks to the sponsor to provide most of the text and the artwork. You should be aware that some journalists wear several hats. They might write for a daily paper, have a monthly magazine column, and serve as TV commentators. While all journalists should be helped in performing their job, it is important to determine who the "movers and shakers" are within the sportswriter and broadcaster group. In seven years of dealing with hundreds of sportswriters, I have developed a high regard for them with just two exceptions. In most cases, they are not likely to produce scandalous stories, but rather try to do a very professional job in writing about the sport. Most of them want to see the sport they cover thrive and succeed since they have a vested interest in the continuation of their employment as sportswriters. With the sports press, as long as you are straight and truthful with them, they will lean over backwards to cover your event fairly.

Advance Press Conference

A wonderful device to introduce your special event to the community is an advance press conference. If you can have athletes, celebrities, and politicians present at the conference, it enhances the event and adds importance to it. Such a press conference (see figure 18.4) can generate an enormous amount of advance publicity for your event and help increase ticket sales. If you can get one of the athletes or stars to come in for a few hours in advance of the event, you can usually schedule television talk shows and radio interviews in addition. On occasion in the past, we have worked with dozens of stars, including Billie Jean King, Chris Evert-Lloyd, Tracy Austin, Martina Navratilova, Pam Shriver, Evonne Goolagong, Andrea Jaeger, and others. On many occasions we only had a few hours of their time and were able to generate enormous amounts of coverage.

In the smaller cities, even an unknown athlete can be built into a star attraction and get extensive coverage.

At the press conference, of course, you must keep things fast moving and have complete press kits with abundant background information in case the press wants to do an in-depth feature story. Many TV personalities want to speak privately with the star for a few minutes to get an exclusive interview for their station with their own appearance on camera. This can easily be accomplished if it is all arranged in advance. You should also have on hand a videotape of the player in action since the stations might want to use this with voice-over on the newscast. Providing this tape for them can assure you of extra time on the air. If your logo appears in the background of the footage, it's an added bonus.

It is a nice gesture to provide a small memento of the press conference— a product that is related to the event in some way is appreciated. As a consumer goods company with over 700 items in our line, it is not difficult for us to select an appropriate product. Depending upon the time of day of the press conference, we will normally have appropriate refreshments available. It is important that the podium have a sign indicating the name of the event, as well as a backdrop behind the podium in a television interview area with

Figure 18.4 William J. Corbett, Avon Director of Public Relations, discusses upcoming media interviews with Chris Evert-Lloyd during a press conference promoting the Avon championship tennis event. A banner bearing the Avon championship logo appears in the background. The press kit cover utilizes the Avon name in a repeating pattern.

prominent mention of your company or client. It is better to repeat a small logo over and over again, rather than have one huge banner, since large lettering is lost when the photos are cropped down or when the TV cameras take a tight shot. This way your logo stays in the picture. You should also provide for a plug-in device to accommodate numerous "jacks" so that the reporters will not have to clutter up your podium or table with their microphones and recorders. Some will, however, want their microphones showing so that their call letters appear on television and in the paper, which is promotion for their stations. We once held a press conference where we had so much television coverage, with extra lighting and electrical requirements, that the electrical circuits became overheated and threatened to cause a fire. Always check in advance that there is an adequate electrical supply to avoid trouble and danger. When possible, the podium or table should be raised so that those in the back can see very clearly. Risers should also be provided for the television cameras so they can shoot over the heads of the press seated at the conference. If risers are not available, you should always have a center and side aisle for the TV cameras to have a clear view from the back and to give them room to maneuver.

Working Press Room

During your event, be it one night or a week-long tournament, the working press room will be the nerve center of the entire public relations operation. It is in this room that stories will be filed, information disseminated, and media requests filled. When you are planning an event, do not just assume that the existing press facilities will be adequate. Quite often they are not, and you will have to improvise by curtaining off storage areas, bringing in mobile homes or trailers, or setting up a press tent.

The room must be staffed at all times, almost around the clock, if your event is large enough. Even if the event is not scheduled until late afternoon or evening, someone should be there to answer the phone and serve the media who arrive early. There should be a large bulletin board with the event schedule, notices, results, statistics, times, etc. This saves your staff from answering the same questions over and over again.

At a large event, there should be a message center for the press, and while some will install their own telephone lines, an adequate number of phone lines must be provided. Once again, do not assume that every large and well-known sports arena will have adequate phone service. Often you must have phones installed yourself. Normally only local calls should be free, and most journalists will have credit cards or will reverse the charges. Many journalists carry with them lightweight, portable computer terminals to enable them to input by phone line to the computer at their publication. Phone lines and electrical outlets must be provided for this purpose. To avoid getting unnecessary calls in the press room, it is wise to make sure the building switchboard has a copy of the time schedule and ticket prices.

Equipment to be provided in the press room will include typewriters, copy machines, tables, telecopiers, and a large newspaper clipping board or bulletin board. In addition to all the fact sheets you provide, put up all the local newspaper stories pertaining to your tournament. Some of the reporters like to see their stories displayed, and it is impressive to show your visitors the coverage the event is generating. If your event is on television, several television sets should be placed around the press area.

Restrictions must be set up for the press area. Press, public relations staff, and athletes or stars should be the only ones permitted in the working press area. At tennis matches, lines people and officials will often drift into the press area to sample the food and to pick up information off the press table. Screen everyone who comes into the press or press interview room. You should always set up a mechanism to screen the press and to cull out those who inevitably surface when there is complimentary food, beverages, sample products, and an event to be watched free of charge. Do not be misled by looks though, since many sports journalists are very casual in their dress and demeanor.

At large events, a working photographer is often hired to deal with the still and motion picture photographers to insure that they are all equitably handled.

Interview Room

There should be a special room set up for the media to interview the athletes immediately after the event. The athlete will generally sit before a table during the postmatch press conference. Risers, sound systems, backdrops, and an adequate electrical supply system are important items not to be overlooked.

SPECIAL AWARDS DINNERS

Award dinners are a special-event technique used by many nonprofit or trade associations in raising funds to support their worthwhile programs. As a public relations person, you are no doubt going to become involved in many of these special events. You can take even the most modest participation in a dinner and make it a worthwhile promotion for your company or client.

First, a senior member of your management or your client might be asked to be the chairperson of such an event. If he or she accepts, they have the task of insuring that the event is both a social and financial success. Some charities have a very professional year-round staff which produces many such events and really only want to use the name of your client as a drawing card. They will ask little of him other than the use of his name. Other charities may have an outside firm to promote and manage the dinner. No matter what the situation, the public relations person is well advised to stay involved to protect the client's interest and reputation.

The next step is for your prestigious client to hold a small luncheon or cocktail party for other top corporate executives whom he wants to serve on the dinner committee with him to lend their prestige to the event and to insure that they purchase one or more tables. Realizing how busy senior corporate officials can be, the meetings are usually attended by others, often public relations staff persons who have been assigned to the project.

There are some people who will lend their names to almost anything. Some years ago when I used to review most of the dinner invitations sent to my company, I noted one person whose name was on almost all of them. Once we received two invitations for a dinner on the same date at two different hotels for two different charities from the same person. Once when I was on a dinner committee with this person, we discovered that he did not even buy a single ticket to the event. It seems that he probably only wanted the publicity of having his name on all of the invitations.

Another situation in which the public relations person becomes involved is when your client or your company is being honored at the dinner. Besides their good works, another reason for honoring such people or companies at these dinners is to insure the success of the dinner by selling tickets to their friends, employees, clients, suppliers, and customers. The person being honored also has an obligation to sell tickets to avoid the embarrassment of a small attendance, which might imply that the honoree is not an extremely popular person.

Some charities or professional organizers will have multiple awards, one for each company—sometimes as many as 50 or 100 at the same dinner. In this way, each company will take 10 or 20 tickets to insure that the event is a financial and social success, and to honor their employee or the company.

Some organizations will honor a government official, or a political figure, as the dinner attraction so that his or her supporters and friends will come. In addition to the money raised for the worthwhile cause, the government leaders profit from such events since they become identified with a worthy cause, have a picture in the local paper, and have another nice plaque to put in their waiting room or office to continually impress their visitors. Also, year after year, as the organization has its annual dinner, it usually prints a list of past recipients and past chairmen, thus putting your honoree or chairman on a list of illustrious people.

Very often an organization will take the current year's honoree and ask him to be the chairman of the dinner the following year. Also, this is reversed and the chairman of this year may be the honoree the following year.

When your client or company is involved, it is wise to check out the small details in advance. Many groups that sponsor such dinners are not "buttoned up" and are very disorganized. Insist on a written flow of events and script so that everyone knows the game plan well in advance. Have dais name cards and a dais list well in advance. Personally check out the sound system early on the day of the event so that you have time to make changes and upgrade the system, if necessary. Check the lighting in advance to be sure that your client will not be blinded and unable to read his speech. Insure that there is a light on the podium. Check months in advance on the audio-visual presentations since they might need professional help. Most of the chairpersons and honorees have been this route before, and are flexible and will know the drill. In any case, offer them a briefing if it will make them more at ease. They will also have more confidence that you are there doing your job and protecting their interests if you offer a briefing. Obtain the guest list in advance for your people to study so that they can refresh their recollection of the names and relationships of the guests. You should, as a public relations staffer, carefully review the list yourself since you are expected, as part of your job, to know who's who if asked. Help your client to feel at ease by making introductions and saying the other person's name just in case he or she has forgotten. Name tags are often lifesavers in this respect.

As a practical matter, the publicity value for such a dinner is quite limited unless you have a very famous person as the honoree. Certainly, your corporate internal newsletters will cover the event and the trade magazines will use it.

Since you have to buy some tickets anyway, why not offer them to the trade press to bring their spouses and to sit at your table. This makes it more likely that they will mention the event in their publication, and it will help you to get to know them better on a personal basis.

You might even consider producing a videotape of the event to send to your branches or overseas locations. When sending videotapes overseas, be sure to check your local management since they have different systems in different parts of the world, and it is sometimes less costly to make the conversion in the United States before shipping. Many countries will charge several hundred dollars in duty to import a finished tape.

A photo session should always be held prior to the reception which normally precedes the event so that press can get photos of the honoree and the chairman, and get the story into their papers in time for the next morning's deadline. All of the usual publicity techniques come into play here. The receipt of the award might well provide a vehicle to get the recipient on radio and television talk shows to talk about the organization and the client's activities.

If you represent a consumer goods company, you undoubtedly have seen hundreds of requests for merchandise for use as table favors for such dinners. This really has a very limited value from a publicity or promotional standpoint, but if your company is involved in a dinner, it is difficult to say no. If you decide to provide table favors, it is best to give small items as they are easier to place in a woman's purse or a man's pocket. Bulky items also clutter up the table all evening and get in the way. It is often wise to place the gifts on the table yourself; but when it is a huge dinner this is impossible, and the waiters, for an appropriate gratuity, will do this for you. Be sure to send enough products for each waiter to take one home and let the maitre'd know this in advance. This will help to insure that you will not have lots of products "walking away" and end up being without gifts for your guests. Occasionally you will have union problems if you try to distribute the gifts yourself.

In planning special-event dinners, you should think of the guests convenience in setting the dress requirements. In New York, for example, many of the executives who live in the suburbs attend numerous dinners each year. For a weekday dinner, formal dress is very inconvenient. It is not only the cost of the tuxedo, which most executives already have, but they may also have to rent a hotel room to change, and sometimes these accommodations can cost more than the dinner ticket. Formal dress is not as difficult on weekends, since people come from home and usually bring their spouses or dates.

Where dinners run very late, it often forces the suburbanites to stay overnight at a hotel, which adds to the cost of the event attendance. Having gone to hundreds of these dinners, I think it is imperative for public relations people to properly counsel their client that long speeches are not appreciated and really cause difficulty for a lot of people. I often look around at dinners when it reaches 10:00 P.M. and usually see a large number of people who are dozing or sleeping. The reason that they leave the houselights out most of the time at these dinners is probably so the speakers cannot really see how many people are not listening to the words of wisdom.

A situation in which you are only taking a table and are not otherwise involved in the dinner can also, with planning, be used to good advantage. You can consider using the tickets for some of your employees who do not usually get to go to such affairs, along with their spouses or dates. A night out at company expense is an added employee benefit which many of them appreciate and for some people it is a very special treat. You might also invite press friends to come with their spouses for a social evening and a nonworking event. Often, you can precede the dinner with cocktails for the people at your table. Seating should not be left to chance, and you should go early and put place cards at the seats so that you can have the proper mixing of your guests. It is also a nice gesture to have a small product gift or a memento of the evening to give to each of your guests. Be creative and it is possible to turn a routine dinner into a great social success.

CONCLUSION

In this chapter, we have covered in a very brief manner some selected techniques to use in presenting a special event. The opportunities in this area of public relations are limitless. Aim high—nothing is impossible with enough dedication, innovation, and funding. There is no question that a well-run special event can achieve many times the exposure and penetration of a similarly priced advertising campaign. The growth and proliferation of special events is proof that enlightened clients and management realize that this is one of the most worthwhile methods and techniques of promotion for their corporate identity and meeting their objectives.

19 FUND RAISING

Howard A. Rusk, Jr.

President, Chief Executive Officer
World Rehabilitation Fund

Fund raising and public relations exist in a tough world, and it is getting tougher all the time. The demand for the philanthropic dollar is at an all-time high. Nor is there any reason to expect that this competition will do anything but increase. Likewise, the competition to capture the public's attention and interest in order to convincingly present facts or a point of view is at an all-time high.

Faced with this reality, practitioners of both arts should, indeed, must join forces if they are to succeed in meeting their needs. I have presented several axioms which perhaps to some may appear to be obvious. But they are axioms that have proven their true merit for a very long time. The examples given from my own experience have borne them out. They should be your North Star in the planning and implementation of your programs. Using them as your guideline, innovative approaches, timeliness, and skillful execution will only add to your success.

FUND RAISING AND PUBLIC RELATIONS: A PARTNERSHIP

Any individual or organization that endeavors to raise funds on a systematic basis that ignores public relations does so at its own peril. By their very nature, these two functions are closely intertwined in a symbiotic relationship. The attempt to separate and/or exclude one from the other

---

Howard A. Rusk, Jr. became president and chief executive officer of the World Rehabilitation Fund in 1972. Prior to this, Mr. Rusk had his own firm which specialized in fund raising/management counsulting for clients in the health and social welfare fields.

He was a former vice president for Development and Alumni Relations at Columbia University reporting directly to the president. During that period, Columbia University established eight fundraising records.

Mr. Rusk has held various directorships at National Hypertension Association, the Churchill School, the American Association of Fundraising Counsel, Inc. He is a graduate of Harvard University.

places the operation in jeopardy and threatens the success of a campaign. If one accepts what I feel to be an axiom—that public relations and fund raising are inseparable—an important first step must be taken. This first step is as essential for public relations as it is for fund raising, and I am confident that it is a recurring theme throughout this book. That step is the need for careful in-depth planning.

In this process, it is necessary to define your objectives on both a short- and long-term basis. Only when this is done, can a comprehensive, cohesive plan evolve. Careful planning will enable an organization or institution to determine what its priorities are and how they should be ranked in order of importance.

It is at this point that the creative process begins to be concerned with how to meet these objectives. Planning will enable you to determine the organization of the fund-raising and public relations campaigns and how they interact. It will also determine what resources must be mobilized toward this end and will provide a timetable for implementation. From this, one can then logically and accurately determine how the campaigns should be staffed on a staged basis, and at what point staff and their skills will be required, and what volume of space, equipment, and supplies will be needed. After this planning is accomplished, realistic budgets and timetables can be projected.

If these tasks are carried out in a thoughtful, unbiased, and realistic way, the chances of success are greatly enhanced. On the other hand, if they are undertaken on a cavalier, egotistical, and/or naive basis, the campaigns will undoubtedly run into severe difficulties which can threaten a successful outcome.

Once this in-depth planning is accomplished, there is a second cardinal need which, again, is a recurrent theme and that is the need for effective communication. Your fund-raising and public relations campaigns must be presented to your leadership and the staff that will help carry out the programs. There must be a full and open discussion of what you intend to do and the reasons behind the decisions reached. Indeed, some of the key leaders should play an active role in the initial planning.

When this initial plan is presented to the larger public who will be involved in the campaigns, their views must be taken into consideration and, if need be, appropriate adjustments made. Your objective in all of this is to have a consensus of opinion, and a unified commitment and dedication to carry it out. It is essential that the leadership and staff see evidence that their views are valued, and that they have had a real and meaningful role in structuring the campaigns. Effective communication should impact to them the feeling that, as a member of the inner circle, they have played an important part in structuring the plan and they have a real responsibility to participate in it.

THE ROLE OF LEADERSHIP

In fund raising, as in public relations, the role of leadership is of utmost importance. A successful outcome of the program often hinges on who are selected to be spokespersons, what they say, when they say it, and whom they say it to. It is also important to select the right kind of leadership to be recruited to serve in a visible way on the board of trustees of the institution undertaking the campaign, the actual campaign committee itself, and the various subcommittees of the campaign such as special events, program, major gifts, and publicity.

In my view, one should always strive toward the objective of having the caliber of leadership be at the highest level. However, that leadership must have relevance to the cause and it can come from many sources. For example, when major universities contemplate large capital campaigns, they most frequently turn to their own boards of trustees and major alumni donors to fill the top positions in the campaign structure. In turn, the university officers and their professional staff work with this leadership in the selection of others to be recruited to serve the cause. Hopefully, the end result will be a prestigious and balanced group of individuals who have extensive outreach to a wide variety of publics, and also have the capability of giving and getting substantial gifts. In addition, they should have the capability of serving as respected spokespersons regarding the various objectives of the campaign and the importance of the acceptance and support of those objectives.

Again, careful planning and research on the activities and outreach of your leadership is of signal importance. Done properly, you will be able to pinpoint your targets and make campaign assignments in the most effective manner.

THE FIVE PARALLEL STEPS BETWEEN FUND RAISING AND PUBLIC RELATIONS

There is a striking parallel between the effective use of direct mail in fund raising and the effective use of public relations in shaping public opinion. Both utilize the same five principles in meeting their goals. For example, in raising funds by direct mail, the first objective is to make the readers aware of the need. Until this is accomplished, the rest of the process cannot take place. The same is true in public relations because an uninformed public may be in agreement with what you espouse, and yet they may harbor contrary opinions which might be based on misinformation or prejudice, or they may be totally uninformed on the issue.

The second challenge of direct mail is to gain the reader's interest. This can be achieved by providing the readers with information they may not have possessed and by providing one or more reasons why the cause has relevance to their lives. The same is true in public relations. When you have captured their interest, these individuals have taken in what you are trying to impart and they will automatically relate it to their own experience in a personal way.

The next objective is to gain the reader's real concern about the problem and the unmet needs underlying the cause. Now that the reader has an educated and personal opinion, he or she should be made to feel that the cause has a real importance. The same is true for public relations, because the amount of time and attention that readers attach to an issue is related in direct proportion to the amount of importance they give to it.

Once these objectives have been realized, the readers must be made to feel a personal commitment to the issue. They must feel a real desire to do something directly to effectuate change and to have a sense of urgency in doing so. To the public relations practitioners and fund raisers, the ability to put people in this frame of mind is a cherished goal.

Lastly, in direct mail, readers must be provided with the means to translate this commitment into action. And they must be informed of what the results of their action will be. In large-scale mail campaigns the most commonly used vehicle for this purpose is the business reply envelope. Since you are reaching the public in a way that allows no personal dialogue, great care is taken to facilitate the giving process. Postage is prepaid and the address is printed on the envelope. In most cases, the name and address of the donor is affixed to the envelope or the reply card, which also includes information on how to make out the check and a gift table in varying amounts that the donor can check off.

In the case of public relations, the final objective might merely be the swaying of public opinion. However, if action is deemed desirable, members of the public are informed on what they can do. Depending upon the desired objective, the action may be contacting a legislator, writing a letter, joining a committee, signing a petition or corporate proxy, attending a meeting or rally, purchasing a product.

While the techniques and degrees of success will vary, the underlying principles do not. They involve an individual's intellect, emotions, and experience in a logical and progressive process. They also demonstrate how intimately public relations and fund raising are intertwined. To separate them would be folly. Rather, the goal should be to have them work together as closely as possible.

THE POWER OF CREATIVE THINKING
FROM A SINGLE IDEA

A cardinal ingredient for success in combining fund raising and public relations is creative thinking. As in a successful marriage, the needs of both partners must be fulfilled. Each should have a real and abiding feeling that this relationship has true value and meaning. If this is accomplished, there will be an ongoing motivation to continue and deepen the relationship.

Two examples from my own experience demonstrate this point. Several years ago, I counseled a nonprofit client that was providing services for people with impaired speech and hearing. This institution was experiencing great difficulty in raising sufficient funds to meet their annual operating budget. Although the need for these services had been manifest for a long time, there had been no expansion or modernization of the client's program. In addition, the organization had a very limited visibility to the general public, the prospective donors, and the handicapped population it wanted to attract as patients.

Clearly, the reasons that the client came to me were to raise a great deal of money to support the institution's programs and to achieve greater visibility for its overall objectives. Knowing its past history, my challenge was to make a truly significant impact while providing a long-range source of income.

In analyzing these problems, it suddenly dawned on me that this client's greatest need could be summed up in one word—communication. Taking this insight to the next level, I then proceeded to try to determine how an effort could be organized by the institution to generate greater communication. Coupled with this was the question of who should be involved in this process who would also reap tangible benefits from the effort. It occurred to me that since speech and hearing are such a basic and integral part of communication, the ideal partner was the communications industry itself.

The next step in the creative process was resolving how this relationship should be structured. I came to the conclusion that the ideal platform would be to create a dinner at which the institution could present a Communications Award. The award would be given to a corporation or individuals who had made a significant contribution to assist the handicapped by means of communication.

The concept of the award was met with a great deal of enthusiasm by client's board of trustees. As a result, the first recipient of the award was the American Telephone & Telegraph Company. The dinner generated a good deal of favorable publicity, while at the same time bringing in a considerable amount of new monies from donors who had previously not been associated with the institution. These funds were then used for the provision of services to an expanded patient population.

I deliberately structured the Communications Award to become an annual event. Although no longer associated with the institution as the "father" of the idea, I am proud that the Communications Award continues to flourish to this day. Among the honorees in subsequent years on an individual basis have included Bob Hope, Richard Rodgers, Pearl Bailey, Beverly Sills, Alistair Cooke, Benny Goodman, and Danny Kaye. Some of the corporations being represented in the past decade are RCA, Time, Science Research Associates, Dow Jones, Mobil, Exxon, ABC, Chase Manhattan Bank, United Technologies Corporation, and ITT. With a lineup of such superpowers, it does not take much imagination to discern the outcome. Each year, hundreds of thousands of dollars are realized to aid those suffering with speech and hearing disabilities. Those corporations and individuals who have been actively involved in helping the handicapped have received national recognition for their efforts. As to the future, the Communications Award has achieved such stature that the honorees know that they are joining a group which must be categorized as first rank.

Here is another example of the power that can be created from a single idea. I represented a small U.S. committee of an international organization seeking support for the perpetuation of Dr. Albert Schweitzer's philosophy and ideals, and of the hospital he established in Gabon, Africa.

This committee had been in existence for many years. In the past it had received its funds in a traditional fashion, mainly from direct mail, gifts from a few concerned friends, and an occasional fund-raising luncheon or dinner. Their support base was relatively small and the funds raised were quite modest in comparison to the overall need.

As with the first example, the client needed a great deal of money because the committee wished to construct a surgery wing on the hospital for the rehabilitation of patients with leprosy.

It occurred to me that there might be a possibility of securing support from the U.S. government, which previously had never assisted Dr. Schweitzer's hospital.

I took the president of the committee to meet with a friend of mine who was an international lawyer of great renown. The lawyer saw merit in the idea and called his partner in Washington, who agreed that it was worth a try. On subsequent trips to Washington, we worked with this partner and a young lawyer from his firm in contacting key officials in the State Department and the White House. We met with Senator Edward Brooke of Massachusetts, who agreed to sponsor a bill in the Senate which would be included as part of the Appropriations Bill. He in turn got eleven of his fellow senators to cosponsor the bill. The result was an appropriation of $1 million for Dr. Schweitzer's hospital, with the grant administered by the U.S. Agency for International Development. To my knowledge, this was the first name-line appropriation for a non-U.S.-based organization in the history of the Foreign Assistance Act.

Because of the uniqueness of this event, I felt that there was an opportunity to generate publicity for the organization. Since President Nixon endorsed the bill and signed it, the committee gave the president a special award. On that occasion, there was considerable press in attendance, which resulted in coverage on network news as well as international wire services. Shortly thereafter, Senator Brooke was honored for his leadership role with a testimonial dinner in New York. This generated additional income and publicity for the cause.

While it took many months to accomplish all of this and a considerable amount of work, it all came about as a result of a single idea.

HOW LEADERSHIP CAN BE USED EFFECTIVELY

I once worked with a client that had a national program which dealt with alcoholism. This is a cause that has very strong emotions tied to it. The fact that alcoholism is a disease is not universally accepted. Further, there was and is a great deal of misinformation and in some cases a total lack of information about the disease on the part of the general public. Nor was there any general consensus about what should be done for alcoholics and their families.

What was known was the visible extent of the problem. Several millions of Americans were afflicted, with hundreds of thousands of people dying from alcoholism each year. The cost to industry due to illness, accidents, absenteeism, and miscalculation due to impaired judgment ran to several hundred million dollars annually.

Clearly a program on a very large scale needed to be launched as soon as possible. The organization noted that an earlier program involved worker education and detection of the alcoholic at the work site, coupled with medical intervention and counseling. This program had shown promising results. It was decided to promote this program on a national level. To reach this objective it was felt that a labor/management committee should be formed. George Meany, president of the AFL-CIO, and the newly retired president of General Motors, James Roche, agreed to serve as cochairmen of the committee. Recruitment was undertaken at the highest level, resulting in a blue ribbon committee of top leadership from the corporate world and within the labor movement.

Shortly after the committee was organized, a series of regional meetings and two national meetings were held. The purpose of these meetings was to formulate a detailed plan of action. Some seed money had come in during this period but not enough properly to do the job. At that point it was decided to undertake a joint public relations and fund-raising effort in which the members of the committee could flex its considerable muscle.

Members of Congress and key government leaders involved with our health care delivery system were contacted and wherever possible visited personally. Complete details of the program and how it was to be implemented were presented. This intensive phase of education and solicitation lasted for several weeks, culminating in a request by the government to make a formal presentation. This resulted in a four-year grant in excess of $3 million from the National Institute of Alcohol and Alcohol Abuse.

This example shows how leadership can play an important role in a critical phase of a campaign. But leadership cannot function in a vacuum. The other important axioms I have alluded to earlier were activated to make success possible. Careful in-depth planning involved the leadership where they could play an important role in formulating policy. Recruitment was at the highest level, and those selected had a relevance to the cause. All of these factors helped make that one grant a reality.

In some cases leadership of a campaign can revolve around one man. One client had a project which included securing American support for the restoration of one of the world's most revered cathedrals. I had a banker friend who had worked with me on an earlier campaign and felt he would be interested in this program. I paid him a visit and told him what we wanted to accomplish. He agreed to lead the campaign. Then he said, "I don't want any formal committee and meetings. I can do the job here in New York but I've got some friends in other parts of the country who can help out too."

We discussed which major metropolitan areas should be involved and what their quota for the American campaign should be. He then took from his desk a directory of members of a banking association and matched cities with friends. In all, he made 16 calls and got 16 acceptances from his fellow bankers. From that point on, the fund raising was coordinated by telephone and mail. Publicity for the campaign was handled with the public relations officers in the 16 cities involved in the campaign. There they used their own press contacts. This resulted in very good local coverage.

This illustrates again the importance of choosing the right caliber of leadership and imparting a sense of what you are trying to do. There must be intimate involvement. Although the major catalytic force for this campaign was just one man, it demonstrates the importance of selecting dedicated people who have sufficient outreach to contact those who have the capability of giving or raising substantial funds.

THE ROLE OF TELEVISION

Television is probably the most powerful tool available to communicate with the public. It is indeed true that sometimes a picture is worth a thousand words. Television is an effective means for some charities graphically to portray their work. But it is not suitable for every organization.

Some of the larger charities employ telethons as a means of raising money. However, before proceeding with this type of fund-raising activity a word of caution is needed. Telethons are expensive to run. Organizations need large, well-trained staffs to run them. Securing advance gifts which will be announced on the air takes place over many months prior to the event. The charity itself must be highly visible, known, and accepted by the general public. The charity should have one or more celebrities who are dedicated to the cause and will give generously to it, as in the case of Jerry Lewis and Danny Thomas. While telethons can raise large sums of monies, they are not the answer for most organizations.

A considerable number of charities utilize public service announcements. These spot announcements run for 10, 30, and 60 seconds. The most commonly used spots are 30-second spots. It is very difficult to impart much information in that period of time. Further, since these announcements run between program segments, the viewer can be distracted.

Realistically, charities should hope that the spot will gain the awareness, attention, and perhaps the concern of the viewer. It has been my experience that the elements of commitment and action are not implemented by the viewer of public service announcements to any marked degree. The one exception to this general statement is a crisis in which the viewer is already at the level of commitment and wants to act. However, public service announcements are a good way for a charity to tell its story. If they can be tied into other fund-raising activities such as mailings or door-to-door solicitation drives, they can be helpful.

If an organization is fortunate enough to be aired as a special, as a segment of a show, or even have professional news crews film it, this can be very effective. For example, Howard K. Smith did a short film for an organization which was helping to rehabilitate disabled people. This organization showed the film at their annual dinner and a testimonial luncheon. It received standing ovations on both occasions because it showed exactly what could be done for disabled people in a very moving way that words alone could not accomplish.

For the most part, I feel that the role of television should be utilized more for its public relations and education values than for fund raising. But it is a powerful reinforcement to a fund-raising campaign.

THE IMPORTANCE OF THE SELECTION OF A SPOKESPERSON

In fund raising as in public relations, great care should be taken in the selection of your spokesperson. Some years ago a small college in the Middle West wanted to create a fitting memorial to Sir Winston Churchill because it was on the site of that college that he delivered his famous "Iron Curtain" address.

Because Sir Winston was such a widely respected world leader, it was decided that direct mail would be an effective means of raising funds for this program. The selection of the right spokesperson, in this case the letter signer, was a key element to success.

In thinking about the problem, I felt that the signer should have the same attributes as Sir Winston. That is, he should be widely recognized and respected. At that time, the pollsters identified a small group of leaders whom the American public held in highest respect. Among them was an individual who I thought would be the ideal spokesperson. I went to see him and he agreed to lend his name to the cause. The ensuing campaign provided the major source of revenue to complete successfully the memorial to Churchill. I feel it was due in large measure to its spokesperson. The signer was news commentator Walter Cronkite.

THE EFFECTIVENESS OF NEW APPROACHES

Early in my career, I was employed by a firm whose founder demonstrated the power of using public relations effectively to reach concerned people. He created a vehicle by which funds could be raised on a major scale. He was the first person to use full-page newspaper ads for nonprofit organizations.

One of the reasons for the success of this technique is that it follows the five principles of direct mail, that is, awareness, interest, concern, commitment, and action. These ads were generally placed on a tie-in to a crisis of some magnitude. A clear example of this is the Hungarian Revolution. Most Americans were shocked and angered by this turn of events. They were also frustrated because of their perceived inability to do something about it. Our firm represented an organization which at the time was supplying relief services to refugees from all over the world. A few days after the Hungarian Revolution broke out, we ran newspaper ads informing the American public about the work of this organization and told them what effect their support would have. Most important of all, our ads told them how and where they could respond. The result was an unbelievable outpouring of support for the organization, because now the American public had been provided with the means to take action.

In addition, these ads for this organization were reproduced and used as enclosures for large-scale direct mail campaigns. At that time, this also was a new approach because it combined two ways of reaching the public, newspapers and letters, into one fund-raising activity. It is rather commonplace now to see such ads; success has many imitators.

FUND RAISING FROM THE CORPORATE POINT OF VIEW

With the current sharp cutback in government spending, philanthropic institutions have been forced to turn their fund-raising attention to the private sector with ever-increasing intensity. In the past few years, several national groups have been mobilized to exert such pressure on corporations to increase their charitable giving and with noticeable results. However, these increases are truly inadequate to close the gap.

As a result of the increased demand for support, many corporations are taking a much closer look at their giving practices as they relate to corporate management objectives. A policy of general support is being replaced with more specific guidelines concerning what type of programs corporations will support and under what conditions. Contribution committees are more sensitive to the relevance of their charitable support and how it relates to the services to be rendered, as well as to geographic location and impact. There is a greater emphasis on employee–matching gifts programs because of the desired multiplier effect of the corporate gift. This policy promulgates the concept that both employer and employee are supporting causes they both deem worthwhile.

Another trend is the desire to increase corporate visibility in positive ways. Support is increasing for projects that further the image of a corporation as sensitive and responsive to important needs; programs that are innovative and forward thinking, timely and pertinent to corporate objectives are receiving more favorable consideration.

In turn, fund raisers must be more sensitive to corporate public relations as it relates to philanthropy. The good fund raisers are doing just that. Careful planning and research again are the hallmarks of success. Existing or contemplated programs are matched more closely to corporate guidelines. More donors and prospects are identified with their corporate connections and urged to participate in matching gift opportunities. Campaign leaders are being briefed in more detail on what to ask for and why their proposal merits support.

Increasingly, both the charity and the corporation realize the value of working in partnership to bring their actions to the public's eye in a positive way. Media of all types, promotions, special events, and other means are being employed to increase exposure to a greater extent than ever before. Not only does this increased visibility benefit both groups, it often generates further support from other sources. In effect, the one and one of public relations and fund raising become three.

SUMMARY

I would like to end with the thought stated at the beginning. Public relations and fund raising are intertwined in a symbiosis and they are inseparable. To ignore this fact is at your own peril. To build and strengthen this relationship can only reap benefits for all.

CHAPTER
20

RESEARCH

Peter Finn

Chairman

Mary-Kay Harrity

Director of Development
Research & Forecasts, Inc.

It has been said that public relations executives rely too heavily on their instincts in planning and evaluating their programs and not enough on the scientific tools at their disposal. Others argue that research is unnecessary in public relations—that it is too expensive and often only confirms intuitive beliefs.

The public relations community seems evenly split between these two points of view. A survey of top communications executives at Fortune 1,000 companies revealed that 48 percent use public relations research, while 52 percent do not.

The most serious objection to public relations research appears to be its cost. If a corporation is ready to spend $50,000, $100,000, or more on a communications program, does it make sense to add $25–35,000 up front to

---

Peter Finn, chairman, directs overall operations for Research & Forecasts, Inc., as well as major research projects. He has guided Research & Forecasts from a small division of Ruder, Finn & Rotman into one of the leading communications research organizations in the country.

Mr. Finn has led Research & Forecasts in pioneering the merging of public relations thinking and research techniques to solve complex communications problems. He has a master's degree from Columbia University.

Mary-Kay Harrity, director of development and communications, has worked as a newspaper and radio reporter. She has also anchored a weekly TV news show on Connecticut public television. As a reporter she specialized in business, health, and environmental reporting.

Ms. Harrity coordinates new business planning and communications activities at Research & Forecasts. She is an active member in Women in Communications and has a B.A. degree from Emmanuel College.

help plan that program? What about a similar amount for postprogram evaluation?

Many practitioners believe that the money would be better spent on another program or hiring a staff member to follow through on existing programs. Many others realize, however, that $25,000 can actually save $100,000 if used for research that directs a professional to *effective* programs—and away from costly, misguided ones.

There is, of course, no easy answer to the question of whether public relations research is essential for program planning and evaluation. What many people fail to recognize is that research can assist public relations in a variety of ways. Before you decide if research is appropriate in any given circumstance, you should understand the different research applications.

AUDITS

The most popular type of public relations research is the audit. A recent Research & Forecasts study shows that two of every three Fortune 1,000 public relations directors who use research say that they have conducted financial relations audits (68%) and employee relations audits (67%). Virtually all of them report that these audits are useful.

An audit is a survey of a company's key audiences. In attempting to respond to perceived or actual problems, or simply to target a communications program to a particular audience, top executives usually rely on their own perceptions, which sometimes are based on faulty or insufficient information. An audit will accurately identify problems and suggest possible solutions because it draws conclusions directly from interviews with the audiences of special concern to the corporation. Among the groups that might be surveyed are financial analysts, journalists, a company's own employees, a segment of the general public, professionals, and community leaders.

There are at least four circumstances under which a public relations manager might decide that an audit would be useful.

1. When there is a new CEO or top public relations executive, an audit can familiarize the new executive with perceptions of the company among key audiences. Such an introduction to the company clarifies public relations goals, thereby indicating the potential value of existing and proposed public relations programs.
2. When the senior public relations executive is planning a particular program, an audit can provide management with a detailed portrait of external perceptions that indicate a need for the planned program.
3. When there is a dramatic change in a company's financial condition, management structure, or overall business strategy, an audit of the

financial community can provide insight into how these changes are likely to affect analysts' recommendations regarding the company's stock. In such situations, an audit of the media also can offer important information on how these developments will ultimately be perceived.

4. When employee dissatisfaction surfaces, whether subtly or openly as in a strike situation, an audit can determine how deepseated the dissatisfaction is and can identify both the cause of the problems and potential solutions.

5. When a periodic measurement of progress or a reassessment is needed for either a particular public relations program or a particular audience, an audit can serve as the measurement tool.

Since a public relations audit is a serious inventory of key audiences, the research design and techniques will vary with each situation. Most frequently, an audit is a problem solver. Its twin objectives are to uncover *why* a communications breakdown has occurred and to point the way to public relations programs that will correct the problem.

Several years ago, an audit helped a major chemical producer in Louisiana overcome the stone wall it ran into when trying to communicate with the local community. The company had weathered a recent strike, compounded by a subsequent negative National Labor Relations Board ruling on charges of an illegal lockout. Needless to say, the company's relationship with the community, which had never been the best, only deteriorated further.

Alert to the healing power of good communications, top management decided to initiate a badly needed public relations program. They had some assumptions about what the community's feelings were and the approach the new program should take, but they could ill afford false starts. To assure themselves that public relations efforts would open up communications, the company wanted to know in advance how local residents would react to different messages and programs.

They commissioned an audit to give them the necessary information. The research was designed to pinpoint the issues that most bothered the community's opinion-shapers, because their reaction to the company was followed closely by the general public. Community members were surveyed by telephone to check for additional, unexpected popular concerns. The leaders' and community's expectations of the company were also explored.

The audit conclusions surprised them and confirmed their wisdom in gathering planning data before launching a community relations campaign. Before the audit, they had reasoned that economics were the principal concern in the area. Since the company was bringing in many jobs, that aspect was to be featured in company communications to offset the impact of the earlier strike.

Fortunately, management waited for the audit results, which informed them that the community was really upset over environmental issues and worried whether the chemical plant was a polluter. In addition, the community wanted the company, a division of a larger corporation "up North," to act in the Southern tradition and to sponsor social and civic events.

The chemical manufacturer shifted its community affairs focus from jobs to the environment, successfully turning around the negative community sentiment.

Without the audit information, the company would have poured time and money into well-intentioned programs sending the wrong messages. No matter how clearly employment facts and figures were packaged and transmitted to the community, the company's attempts to communicate with local audiences would have been a frustrating experience. The audit directed the way to meaningful and *cost-effective* public relations.

It may not be difficult to appreciate that research may be required to discover what external audiences think about a company, but what about internal constituencies? Is a formal audit necessary to find out how managers and nonmanagement staff think? Sometimes the closer we are to a key public, the less clearly we see and hear them.

In the case of a major insurance carrier in the Midwest, a structured internal audit assisted management in fighting a general lack of enthusiasm among its staff and its community. Senior executives were at a loss to explain why employee morale appeared low and the community seemed cool to the firm—and looked to an audit to determine why.

The audit, utilizing qualitative research techniques (i.e., in-depth interviews), first investigated what senior managers expected the staff and community to think about the firm, and then what employees and community leaders actually thought. The gap was startling.

The company's decision makers had assumed that the company's "good works"—its behavior as a model corporate citizen and especially its new downtown headquarters built as part of the urban recovery effort—spoke for themselves about the company's commitment to the area. Not true.

The audit revealed that the company's low visibility, which was also a company trademark, was undercutting the impact of its community activity. Employees had little sense of the company's identity or pride in belonging to a well-regarded organization.

Judging their employees as the firm's most important ambassadors to the community, management realized that the first public relations program must be conducted in-house before other group's attitudes were considered.

Always keep in mind as you design or commission an audit that information is worthless unless you know how you will be able to make it actionable. Every audit report ought to conclude with a statement of what the findings mean for your operations as well as recommendations for follow-up action.

PUBLIC ISSUE STUDIES

One of the most exciting types of public relations research, the public issue study, is ironically one of the most neglected. Unlike other research techniques, public issue studies *become* public relations programs. This relatively new research tool is used to generate widespread attention for its sponsor.

Possibly because of their newness, public issue study programs appear to be a foreign concept to most practitioners. Since they have impressive potential for creating news events and ongoing media coverage, these programs should be familiar to all communications professionals.

Beyond publicity, an issue study can position an organization in a unique way before elite audiences as well as the general public. Each study delves into a major issue confronting the public, policy makers, and the press, offering them fresh information on the subject. This places the sponsoring organization in the enviable and credible role of authority on a topic that concerns its business or perhaps its chief executive.

Versatility is one of the most significant benefits of a public issue study. If the research has included several sample groups and probed a variety of attitudes and opinions, the results will generate innumerable news story angles appealing to the general press and specialized publications. In addition, the findings can be presented at press conferences and in radio interviews, by-lined executive articles, speeches for top management, booklets, ad copy, and other outlets. Each exposure of the study to a key audience, especially in the media, gives a "third-party" endorsement to the organization's effort in undertaking the study.

Like an audit, a public issue study can be developed as the basis for a comprehensive public relations campaign or to meet a single-problem situation.

Miller Brewing Company looked to its recently released study *The Miller Lite Report on American Attitudes toward Sports 1983* as an umbrella program that would reinforce the company's identification with team sports. For years, Miller had been highlighting sports personalities in its advertising and underwriting sporting events across the United States. And it was generally recognized that Miller was "a" sports-minded company. Now it was time to consolidate that position and become "the" sports-minded company.

No other national study of Americans' relationship with sports had been conducted since 1929, when the Carnegie Institute released its study *American College Athletics*, based on personal interviews with players and coaches. The *Miller Report* presents the results of over 1,000 interviews with a representative sample of American adults, and additional interviews with teenagers, sports reporters, coaches, and physicians specializing in sports medicine. Sports issues such as sports as a family activity, the role of competition, opportunities for women and minorities, and athletic violence were included.

The *Miller Report* was released at a New York press conference that attracted reporters from publications as diverse as the *New York Times*, *Reader's Digest*, *Working Woman*, and *TV Guide* and electronic media such as ABC Radio Sports, CBS Sports TV, WNBC-TV News, and USA Cable. The subsequent coverage was nationwide, positive, and continuing. Feature stories appeared in publications ranging from *Sports Illustrated* to the United Airlines in-flight magazine, articles in newspapers from the *San Francisco Chronicle* to the *Chicago Tribune*, the *Miami Herald*, and the *Boston Herald*. More important, the study became a reference almost immediately for sports journalists writing about a range of sports topics.

Complaints of bias and glibness often prevent a fair hearing among policy makers for a corporation involved with a sensitive national issue. The corporation's viewpoint, no matter how fact based or thoughtful, is dismissed because of presumed "special pleading." A serious study on the issue in question can open positive communications between the corporation and leaders deciding national policy.

In the midst of heated national debate over U.S. environmental policies, The Continental Group, Inc., commissioned a landmark study to disseminate new, objective perspectives on the basic controversy: how to balance economic progress and environmental protection. As an international company with divisions in packaging, forest products, energy, and insurance, The Continental Group had long manifested its commitment to environmental conservation.

Determined to provide a catalyst to better understanding of the trade-offs necessary in settling questions involving natural resources and economic growth, the company initiated a study of the attitudes of the general public, business executives, and environmentalists towards these issues. The study revealed that most Americans seek to balance economic and environmental considerations, even if balanced growth means moderating extreme economic and environmental objectives.

A distinguished advisory panel guided the project so that it focused on the most salient facets of the environmental debate. More importantly, these individuals brought a range of expert insights to the study development and analysis. Their involvement was a significant factor in producing a landmark study. The panel included Gerard Piel, president and publisher of *Scientific American*; Ruth Hinerfeld, past president of the League of Women Voters; Jay Iselin, president, WNET/Channel 13; Riley Dunlap, associate professor of sociology, Washington State University; William D. Blair, president of the Nature Conservancy; Zachary Morfogen, director of cultural affairs, Time, Inc.; Harlan Cleveland, director of the Hubert H. Humphrey Institute of Public Affairs; Michael Sovern, president of Columbia University; Thomas D. Nicholson, director of the American Museum of Natural History; and Seymour Martin Lipset, professor of political science and sociology, Stanford University.

To provide a well-rounded view of environmental/economic concerns, the study entailed interviews with a scientific sample of over 1,300 adults, over 260 top executives from Fortune 500 companies as well as smaller businesses, and 343 members of four major environmental advocacy groups. On-site examinations of five U.S. communities—Smyrna, Tenn., Montpelier, Vt., Seattle, Wash., Phoenix, Ariz., and Columbus, Ohio—were conducted to study how residents and community leaders had dealt with real decisions on environmental/economic trade-offs. In total, more than one million "bits" of data were collected for the study and interpreted using intricate statistical procedures.

More than 60 journalists from major print and electronic news organizations attended the New York press conference announcing the study results. Intended as an program to spark new discussion of the need for balance in environmental planning, the study was featured on editorial pages in over 40 newspapers across the nation, and news stories appeared in publications such as the *New York Times, Wall Street Journal, Washington Post, Los Angeles Times, Chicago Tribune, New York Daily News,* and *USA Today,* as well as other metropolitan dailies and weeklies. National magazines and trade periodicals also covered the study, which has relevance for all segments of the national population.

Since its release, the study has become source material for journalists, and S. Bruce Smart, chairman and chief executive officer of The Continental Group, has been frequently quoted in articles on environmental matters.

Leaders in business and government have recognized The Continental Group's efforts and the importance of the study itself. Two company executives and the research project director were invited to the White House to discuss the findings of the report with members of the Office of Policy Development and with representatives of Vice President George Bush.

The National Science Foundation distributed information about the study to the scientific community, key influentials in the environmental debate, by citing the report in the Foundation publication *Science Indicators.*

PLANNING AND CONDUCTING A STUDY

The first question that must be answered in planning a research effort is whether or not it should be handled in-house. There are several factors which come into play in making this decision:

- Do you have a budget for an outside firm?
- Does anyone on your staff have research expertise including questionnaire design, sampling, data collection quality control, and survey analysis?

- Will those who have the expertise be able to give enough priority to the project to ensure that it is monitored carefully and is not consistently put aside for other projects?
- Is there any danger that survey participants will not be completely open in the interviews because they feel they are not speaking to an objective third party?

Costs can of course be kept quite low if the project is handled in-house. There is a much greater risk, however, that some serious flaw in the methodology or lack of objectivity in the questionnaire design, data collection, and analysis will make the results unusable. If no one on staff has the experience to detect such problems, you run the risk of making policy decisions based on incorrect information. It is without a doubt safer to utilize an outside firm with the required expertise and objectivity.

If you do contract with a research firm, it is essential that you work closely with those directing the project to ensure that they fully understand both your objectives and the subtleties of your organization's communications environment.

Whether you are conducting the study in-house or working with an outside research house, you should have a thorough understanding of how a study is planned and carried out. A full-scale research effort involves the following basic steps:

- Planning the study and setting objectives
- Determining groups to be surveyed, data collection method, and sample sizes
- Background research and exploratory interviews
- Questionnaire design
- Questionnaire pretesting
- Data collection
- Computer analysis
- Report preparation

A small-scale research effort may only involve a few of these steps. An informal qualitative community relations study, for instance, may entail only giving some thought to the study objectives, making notes on the questions you want to ask, meeting with or talking on the phone with a few community leaders, and preparing a written summary of your conclusions. This could take from a few hours to a few days. A serious research effort, by contrast, can take from a few months to a year, depending upon the number of audiences surveyed and the depth of the interviews and analysis.

OBJECTIVES

Only you can determine your objectives. *This is the most critical stage of a research effort.* If you don't articulate the objectives at the outset, it is unlikely that the final product will be satisfactory and useful. You may find that outside research consultants can help you clarify your objectives based upon their experience with other organizations and a discussion with you of your specific needs. Be sure, however, that before the study begins you have a detailed, written statement of objectives that everyone involved with the project agrees are realistic.

SAMPLE

After agreeing upon objectives, it is easy to select the audiences. Be sure if any special criteria are required for a respondent to qualify, that these are taken into consideration when the study is designed. If you are doing a financial analysts' survey, for example, you will want to interview only analysts who are familiar with your company. Starting off with a general survey of all analysts following your industry may leave you discovering too late that you have to discard half of the interviews because 50 percent of the analysts were unable to answer questions specifically about your company. The percent of those who qualify to be interviewed in a particular audience can significantly affect the data collection costs. Whether you are using an outside firm or not, you should give careful consideration to this factor.

Another important decision that has to be made in the study planning phase is how large the sample should be. There are two factors that are important in determining the sample size. One is the degree of accuracy required, and the other is whether or not you want to analyze the responses of subgroups within the given population.

If you are planning an employee survey, for instance, and want the results to be fairly precise, you should plan for a sample of approximately 500. This will give you results with a maximum margin of error of 4.5 percent. This means that if 45 percent of the employees surveyed say they feel your company doesn't really care for them as individuals, the results from asking this question of *all* employees would be no more than 49.5 percent and no less than 40.5 percent (see table 20.1 for estimate given other sample sizes).

PRETESTS

Since it is often difficult to estimate what percent of a population will qualify when doing quantitative research, it is often useful to do pretest

TABLE 20.1   MARGIN OF ERROR TABLE: ESTIMATED SAMPLING ERROR FOR A BINOMIAL (95 PERCENT CONFIDENCE LEVEL)*

Sample size	Binomial Percentage Distribution				
	50/50	60/40	70/30	80/20	90/10
100	10	9.8	9.2	8	6
200	7.1	6.9	6.5	5.7	4.2
300	5.8	5.7	5.3	4.6	3.5
400	5	4.9	4.6	4	3
500	4.5	4.4	4.1	3.6	2.7
600	4.1	4	3.7	3.3	2.4
700	3.8	3.7	3.5	3	2.3
800	3.5	3.5	3.2	2.8	2.1
900	3.3	3.3	3.1	2.7	2
1000	3.2	3.1	2.9	2.5	1.9
1100	3	3	2.8	2.4	1.8
1200	2.9	2.8	2.6	2.3	1.7
1300	2.8	2.7	2.5	2.2	1.7
1400	2.7	2.6	2.4	2.1	1.6
1500	2.6	2.5	2.4	2.1	1.5
1600	2.5	2.4	2.3	2	1.5
1700	2.4	2.4	2.2	1.9	1.5
1800	2.4	2.3	2.2	1.9	1.4
1900	2.3	2.2	2.1	1.8	1.4
2000	2.2	2.2	2	1.8	1.3

* How to use this table: Find the intersection between the sample size and the approximate percentage distribution of the binomial in the sample. The number appearing at this intersection represents the estimated sampling error, at the 95% confidence level, expressed in percentage points (plus or minus).

Example: In a sample of 400 respondents, 60% answer "Yes" and 40% answer "No." The sampling error is estimated at plus or minus 4.9 percentage points. The confidence interval, then, is between 55.1% and 64.9%. We would estimate (95% confidence) that the proportion of the total population who would say "Yes" is somewhere within that interval.

interviews. This consists of doing 5 or 10 test interviews. If you must eliminate 10 people to find 10 qualified individuals for the pretest interviews, you have some basis for projecting the incidence (the percent of an audience that will meet your criteria).

Pretest interviews also will give you an idea of how long each interview is likely to run. If the survey is to be conducted by phone, the interview length has a direct relationship to your expense costs. Pretesting will also give you an idea of how many interviews can be completed per hour, thereby indicating how many interviewers you will need for how many hours. This will most likely affect your timetable, which you prepared in the study planning phase.

If you know that you need to analyze separately the responses of male and female employees or black and white employees, you may well have to increase the sample size beyond 500. If Black employees represent only 10 percent in a sample of 500, then you will end up with only 50 Blacks in your survey. You will probably want to increase this number to at least 100, giving you a margin of error of 10 percent. If greater accuracy is needed, it may be desirable to increase the size of the Black portion of the sample even more.

If the number of Black employees in the sample is increased to 100, this doesn't mean that the entire sample of employees must be increased from 500 to 1,000. You can use a process called oversampling to augment the sample segment of Black employees. If the data is collected by phone during the oversampling, you can use opening questions called "screeners" to eliminate all non Black respondents. This will allow you to supplement the number of interviews with Black employees so that you have a number large enough to analyze statistically.

You won't want Black employees to be overrepresented, however, when you are reporting on the results of the employees as a whole. This means that the Black portion of the sample should be weighted down in the computer analysis to correspond to its true percentage of your employees. This same process could be used if you wanted to oversample males or females, middle-level executives, secretaries, assembly line workers, or any other subgroup. If you are unfamiliar with oversampling and weighting the results, it is unwise to try these procedures without the guidance of research professionals with the necessary experience.

GETTING THE STUDY STARTED

Background research is indispensable, whether you are designing an audit for use in planning a public relations program or an issue study to publicize your company. Only the most significant issues under consideration should be covered in a survey questionnaire. Clear objectives will assist the development of a good questionnaire because extraneous topics will be easy to recognize and delete. This is helpful but not sufficient for devising the most effective or interesting survey. To guarantee that your survey will probe pertinent subjects, additional preliminary work is required.

While preparing for a press relations audit, you might want to have two or three freewheeling, presurvey interviews with editors. If they indicate that a hastily canceled press briefing a year ago left a bad impression of your company, and you had planned to question reporters only on their view of your financial reports, you would have failed to probe an issue that may be doing more damage than you would have ever imagined. Whether the canceled briefing is affecting your relationship with the majority of journalists is something you can expect to uncover from the larger survey—if you know ahead of time to include that topic in the questionnaire.

For a public issue study, background research is essential. A study intended for public release to establish both the credibility and authority of your organization must offer opinion-leaders and the public new information. That will happen only if the study begins where the latest data stops. A thorough literature review and interviews with experts can pinpoint the salient aspects of your topic; they can protect you from duplicating others' research while allowing you to build on the most recent research findings in your subject area. The value, and the media coverage, of your public issue study will be in direct proportion to the fresh insights and perspectives you bring to the study report.

QUESTIONNAIRE DESIGN

Once the background research is completed, the questionnaire design begins in earnest. Draft questions will have already emerged from the literature you have read and from interviews with experts in the field. The construction of the actual questionnaire, however, is a precise, technical process. The simplest questions are often the hardest to frame so that everyone being interviewed will understand what is being asked and the response options.

Consider this question: "How many children do you have living in your household?" If the respondent lives with her sister and they both have children, does she give the interviewer the number of her children only? Or all the children in the house? If you want to know the total number, it would be safer to phrase the question: "How many children are there in your household?" A good questionnaire will be objective, unambiguous, and easy to administer.

Pretesting plays an important role in ferreting out any questionnaire items that might be troublesome in the full survey. Through testing and refining, the final questionnaire should meet the criteria for an unbiased survey instrument. Once formatted, the questionnaire must be properly coded before the survey so that the responses can be quickly processed and analyzed by computer.

DATA COLLECTION

In public relations research, data is generally collected through telephone interviews or mail surveys. If telephone data gathering is used, interviewers should be trained carefully with each new survey instrument. Even highly skilled interviewers will have questions about a new survey form. No matter how experienced and efficient the interviewing team, the data collection should be continuously monitored by a supervisor who can spot and correct problems in administering the questionnaire. This is crucial to maintaining quality throughout the data collection.

Special procedures are needed during the data collection to produce a statistically valid, projectable sample. At least four callbacks should be made to those who resisted participating or who failed to complete an interview because they were too busy or could not be reached because of a busy signal or no answer. If the sample list was drawn up as a randomly selected sample, deviating from the callback procedure will compromise the representativeness of the sample and the survey results.

Mail surveys are often used in surveys with groups which are difficult to contact by phone, for example, airline pilots, whose home addresses may be available through a trade organization but who do not work in one location. A serious drawback to mail surveys is the inability to control the representativeness of the sample. Since those who return survey forms may be significantly different than those who don't, there is no way to determine how the broad range of group members react to the survey topic. Mail surveys usually take much longer to complete than phone surveys and frequently require incentives and repeat mailings to generate enough responses to analyze with precision.

COMPUTER ANALYSIS

There are two major categories of analysis for quantitative studies, that is, studies designed to produce statistically valid findings: frequencies and cross-tabulations. Frequencies (also called marginals) give you the percentage tally of all those in the sample who answered a question the same way. For example, if an employees' survey asked how well informed employees thought they were about the company's goals, the survey frequencies might show that 58 percent thought they were very well informed, 20 percent believed they were somewhat well informed, 19 percent responded that they were uninformed, and 3 percent had no opinion.

If this were the full picture, the company might reasonably feel that its employee communications program was on track. However, when the answers of those who had been with the company varying lengths of time are compared, a far different picture may emerge. For example, if workers with fewer than five years on the job made up 80 percent of those who felt they were less than very well informed, and this same group also reported a high degree of dissatisfaction with their work, the results would indicate the need for some corrective action. Management might consider a new communications program targeted to that group to stem their discontent before it caused high turnover and low productivity.

Although this analysis can be conducted without a special computer program, advances in survey research make it impractical to do so. The public relations professional can learn a wealth of information if the raw survey results are analyzed by sophisticated computer techniques.

In major public issue studies, the computer analysis can and should produce truly fascinating and intriguing results. Procedures such as multivariate analysis and regression analysis can construct scales or models of beliefs or opinions that help to explain in depth why people behave the way they do.

STUDY REPORTS

The study report is a summary of all the work that has been done during your research project. A comprehensive and useful study report will document the objectives that gave rise to the project, the study's findings and how they meet the objectives, and the research methodology.

At the conclusion of an audit, the report should explain how the results relate to your goals and what they suggest for program evaluation or future planning. Senior management will look for a solid connection between your plans for effective public relations programs and the expenditures for research. Therefore, the report should be as concrete as possible in its recommendations.

The report for a public issue study should be simultaneously enlightening and entertaining. Since these reports are generally distributed widely to leadership groups, the press, and public, the major findings arising from the statistical results need to be explained clearly and precisely so that the casual reader will grasp fully the study's implications.

Graphics are extremely useful in helping readers to understand the research. Media placement is also facilitated by camera-ready tables and charts illustrating your study news releases.

CONCLUSION

What we have discussed here is not whether public relations professionals can operate without research. They can. The critical point is that they can operate better—more effectively, efficiently, and economically—with research.

Research techniques developed expressly for communications are contributing much to public relations as a profession. For many reasons, there is no turning back to program planning without research. With mass audiences breaking down into far narrower segments, each with its own interests and concerns, research is the only certain method for knowing that a communications program will reach its target. Audiences, narrow or broad, are increasingly savvy about the communications process. They have less and less patience with messages that do not speak to them in their own language about issues of importance in their lives.

Moreover, as public relations functions become more specialized, research will be vital for providing reliable information to professionals who do not have ongoing, direct contact with their organization's key publics.

Whichever research format or methodology you choose for planning programs or creating them, there are two ground rules for public relations research: (1) without a commitment within your organization to act on the research results, the most exact and valuable information will be wasted; and (2) research is only as reliable as the procedures used. Misapplied techniques or careless data analysis can be more harmful than helpful, directing staff time and resources to ineffective programs.

PART

III

HOW PUBLIC RELATIONS IS MANAGED

An Overview

Chester Burger

President
Chester Burger & Company, Inc.

Long ago, some of the public relations pioneers established a pattern of operations that persists to this day. They emphasized action, imagination, daring, improvisation. The best of them produced results that satisfied those who paid the bills.

But while their results satisfied clients and employers, their methodology didn't. These people showed little interest in meticulous planning, careful budgeting, cost controls, and the like. Business management was missing from public relations programs.

The corporate financial executive, the manufacturing executive, or the personnel executive, of course, wondered why public relations couldn't be managed as any other discipline was managed. To ease their disquiet, some public relations professionals thereupon resorted to mystique to cover their

Chester Burger founded the management communications consulting firm bearing his name in 1964 and has counseled senior management of many leading companies.

Mr. Burger's career in communications began in radio and television at CBS. He organized the network's original television news operations and served as national manager of CBS Television News. He was writer-producer for the "Omnibus" series for the Ford Foundation.

Among his many awards are the Distinguished Service Citation of the United Negro College Fund. He serves as a member of the National Panel of Arbitrators of the American Arbitration Association. He is also one of the few men elected to membership in Women in Communications. His five published books include *The Chief Executive*.

lack of interest in management. They got away with it for a long time, not being held to standards of accountability. But finally, improvisation became a liability. The very mystique they propagated caused management to regard public relations people as somehow outside the normal range of management disciplines and therefore limited in their growth potential within the company.

Times have changed. The best public relations professionals now pride themselves on their ability to manage prudently. Public relations firms, which once emphasized their creativity, now emphasize to prospective clients not only their creativity but their careful use of clients' funds, their management control, and their accountability.

I remember more than one occasion when the heads of large public relations agencies lacked information (except "seat of the pants" guesses) as to whether any particular client program was being executed on schedule and according to budget. I recall another case in which a counseling firm's owner had not studied his financial results for almost a year. And I recall many cases in which heads of corporate public relations departments simply didn't know whether their principal activities matched management's expectations.

So we've included a whole section on the subject of planning, administering, budgeting, and evaluating public relations. The authors write from extensive management experience, having won acceptance as part of the senior management teams in their corporation. In the case of AT&T's pioneering work in measurement and evaluation, you'll find a complete report on the most advanced and sophisticated techniques yet employed in the public relations field.

Good management doesn't impair good public relations; it enhances its effectiveness. Our experience convinces Bill Cantor and me that you should pay attention to the content equal to the attention you pay to the management of your work. Emphasizing one over the other marks an amateur, a person without a future in a world of increasing professionalism.

PLANNING

Quentin J. Hietpas

Vice President of Public Relations
Control Data Corporation

Whenever I approach the planning process I remember the dialogue in Lewis Carroll's *Alice in Wonderland* when Alice came face to face with the pussy cat.

> "Cheshire Puss," she began, rather timidly, "would you tell me, please, which way I ought to walk from here?"
> "That depends a good deal on where you want to get to," said the Cat.
> "I don't much care where," said Alice.
> "Then it doesn't matter which way you walk," said the Cat.

Alice's dilemma applies to public relations planning. Planning builds a path from the start of a communications project to its completion. So it's important that you have good planning skills.

The definition of public relations I like best is: A *planned effort* to influence public opinion through good conduct and based on two-way communication. Note the emphasis: "planned effort."

Planning is a management necessity in successful corporations. Most businesses routinely assemble five-year plans—including support planning down to the lowest operating rungs. But sometimes public relations operates in a vacuum, in response to events or emergencies, without much thought to carefully planning for desired results.

Quentin J. Hietpas is vice president of public relations for Control Data Corporation. He previously held similar positions at The Pillsbury Company, International Multifoods, Apache Corporation, and Data 100. Mr. Hietpas is an attorney, a former newspaperman, and an accredited member of the Public Relations Society of America. He served for two years in the U.S. Air Force; and for the past eight years he has been adjunct professor of journalism at the College of St. Thomas, St. Paul, Minnesota, teaching public relations.

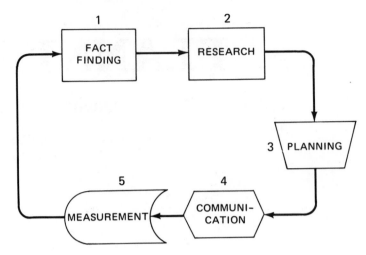

Figure 21.1   The programming cycle.

THE PROGRAMMING PROCESS

Planning is one of five steps (see figure 21.1) that should be followed in devising any overall communications program. Let's suppose you're a public relations counselor and are asked to conduct a program for a client.

You would start by doing basic *fact finding* (listening) about the client—its charter, products, markets, audiences, competition, corporate and marketing objectives, and strategies behind those objectives.

Then you would do careful *research*. Research determines the base for your plan. Remember, public relations is "a planned effort to influence public opinion" and you're seeking to neutralize hostile opinions, retain favorable opinions, or sway unformed opinions in your favor. However, you must first learn what those opinions are. You must be a good listener to collect the necessary feedback for your plan. That's what research is—good listening.

Then you would carefully do *planning* for the program—based on your fact finding and research.

Next, you would implement that plan—*communication*.

Finally, you would evaluate results achieved against desired objectives—*measurement*.

Let's focus on the third step—how to devise a public relations plan. The following model (see figure 21.2) has proved successful hundreds of times at Control Data Corporation.

PLANNING: A SUGGESTED APPROACH

An *overview* at the beginning should emphasize results of your fact finding and research. It will set the stage for the actual planning process.

A good way to remember the basic steps of this process is to borrow from a lesson journalism students learn in their first writing course: a complete story must answer who, what, when, where, why, and how.

By rearranging those five Ws and an H into a slightly different order, you have a simple checklist for public relations planning. The checklist can be used when structuring a short-range plan (for a single communications project), or for broader one-year or five-year plans. Here are the steps:

Why am I communicating? This means setting good *objectives*. It's important to know where you're going and to remember that you never communicate for communication's sake. By starting with meaningful objectives—and making sure that everything in the plan relates to those objectives—you will ensure that your plan is heading in the right direction.

Who do I want to reach? This means careful analysis of your publics. A big mistake in the planning process is not carefully determining who you want to reach.

Where will I communicate the messages? This means selecting the media you will use.

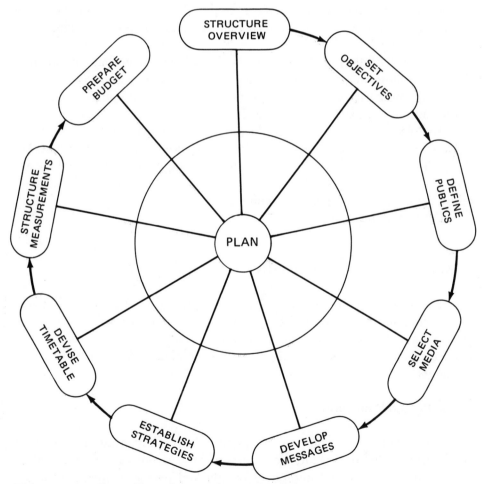

Figure 21.2 The public relations planning model.

What do I want to say? This means key messages or copy points that will be incorporated into the communications that result from the plan. This process determines images and positioning.

How will I say it? This becomes your strategy, supported by a series of action-oriented communications programs.

When will I communicate? This becomes the timetable. Timing can mean success or failure of a program. The timetable disciplines the entire plan.

So there you are. Whether it's a simple one-time communications project (such as a special event), or whether it's a full-blown, long-range plan, you won't go wrong if you carefully answer those six questions. Two additional elements are needed to complete the plan:

Measurements should follow the timetable. Measurement techniques will enable you to evaluate your results against your objectives.

Budget should be added at the end, after all the other steps have been completed.

To sum up, the major elements of the planning process are: (1) overview, (2) objectives, (3) publics, (4) media, (5) messages, (6) strategy, (7) timetable, (8) measurements, and (9) budget.

If carefully followed, these steps will produce a plan that should stand the test of close management scrutiny. The real secret is to carefully and thoroughly prepare each of the steps in written format. A good format to use is the outline approach: I, A, 1, a, (1), (a).

The plan is a communications document between you and your boss, and between you and your subordinates. It's a commitment to accomplish certain things in a certain time and in a certain way. The plan gives symmetry and body to your entire program. If not carefully written—or if it lacks time, effort, and creative thought—it won't be effective.

Let's examine each step.

STRUCTURING THE OVERVIEW

The overview is the prelude to the guts of the plan—the bridge between fact finding and research, and the plan itself. It is where you make certain your communication with the organization you are serving is sound— particularly as it relates to assumptions and problems. The overview has five elements.

Strengths and Weaknesses

Understand the strong selling points of your organization, client, or product. Equally important, be aware of any weaknesses that might be perceived by your target audiences or attacked by the competition or the media. Strengths and weaknesses should manifest themselves during fact finding and research. It's important to put strengths and weaknesses in writing—debate them, if necessary, for consensus.

Company Objectives

If the plan is to be effective, it must be geared to one or more of the client's objectives. Top-level managers of well-run corporations make every action they take relate to their corporations' goals. Public relations people should be no different—they should be in the mainstream of where the organization is going.

Actually, it is from this part of the planning process that the definition of public relations planning takes shape: *Public relations planning begins by determining the organization's objectives; then it relates those objectives to the interests and concerns of the organization's audiences; and then it uses communications strategies to influence public opinion to achieve those objectives.*

How do you determine your organization's objectives? Many companies have plans with five-year, ten-year, or even longer-term objectives—and they have one-year plans with short-term objectives. If you work for an organization that doesn't have clearly delineated objectives, it's up to you to clarify them for your planning.

Carefully determining those objectives—and then relating your planning to them—will be recognized by top management and will help build your credibility.

Results of Research

At this point in the plan, a succinct recap of audience attitudes and opinions—as determined from your research—can be spelled out. It's here you determine whether opinions need to be swayed, retained, or neutralized. It's here that the bridge between research and planning takes place. It's from this segment that messages will be developed and audiences prioritized at a later stage.

Assumptions

Remember, the plan should facilitate communication between the planner and the boss/client. It's important that assumptions be clarified early in the planning process. For example, make sure the program will have necessary funding. Determine what is being requested of you as opposed to others in the organization. Address conditions beyond your control. A host of similar questions can be cleared up in this part of the planning process.

Problems

You should know from your fact finding which problems might need special attention—problems that might impede success of the plan. Put them in writing early so agreement can be reached. A discussion might bring to the surface other problems not touched on through your fact finding.

SETTING OBJECTIVES

Setting objectives is a painstaking process. In the words of pussy cat to Alice, you are determining "where you want to get to." It's what you strive to achieve. Yet public relations people too often treat this phase of planning in a cavalier fashion. Objectives in many plans are merely general statements of goals. Be specific. It takes a lot of thought to write a good objective.

Remember, it's usually the achievement of the objective that determines in your client's mind whether your plan has been successful.

An effective plan spins off the objectives agreed on by you and your client. A good objective should meet six criteria and be:

Related to overall objective(s) of the organization. A meaningful plan contributes to the organization's success. Test your objective against your organization's, as defined in the overview. Objectives must relate directly to every communication you produce. Again, never communicate for communication's sake.

Improvement oriented. Obviously, the plan is attempting to achieve improvement over something—for example, a 10 percent increase in sales leads; a 15 percent gain in productivity. Improvement factors should be clearly stated in the objective.

Clearly defined. The objective must be free of ambiguities.

Specific. The objective must be specific. Generalities have no place in a good objective. Quantify. Be specific. It would be too general if an objective merely said "...to avoid mass resignations." By elaborating it to "...hold turnover of employees to 4 percent during the six months following the announcement" is an objective capable of measurement.

Measurable. If the objective is to be evaluated at the end of the planning cycle—after communications have taken place—you must be able to say to your boss: "Yes, I achieved what I set out to achieve," or "No, I fell short." That will be possible only if clear measurement is built into the objective. Measurement should be quantified and should be ascribed to a specific time period.

Attainable. Inexperienced public relations planners will too often frame an objective in such broad terms that it's impossible to achieve. When they realize they can't accomplish it, they lose interest and the whole program flounders. For this reason, make certain you evaluate the objective for attainability, but allow enough "stretch" to make accomplishing it an achievement.

How do you apply these criteria? Here's an example:

About a dozen years ago, an organization in a suburban city was established to counsel teenagers with their problems. The organization hired several professional counselors, but needed funds to maintain operations and to grow.

The organization's objectives—the first year—were to raise $100,000 and to double its case load. The organization received a commitment from business leaders, who said they would match contributions from private citizens on a five-to-one basis.

As the public relations plan was put together, these objectives were set:

- Raise $20,000 from private citizens in the community by January 1.
- Double the case load to a minimum of 50 cases by the end of the planning year, November 30.

Note how these two objectives met the six criteria of good objectives:

Related to organization's overall objectives: There was a clear relationship between the plan's objectives and the organization's overall objectives: to raise $100,000 and to double the case load.

Improvement oriented: Private citizens in the community had contributed nothing thus far, so there was obvious improvement orientation from $0 to $20,000; and there was also an improvement orientation in terms of case load—from 25 to 50.

Clearly defined and specific: The two objectives left no doubt about what had to be accomplished. No generalities or ambiguities existed in either objective.

Measurable: At the end of the communications phase of the program, there would be little doubt whether the objectives had been attained— $20,000 would or would not be raised by January 1; the case load would or would not be doubled by November 30. Note how those objectives were quantified to avoid ambiguity in the measurement and how they were ascribed to specific periods of time.

Attainable: At the program's outset, the planner felt the objectives were attainable. Would results prove him correct? The communications program—writing, printing, and mailing brochures to every home in the community—succeeded in getting the necessary level of citizen contributions. And the case load at the end of the year had increased to 65. Thus, attainability existed in both objectives.

In summary, take time to frame objectives and carefully test them against the above criteria. Then discuss the objectives thoroughly with your boss/client to make sure expectations on both sides are understood.

Now you are ready to proceed with your plan.

DEFINING TARGET PUBLICS

Once objectives have been set, you can determine the publics or audiences you will try to influence.

Howard Hill, once regarded as the world's greatest hunter with bow and arrow, was quoted: "Unless you know your game's feeding, sleeping, and daily habits, unless you plan your hunt in great detail and follow your plan with precision, you are not hunting at all. You are merely walking in the woods."

That's what audience analysis is all about. Effective communications relates the organization's objectives to the interests and concerns of its publics. Your publics don't give a damn about your objectives—or the objectives of your organization—unless they can identify them with *their* interests and concerns.

Know your public. What is a public? It's a group of people with common interests who are affected by the acts of an institution or whose acts affect that institution.

To accomplish the plan's objectives, you must be specific about the publics you want to reach. The following process (see figure 21.3) may guide you:

First, avoid the "general public." It's almost impossible to define interests and concerns of the broad and amorphous "general public." Howard Hill would say, "You are merely walking in the woods" if you try.

Second, define broad audience categories that affect your institution or that are affected by your institution. This is where audience analysis really begins. On a large blackboard categorize broad audiences which affect your institution or whose opinions are affected by the institution.

Using Control Data as an example, its acts and policies affect such broad audiences as 58,000 employees, some 300 communities and 50 countries in which it operates, investors, and thousands of customers. There are many more audiences too. The acts and opinions of those audiences, in turn, can affect the corporation. For example, if the corporation doesn't perform well, its investors may become dissatisfied and sell their stock.

Third, break broad audience categories into smaller, more definable groups. Remember, the more specific you are in defining your audiences, the better you will know their concerns and interests—and the better you will communicate. For example, we can narrow the broad "employees" category into "clerical," "general management," "sales management," "sales force," "research employees," "production workers," and so on. Those categories

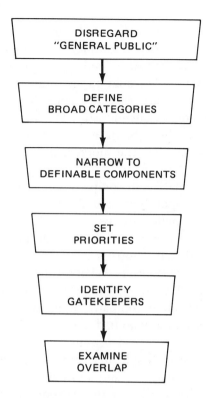

Figure 21.3 The audience selection model.

can be narrowed even more. For example, "production workers in large cities" and "production workers in small communities." Each of those smaller groups has different interests and concerns.

Careful analysis at this stage will allow you to better aim your communications "arrow" at as specific an audience target as possible.

An example may help. One young electronics company had very specific needs to raise capital. Its initial focus was on its broad "investor" category. Then it narrowed that category to "current stockholders" and "potential stockholders," "large institutions," "debenture holders," and "security analysts."

Another company—planning a product publicity program—narrowed customers into various users of its products.

All that effort is obviously aimed at a later step in the planning process, selecting the proper media to reach your target publics.

Fourth, set priorities. Who's most important? This step is crucial for success of the audience selection process. No matter how many resources you have at your disposal, it's virtually impossible to address each of the audiences you've identified.

Realize that you not only won't be able to do everything you want to do, but that it's better to do a few things and do them well. At this point, you should zero in on one or two—three at the most—key audiences. Explain why they should be high priority. Example: one company—in its plans for a merger announcement—narrowed its employee audience until determining that its sales force of 300 people would be the number one priority audience. The company's explanation was: "Research consistently shows that our sales force is considered the best in our industry. We know recruiters from other companies are trying to lure them away. Thus, the sales force must understand not only reasons for the merger, but also how the merger will benefit them."

Another example is that small company mentioned previously that was eager to get additional operating capital. As it narrowed its "investor" category to increasingly smaller groups, it identified security analysts as its number one target. Why? Because analysts could have enormous influence on how investors viewed that company.

Fifth, identify the gatekeepers. What's referred to here are opinion-leaders—people others follow. If you can pursuade them, they will influence others. That's what that small company in need of future capital did. It selected 50 analysts, by name, who had ability to influence their colleagues because of their reputation as specialists in the electronics industry.

Think how that decision made it easier for the company to focus on media selection, message analysis, and strategies.

That principle was applied by another corporation that sold its products to doctors. In looking over its customer lists, it found a well-known surgeon who was regarded by his colleagues as one of the best physicians in the country. The company made him a special target—a gatekeeper or opinion-leader—and used him as a spokesman to endorse its products in special by-line articles in medical publications.

Sixth, examine overlap. People are often members of different and overlapping publics. The fastest way to lose credibility is to address a message to one audience that is different from—or conflicting with—a message addressed to another audience.

One company, with many employee shareholders, forgot that principle. In its company newspaper, it told employees how it regretted the layoff of several hundred employees because of recession. Yet, in its quarterly report, the company boasted about the substantial savings realized through reductions of "almost 1,000 people since the beginning of the year." The two messages not only had conflicting facts, but conflicting tones—apologetic in one case, braggadocian in the other. That company lost credibility with employee stockholders who read both messages and with security analysts who might have read the company newspaper.

SELECTING TARGET MEDIA

After defining and prioritizing your publics, you can begin the important step of media selection. Public relations people too often focus only on external broadcast or print media. Actually, you should follow a much broader approach.

Certainly media includes newspapers, magazines, television, and radio. But it can equally include a letter, a conversation (suppose I want to convince the president of my company to change his course of action?), a payroll stuffer, a speech, or an audio-visual presentation.

Carefully examine the advantages and disadvantages of two types of media channels: controlled and uncontrolled. There are times when the need for pretesting and presenting a message "exactly right" mandates a controlled channel. There are other times when the need to have an objective viewpoint—as reflected in a newspaper editorial or magazine feature— dictates the use of an uncontrolled channel. Frequently, a combination of the two—controlled and uncontrolled—is the answer. Here are some factors to consider regarding this choice.

Controlled media channels: The sender has complete control over the message.

The advantages are (1) control; (2) high planning content, which allows the sender of the message to say it "just right"; (3) timing, which permits the sender to time the message to the day—or in some cases, hour, or minute —desired; (4) the opportunity to pretest the effectiveness of the message by trying it out on a group of people—perhaps in a focus group.

The disadvantages of controlled media are (1) the message has less credibility because the receiver knows the sender controls content and timing; (2) there is the realization that the sender is probably presenting only a particular viewpoint; and (3) the time and cost is often greater.

Important controlled channels often overlooked by public relations planners are media and direct mail advertising, audio-visual presentations, trade show appearances, letters, management bulletins, bulletin boards, and the grapevine.

At Control Data, we consciously team advertising professionals with public relations professionals to prepare communications plans. They consider such controlled media as formal word-of-mouth (speeches), which can be completely controlled; informal word-of-mouth; and face-to-face meetings— including luncheons with editors or visits with community leaders, where the objective is to persuade and where there is instant feedback through facial expressions and voice inflections.

Institutional advertising is growing rapidly as a public relations medium—and is highly successful when control is extremely important.

At Control Data, we began using institutional advertising several years ago to supplement our corporate public relations efforts. Advertising became the principal medium used to carefully position the company with certain target audiences. Now we use publicity to supplement that advertising.

Uncontrolled media channels: The sender has little or no control over the message. Examples are a radio or television news conference, or a magazine or newspaper interview.

Advantages of uncontrolled media are (1) objectivity—the receiver of the message knows it was filtered through a news reporter and editor; (2) it might be easier in some cases, because the reporter does much of the work; and (3) in many cases it is less costly and takes less time.

Disadvantages are (1) there is greater chance for error; (2) there is an inability to plan how the message appears; (3) timing is problematic and you can't be sure the message will ever appear; and (4) it is difficult to pretest the effectiveness of the message.

Uncontrolled channels require special publicity placement and news media relations skills. The rewards can be great in terms of the added objectivity that a well-placed editorial, feature aritcle, or television spot can bring to the strategy. However, distortion is possible if the publicist isn't skillful in media relations techniques.

There are many aids for selecting external media, including the *Editor and Publisher Yearbook*, *Ayer Directory of Publications*, and *Working Press of the Nation*. Those publications help determine readership qualities of daily and weekly newspapers, and consumer and trade magazines. The *Standard Rate and Data Service*, *AP Broadcast Services*, *Hudson's Directory*, and *Bacon's Publicity Checker*—along with a host of other directories—are also invaluable in media selection.

The needs of your project might indicate that you use more specialized directories: *Bacon's International Publicity Checker*, *Burrelle's Special Groups Media Directory* (minority audiences), or the *Directory of College Students Press*.

Regional directories also are available in most cities and states that list local media. Listing of TV talk shows, syndicated columnists, or government publications are also available.

It takes time, thought, and creativity to select the best media for the plan—judgments shouldn't be superficial.

The same process used for selecting public(s)—as defined above—should be used for media selection. Begin with brainstorming all possible media and gradually narrow options until final media are selected.

When considering, for example, "uncontrolled media magazines," you need to know which magazines are read by your target publics. (That capital-seeking company could place a feature article in *Institutional Investor* magazine, which is read by the security analysts who were chosen as the target public.)

Or, when considering controlled media, informal word-of-mouth, face-to-face meetings, or small group meetings might be another way of reaching those analysts—as might a controlled direct mail program.

All of those considerations come together when strategies and messages are formulated later in the plan. It's important in the media selection process that you delay final decisions—make only preliminary selections—until messages and strategy are devised. Then finalize your media selection.

DEVELOPING THE MESSAGE

When objectives have been set, publics have been identified and prioritized, and decisions about media have been made, you can focus on the messages to be communicated.

Consider three principles when defining the message.

First, never forget you're seeking to influence public opinion—that's the primary objective of public relations.

Second, remember you're seeking to create a particular kind of image. Good images are fragile and must be carefully nurtured. A good friend once said to me in another context: "Those who are lucky enough to catch a rainbow must be very careful to protect its fragility." That's good advice for creating and maintaining an image for your organization, client, or product.

Third, to be understood, your message must relate to the interests and concerns of your audiences—before a light can go on for communication to happen, your public must be able to identify its needs in your message. The following guide might help in the message section of your plan.

First, determine what people think of you. Your message will be worthless unless you know how your publics perceive you. That information should be available from your fact finding and research (and should be spelled out in the overview at the start of the plan).

For example, consumer research showed that a food company was regarded as having old management and as being production oriented, stodgy, inept at planning, and unpredictable in terms of annual profits.

Second, establish what you actually are. In the example above, the company made changes in management, philosophy, and in its approach to the marketplace—all of which began to produce exciting results, both in terms of marketing mix and improved profits. However, because the public didn't perceive those changes in the marketplace, perceptions and actuality were markedly different.

Third, establish your desired image. The concepts your client wants communicated to its key publics should be put in writing. Use succinct image statements with the phrase: "We want to be thought of as . . ." For example, "We want to be thought of as a company that is changing and diversifying into a variety of new consumer-oriented products." Frame those statements carefully—and get client approval—because they will be the basis for the next step.

Fourth, reduce image statements to key words. Key words and phrases should be visually and vocally appealing, and should be repeated over and over in the media selected.

Key words for the food company example above might be: "changing," "new," "turnaround," "new products," "consumer focus," "marketing oriented," "consistent profits" (utilizing percentages of increase). Those key words and concepts would be used in speeches, company literature, preinterview briefings, news releases, prepared Q&As, fact sheets, position papers, brochures, ads, direct mail pieces, annual meetings, annual and interim reports—in all the media selected to reach the target publics.

Frequent communication of key words will slowly but surely change old images and build new ones. However, they should be part of thoughtfully conceived communications strategies that emphasize frequency—and reach—of the messages to be communicated.

ESTABLISHING THE STRATEGY

All of the above steps have laid the foundation for establishing the strategy—objectives have been set, publics have been identified and prioritized, media has been analyzed, and messages have been formulated.

The strategy will make all of that come to life.

The creativity of the planner is especially crucial. Effective strategy must have *action* built into it—it must make things happen that relate to the plan's objectives. Amateur planners get carried away creating their strategy and forget that the purpose of the plan is to accomplish certain very specific, measurable goals.

Strategy has two parts—a summary statement (of the strategy), which should be brief; and a series of detailed action programs.

A company that decided to close two of its factories—in two cities— because of declining profits, said in its *strategy statement*: "All measures must be taken to treat affected employees as fairly as possible. Measures should include new benefit programs, liberalization of retirement and severance pay, and programs to help employees find new jobs. Communications must inform employees first, then their families, and then other publics in order of importance."

The series of *action programs* must drive off a strategy statement and must relate to each other. In the case of the factory closings, some of the tactics were:

Action Program 1 Organize committee of public relations director (chairman), vice presidents of personnel, labor relations, and marketing, to plan execution of the strategy. All meetings held away from offices—all information kept confidential until last possible moment.

Action Program 2 Plant managers of the two factories report to company headquarters the day before announcement, are told of decision, are carefully rehearsed in speeches they will give, and are rehearsed in answering possible questions. On evening before announcement, two teams—each composed of a public relations specialist, a personnel specialist, a production specialist, and a labor relations specialist (plus the plant manager)—leave for factory sites in chartered planes.

Action Program 3 Employees at sites assemble for 8:00 A.M. simultaneous meetings. Plant managers announce factory closings; employees told to phone or drive home to tell their families.

Action Program 4 While employee meetings are being held, production managers visit preselected opinion-leaders in each city, and tell them about closings and how employees will be treated to minimize hardships.

Action Program 5 At the same time, public relations people notify the evening newspapers, provide press kits, and answer editors' questions, while personnel and plant managers begin meeting privately with each factory employee. Employee group opinion-leaders are interviewed first to start "grapevine" communication. Key information is carried via grapevine and will assist management by reducing meeting time with each employee (most employees learn significant details through grapevine).

Action Program 6 Radio stations receive prepared statements in early afternoon, while headquarters wires news to managers at all other plants (who post notices on bulletin boards). Thus, before general public is aware of the news, all employees at some 60 company locations in North America are informed.

Action Program 7 Marketing telephones key customers and guarantees uninterrupted supplies.

Action Program 8 Newspapers circulate stories later in afternoon; stories are quickly checked for accuracy.

Action Program 9 The next day, letters from plant managers are received at home of each employee, reinforcing the previous day's communications. Full-page ads published in newspapers at both site locations— making certain that the company's message was accurately portrayed to the communities.

DEVISE THE TIMETABLE

Effective strategy requires a carefully devised timetable. It is in this part of the planning process that important discipline is imposed. The timetable needs day-by-day, hour-by-hour, and minute-by-minute *detail*. It should spell out *assignment* of duties (who will do what?). It should be *thorough*, making sure nothing is left to chance. And, it must be *attainable* (don't promise more than you can deliver).

The following timetable was prepared and followed by Data 100, a Minneapolis corporation, for its announcement of a joint venture agreement with Sumotoma, a Japanese company.

This timetable shows why detailed timing was crucial and how it paid off

TIMETABLE: DATA 100—SUMOTOMA ANNOUNCEMENT

A. *Monday*
   Jan. 5   Prepare press packets.

B. *Wednesday*   Make advance press appointments.
   Jan. 7

C. *Monday*
   Jan. 12

   7:30 A.M.   Hietpas (Data 100 vice president of PR) calls agency account representative to check status of Boston, New York interviews.

   8   Data 100 executive and Data 100 president briefed by Hietpas, and Data 100's director of PR and acquisitions manager regarding possible media questions and answers.

   9   Data 100 executive VP to do phone interview with *St. Paul Dispatch Pioneer Press.*

   9:20   Data 100 executive VP and Hietpas leave for airport. Data 100 president and Data 100 acquisitions manager leave for *Minneapolis Tribune.*

   9:30   Data 100 PR director to complete phone contacts, including *Computer World* in Boston.

   9:50   Data 100 executive VP and Hietpas leave for Chicago.

   10   Data 100 PR director to service *Corporate Report*—suggest profile of Data 100 executive VP.

   10   Data 100 president, supported by Data 100 acquisitions manager, interviewed at the *Minneapolis Tribune.* (Story to run Jan. 14.)

   11   Data 100 acquisitions manager leaves for New York, delivers packets to agency office upon arrival.

   11:45   Hietpas and Data 100 executive VP arrive at Midday Club at Clark and Monroe Street in Chicago for *Chicago Sun-Times* interview.

   Noon   Data 100 PR director to send, via overnight delivery service, advance packets to *Datamation, Electronic News, Computerworld, Computer Decisions, Modern Data, Infosystems, Data Communications, Data Communications Users,* and *Canadian Data Systems.*

   2:30 P.M.   Hietpas and Data 100 executive VP at Channel 26 in Chicago for interview on stock market program.

   3   Data 100 acquisitions manager arrives in New York, delivers press packets, begins briefing the Sumotoma spokesmen.

   4   Hietpas and Data 100 executive VP leave Chicago, arrive in New York at 6:54 P.M.

   8   Photo session at Data 100's New York office. Data 100 acquisition manager brings Sumotoma executives, who will be in photos with Data 100 executive VP. Photos printed overnight and delivered for inclusion with captions in key press packets.

   9   Data 100 acquisition manager and Data 100 executive VP have dinner with Sumotoma executives to complete briefing; Hietpas to have dinner with agency to review final details.

   midnight   Story released at a Sumotoma press conference in Tokyo where it is 2:00 P.M.
   Jan. 12   (Jan. 13).
   (New York
   time)

D. *Tuesday*
   Jan. 13   (Note: All times are New York time.)

   9 A.M.   Basic news release transmitted via teletype to all "prompt disclosure" outlets,

including Dow Jones, Reuters, Associated Press, and United Press. Also included is a wire to the *Providence Journal.*

9	Press packets delivered to media in London. (It's 2:00 P.M. in London.)
9	Japanese press in New York get press packet.
9	Data 100 executive VP and Sumotoma executives interviewed at Waldorf-Astoria by Reuters News Services. Breakfast meeting.
10	Press packets delivered to key Chicago media by agency's Chicago office (9:00 A.M. in Chicago).
10	Data 100 executive VP and Sumotoma executive interviewed at Waldorf by reporter for *Financial Times.*
11	Data 100 executive VP and Sumotoma executive interviewed at Waldorf by *Time* magazine reporter.
11	Press packets delivered to *Los Angeles Times* and other key West Coast media by agency's Los Angeles office (9:00 A.M. West Coast time).
1 P.M.	(Noon Minneapolis time) Data 100 PR director finished calling market markers and is available to handle analyst calls.
1:30	Interview with *Business Week* magazine. Note: There are interviews pending with United Press, New York bureau of *Chicago Tribune,* the computer editor of *Business Week*, the *Journal of Commerce*, and Associated Press.
3	Interview of Sumotoma executive and Data 100 executive VP with *New York Times.*
4	Press party—Sumotoma and Data 100 executives are hosts. Invited are key members of New York's financial and business press; also, the Japanese press and the international press.
4:30	Data 100 executive VP interviewed during press party by international editor of *Datamation* magazine.
Dinner	(Left open for possible interviews.)

E. *Wednesday*
  Jan. 14

7 A.M.	Data 100 executive VP leaves for company plant in Providence, R.I., to brief press.
8	Data 100 executive VP and Hietpas have breakfast interview with *Electronic News* reporter in New York.
9	Data 100 acquisition manager interviewed by *Providence Journal.*
9	Phone interview by Data 100 executive VP with editor of *Data Communications* (agency to give him press packet the day before).
9:30 to 11	(Open for interviews with financial writers who couldn't attend the day before.)
Afternoon in Boston	Tentative interviews of Data 100 executive VP with *Boston Globe* and *Christian Science Monitor.*
Dinner	With a reporter from *Computer World.*
By 5 P.M.	Release mailed to 2,200 people on financial mailing list.

F. *Thursday*
  Jan. 15

7:26 A.M.	Data 100 Executive VP and Hietpas leave Boston for Chicago.
10:30	Data 100 executive VP interviewed by editor of *Infosystems* magazine.
Lunch	With editor of *Investment Dealers Digest.*
Return home	
4 P.M.	Early press clippings posted on company bulletin boards.

in announcing a complicated business venture that spanned eight cities in three countries with five different time zones.

STRUCTURING MEASUREMENTS

You should indicate near the end of the plan how you intend to measure your results. This relates directly to the objectives you set at the start of the plan.

Suppose a plan was being devised to communicate to employees of a young, but successful technology company, a proposed merger with another company. (The company wants employees told in such a way as to prevent mass exodus of its highly regarded sales force.)

One of the objectives might be to hold turnover in the sales force to less than 4 percent during the six months following the announcement. You would indicate—in the measurements section—how you would establish a system to obtain that information.

Or suppose a plan has an objective to generate 500 qualified sales leads for the sales force by June 30. Your measurements would describe how leads are to be identified, tracked, qualified, and followed up—after they were received by the corporation.

Or suppose an employee communications plan has an objective to increase understanding of the company's retirement program by 10 percent in 12 months. The measurement section would probably contain a benchmark study showing current levels of employee understanding. Then another study would be conducted following the communications, to measure increased levels of understanding.

As stated at the outset, the plan is a communications vehicle between the planner and the client/boss—so it's important that measurements be established to determine if the plan meets its objectives.

PREPARING THE BUDGET

When the plan is complete, you can detail costs for implementing it. The budget should be complete and should be a measure of your accountability.

Costs must reflect all items needed for implementing strategy, time-table, and measurements. There are two types of costs:

Fixed costs that will be incurred over the life of the plan and which can be anticipated and held constant—salaries, office space, and other costs.

Variable costs that will change depending on circumstances. An example is airfare for people to accomplish goals. Entertainment costs are another variable, as are the costs of public relations help and photographic fees.

A plan without a budget is useless—it would be returned from the client with the terse request: "What does this cost?"

CONCLUSION

If public relations people feel their function is not appreciated, it's because they forget they are being held to specific standards. Peter Drucker, the dean of management consultants, says: "The definition of business management is that it is an economic organ...every act, every decision, every deliberation of management has economic performance as its first dimension. The business manager can justify his existence only by the economic results he produces."

Public relations managers are no different from personnel, marketing, or production managers. The bottom line expectations are the same.

It is imperative that public relations people be viewed as good business people. Management is more receptive to public relations programs and ideas if there is respect for the business judgment of the person submitting them. Public relations managers must compete with all other departments—marketing, advertising, sales, engineering—for operating funds and staff. If they are not perceived as efficient, well organized, bottom line oriented, and acting in concert with the company's objectives, they will come up short at budget time.

That's where good planning comes in. Developing a planning mentality is the only way public relations can be managed. Every successful public relations department has that mentality. It is a mentality designed to avoid the Christopher Columbus syndrome: When Columbus left for America, he didn't know where he was going. When he got there, he didn't know where he was. And when he returned, he didn't know where he had been.

22
ADMINISTERING

Neal Ball

Vice President, Public Affairs
American Hospital Supply Corporation

An important milestone toward successful administration of corporate public affairs is reached when the senior public affairs executive begins referring to top management as "we" instead of "they."

This is no small step. It is rather a giant leap forward. And it is a move that can be made by invitation only.

It is an informal invitation, but it is never issued until the groundwork for acceptance is carefully prepared and assured.

Key to that preparation is the manager's readiness to serve as an executive of the company. Unfortunately there usually are no handy models available. For the truly management-integrated public affairs function is a fairly recent business development, spurred by (1) the changing responsibilities of chief executives and (2) the increased management orientation of public affairs professionals.

The first point has been widely discussed. We all know that the CEO's role has changed markedly in the past two decades. Expanded international interests, the need for longer-range planning, the complexity and scope of government regulations, new definitions of social responsibility, greater demands for accountability—all are aspects of that change.

The second point has been less discussed because it is often assumed that the effective public affairs function simply flexes with the changing CEO

Neal Ball joined American Hospital Supply Corporation in 1960. As vice president of public affairs, he is responsible for public and government relations, investor relations, corporate philanthropy, employee communications, and community and consumer relations.

He is president of the American Hospital Supply Corporation Foundation and in 1982 was appointed to the corporation's management committee. During a two-year leave of absence, he served as deputy press secretary to the president of the United States.

Mr. Ball is chairman and founder of American Refugee Committee and also holds directorships in several international organizations. He won the UNICEF World of Children Award in 1980.

role. Since the CEO's evaluation of the function is paramount within the corporation, the function is considered successful by some when he pats heads instead of pounding desks. There is some value to this but, in reality, not enough to assume any significant contribution to corporate goals. Nor should approval-based activity suggest professional security.

So, what does a manager in public affairs do to become an integral part of a management team that is the driving force of any company? One answer is to worry less about organization charts and more about the corporate plan. It's not the "box" position of the function in the corporate structure that determines its usefulness or importance (although the box may acknowledge it); instead, the test is whether or not it actually is (and also is widely perceived as) performing a critical function in helping formulate and achieve precise corporate goals.

For example, trends in public opinion may indicate a marketing opportunity. The effective public affairs manager is one who has not merely analyzed those trends, but who has then gone on and taken the initiative in having them integrated into strategies that can be put to work in a practical fashion. By contrast, the person who merely holds the job is inclined simply to wait to be asked to help with product publicity once someone else has figured out what is worth publicity effort. The public affairs function thus must help management determine corporate objectives, rather than simply provide tactical support to implement them.

When that happy state is arrived at, the public affairs executive may feel himself truly part of management—except there's a catch. It doesn't come about at all unless he already has managed expertly.

What is that required expertise? For one thing, there must be a good grasp of the functions, techniques, audiences, and dynamics of all the activities discussed elsewhere in this book. The hard part is getting them done through other people, accepting full responsibility for results (or lack of them) while delegating authority, resources, and recognition.

There also comes the need to achieve results in a way that allows future and perhaps different results to be accomplished. The people supervised may be adequate for the present, but training, assessing skills, and counseling have to be part of even the best situations if any real growth is to occur. Delegation without development can't work for long.

It is a wrenching experience when the writer, designer, economist, lawyer, publicist, or whoever moves into a position of supervisory authority and now must manage his former function while taking responsibility for additional functions. He must grow into his broader responsibilities and recognize that his new job is to manage the work of others. Unless this turns out to be tougher on the promoted employee than on those supervised, it's not working. Real personal growth comes harder than simply exercising newfound authority to reshuffle other people's responsibilities.

The drawing board, typewriter, or other implements of a craft are replaced by policy manuals, personnel forms, meeting agendas, etc.; and they seem at first to be rather flimsy tools.

(I once heard this described as "moving from doing to thinking"; and I remember challenging the notion, even though it may have contained a grain of truth, that any professional had done anything without thinking or might now think but not implement ideas.)

A still greater surprise awaits the newly promoted supervisor—there are no buttons to push. Or, if there are buttons, pushing them doesn't do much. The actor playing manager in a movie barks into an intercom and convinces only the film audience of his authority. The real-life manager finds the power he's been given more like that defined by Harry Truman as "the power to persuade." (His successors learned the hard way. John Kennedy during the Cuban missile crisis, was surprised to find that a U.S. base near Russia was in operation although he had long ago ordered it closed. Another commander in chief, Richard Nixon, ordered the Marines to open their beach at a California base to the public, only to find that while they might always be faithful, they were not always responsive; it took months of discussion and confrontation to open the beach.)

It's sometimes assumed the transition to supervisory or managerial responsibility is tougher on the "creative" public affairs employee than on someone in line or other staff responsibilities. Not so. The sales representative, laboratory technologist, computer programmer, or auditor finds it no easier. Management creativity (as opposed to artistic skill alone) consists of skillful use of personnel, resources, and policies to produce productive results.

But now that application of creativity is required somewhat less for tactics and more for strategies. (Instead of writing a public service announcement, and in addition to being able to cause a good announcement to be written, the manager's creativity goes to an exploration of all the devices which might better accomplish the same result. He devises and initiates solutions rather than just communicating the existence of problems.) Later, creativity will be even more needed for determining and reaching corporate rather than departmental objectives.

Having taken away the new manager's typewriter, slide rule, or other specialist's instruments and the creative "isolation" of his cubbyhole, what do you replace them with? I recommend the same intangible but essential managerial awareness given (read that "required of") me by our own chief executive officer.

It's an awareness transmitted both by example and instruction and it has four inseparable elements: planning, motivating, organizing, and controlling.

What could be easier? Flying without using a plane, that's what.

The appearance of simplicity only adds to the difficulty. A list of the manager's daily activities could easily be reassembled under those four headings, bringing satisfaction that "now I am a manager." But these are not so much labels as challenges; they are less a series of precise steps than general descriptions of complex practices and multiple disciplines.

There *is* a logical sequence given any well-defined goal: plan objectives, strategies, and tactics; organize adequate and appropriate resources to accomplish the plan; motivate (meaning implement or impel) the process; and finally, control (analyze and measure) results.

The effective public affairs or public relations manager understands that he or she must question assumptions on which the plan or program is based. A public affairs perspective must be broader in its vision and experience than a perspective deriving from a narrow technical discipline.

In short, a public affairs manager should be able to draw on specific expertise and data to be a source of sophisticated information and valuable counsel to senior management for assessing the current business climate and predicting future modifications.

With that input and similar input from other public affairs managers and from financial, personnel, legal, planning, marketing, and other staff areas, some environmental assumptions can evolve and be challenged, modified, and adopted. It is the world as best we can know it from our experiences and for our purposes—and for a given period of time. And a measurement of managerial ability is how much the manager brings to this crystal-ball process.

Planning is discussed elsewhere in this book as it relates to public affairs. But the successful administration of public affairs depends greatly on how well that planning meshes with the planning of other staffs and how well integrated all of those plans are in achieving common or corporate objectives. This requires what is sometimes now called "negotiation" and used to be called "discussion."

In candor and completeness, the manager responsible for investor relations, for example, needs to discuss proposals with managers in planning, financial, legal, and other areas. The process is investigative, informational, and even, at times, confrontational. The process doesn't seek peer permission to proceed; it invites informed reaction, thorough questioning, and useful information. It helps to clarify goals and can encourage peers to share them. In many cases resources outside of one's own department can be drawn upon to help achieve those goals.

Planning and personnel administration are inextricably linked. Every member of the public affairs staff can and should contribute to the final plan. This is not so much consensus management as it is common sense; each person has at least a fairly clear idea of resources required and will have some ideas on how to do things better, quicker, or cheaper—maybe all three.

The discussions within each department of the public affairs staff, among the departments with other staff and operating groups, and with external resources (e.g., agencies, associations, and consultants) require significant amounts of time. And they continue, more or less intensely, formally and informally throughout the year as plans are developed, implemented, modified, and evaluated.

A useful administrative step in the planning process is to have the suggested tactics, strategies, and goals reviewed by an outside consultant. The expertise sought here is not goal definition nor even priorities setting; it's an objective review with the contributors to the plan of whether or not all of the steps necessary and only the steps necessary to reach certain objectives have been built into the plan.

A detached view can be of invaluable help at the right time in the process. It may also be more quickly accepted from without.

At American Hospital Supply Corporation, we began an emphasis on public affairs planning about ten years ago. Until that time a results orientation, supportive of corporate goals and meeting the management's perceived needs, seemed sufficient. Prizes, awards, and commendations came often enough to keep everyone happy; and financial controls and measurements of return on investments were favorable.

What the absence of informal planning process for public affairs really meant was that we were not then fully involving managerial and professional skills in determining objectives nor in accomplishing those objectives.

We had annual sales of about $700 million, plans to more than triple those sales in 10 years, and a history of meeting such plans. We also knew that resources for corporate staff functions should not simply grow as a percentage of sales or earnings. Budget increases determined annually for the coming year could not be considered either a kind of departmental bonus nor a grade for the work done the year before. And if a manager was to understand that a projected dollar cut in her plan, at the same time another department's plan was increased, was not a judgment on the value of her function, then greatly increased communication and involvement in planning would be required. And that involvement comes not only from how the group is directed, but from its very organization.

Plan...organize...motivate...and control. Organization is frequently underestimated as a management tool. It obviously fits with planning and motivation. But it is also vital in its link with control, since inappropriate organization can almost guarantee failure while well-structured effective organization virtually invites success in that it helps sound alarms of impending management breakdowns early enough for them to be corrected.

Numerous texts on organization theory were helpful in developing our plans. In general, the most prudent advice was to form the organization which best produces desired results for today, yet is structured to accommodate changes in direction or goals tomorrow.

While some experts gave ideal fixed numbers for "span of control" (the number of managers reporting to the senior manager), most found no magic in any given number.

We sought an organization that would involve all of the talent we had in a

more productive way, with a flexibility to accommodate evolving requirements and objectives. It would have to offer career paths within public affairs
and exposure of potential managers to responsibilities they might one day be
asked to undertake. It also had to take into consideration the structure of
departments and groups beyond public affairs. The organizational expertise
of various corporate personnel departments had to be called upon.

The corporation was effectively organized around markets and was
largely decentralized. Keeping as many decisions as possible as close to the
customer as possible, minimizing central policy (our corporate policy manual
is less than a quarter-inch thick), and promoting from within were all
well-established and effective concepts which had to be considered.

For public affairs, "audiences" replaced "markets" and audience
manager positions were created for each of the usual constituencies—
customers, employees, shareholders, etc. Except for clerical help, none was
assigned any staff, and all were asked to draw upon writers, designers,
logistical support, and research and planning capabilities in a new communications services division.

The audience manager then became an expert for a constituency, knew
what had to be accomplished within that group, and could contribute from
that expertise to larger plans and objectives relating to it. The manager also
became an advocate for a constituency, competing with other audience
managers for resources from the communications services division. At the
same time, cooperation with other managers to get the fullest impact from
shared resources became an even greater necessity.

Two results surfaced immediately. One was the audience manager's
discomfort at not having a staff of two or three assistants. The other was
the assistant's discomfort at losing a title such as "supervisor," "assistant
manager," or whatever and becoming instead an editor, researcher, or other
specialist. It was a "loss-of-executive status" syndrome, and it took awhile to
reduce itself to the semantic problem it really was.

In time, the manager learned he had more resources than ever to draw
upon and that these were more able, more varied, and more informed
resources than had been available earlier. On the other hand, an editor, for
example, was no longer limited to one area of interest or to one part of a
process. Because the job was broader and more demanding, improved salary
ranges and increased visibility also resulted.

Where a division product research manager earlier had new product
interviews with writers from investor relations, employee communications,
and market communications, that interview now could be done once with an
editor who prepared a variety of materials for various communications needs.

What had been fairly frequent requests for additional staff, for all the
usual good and not so good reasons, became only occasional and tentative
requests. Additional help needed from the communicating services "pool"
could be requested when "capacity" was reached; priorities could be

established against the overall plan. In order to assure resources for a project, longer-term planning increasingly was required. Overwork peaks and sluggish valleys were largely eliminated.

Benefits from the new organization probably couldn't have occurred as readily if the employees themselves had not been included in discussions on objectives, desired results, work problems, and opportunities. There were not "touching base" sessions simply to reduce resistance to a management decision; many of the best ideas incorporated came from these meetings.

(They were accompanied by fairly far-out ideas, too. And some highly creative suggestions died sudden and colorful deaths, not at the hands of management but from fellow workers. For example, the suggestion that audience managers would be able to work more cooperatively and with better intercommunication if they all sat around one large desk, newsroom-style, was, to be kind, ahead of its time.)

Over the years, the structure has been modified somewhat and in fact is characterized by being changeable without serious disruption.

The number of employees has increased only slightly in a decade, an impressive fact in view of highly increased productivity and added responsibilities. And broader examination of marginal activities and clearer managerial priorities help eliminate enticing and traditional projects whose time has come and gone. New technologies not economical for individual departments often are productive and cost effective when utilized by the group as a whole through its communications services division.

Motivation or implementation as the third element of management follows planning and organization. The "matrix" organization outlined above, for example, requires clearer and more frequent communication between the people in the organization and definitely additional time from the senior manager. There are more frequent "communications problems." These usually turn out to be a variety of problems which would come to light less readily in another structure.

Implementation is easier when more of the people involved know why something should be done and understand the consequences of delay or failure for those with whom they work as well as for themselves.

I prefer the word "implementation" to "motivation," for while the latter means stimulating to action, it sounds more like something a manager does to his people rather than with them.

Every manager has resources, rewards, and recognition to offer, and there are restraints which can be applied. But these generally have only a temporary effect. Manipulative techniques don't develop managers. Effort is more effectively—and more honestly—spent in careful evaluation and in initiating developmental activities.

One looks for a degree of discipline within any organization. But only when that discipline is self-discipline and includes the manager's willingness to challenge himself is it productive instead of disruptive.

The control function, using thorough evaluation supported by meaningful measurement techniques, is the loop-closer. There is no single bottom line for most activities—any venture can bring short-term profitability and longer-term chaos if not properly implemented. The measurement of results therefore includes not only what was accomplished, but an evaluation of how those results were achieved.

I recently outlined the application of "plan-motivate-organize-control" to a public affairs seminar, and one of the executives said, "Sounds great, but is it fun?" I said we call it work, but if you can make it work for you, then you might call it fun. Work or fun, the application to public affairs of management techniques tested in other corporate areas does bring results and also a sense of achievement to those producing them.

BUDGETING

John A. Koten

Vice President Corporate Communications
Illinois Bell Telephone Company

The public relations budget is a communications opportunity for practitioners that may go unrecognized amid the unaccustomed exercise of dealing in numbers rather than words. The budget process offers a chance to show top management what the communications department is doing and why it's a sound investment for the corporation, association, or institution. It's an opportunity to demonstrate that public relations is well managed and cost effective.

Public relations counseling firms must budget effectively to satisfy their clients. Their charges are constantly reviewed by their clients, necessitating a continued review of cost/benefit relationships. The same is true, often less obviously, for the public relations budgets of corporate and institutional organizations. Unfortunately, many practitioners in corporate or association public relations departments are not trained in this essential management skill. Mastering it is a key to achieving the top positions in the industry.

An annual budget is a request for resources: staff, equipment, and program. Ultimately it is expressed in dollars. The communications department must compete with other departments to get the resources it needs. This means public relations practitioners must define what they intend to do and convince top management that the organization will get a measurable return for every dollar allocated to communications.

No organization, be it corporate or institutional, can long survive without the consent of its publics. This makes it imperative that the

John A. Koten is vice president of corporate communications of Illinois Bell Telephone Company. He heads a staff of 165 persons with an annual budget of $22 million and is responsible for media relations, government affairs, employee information, advertising, community and urban affairs. In 1974 he was named public relations director at AT&T in New York, was elected vice president public relations of New Jersey Bell in 1975, and was named to his current position in 1980.

He is a director of the Arthritis Foundation, the American Symphony Orchestra League, and a member of the Association of Governing Boards of Universities and Colleges.

organization be sensitive to what others say about it and that it communicate its position to its audience so that it will gain understanding and support. No one can speak better or with greater clarity about the organization than it can do for itself.

The budgeting process helps accomplish this objective. To the extent the senior communications person can develop understanding for this principle with the chief executive, determination of the overall budget is simplified.

The process of competing for resources does not end with management approval of the annual budget. As an ongoing responsibility, communications managers need to track expenses and hold professionals accountable for cost-effective performance. They must redirect resources and occasionally seek additional funds to handle crises and new opportunities. Similarly, they must return unused resources to the organization. Finally, communications managers must measure results and relate them to expenses.

Financial management is an essential skill that's as important to practitioners as traditional communications expertise. Proficiency in this aspect of the job can actually create more opportunities for creative work, save time in the long run, and increase the value of public relations to the organization.

This chapter describes some of the methods used by successful public relations departments. It concentrates on the problems of the in-house public relations department of a corporation, nonprofit association, or government agency rather than attempting to include the unique financial management concerns of counseling firms. It should be noted, however, that by knowing the "true" costs of running an organization, the manager can make better decisions about when to perform an activity in-house and when use of an outside agency might be the best use of resources.

The budget process is different in different organizations, but the end objective is the same: to make available sufficient resources to enable the department to help the organization accomplish its mission. By applying the basic principles of these models, any public relations department, whether it's a one-person staff or a large corporate organization, can improve its ability to take advantage of budget opportunities.

The process of formulating an annual departmental budget can be as formal or informal as the organization wants to make it, ranging from sophisticated computerized printouts to handwritten notes and informal discussion. The most successful practitioners integrate their annual budget with a plan of activities for the coming year rather than confining their attention to dollars and staff headcounts. It is important that whoever reviews the budget also understands what it will accomplish.

Introducing a description of activities into the budget process gives the communications manager a chance to review existing activities in the light of anticipated needs. Obsolete programs may be altered or eliminated and new programs may be introduced or adopted. Linking communications functions and activities to a funding request lets top management know how the communications budget is supporting its overall objectives. This makes the budget a series of concrete decision packages rather than an arbitrary request for dollars.

Many communications departments use the current year as the basis for budget requests. Then as new activities are deemed helpful they are added to the existing budget. Other activities which won't be repeated are deleted. For example, a new employee publication, a major corporate anniversary, or other new planned activity is tied to a request for existing funding and submitted for approval. Annual events provide a ready opportunity to combine planning and budgeting into a single decision-making process.

The National Safety Council's communications program, like that of many associations, includes such annual events as safety week promotions. The council's public relations staff uses its calendar of events as a primary planning tool. The current year's actual expenses for each event are reviewed to formulate a budget request for the following year. Each event is evaluated and a decision is made to change, expand, or reduce it. The result is both a specific plan of action and a request for funds, laid out in detail for approval by management.

Sometimes it's possible to plan programs many years ahead, and budgets can be built accordingly. The automobile companies are accustomed to lead times of three to five years before new models are introduced. Boeing started its introduction of the 767 two years before United inaugurated the first commercial flight. United in turn announced its intention to fly the 767 six months ahead of its maiden flight. Successful introductions don't just happen; they are planned years in advance. Eastman Kodak, for example, planned its successful introduction of the disc camera over a five-year period.

Perhaps the most effective planning method is to use organizational goals as the basis for formulating and budgeting communications activities. The public affairs department of Baylor College of Medicine uses an organizational mission statement, overall objectives for the decade, and annual priorities to aid communications planning.

Often a public relations department can plug into an established corporate planning system. Many companies use an annual business plan as a basis for their activities and budgets. Apple Computer, whose industry is particularly volatile, uses a rolling quarterly business plan to respond quickly to fast-moving technology and markets. The public relations department revises its programs accordingly in order to keep the company positioned ahead of the market.

Some companies use a formal management-by-objectives process. At Illinois Bell, company officers formulate each year's corporate objectives: a comprehensive but simply worded statement of management direction that outlines areas of emphasis for the coming year.

Each officer then expands on the corporate goals with a set of departmental objectives. These objectives indicate how, in general terms, each department will contribute to the corporate goals. Every department generally will formulate objectives to support each broad corporate goal, but emphasis varies according to function: operating departments' objectives tend to focus on efficiency and quality, while the marketing department will stress sales goals and market plans. The corporate communications department develops internal objectives to assist each of the departments to achieve their targets and the external objectives that help the corporation achieve its expectations.

The next step is a bottom-up process to formulate specific action plans supporting the top-down goals and objectives. In the corporate communications department, each professional develops a series of specific action plans that define what that individual intends to do, within the scope of his or her job, to contribute to the organization's objectives. These action plans are reviewed through supervisory channels, where negotiation between practitioners and their supervisors develops a set of action plans for each group. The result is a comprehensive corporate communications plan for the coming year that defines specific projects, timetables, and action steps and identifies the individuals accountable for each action plan (see figure 23.1).

Once plans are formulated and approved, they become a year-round management guide. Action plans are reviewed quarterly with each person's supervisor: from first-level supervision all the way up to the chief executive officer. The review process tracks progress toward corporate goals and provides an opportunity to negotiate new or modified action plans to meet changing situations. More important, it forms the basis for individual performance appraisals and annual salary treatment.

While outlining the specific action steps may seem cumbersome, particularly in a large organization, this specificity makes the planning process a useful budget tool.

First, the discipline of making an annual plan forces practitioners to work ahead, the farther the better. Breaking a project into its component tasks and assigning responsibility to individuals has the effect of allocating resources to a project in advance and helps estimate the manpower and expenses needed.

Second, this process makes individuals accountable for results. Reviewing action plans and reporting progress regularly creates an automatic follow-through mechanism: individuals know in advance what is expected of them and must take personal responsibility for the results they produce.

Third, individual accountability demands that practitioners measure the results of their work and compare those results to the objectives they're intended to support. The same individual accountability also extends to the cost-effective accomplishment of assigned tasks. This system also permits employees to keep track of how well they are doing relative to what's expected of them.

Even when a formal, companywide goal-setting process does not exist, a communications manager can initiate this discipline within his or her own

Corporate Goal: Win public confidence in our business.
—Build understanding and support for the company's position on public policy issues.

Corporate Communications Objective No. 11 (of 13):   Identify, analyze, and monitor emerging issues and events that will enhance or impede achievement of corporate goals. Inform the public and employees about our positions on key issues and the reasons for those positions.

Action Plans	Responsibility	Completion
Background news media on privacy issues such as wiretapping and annoyance calling.	Johnston	December
Add 24 trained spokespersons to statewide resource pool currently available; schedule "hands on" video training.	Johnston	December
Conduct eight regional share-owner information meetings excluding Chicago, minimum 800 attendance.	Jernigan	October
Produce video program on IBT impact on state's economy for use at high technology task force meeting.	E. Smith	June
Develop two new volunteer speaker talks relating to restructuring and technology.	Jakubs	September
Conduct study to determine relative importance of community relations activities on customer attitudes.	Gardner, Hill	June

(*Note*: The department listed more than 150 specific action plans supporting this objective.)

Figure 23.1   Illinois Bell objectives and action plans.

department and use it in presenting a budget request. It's always possible to formulate some overall goals with which management is likely to agree, then list activities supporting these goals and seek access to top management during the annual budget cycle.

One cautionary note: Planning activities and linking them to a budget proposal should not be confused with formulating job descriptions for communications staff members. Job descriptions are useful for determining the caliber of practitioner needed to fill a staff position. Activity plans describe, in specific terms, how an activity will contribute to organizational objectives. Using these plans as a budget decision package demands a clear statement of what the public relations department intends to do, who will do it, how much the activity will cost, and how it will deliver value.

The process of formulating the annual budget demands that the chief executive officer evaluate the relative worth of the communications effort and translate this assessment into a budget decision to allocate resources. If the CEO is not committed to support specific communications programs, the resulting decision is likely to be arbitrary. Often the budget allocation is based on the assumption that the current year's activities will be perpetuated—with a percentage added to the budget to account for inflation—or reduced by subtracting a percentage of the budget allocation.

When this decision is made without the participation of the departmental chief, the communications department may be foreclosed from taking advantage of new opportunities to enhance its value to the organization. Worse, if communications is viewed as a discretionary expense, rather than an investment in accomplishing corporate goals, the department may be the last to expand its resources and the first to cut programs in a tight economy or under a change in ownership or administration.

FORMULATING A BUDGET REQUEST

Forecasting: Translating Plans into Dollars

Once the prospective program has been determined, attaching price tags to it to formulate a budget recommendation is a matter of experience and research, with some well-educated guesswork thrown in where necessary. Nearly all budgets are for 12-month periods, usually beginning January 1. More sophisticated organizations budget for two, three, five, and even ten-year periods.

Like predicting the weather, forecasting expenses a year or more in advance requires patience and a good data base. If the communications department has done an effective job of tracking current expenses and accounting for results, it's possible to estimate expenses as accurately as any other department in the organization and manage within them. Without good data and tracking mechanisms, the job can be very difficult. Here are some factors to consider.

Staff

This is the largest budget expenditure of most public relations organizations. You already know how many people you have and how much they're paid. The schedule of salary increases consistent with your company's practice should be factored into your budget. (In a large organization, the personnel department may provide some guidance here.) If you are recommending additional staff, you should be able to estimate how many you need, their skill level, and how much their salaries are likely to be.

Salary surveys, available from professional publications and industry associations, are a useful guide. Your company may conduct salary surveys of its own. If so, be sure that the jobs measured in your field are compatible to the ones in your industry for organizations of relatively similar size.

Staff additions generally require top management approval in most organizations and must be thoroughly justified. Because staff are the public relations department's principal resource, the communications manager should be sure that the people in his department are capable of doing the job that needs to be done. Unproductive staff are a luxury no organization can afford. This is particularly true in a field where it's often difficult to precisely measure results. The manager should be the best judge and should constantly look for ways to improve effectiveness.

Employee-related Expenses

Travel and conference expenses, professional membership dues, etc., can be estimated based on your group's experience and your own assessment of whether travel, for instance, is likely to increase in the coming year due to the programs you have in place or anticipate.

Outside Services

Such expenses as agency fees, photography, graphics, and printing can be tied to specific projects, based on past experience with such projects and your estimate of what future prices may be. It's a good thing to talk to your suppliers and get a feel from them about the trends in their fields.

Publications

Printing, typesetting, postage, and paper costs can be estimated based on past expenses. Suppliers can be particularly helpful here. You'll want to be familiar with the expiration dates of your contracts and what their provisions are as they relate to your budget. The fewer "surprises" you have in your budget, the better manager you will become.

Capital Expenditures

Typewriters, audio-visual equipment, furniture, etc., are often considered capital items (rather than consumable commodities) and may be accounted for in a separate budget. Capital equipment is depreciated over a period of years and, like a piece of machinery in a factory, must demonstrate a return on the company's investment. You'll want to figure out the average life cycle of the various kinds of equipment you use, so that you can have a replacement program in place that will enable you to "modernize" your facilities to some degree each year. The resulting accounting procedures usually call for thorough justification of new purchases and careful tracking of inventories. In some cases, such as the acquisition of a word-processing system, you may be able to show that the new equipment will result in expense reductions, thereby justifying their cost right up front.

Overhead

Typically most corporate and association people do not need to include the cost of space, heat, light, telephones, maintenance, etc., in their budgets. However, budget planners should be aware of what these costs are. Increasingly, this information is available on a unit by unit basis and needs to be considered when assessing the value of the activity to the total enterprise. Such costs need to be considered in the budget allocation process and could be used to determine whether it is more cost effective to maintain or enlarge a function as opposed to going "outside" to have the work performed. There are other considerations that will be part of such a decision, but awareness of "true" costs could play an important role.

Cross-Charges

It's also important to know who can or does cross-charge expenses to your accounts. Ideally these will be budgeted in advance and you will determine whether they are suitable expenditures. If others have access to your accounts, be sure to have a mechanism to know when these expenses are likely to be made. Otherwise your careful forecasting may be knocked out of kilter.

Supplies

These range from routine consumable items, like typing paper and pencils, to special supplies for specific projects, posters, brochures, and promotional items. Previous experience is the best guide here, unless you're forecasting some unusual activity.

Advertising

These costs include media space and time, production expenses, and talent fees. Advertising agencies can help forecast these costs based on your anticipated plans.

Special Events

Meetings, conferences, and trade shows all have identifiable expenses such as hiring a hall, purchasing refreshments, decorations, name tags, materials, etc.

A mature communications department can rely on considerable experience in forecasting costs based on past experience. If past expenses have been adequately tracked and compared, you can often forecast future expenses easily and accurately. For example, the National Safety Council logs specific expenses for each of its annual meetings and uses these expense breakdowns to forecast expenses for the following year.

While a newly formed or growing public relations staff may lack the benefit of this experience, it's still possible to get good information on cost trends from other companies in the same industry, professional associations, and other communications professionals.

No management likes surprises when it comes to budgets, and you will do well to keep them at a minimum.

Sources of Funding

Most public relations departments receive an annual budget allocation to fund communications activities as part of an overall budget. But the departmental budget may not be the only source of resources. Some practitioners may charge some or all of their program expenses to the in-house "clients" they serve—in effect, acting as an internal agency.

Standard Oil Company (Indiana), for example, prorates its corporate public relations budget among the corporation's operating subsidiaries. The annual share charged to each subsidiary is based on the proportion of the department's effort that goes toward servicing the subsidiary. Both the current year's activity and anticipated demand for the coming year are considered in calculating the annual budget allocation. In this process the operating units can, and do, ask for justification of the public relations budget.

A number of other communications departments charge specific programs and services to their internal "clients." The public affairs department at Baylor College of Medicine gets a budget allocation from the college, but also uses other sources as well. When a faculty department requests assistance on a major communications project, the out-of-pocket cost of this service is charged back to the client department. Since Baylor faculty members often obtain grants for major research projects, they are encouraged to incorporate communications expenses for their projects—such as the cost of recruiting subjects for experiments—into their original grant request. In one case the grant for a National Heart and Blood Vessel Research Center included a budget for a communications director and staff needed by the center.

Similarly, some organizations fund major projects with separate, interdepartmental budgets that include a public relations component. A major trade show sponsored by Jewel Food Stores in Chicago, for example, was funded in a separate budget that included public relations expenses allocated to this project.

At Illinois Bell the corporate television center cross-charges its services to operating departments for which it produces employee information and training videotapes.

Setting Priorities

Inherent in any planning and budgeting process is the assumption that people can always think of more activities than they can reasonably accomplish and managers aren't likely to get all the resources they would prefer to have. Obviously some method of setting priorities is necessary.

Most communications managers arrive at priorities in the course of negotiating budget requests with their bosses. The communicator, ideally guided by organization goals, submits a list of activities for funding. The chief executive officer determines what the organization can afford. Together they assess the value of each project to the organization and determine which ones to support with people and dollars.

For example, the public affairs staff at Baylor College of Medicine builds negotiation of priorities into a bottom-up process of formulating budget requests tied to activities. Using the college's mission statement and organizational goals as a guide, staff members recommend specific activities. Supervisors work with each professional to determine priorities. As part of the process, supervisors are asked to indicate where they would cut if they had to cut 10 percent from their budgets and which activities they would expand if their budgets were increased by 10 percent. The public affairs vice president's negotiation with the college president and treasurer determines the final priority ranking of the department's activities.

Zero-based Budgeting

Zero-based budgeting provides a mechanism to reevaluate every one of an organization's functions every year. The concept is relatively simple and straightforward. Imagine that your department is starting from scratch every year with no activities, no people, no budget. Begin by determining a threshold—the minimum level at which the department can reasonably provide only those services which are absolutely necessary to the organization's survival.

The manager then builds on that threshold by adding a series of increments in declining order of importance to the organization. Each increment identifies a specific activity or function, lists requirements for staff and resources, and defines the consequences to the organization if that increment is not funded. The result is a series of decision packages ranked in order of priority and identifying the trade-offs for each component. Theoretically, the organization can function at any level of funding at or above the threshold.

Illinois Bell uses a computerized version of zero-based budgeting (see figure 23.2; pp. 330–331) to organize its funding priorities. Each work group organizes itw own ranking "tower," with the threshold at the bottom and optional activities at the top. Department heads review each manager's ranking tower and combine them into a ranking tower for the department. This process, which eventually builds up to include the chief executive, ultimately produces a comprehensive ranking tower—or priority-ordered list of activities—for the entire company. The funding decision is then made by drawing a line at the level of available resources, thereby funding activities below the line and withholding support from those increments above the line.

Informal Prioritization

Although the discipline of zero-based budgeting is a useful tool to the public relations practitioner, the process of setting priorities doesn't always take place in a highly structured environment. Union Carbide Company sets funding priorities for its public relations department informally by communicating closely with top management and gauging the degree of need for each communications function or program. In using an informal process, it's essential that the top manager accurately gauge which programs are most important to top management. If this consensus is clearly recorded in the minds of the chief executive officer and the communications officer, it's an informal but useful guide to operating the communications effort and allocating resources.

Budgeting for Flexibility

No public relations practitioner can forecast everything that is going to happen in the next year. Communications work is volatile by nature. While it's possible to plan an organization's intended direction and program many proactive projects in advance, every practitioner must be prepared for crises and unforeseen opportunities. That means building enough flexibility into the budget to manage the unpredictable. Funding of public relations activities should support the basic position that drives the existence of the communications function: that public support is essential to the corporation's survival; and that the organization must represent itself to its publics with the strongest possible voice and not abdicate this advocacy to others. If management agrees to this fundamental, resource allocation should not be troublesome. In the end, the ability to deliver is paramount.

Contingency funds inevitably must be built into the communications department's budget, formally or otherwise. Illinois Bell uses an "unallocated reserve" fund under the direct control of the corporate communications vice president. This is not a blank check. Sooner or later practitioners are held accountable for the reasonable accuracy of their estimates. Overestimating or underestimating by more than a small margin is a game that's usually unwinnable.

Even if an organization tends to be crisis-ridden, it's usually possible to "guesstimate" the anticipated crisis workload for the coming year, and plan for the resulting increase in consumer and news media interest. Expense tracking systems are of particular value in learning from actual expenses and past deviations from budget estimates.

Standard Oil Company (Indiana) finds it necessary to build flexibility into its public relations budget because of the nature of its business. Some company activities, such as exploration plans, are highly proprietary; plans often are closely held even within the company. Some crises, such as an oil spill or tanker mishap, are virtually impossible to forecast. In either case, when the time for action occurs the department must be in a position to respond.

In some instances a communications staff has no alternative but to do what has to be done to handle a crisis situation regardless of expense, then redirect resources later, or seek budget relief to cover any shortfall that cannot be absorbed in the departmental budget. There's no way a plane crash, hotel fire, bottle tampering, or nuclear accident can be anticipated. When these events happen, you can only hope you have an experienced staff in place that knows the business, and has the confidence of its management and the media. No accurate value can be placed on this, but at that moment the organization can get the biggest return on its *investment* in public relations instead of the *expense* of public relations. With no investment obviously there's no return. If the organization's chief executive officer supports the basic principles of public relations outlined earlier, the need for the organization to speak out in an emergency will be evident and unquestioned.

FINANCIAL MANAGEMENT

Budget Tracking: How to Keep Abreast of Expenses

Tracking expenses is the first requisite of managing a communications department budget. Communications managers responsible for their own budgets need a continuous handle on costs in order to control them and ought to be the first to know if their department is in danger of exceeding its budget. Accurate tracking of expenses also is essential, as outlined earlier, in forecasting future costs. Tracking methods range from sophisticated computer systems to simple, handwritten logs. The objectives of these systems are the same:

Rank	Program	Impact If Not Funded	Staff
EMPLOYEE INFORMATION RANKING			
3	Information support of personnel policies and 2-way discussion programs.	Less employee understanding of personnel policies and lack of 2-way communications.	4
2	Employee magazine	Reduced understanding of complex corporate issues; no regular medium to reach retired employees.	5
1	Employee bulletins and phone-in newsline.	No timely employee information on company developments; outside media and rumor mill become primary information sources.	3
MEDIA RELATIONS RANKING			
2	Issue press information on technology advances; respond to media queries on service.	Low-technology image, more competitive losses, more service complaints to regulatory agencies, more adverse coverage on service.	1
1	Provide press information on rates and legal matters; act as spokesperson and coordinate press information.	Poor media representation and less favorable regulatory decisions.	2
ADVERTISING RANKING			
2	Bill inserts to specific customer groups on service matters and dialing changes.	No efficient way to get local service information to customers; more use of 1st class mail; lost sales opportunity.	2
1	Twelve issues of bill insert newsletter to 3.6 million customers.	No recurring way to inform customers statewide of rates, service developments, and new products/services. Lower sales, reduced revenue.	2

Rank	Program	Impact If Not Funded	Staff
DEPARTMENTAL RANKING			
7	Information support of personnel policies and 2-way discussion programs.	Loss of employee understanding of personnel policies and lack of 2-way communications.	4
6	Bill inserts to specific customer groups on service matters and dialing changes.	No efficient way to get local service information to customers; more use of 1st class mail; lost sales opportunity.	2
5	Twelve issues of bill insert newsletter to 3.6 million customers.	No recurring way to inform customers statewide of rates, service developments, and new products/services. Lower sales, reduced revenue.	2
4	Employee magazine	Reduced understanding of complex corporate issues; no regular medium to reach retired employees.	5
3	Issue press information on technology advances, respond to media queries on service.	Low-technology image, more competitive losses, more service complaints to regulatory agencies, more adverse coverage on service.	1
2	Provide press information on rates and legal matters; act as spokesperson and coordinate press information.	Poor media representation and less favorable regulatory decisions.	2
1	Employee bulletins and phone-in newsline.	No timely employee information on company developments; outside media and rumor mill become primary information sources.	3

Figure 23.2   Illinois Bell budget decision packages.

- To know how much the department is spending at any given time and whether expenses are on target;
- To have enough information about budget status to make intelligent spending decisions and manage costs;
- To compile an accurate, historical record of costs as an aid in forecasting future expenses.

Some organizations require that the budget forecast be broken down month by month. This is essential in forecasting the company's cash flow, because many firms use short-term debt to meet commitments that revenues don't cover: they may synchronize such borrowing in order to manage the company's cash resources daily. Hence the ability of managers to anticipate and track monthly expenses accurately has an impact on the organization's profit and loss statement.

Most organizations supply the public relations department head with periodic accountant's reports of expenses. Illinois Bell's corporate communications department gets monthly printouts detailing each management unit's actual expenses. Included are both the previous month's actual expenses and running totals of year-to-date expenditures in each budget category. At the department head level, these reports show how each subordinate unit is doing—thus equipping the department head to track how well programs are being met and to initiate cost control measures and shift budget allocations between units, if necessary.

Although each group within the department has its own budget, financial control is centralized under a single manager reporting to the vice president. (In an agency this function would be done by the business manager, financial officer, or treasurer.) A manual tracking system supplements the company-provided expense reports at the point of departmental budget control to provide such information as a daily log of all bills processed. This provides immediate information on how much money is being spent, by whom, and for what—and enables the budget coordinator to head off potential budget problems.

In a similar system at Bank of America, an operations manager in each organization tracks the budget and informs managers when they are over or under their allocations. The public relations staff at Jewel Food Stores requests, and receives, a monthly breakdown of expenses from the accounting department. This report tracks actual expenses month by month with previous-year and year-to-date comparisons. Similarly, the National Safety Council gets an accounting report that compares actual expenses with the amounts budgeted for each month.

However, even detailed companywide tracking systems may not give communications managers enough information to manage their expenses. Because communications department expenses tend to be unlike those of other operating units, the standard accounting categories designed for the rest of the company may lump a variety of public relations expenses into "other" or "miscellaneous" categories.

Practitioners may want to track expenses as they are incurred instead of waiting for the following month's report. At Standard Oil of Indiana, public relations managers supplement monthly budget printouts with a manual log of expenditures to identify specific items of interest to them.

The National Safety Council uses a manual tracking system to supplement the monthly budget reports for public relations staff members. A typewritten budget sheet for each activity or project breaks down expense components for distribution to each professional involved in the activity. The same sheet includes room to record actual expenses as they're incurred for comparison at the time and to fine-tune the following year's budget forecast. In addition, a daily log of expenses in each category includes a running total of expenses to date and the amount left in each budget category—much like a checkbook.

Managing Expenses

Most methods of managing expenses are informal and common sense: avoid spending more than you have to; evaluate major expenditures in advance; track the budget and reduce or eliminate expenditures when they begin to exceed budgeted amounts. Here are some ways communications managers can control their budgets during the year:

- Build in accountability by making each professional responsible for meeting the budgets for their projects and making sure they participate in planning, tracking, and evaluating expenditures. This encourages practitioners to be good money managers as well as effective communicators.
- Seek competitive bids on major purchases—perhaps by telephoning several suppliers—to get the best price commensurate with quality and service needs. It's a good idea to review existing contracts with suppliers and open them up for bids periodically. Avoiding any appearance of "sweetheart" deals with suppliers helps keep the communications department invulnerable to criticism.
- Negotiate with regular suppliers, such as printers, to minimize such expenses as overtime by adjusting deadlines, delivery routines, etc.
- When hiring photographers, have a good idea of what you want in advance and discuss it completely. Ask for proof sheets before you make your final selection.
- Plan your rehearsals for CCTV production in advance so you don't waste expensive studio or camera crew time.
- Minimize alterations to typeset material by developing approval routines that take care of changes at the rough copy stage. Making editorial

changes at the galley or page proof stage can escalate costs dramatically.

- Use the approval process to maintain control over expenditures as they occur. Many organizations do this automatically by setting ceilings on the dollar amount each level of management can approve.

Cutting the Budget

Sooner or later most public relations practitioners must cope with a budget cut. In most cases, such cuts are part of an organizationwide expense reduction. Usually the communications department is told to reduce its budget by a prorated percentage or dollar amount. When the cut is a modest one, standard cost-control measures can tighten the department's belt a notch or two without major cuts in communications programs. Often a near-future plan can be postponed, reduced, or eliminated, or a publication schedule adjusted by an issue or two.

If the budget cut is a major one, however, practitioners must eliminate existing programs. If the communications department's budget is based on a prioritized list of activities to begin with, cutbacks are easier to manage without jeopardizing the department's ability to accomplish its essential mission. When this is the case, it may be possible to negotiate budget cuts with top management, eliminating specific activities and evaluating the resulting trade-offs and relative disadvantages.

A budget cut can even provide an opportunity to improve a communications program. At Western Electric's Hawthorne Works in Chicago, a local advertising budget was targeted for a budget cut during a period of corporate retrenchment. The budget cut prompted the public relations department to take a hard look at the advertising program in question. To cut this budget the department withdrew from its long-standing sponsorship of a once-a-year television program and started a series of spot radio commercials. The result was an improved advertising program: more exposure to a more select audience at a substantially lower price.

In addition to providing an opportunity for smarter management, a budget cut also is a potential communications opportunity for the public relations practitioner (see figure 23.3). Although the chief executive may not initially think of communications as an aid in solving a financial problem, a communications program that helps increase revenues or cut expenses could justify an increase in the public relations effort rather than a cutback. A downturn in sales, for example, may call for a new advertising or sales promotion program. Cuts in advertising budgets could lead to increased public relations efforts as the most efficient way to promote the company. Or a corporate retrenchment such as a plant closing may create the need for expanded employee information or community relations efforts.

Illinois Bell initiated an employee information program to generate employee support for a companywide budget cut. Because the individual

Figure 23.3 Investing in specially-designed costumes helped Illinois Bell call public attention to an upcoming change in the procedure for dialing long-distance phone calls. Though not inexpensive, the costumes and other expenses combined with public appearances cost considerably less than paid advertising. Results of the campaign proved that this unusual expense was an economic and worthwhile investment.

actions of employees at all levels affect the cost of doing business, management needed the active cooperation of every employee. The corporate communications department produced a videotape in which the company president and other officers explained the company's financial situation. This was supplemented by a supervisory discussion package for use in employee meetings, along with follow-up articles in the companywide employee magazine and departmental newspapers.

All employees were asked to help find ways to save money. The program more than paid for itself, as employees, understanding the need and the link to their own jobs, generated hundreds of money-saving suggestions. If the budget is built properly in the beginning, the downside risk of any cut will immediately be known; and it can be assessed with all other cuts so that its comparative impact will be known.

Redirecting Resources to Targets of Opportunity

Every public relations practitioner needs to be agile enough to respond to unforeseen communications needs and opportunities to meet organizational goals. Usually this involves securing additional resources to take advantage of the opportunity, either from within the departmental budget or in a supplemental allocation approved by top management.

For example, when the Chicago Symphony Orchestra reversed a long-standing policy and decided to allow local radio broadcasts of its concerts, it presented an unique advertising opportunity for Illinois Bell. The company already used cultural radio programming as a way of "rifling" its advertising messages to business decision makers. Broadcasts of the popular symphony were certain to attract corporate sponsors immediately. When Illinois Bell was offered the chance to sponsor the program it had to act quickly—otherwise another sponsor would be found and the company could lose the opportunity to participate in these broadcasts for years to come.

The corporate communications department quickly made a recommendation outlining the advantages to the company's marketing effort and got the additional budget allocation needed to take advantage of this opportunity.

Bank of America got an unexpected chance to host a meeting of political cartoonists: a unique press relations opportunity. Although the event hadn't been incorporated in the public relations department's budget, the department was able to shift resources internally to fund this activity without exceeding the overall budget.

One method that improves a communications department's agility is to keep unallocated reserve funds as a separate item in the budget. Illinois Bell's practice is to keep the budgets of subordinate work units lean, with resources earmarked for specific activities, and use funds at the point of departmental budget control to build in the flexibility needed to keep the department responsive and agile.

MEASURING RESULTS

To receive budget allocations it is essential that some measure of the return be available. Thus, measurement of public relations results is as essential to the public relations budget as planning and financial management. Because the department's budget allocation is a measure of top management's investment in communications, results of communications activities (see figure 23.4) provide the return on this investment that managers expect.

Most public relations programs can be quantified in some fashion even if "hard" figures on actual results are not available or cannot be identified:

- Numbers of releases, numbers of press clippings, attendance at shareowner meetings, numbers of public talks and attendance figures, numbers of uses of exhibits and displays—all satisfy the need to indicate audience size in the common management language of numbers. The numbers are only meaningful, though, if they are compared to predetermined objectives.
- Advertising programs usually are measured in the course of their

Figure 23.4 Producing a high quality employee magazine on a budget takes careful forecasting and expert expense management. As part of a company-wide budget cut Illinois Bell reduced its employee publications expenses by 40 percent without eliminating any publications.

implementation with media measurements and sales figures. Advertising and promotional programs also may be measured by offering a premium or free literature and tracking response.

- The cost of some projects can easily be compared to the cost of other ways of reaching the same audience. For example, a promotion program to inform Illinois Bell customers of a major service change (dialing an extra digit for every long distance call) was approved enthusiastically when its projected costs were compared to more expensive paid advertising.
- Formal research, measuring public and employee attitudes and levels of knowledge, is designed to help formulate and evaluate communications programs, but also can be useful in the budget process. At Illinois Bell, vice presidents of the company's operating units get results of employee surveys annually to assess their departments' needs for employee communications—assessments that often lead to departmental information programs funded by the departments themselves.

Comparing budget expenditures to program results also is helpful in building knowledge and factual evidence to formulate future budgets—both for the benefit of the communications manager looking for ways to get the most out of the department's budget and to assure the organization's top managers that the communications effort is cost effective.

For public relations practitioners, the bottom line of the budget process is not merely a matter of getting the resources needed for current programs. It's an opportunity, perhaps the best opportunity, to enhance the stature of the communications function by building credibility within the organization, demonstrating sound management, and using management's investment in communications to yield results.

EVALUATING

Rudolph Marzano

Media Relations Manager
AT&T Information Systems

The scene: The Oval Office of the White House on March 21, 1973. John Dean has told President Nixon there is a "cancer" eating at his administration, that his presidency is in mortal danger, and that some of his top aides and other members of his reelection team may face jail if convicted of obstruction of justice.

The president seems unshaken as Dean shifts to specifics, citing people, possible perjuries, cover-up tactics, and even the spectre of blackmail by the Watergate burglary team. Finally, as Dean outlines the possible felonies involved in the "dirty tricks campaign," the president says:

"I have been sick about that because it is so bad the way it has been put out on the PR side. It has ended up on the PR side very confused."

In those two sentences Mr. Nixon touched on what may well have been the fatal flaw in his administration: the belief that news could be doctored, events maneuvered, people constantly fooled. In brief, that when things go badly, one can always "PR it." They also show that Mr. Nixon—the candidate, the president, the lawyer—hadn't the least notion of what PR is all about. And, judging from events, he had plenty of company, among them many people who should have known better.

What then *is* PR—the profession of public relations—all about in this, the final quarter of the 20th century? How does one spread understanding of this vital aspect of corporate life, one in which thousands of highly skilled men and women work at the very heart of every large company in America?

One step toward understanding is to banish the word "practitioner" to

Rudolph Marzano joined the Bell System in 1966 with the Western Electric Company and transferred to AT&T in 1970. In writing this article, he drew on 20 years experience in corporate public relations. Mr. Marzano started his career as a reporter on the former Newark *Evening News*.

Mr. Marzano's chapter was written just prior to the court-ordered breakup of the Bell System and therefore presents the cumulative experience of the entire nationwide organization with respect to evaluating.

the world of press agentry, where it belongs. One practices press agentry, one lives public relations. If Mr. Nixon and his cadre of aides had been aware of this basic distinction, Watergate might indeed have remained a third-rate burglary. Further, it might never have happened at all.

Another is to mark how far the profession has come since the one-man shops of the 1920s, those years when, in too many instances, public relations and sales gimmickry went hand in hand—when, for example, one world-famous industrialist, Ivar Kreuger, the "Match King," considered it a public relations coup to have his salesmen spread the word that three on a match is bad luck.

Today, 60 years later, public relations is a big part of big business and most other major institutions. No one-man shop could cope with a combination of media relations, employee information, advertising, community and educational relations, consumer affairs, speechwriting, and corporate contributions—all major activities of a typical corporate public relations department in the 1980s.

In today's business and regulatory climate, the people involved in such activities work long hours at what has become through the years a demanding profession. One cannot "PR it" when faced with a bad earnings report, any more than one can use "publicity" to justify a price increase or product failure. It takes hard work and truthful writing—two basic public relations tools—to cope with such situations.

Amid this complexity, then, perhaps the best way to understand public relations is to measure it and then analyze the measurements to see what they reveal about both the people and methodology involved. Of course there are those who will say—have been saying—that you can't measure public relations, it's a *creative* profession and you can't measure the output of *creative* people.

Well, it has been measured for a number of years now at most Bell System companies, proving that those who say nay are wrong in several important respects.

First, public relations is actually more craft than creativity. For example, putting together a news release, that most basic of all public relations skills, is not a "creative" act. It is one that requires clear thinking, the ability to marshall and understand the facts and issues involved, and the training and discipline needed to put those facts and issues on paper clearly and logically. That is craftmanship, not creativity, and the effectiveness of such craftmanship can be measured, as is explained later in this chapter.

Even speechwriting, which comes as close to the creative act as anything else in public relations, really involves the same kind of understanding and discipline that goes into a news release. The speechwriter's creativity lies in the approach to a given topic and, sometimes, the style with which it is presented.

Finally, down through the years the people of the Bell System have proved that virtually anything can be measured—from the intangible, such as operator courtesy, to the concrete, such as dial tone speed and network call completion, to name just a few of the more than 100 Bell measurement plans currently in operation.

Given that tradition of measurement, it seemed only natural when, in early 1976, Edward M. Block, AT&T's public relations vice president, appointed six Bell assistant vice presidents to a committee charged with developing the first public relations measurement plan in the history of corporate America.

One of the committee's first steps was a study of all Bell System public relations departments to determine the functions they carried out in common. The results highlighted six areas for measurement: media relations, advertising, employee newspapers, community relations, educational relations, and administrative analysis (to track PR expenses). The direction and scope of the overall measurement program were thus laid out, and the areas will now be taken in turn.

MEDIA RELATIONS

The committee's first move in measuring the effectiveness of Bell's media relations was to find out, at the start, how the Bell System was viewed by media people: how effective were the news releases and other material sent to them? and were media people's queries answered fully and promptly?

So the committee asked these questions, by means of 1,600 questionnaires mailed to a random sample of working news people: reporters, editors, publishers, program directors, and station owners.

The results were gratifying, not only in how the Bell System was regarded among the random sample, but by the level of interest shown in the survey itself. Of the 1,600 questionnaires, 1,148 were returned, a 72 percent feedback in a survey area where a 40 percent to 50 percent return is considered very good.

Some of the findings are listed in table 24.1.

With such results in hand, AT&T therefore knew going into its measurement venture that its money would not be wasted and that there was media interest that could be measured on a continuing basis. The question

TABLE 24.1 MEDIA RELATIONS

	Better than most	About the same	Worse than most	No opinion
Relations with media generally	60%	27%	11%	2%
How honest and straightforward the information is	44%	43%	8%	5%
The clarity of press releases	40%	42%	5%	13%

was, were such percentages one-shot temporary results, or could they be sustained over the coming years?

The goal, then, was objective, national media relations data that would reflect both events within and about the Bell System, as well as how those events are perceived by the nation's press over a long period of time.

The project began with help from the Annenberg School of Communications at the University of Pennsylvania. A sampling of stories about Bell in various newspapers was analyzed by the Annenberg people and then broken down into the categories into which most Bell news would be likely to fall: technology, labor, rates, government, etc.

Guidelines were set as to what would constitute a positive, neutral, or negative news story in each category. A coder's manual for those who would decide the tone of each clipping was started and eventually covered 80 typewritten pages, meticulously defining each category and the criteria to be used in adjudging news clips.

It is important to note at this point that the measurement process was set up from the very outset in ways that would guard against internal bias on the part of AT&T. Aside from AT&T's defining its measurement goals, outside groups always performed any function that might conceivably reflect on the integrity of the program.

To be specific, the clips were gathered nationwide by a professional clipping service, which sent them to another outside company for processing. There, a specially trained staff categorized each clip and judged whether it was positive, neutral, or negative as to what it covered regarding the Bell System. The results were entered into a data base that produced quarterly printouts.

When it was felt, early on, that coder consistency should be tested to ensure uniformity of judgment and use of the criteria, this was done by a group headed by Dr. Klaus Krippendorff, professor of communication at the Annenberg School in Philadelphia.

In brief, the clippings were gathered by one non-Bell organization and analyzed as to content and tone by another, whose coders were tested by a third. Again, measurement integrity is involved here. With outside organizations performing these vital functions, the possibility of clippings being doctored or data altered in the interest of any Bell System unit was virtually nonexistent.

Now to the continuing operation of the program; a review of its results; and, where appropriate, an explanation of what those results are intended to reveal.

Gathering the data—the raw material for measurement—is more intricate than it sounds. Some companies had their results broken out by state, others often by cities, and in some instances, even by zip code. As a result, the reporting of the combination of national, state, and local data required some 7,000 pages of computer printout each quarter.

The 7,000 pages encompassed individual measurement results for each Bell entity and material for the national report, a quarterly compilation of printouts, tables, and charts that apply to the Bell System as a whole. It is this report that best illustrates the goals of the program and how they are depicted, with the major components as follows.

Totals

Figure 24.1 illustrates national figures for a quarter picked at random (as is the case for all other examples used). The percentages fluctuate from quarter to quarter so that positive percentages and neutral percentages could be lower or higher for any given time.

The circulation column of figure 24.1 represents potential reader or viewer exposure. In other words, the clips tallied represent a combined circulation of 1.784 billion.

	Clips	%	Circulation	%
Positive	16,207	55.0%	957 Million	53.6%
Neutral	11,142	37.8%	715 Million	40.1%
Negative	2,125	7.2%	112 Million	6.3%
Total	29,474	100%	1.784 Billion	100%

Includes Both Print And Electronic Media; Each Broadcast By A Network Outlet Equals One Clip.

Figure 24.1   Second quarter clips total chart.

Treatment of Clips

Designed for a "quick read," figure 24.2 takes the general figures in figure 24.1 and makes them specific to category, number, and tone. In figure 24.2, for example, customer service, a key Bell measurement, accounts for 15 percent of the quarter's 29,474 clips. Of these clips (concerning customer relations), 81 percent were positive, 16 percent were neutral, and 3 percent were negative. This technique of data collection allows for category results to be seen at a glance.

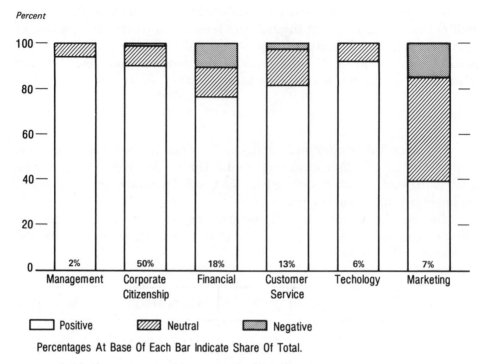

Percentages At Base Of Each Bar Indicate Share Of Total.

Figure 24.2　Second quarter treatment of clips chart.

Rebuttal Ratio

This measurement (figure 24.3) and the following one (figure 24.4) are really the "guts" of the entire program because they reflect not only what Bell media relations people do, but how well they do it. These two measurements, as far as can be told, originated with the AT&T program.

Rebuttal rattio (see figure 24.3) means that the clip analysts are able to identify a certain number of stories that are negative and, therefore, could have had the Bell system's side of the issues that was in question included.

This, then, reflects somewhat how well a Bell System media relations person knows, and more important, *is known by*, the working press in his or her area. In short, did the reporter or editor involved know a Bell System person to call for a Bell comment. In this regard, it should be noted that a "no comment" by a Bell spokesperson in a news account is a plus, for the measurement is based only on whether there was an *opportunity* to comment.

This opportunity factor makes the ratio a measurement for the long haul only. That is, there are too many variables—missed phone calls, deadline pressure, etc.—for it to be used, for example, for just one quarter. But over a span of time, a year perhaps, it takes on meaning.

Percent

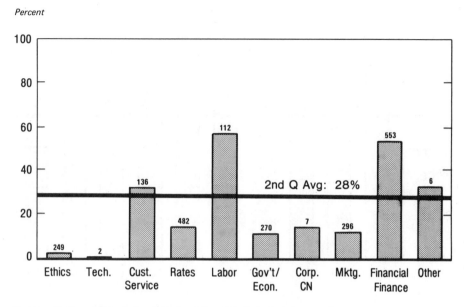

Number At Base Of Each Bar Indicates Clips With Rebutted Opportunity.
No Negative Management Clips.

Figure 24.3 Second quarter rebuttal ratio by category chart.

Using customer service again as the example, the figure 24.3 shows that of 136 negative stories in which a rebuttal was possible, some 30 percent were rebutted. Close enough for a quick read: the actual printout figures were 136 stories, 44 rebutted, for a ratio of 32.4 percent.

Over a five-year period, the Bell System national rebuttal figure was 35 percent, with local company percentages varying somewhat, but generally close to the national average. That 35 percent translates to a .350 batting average, good even for a Ted Williams, and especially good when it is pointed out that many network TV and radio negatives have been included. (These are virtually impossible to rebut because of the nature of network broadcasting: remoteness, inexorable deadlines, and the general lack of time to treat a single item for more than a few seconds.)

Company Input into the Media

This measurement (see figure 24.4), again over a period of time, gives a fairly accurate picture of what media relations is doing for the Bell system in terms that are especially important to any large organization—what is media relations turning out and how much of the material is being published or broadcast.

The input ratio, therefore is based on positive stories that the clip

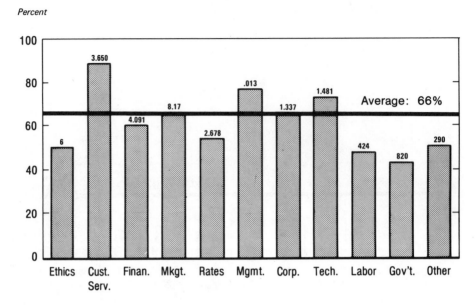

Numbers Indicate Total Positive Clips In Each Category

Figure 24.4   Second quarter company input into media by category chart.

analysts are able to identify as coming from company sources (i.e., news releases, speeches, interviews, or material that results from a personal Bell contact with a writer or broadcaster.

The black "average" line in figure 24.4 means that of all the positive Bell news clips in the second quarter, 66 percent were the direct result of Bell system media relations or other public relations personnel. Of the 3,650 customer service clips, 88 percent were linked to company efforts. The Bell system's four-year national input average was 71 percent.

Treatment by Publication Groups

Figure 24.5 is a simple measure of how the Bell system fared in the various types of publications clipped or monitored. Nothing is startling in this area except for the fact that radio coverage was non-existent. This in part was the result of a misunderstanding with the monitoring service.

Television and radio coverage seem to be the least effective measurements in the program. This is due in a large part to simple matters of cost. The ideal coverage would be local, as is the case with newspapers. However, this would probably cost in the neighborhood of a million dollars, given the number of stations and the high cost of broadcasting. Therefore, national coverage seemed more economical on the grounds that some coverage was better than none at all.

	Positive	Neutral	Negative
Dailies (20,675)	49%	42%	8%
Weeklies (4,116)	73	22	5
Trade Jnls. (1,370)	60	35	4
Bus.-Finan. (786)	61	34	6
Gen. Mags (80)	62	31	5
Network Radio (0)	0	0	0
TV (2,447)	70	30	0

For Print, Number Of Clips; For TV And Radio, Number Of Stations

Figure 24.5 Second quarter treatment of clips by publication groups chart.

Treatment by Circulation Size

Figure 24.6 answers the question, from quarter to quarter, of how the Bell system fared in various-sized publications. If there were a four-year chart the results would be comparable to figure 24.6. From a positive clip standpoint, Bell does better in the very small papers. However, the negative line at the bottom of figure 24.6 proves that the press in general views the Bell system in a positive light.

Treatment by Syndicates

Wire service and editorial treatment of Bell news and issues is shown in figure 24.7, which is a simple compilation of clips divided into percentages. For example, of 10,243 clips off the Associated Press wire service, 43 percent were positive, 48 percent were neutral, and 9 percent were negative. The only difference between figure 24.7 and the average syndicate chart is that editorials are not as negative on the latter chart and tend to cluster toward neutral at a rate higher than 46 percent.

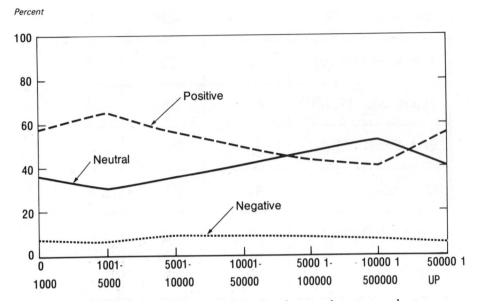

Figure 24.6   Second quarter treatment of clips by circulation size chart.

	Positive	Neutral	Negative
AP (10,243)	43%	48%	9%
UPI (1,817)	38	52	10
Other (1,611)	35	43	22
Average (13,671)	42	48	10
Editorials (356)	15	46	38

Number Indicates Stories

Figure 24.7   Second quarter treatment of clips by syndicates chart.

Category Charts

There are 36 of these charts: a positive, neutral, and negative for all 11 Bell categories. Each chart is a bar chart for the companies involved in the program. Individual clip totals are listed at the bottom of each bar. In this way, the Bell companies can not only see how they have been doing individually, but they can compare their clip totals with the totals of all other participating Bell-system companies. Although these charts (see figures 24.8, 24.9, and 24.10) were not designed as "report cards," some people use them as such. However, the chart's principal function is to make companies aware of areas that require attention. Therefore, if the charts reveal a sharp increase in negative customer service clips, the company involved would know that something may be wrong in the most important area of that company's business—its relations with its customers.

The category charts cannot be interpreted individually, but must be read in their natural cluster of three. For example, Southern New England Telephone (SNET) had a total of 90 customer service clips in the charts depicted. When this total is considered—56 positive, 25 neutral, and 9 negative—that negative bar takes on its true perspective as only 10 percent of the total. In the same manner, the seemingly less impressive positive bar actually represents more than 60 percent of the total.

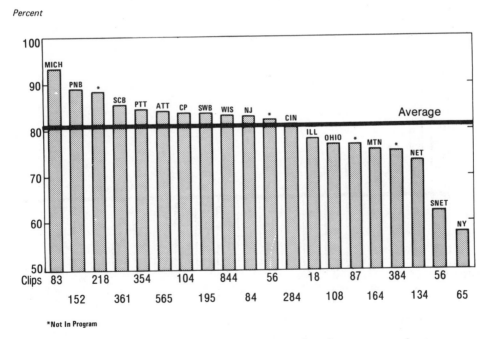

Figure 24.8 Second quarter number of positive clips by company chart.

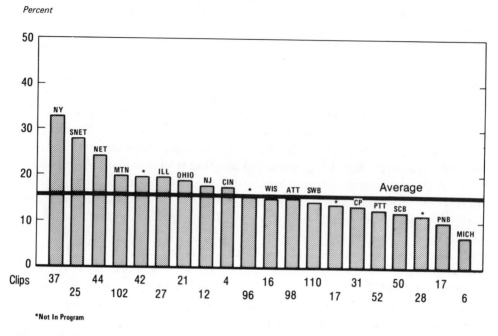

Figure 24.9   Second quarter number of neutral clips by company chart.

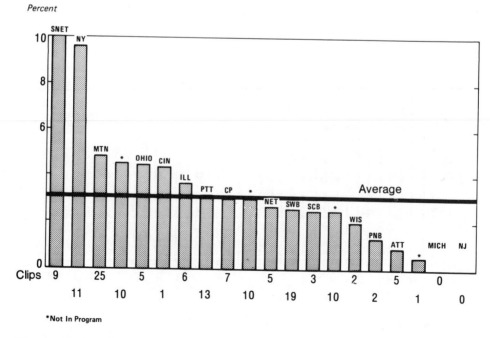

Figure 24.10   Second quarter number of negative clips by company chart.

In closing this media measurements section, some general observations based on almost five years of measurement experience are in order.

The program can be as flexible as desired at any given time. That is, results can be analyzed broadly, by category, or narrowed to individual stories if necessary. For example, media treatment of a speech can be judged with precision using the individual story option.

Whether the speech makes *Vital Speeches* is immaterial when the clips can be made to answer: did the press use the speech at all? if so, were the major points covered? how prominently was it played? was the lead straight or did some editorial bias show through? were there editorials based on the speech? and if so, were they favorable or not?

With measurement properly used, that kind of analysis is possible on any news material issued by any company at any time.

The costs of the program can be tailored to specific company needs. That is, clip categories can be few or many and clips totals can be based on a census (taking all clips available) or a scientific sampling, such as is used by Roper, Harris, and others.

Along this vein, the program should be an evolving one, with changes made to fit circumstances and categories cut when they have outlived their usefulness, since the more categories, the higher the cost. For example, three categories were cut from the AT&T program when, after five years, they had revealed all that needed to be known in those three areas.

Finally, one of the most important functions of AT&T media measurements was to keep the negative numbers in perspective. Bad news not only travels fast, it sticks in the mind, sometimes out of all proportion to its real import. Time and again media measurement has shown that Bell System news is not only treated fairly by the nation's press, but that the negative numbers are nowhere what they seem to be on a given "bad" day.

ADVERTISING

In the area of advertising, AT&T decided to find out in the late 1970s—through measurement—how much revenue resulted from money spent on promoting intrastate long distance calling (Message Toll Service, or MTS) among residence customers.

That question, however important, is a narrow one. It is not concerned with customer awareness of advertising, or recall, or any of the other criteria usually used in advertising research. It addresses itself solely to whether or not the Bell System could show specific dollar return from advertising intrastate long distance calling to residential customers.

Residential intrastate long distance calling was selected for measurement because it is the most uniform advertising done by Bell telephone companies. A major problem was that long distance is a mature service, advertised for decades, and therefore isolating specific effects was difficult. This was overcome, however; and the results achieved were convincing proof that advertising had made a substantial contribution to the development of that service.

Although there had been extensive research on intrastate long distance advertising, most of it was marred by problems in methodology, or was involved in aspects of advertising unrelated to the specific measurement sought. What was needed, therefore, was an econometric model designed to produce data pertinent to the Bell System's needs.

In this vein, any first-year student of statistics can produce such a model, given a batch of numbers and a computer program. However impressive and scholarly the result might seem, it would not necessarily reflect sound measurement. The test of any such statistical exercise would be to compare its methods and conclusions with those of more rigorously designed econometric models, and thus determine validity.

With this in mind, an ad modeling task force was established within the Bell System in April of 1979. The "common form model" (CFM) it subsequently developed is therefore consistent with other econometric models developed by Bell companies for other purposes.

The key elements in the Bell ad model are (1) the variables to be examined are standardized; (2) the numbers that stand for the variables are defined as to source; and (3) a uniform methodology is employed.

The model estimates the contribution to revenue per advertising dollar spent on residence interstate stimulation, with calculations on the "aggregate level"—overall dollars on a state level. Thus the model is frequently referred to as an "aggregate model."

In any case, such aggregate models rely on economic theory and statistical analysis for selection of the variables that best explain the effect of the advertising involved on consumer behavior (demand). Econometric models of this kind are designed to approximate mathematically how consumers respond in the form of purchasing decisions.

The Standardizations

To measure ad performance among the Bell Operating Companies (BOCs), some uniformity was essential. This model defines that uniformity as follows:

- *Time Frame:* The data used in the model are from January 1974 through December 1978—five years in 60 monthly intervals. In some instances the data was available on a quarterly basis only, in which instances the monthly intervals were interpolated.
- *The Variables:* The objective is to predict residential intrastate long distance revenue as an outcome of the interaction of price of service,

income of the customers, advertising, and seasonalities (e.g., very likely less calling in the summertime in some states). The resultant equation may be stated as:

$$\text{Intrastate Residential} = \begin{Bmatrix} \text{price} \\ \text{income} \\ \text{advertising} \\ \text{seasonalities} \end{Bmatrix}$$

- *Data Sources:* To be certain all companies used the same kinds of data, the task force specified the sources for all facts and figures involved in any ad model.
- *The Method:* Uniform statistical methods were required of the companies that used the common form model. The method used for the Bell model employed correlation and multiple regression techniques.

Elasticity

This is an econostatistical term that can be defined briefly as the sensitivity or responsiveness of one variable (e.g., revenue) to changes in other variables (e.g., advertising or price). Specifically, advertising elasticity is defined as the percentage change in revenue due to a 1 percent change in advertising.

One way to visualize elasticities is to think of each of the variables in the given equation (revenue = price, income, advertising, seasonalities) as being five rubber bands all bound together. The pertinent question then is how much does the movement of one rubber band affect a second rubber band when all the others are held constant? In terms of the examples used above in defining elasticity, this would involve calculating statistically the elasticity of advertising, which means its effect on revenue.

The Outcomes

In applying the model in an actual company, the advertising elasticity was 0.026, meaning that a 1 percent increase in advertising expenditures yielded a 0.026 increase in residence intrastate long distance revenues.

In actual application, the elasticity was applied to one company's test data in the following manner:

- 1% of the mean monthly ad expense : $.01 \times \$19,719 = \$197.19$
- 0.026 of mean monthly intrastate LD revenue : $.00026 \times \$2,784,252 = \$723.90$
- Payback ratio : $\dfrac{\$723.90}{\$197.19} = \$3.67$

Or, a $1 increase in advertising expenditures yielded a $3.67 return in residence interstate long distance revenues.

Obviously, however, the Bell companies are likely to vary as to the elasticities they obtain, and therefore in the payback ratios. Some qualifications are called for in talking about these elasticities and payback ratios in any and all situations.

- First, the elasticity factor is an estimate and has "confidence limits" associated with it. That is, the 0.026 may vary plus or minus a specified amount.
- Second, the payback ratio isn't all profit, since there are costs associated with the extra calls generated. In the example cited, the *net* payback ratio is $2.89 per increase in ad expenditures.
- Third, all the outcomes are reported in terms of demand averaged over the day. If the increase in demand is largely in traffic shifts, then other data would be required for the model and the outcomes may vary.

EMPLOYEE PUBLICATIONS STUDIES

In most large corporations newspapers published by the public relations department play a major role in informing employees of developments not only in their individual companies, but in their industry as a whole.

In the Bell System there are more than 200 such employee newspapers with a combined total annual budget of about $7 million. With such numbers involved it seemed appropriate to measure the effectiveness of Bell newspapers at the same time the media measurement program started in 1978. The study was conducted in two phases: one in 1978 to establish benchmark results, and another three years later for comparison.

Both measurements were based on the following six performance criteria:

- *Distribution*: What percentage of employees received the publication on a timely basis? If out of date, the publication loses some value. If some employees didn't receive it at all, some of the publishing costs are wasted.
- *Awareness*: How well did employees recall important articles?
- *Reliability*: Did the paper present both sides of an issue well? Was it a good source of information? Did the employees therefore consider the paper trustworthy?
- *Understanding*: Did the readers clearly understand the company position on important issues and events?
- *Readability*: Did the employees comprehend the paper's contents

without difficulty? (As was expected, this measurement had an effect on the other five.)

- *Cost*: Although not a precise measurement because of differing local conditions (e.g. varying costs for printing and labor), it was felt the cost factor would be valuable as an estimate nationally and for comparative purposes between the two study periods. Estimated cost efficiency was arrived at by dividing total cost by reader awareness, the key measurement in the whole process.

For both studies the participating editors agreed to run five test articles in one issue in addition to the regular news and features. For four of these, AT&T furnished the story concept and main points to be covered, leaving writing and layout up to the editors. The fifth, or "control," article that appeared in all publications was provided by AT&T's employee communications organization.

The story concepts for the test and control articles in both studies were representative of the general run of articles that appeared most often in the publications involved. Although the individual test stories were different, of course, the topics were identical. This gave both tests a uniformity that later enabled the interviewers who conducted the studies to obtain data from each that were comparable, even on a national scale.

At each Bell company, the data were compiled from the results of 50 telephone interviews with randomly selected employees (20 management, 30 nonmanagement) conducted by a professional polling firm, for a total of 1,000 interviews. This sample size produced results that were statistically significant, but too limited to be used as "report cards" for each publication.

The results of the studies are listed in table 24.2.

TABLE 24.2   RESULTS OF TWO TELEPHONE INTERVIEWS

	1978	1979
Distribution Efficiency	71.0%	70.0%
Awareness	38.0%	41.0%
unaided recall	9.0%	7.0%
aided recall	29.0%	34.0%
Understanding	74.0%	70.0%
Readability		
(years of schooling)	10.2%	8.1%
Reliability	22.0%	16.0%
excellent as source	26.0%	20.0%
presents both sides	17.0%	12.0%
Cost Efficiency	$.57	$1.02

COMMUNITY RELATIONS

For many years Bell System companies have had a program of public talks given by employee volunteers to various community groups such as Rotary, Kiwanis, Chamber of Commerce, and Business and Professional Women. These talks have been written by AT&T, by Bell Laboratories, or by local telephone company personnel.

There was little need for formally evaluating them because they were usually written by subject matter experts and were not particularly controversial.

In 1981, however, the Bell System decided to position itself as an Information Age company and a public talk was written at AT&T for use by the operating companies to help that process. Entitled "Information a la Carte," it was intended to explain the Information Age, illustrate why the Bell System was a logical supplier of various new services and equipment, and prepare listeners for even more changes in telecommunications, including the eventual restructuring of the Bell System.

The importance of the subject dictated that the talk be tested more formally than was usual, so the firm of Yankelovich, Skelly and White, Inc., was engaged by AT&T to do so. The talk was presented by an experienced New Jersey Bell speaker on two occasions and by an Illinois Bell speaker on the third. Audiences consisted of 18 members of a Lions club and 16 members of a Rotary Club in New Jersey, and 46 individuals who were specifically recruited in Illinois.

An evaluation showed that the subject was considered an important one to the audience, but that they had little specific information about the role of the telephone company in connection with it.

The speech was effective in imparting knowledge about specific subjects such as digital transmission, and it enhanced attitudes toward the Bell System as an "innovative" organization. Self-administered questionnaires issued pre and post talk indicated improvement in feelings of a significant nature about AT&T's innovative characteristics and commitment to the public interest. There was a significant change in perceptions of how electronic communications would change life styles, and concerns about the future cost of telephone service were mitigated.

A major accomplishment of the speech was in helping to make its audiences aware of events involving the restructuring of the Bell System. The questionnaires showed that many who were unfamiliar with the subject before the speech were able afterward to make the link between restructuring and the Information Age.

Because this was the first time in recent history that a public talk was specifically tested against clear objectives, it was possible to assure the telephone companies that audiences would react to the messages in the ways we had hoped they would and that important messages were successfully communicated.

EDUCATIONAL RELATIONS

A major element of educational relations activity for the Bell System during the 1970s was the development of four classroom game/simulations designed to give college students a greater understanding of the world of business.

Much of the educational and general literature of the period indicated that both college faculty and students, mirroring events of the day, were concerned with such subjects as ethical behavior (particularly as it related to business and government employees), corporate social responsibility, and individual privacy. It was also clear from the experiences of telephone people that there was a general lack of knowledge regarding the economics of a utility company.

Consequently, during the mid-1970s AT&T, with Simile II of Del Mar, California, developed four game/simulations that were tested on more than 25 college campuses, with some 1,000 students and faculty members involved during the various stages of development. Prototypes of the games were played and then modified where necessary, with the entire process taking almost three years.

The games were "Where Do You Draw the Line?—An Ethics Game," "The Privacy Game," "Relocation," and "Trebidies Island." Although they were quickly accepted by many college faculty members and students, as well as military and corporate trainers, it was felt that a further step was necessary: a formal evaluation to prove, or disprove, their ability to alter participant attitudes about the subjects involved.

It was decided to contract with Stevens Institute of Technology in Hoboken, New Jersey, to have faculty and graduate students in the Schacht Management Laboratory evaluate the effectiveness of two of the game/simulations. Subjects were 135 undergraduates at Stevens, and the two games examined were "Where Do You Draw the Line?—An Ethics Game" and "The Privacy Game."

Students were randomly assigned to participate in either an entire game session, a portion of a game session, or no game session. Following completion of the appropriate degree of game playing, students completed a series of questionnaires designed to assess their attitudes and perceptions of issues discussed during the game. The games were led by a professor in the management science department as Stevens, and the games were all videotaped.

Analyses of variance were employed to test for significant effects of extent of game playing (full game, part game, no game).

For the ethics game, significant differences in students' judgments of acceptable behavior and in their perceptions of business people were found as a result of game playing. Students often became quite involved and emotional when presenting and defending their own opinions, and a high level of group interaction was observed.

"The Privacy Game" was effective in changing students' beliefs and attitudes concerning specific privacy issues as well as more general attitudes.

The researchers concluded that: "...participation in game sessions can change the attitudes and perceptions of participants. We believe that the Ethics and Privacy games have important and widespread applications in filling a large void in the educational system. They encourage thought and discussion about very important topics. Both games would be valuable tools for educators...."

ADMINISTRATIVE STATISTICS

This measurement was designed to enable the Bell operating companies to keep track of the relationship between public relations and operating expenses. Through the years it therefore made it possible for the various public relations vice presidents to compare their individual budgets with those of the company as a whole, as well as to compare them with public relations budgets in the rest of the Bell System.

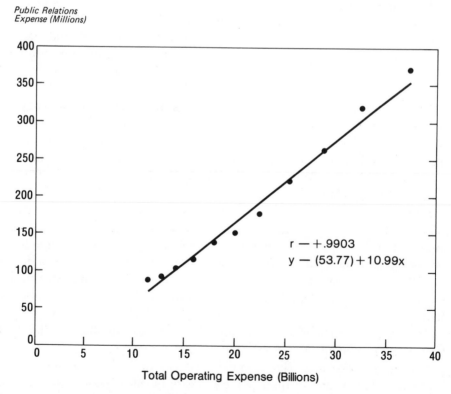

Figure 24.11 Correlation between total operating expense and public relations expense (1971–1981).

The charts for this area have shown that Bell PR departments have held the line on expenses and thereby kept them consistently close to operating expenses since the measurement began in 1971. Had this not been so, had the PR budget practices been looser, the value of the measurement would have been apparent in showing when and in what areas corrective practices were necessary.

Statistical analyses of such things as budgets and manpower allocations are not regularly distributed, but can be prepared from information available in a way that makes for useful comparisons, as illustrated in the following four charts.

Figure 24.11 shows the close correlation, as explained above, between the Bell companies' operating expenses and their public relations' expenses. About 98 percent of the time (r^2 coefficient of determination), there is a clear relationship between the total operating expense and public relations expense. If there were a perfect correlation between the two, all public relations expenses (represented by the dots) would fall on the solid line. Since the correlation is so nearly perfect, figure 24.11 shows clearly that during the 11 years illustrated, there was strict control of public relations expenses.

Figure 24.12 plots operating expenses and public relations expenses over the past 11 years on the basis of the number of main telephones and

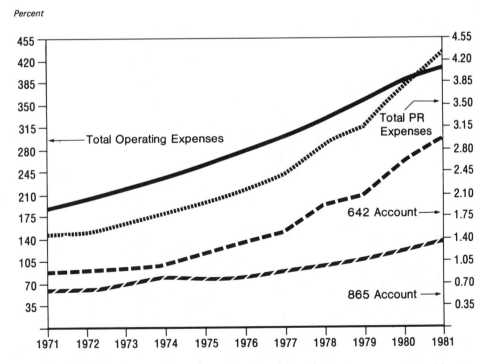

Figure 24.12 Total operating expenses and public relations expenses over 11 years on the basis of the number of main telephones and equivalent telephones.

equivalent telephones (extensions, etc.). The scale on the left side of the figure depicts the total operating expenses and the scale on the right side (at .01 of the operating expense scale) illustrates the public relations expenses.

Figure 24.13 shows public relations expenses as a percentage of total revenue. The top line of the figure represents the highest percentage for a company; the bottom line represents the company with the lowest total. The center line represents the Bell system average. Figure 24.13 does not represent any one company, however. Instead, the method of analysis was designed so that each company could use its own data to plot an annual graph.

Figure 24.14 illustrates the annual percentage change in total public relations expenses. It shows that between 1980 and 1981, the last period for which the expense figures were compiled, public relations expenses in the Bell-operated telephone companies increased by 16.2 percent. In analyzing figure 24.14 bear in mind that the black lines represent increases or decreases from year to year. For example, in the BOC average, the percentages for 1979, 1980, and 1981 were 18 percent, 21 percent, and 16.2 percent, respectively. This indicates that public relations expenses for 1980 increased by 21 percent over 1979, and expenses for 1981 increased by some 16 percent as compared to 1980. In other words, public relations expenses for 1981 did

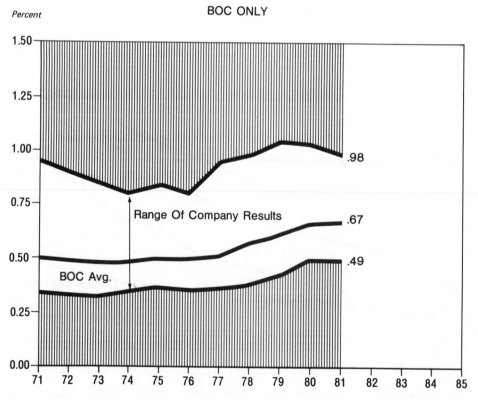

Figure 24.13   Public relations expenses as a percentage of total revenue.

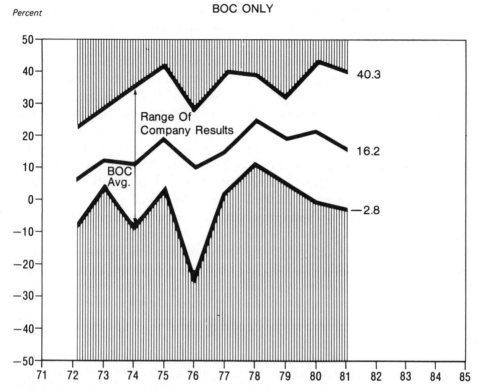

Percent

BOC ONLY

Range Of
Company Results

BOC
Avg.

40.3

16.2

−2.8

Figure 24.14 Annual percentage change in total public relations expenses.

not drop, but increased by a lesser percentage than in 1980 (up 21 percent in 1980 and up 16.2 percent in 1981).

CONCLUSION

In ending this chapter on evaluating public relations, events of the past two years must be taken into account in considering the future of such measurements in the Bell System. With divestiture taking effect on January 1, 1984, that future is uncertain. Some companies may elect to continue public relations measurement, others not. Or, with the telephone companies separated from AT&T, their central organization may elect to measure for the seven regional telephone companies.

In any event, some lessons learned during five years of measurement at AT&T can be passed on so that others who may want to start similar programs may benefit.

Keep the programs flexible in content by monitoring the results periodically so that only useful results are obtained. This applies to all measurements, be they media, advertising, community relations, or whatever. For example, the management category in the AT&T media measurement program was carried far too long. This category reflected how well the Bell System was managed in the eyes of the media and entities such as regulatory bodies that passed judgment on actions of the various Bell companies.

At the end of 1981 the category was reviewed. Among the hundreds of positive clips it was found that there were only 11 negative management clips—11 in four years. With those results it didn't seem necessary to measure the category any longer. The Bell System was obviously well managed.

Keep the programs simple. This can be done by substituting charts and graphs for computer printouts at every opportunity. The Bell experience in this regard has been that people are daunted by such printouts. Charts and graphs proved more practical and easier to comprehend.

Stand apart from the gathering and evaluation processes once a program's goals have been defined. Remember, in considering this, the management example cited above. AT&T can defend the fact that there were but 11 negative management clips in four years because the compiling and evaluation were done by outsiders who had no stake or interest in any possible pandering to upper management. If AT&T personnel had been involved, there would be a natural suspicion of bias. Again, let outsiders do the gathering and evaluating.

In any media measurement program scientific sampling can achieve the same results as clipping everything in sight, and at a fraction of the cost. The necessary consultant fees (an expert who can interpret the numbers and extrapolate from the results) are a pittance compared to the costs of a 30,000 or 40,000-clip quarter.

Give those who get the resultant measurement reports some words to read. As has been pointed out, many people are frightened by computer printouts with numbers alone. A two or three-page narrative explaining the numbers and highlighting major findings has proved useful at AT&T.

Finally, a public relations measurement program cannot be a one or two-shot affair. The results are meaningful over the long haul only. So it has been for the Bell System. Five years of measurement proved, among other things, that the Bell System is perceived as extremely well managed, that Bell technology is seen as of the highest quality, and that Bell System public relations people throughout the country are among the best in American industry. Such assertions would be suspect if based on one or two measurement periods. However, when considered on the basis of quarterly measurements over a considerable span of time, they become hard facts.

The author thanks Donald U. Honicky of AT&T for his work on the community and educational relations sections of this chapter, and Dr. William E. Taylor of Bell Telephone Laboratories for his mathematical and editorial help on the advertising section.

IV

HOW PUBLIC RELATIONS IS STAFFED

An Overview

Bill Cantor

President
The Cantor Concern, Inc.

In many ways, the rest of this book presumes that the "right" public relations people are already working at their jobs. What this section of the book is meant to do is to describe how to make sure that happens.

Hiring people and keeping them, however, only *appears* to be easy. There is that flood of resumes for every ad; five candidates proposed by the search firm. In fact, for many managers hiring and keeping good people is the most difficult and most painful part of their job. It shouldn't be. Like every other skill in business, this one, too, can be learned.

However, it *must* be learned. Great chefs will tell you that the real secret of masterful cooking is to get superb raw materials to work with. The same is true of public relations—or any other part of business. The skill lies in recognizing and using that raw material to its fullest. The best fruit is not

---

Bill Cantor is the president of The Cantor Concern, Inc., a New York City–based executive search firm specializing in the recruitment of public relations/public affairs professionals. He became a partner in Chester Burger & Company, Inc., the management consulting firm which services the public relations field, when the two firms merged in 1982. His concepts have influenced communications management attitudes toward hiring executive employees, maintaining their productivity, and prolonging their tenure.

Mr. Cantor has been widely quoted in the print and electronic media on business and employment trends, interviewing techniques, and related subjects. At the close of the Carter administration he was invited to conduct a workshop at the White House on the psychological aspects of interviewing techniques.

always the fruit with the shiniest peels; the best meat is not always the reddest.

From my own experience, the failures experienced by management in hiring and retaining their "right people" most often happen because management first failed to understand completely what they wanted, why they wanted it, and what they would do with it if they got it. After all, if you don't know where you're going, it doesn't matter who you use to get there.

Hiring and retaining the best people, though, can not only be learned as a skill, it can be an important learning experience for the manager. It can prove to be the time to reevaluate the organization and its goals. It can prove to be the opportunity to prepare for the future. Chapter 25 , I think, lies at the conceptual heart of this book. The moment of hiring is, after all, a moment of transition; and it is at such moments that great gains can be achieved—for an organization and for individuals.

FINDING AND KEEPING THE RIGHT PUBLIC RELATIONS PEOPLE

Bill Cantor

President
The Cantor Concern, Inc.

Far too often, executives try to find a person to fill a new or newly vacant job the way too many people look for a spouse. They know the position is empty. They have a vague, romantic idea of the job. What they really want is to fall in love.

Perhaps that's why there are so many divorces. It's certainly why many companies find it is so difficult to conduct a successful job search.

The public relations mission of an organization can be successfully achieved only by its sole real asset—its people. Their knowledge, skill, and dedication to the function they perform are vital to the organization. To find qualified professionals with the needed skills and experience is difficult enough. But to find them in people who also are compatible with each other and with management is extremely hard.

Look at some of the factors that you must consider in finding and keeping the right people in public relations or in any corporate function.

1. The requirements of the function to be filled
2. The skills and personality of the candidate
3. The skills and personality of the people to whom he or she will report
4. The nature of the organization

Consider, first, the requirements of the function to be filled. Much is at stake for both employer and employee. So it is a wonder that a job description does not exist for every employee in every organization. It constantly amazes me to find an employer who is willing to pay anywhere from $50,000 to $200,000 for an employee (plus the fee for a search firm to find the right candidate for the position), but who does not have a single sheet of paper describing what the person will be expected to do. The expectations are there, of course, in the employer's mind. But there they often remain, like a time bomb waiting to be set off when the new employee fails to meet expectations about which he knows nothing.

A job description, then, is critical to finding and keeping good people. It defines clearly the responsibilities and reporting relationships. Equally important, it can serve, after the job has been filled, as a planning tool and management guide in manpower evaluation, merit ratings, and performance appraisals.

Indeed, development of the job description, as an activity in itself, will prove useful to the supervisor for other reasons. It creates an opportunity for the supervisor to talk in depth with people currently in or around the position to learn how they view the job and whether their perception of what is expected of them corresponds to management's. It also can serve as a management guide for job simplification, work-load sharing, and general staffing needs within the department. In other words, developing the job description carefully helps answer the question: "Who is doing what, and who should be doing it if at all?"

In the hiring process, the job description can save management dozens of hours of time wasted on interviewing the wrong people. Whether the position is filled from within, from "outside" through a newspaper ad, or through the services of an executive search firm specializing in public relations, the people responsible for recruitment will do a much better job of sending the right candidates when they have a clear understanding of what the position entails.

Actually, the ideal person to develop a job description is the person currently in the job, if that is possible. Who knows more about what is really expected (as opposed to what people think is expected) than the person already doing the job? If that is impossible, however, the personnel executive may seek the help of a knowledgeable person within the organization to assist in writing the description. In either case, the procedure need not be complex. Typically, most jobs have no more than a half-dozen functions. All other activities usually can be grouped within these main headings. The more accurate the descriptive wording, the more useful the job description will be.

I have emphasized the job description because it is so critical not only to the hiring process, but also to the successful management of any operation. It is also, in my experience, the most neglected. The second factor to be considered in staffing is the personality of the desired candidate. What kind of person do you seek? Do you want a "star?" Do you want a team player? How will he or she interact with the present staff and with the other people with whom he or she will be working?

The job description will portray the skills you need. It will not answer the preceding questions. Yet the personality of the individual, at least as much as the skills, will determine the individual's success or failure. And personality is also difficult to discern in the hiring process, although experienced interviewers can see through the mutual "selling situation" that constitutes most employment interviews.

Third, there remains the nature of the employer. Each organization has its own personality, which is generally determined by or through its chief executive officer. Some CEOs are highly dictatorial and authoritarian in their style of management; their organizations reflect that style. Other CEOs concentrate on exercising their own skills, preoccupied with what they can do and less concerned with using the power of their position to support others in the organization. Still others are extremely sensitive and overly concerned with their own image. They bend over backwards to avoid offense to anyone and to be liked by everyone.

Without discussing what is the "best" style, if any, it is critical in the hiring process to understand that style and how it affects the organization's culture.

Note that understanding each of these factors requires both objective and subjective judgments. A clear understanding of these factors is the key to successful hiring and retaining people. Who, then, is best equipped to make these judgments and thus to carry out the hiring process?

The professional personnel executive is the one, in my experience, who often holds the responsibility for public relations staffing. Yet he or she usually has little opportunity to understand the profile of the ideal individual needed to meet the company's needs. Education or personnel experience have not prepared this person, to understand corporate public relations needs in any depth. Those in the public relations department who place the executive search order with him generally fail or are unable to provide the information he requires, or the job description he would insist upon before trying to fill virtually any other staff position in any other discipline.

There are two reasons for this. First, the personnel executive is the natural victim of the failure of public relations to establish agreed-upon standards or terminology for its functions or its people. Whether or not public relations is a profession or whether accreditation of education in public relations is necessary or even possible is arguable. Nonetheless, the fact that these arguments have been going on for more than 50 years is symptomatic of a definitional problem that afflicts public relations and those who deal with it. It's hard to shoot a bear if you don't know what a bear looks like.

The personnel executive may also fall victim to his or her own "insidedness." Usually too close to the organization, to its personality, to its politics, to its individuals, the personnel executive often finds it difficult to make both the objective and subjective judgments, and realize it. Moreover, when problems in the hiring process crop up, as they usually do, the personnel executive often yields to demands of those inside the company, to the detriment of the search.

Recently I was asked to find the "ideal candidate" for a middle-level public relations job. (For some reason, I am always asked to find the "ideal candidate," as if he or she ever existed; perhaps someday I will be asked to find the "less-than-perfect-but-good-for-us" candidate.) I submitted four candidates. After reviewing the dossiers and interviewing the individuals, the personnel executive called back to report. The first candidate was "too good, too strong," I was told. "She'll be bored with this job." The second and third candidates were a bit too weak, but the fourth intrigued them. My client interviewed the fourth candidate three times. At last, I was called again.

"Bill, this person is very good. But she is a bit light in the issues area. She needs eight or nine months more experience in that field and then she'd be perfect. I think you better find us more candidates."

"Wait," I said. "Don't you think that if she gets eight or nine more months experience, you'll then think she's like the first candidate? You'll think she's too strong, too good for the job?"

There was a long silence at the other end of the line. Finally, "Oh, yeah. You're right."

They hired her.

Please understand, I don't denigrate personnel executives or the personnel function. But public relations is not only relatively undefined, but is changing and evolving constantly. Subjective factors mean relatively more than in most other corporate functions. In this situation, internal people are faced with an extremely difficult task in the hiring process.

Yes, this is my self-serving plea for recognition of the value of the specialist in public relations executive search. At the risk of being ingenuous, you just wouldn't have your appendix removed by an opthalmologist. The same thinking should prevail in using executive search services.

But what kind of executive search services?

In March 1982, *The Recruiting & Search Report*, an industry newsletter, looked at the dilemma of clients seeking to hire the right search firm and classified four categories of searchers available for clients:

> Look again at the relative advantages/disadvantages associated with each category of firm[1] from the client's viewpoint. Even though each category of recruiting firm is theoretically capable of successfully completing any assignment, it should be obvious to client and recruiter that recruiter selection must be judgmental: the Acme Agency is unlikely to be able to locate and bring about the successful hire of a Fortune 500

1. Firms are categorized A, B, C, and D for purposes of this discussion.

divisional general manager. But the well-known retainer-only firm is just as unlikely to be able to locate a junior secretary in Biloxi, Mississippi. Different jobs require different staffing tactics.

Recruiters often overestimate their capabilities; clients overestimate their recruiting needs just as often. The reverse is also often true for both—just as the recruiter may expend time and effort on assignments that aren't worth the trouble when compared to his strengths, client firms may select "under-powered" recruiters for assignments beyond the recruiter's capability. Again, recruiters and client firms must work hard at picking each other. Poor recruiter/client selection is a major cause of many frustrations and disappointments surrounding this business.

Back to the client side—How do you know what sort of recruiter you are dealing with when you are approached? Let's consider some indicators:

A's are often effective as camouflage; since they will often be orchestrating a candidate's job search behind the scenes, you may not be aware of their existence. Some clues: resumes that are too slick for a candidate's background—these become easier to detect once you have received several from the same source. Word processor cover letters are also a giveaway. *A* firms are masters of hype. With a probability approaching 100%, these candidates are either unemployed or on terminal assignment.

B's will approach clients with "perfect" candidates, often described as such before any vacancies are discussed or described. Or, the "recruiter" will produce an instant candidate for your vacancy. Interestingly, the *B*'s fee schedule is often negotiable (you get what you pay for?). The emphasis is on the quick fix—he's got a lot of projects going. Also, the majority of the *B*'s candidates will be employed, "looking for great challenges," or otherwise motivated to make a change. Remember, the candidate sought out the *B* firm, not the other way around. The loyalty of the *B* to any given candidate is upredictable, because candidates are expendable; the *B* has another "perfect" candidate to replace the rejected one until someone tires of the process.

C's will resist pressure for quick solutions, and will ask lots of questions—probably more than you are used to answering, and often sensitive ones. The *C* recruiter will be stingy with candidates; they are hard to replace. He also tends to be conspicuous in his absence after several of his candidates have met with rejection. Expect resistance to fee negotiating. . . .

D's are the champion name-dropper and buzz-word artists. They prefer thick carpets and 42nd floor offices. While they'll probably be able to tell you who your competitors are and what your earnings per share were last year, knowledge of your industry may be superficial (few *D*'s specialize in an industry or function; they prefer to be "generalists"). Expect self-serving descriptions of recruiter credentials, elaborate proposals, patronizing attitudes toward personnel people, and a very sharp "front man" who will present the proposal.

Obviously I think the *C* people are the best. I'm one. In the discussion that follows, I'll speak about the hiring and staff maintenance process as it should go on. But, as you can see from the above description, which outside firm you choose, should you choose one at all, will affect the results you get.

Every staffing problem or opportunity has in common the three sides of a triangle: the employer, the employee, and the job to be done. Obviously, all three must be equal and in harmony to optimize the prospects for a successful match. If only two elements are in harmony, the chances for success are diminished, though still good. With none of them matching, hiring is possible; success is impossible.

Our basic approach to handling a search assignment is to press our clients for a crystal-clear description of the position they seek to fill. We do this in our very first conversation. Generally, such job descriptions are less than satisfactory. We need to know more, to clarify the position. We probe for answers to such questions as:

- What is expected of the candidate?
- In what period of time?
- Are company executives in agreement on this?
- Are they committed to the success of the public relations department?
- What attitudes and personality does the company wish to project?

Too often, the answers to such questions are not forthcoming; if we cannot get them, we will rarely accept the assignment. While we are paid by the company, we also feel a strong responsibility to the candidates. We will not ask a professional public relations person to go through the upheaval of changing employment and, in many cases relocation, if we do not feel that he or she has a fair chance for success in the new position. In this way, both our clients and our candidates are best served. (Most companies show little awareness of the hidden costs of executive turnover.)

If we do accept the assignment, there are more questions to be answered. These include:

- What problems have you previously had regarding this job?
- Why has (or has not) the current individual succeeded in the department?
- How sincere has the effort been to rectify existing problems in the department?
- What is the salary and fringe benefit package?
- What is the position's upward mobility? Is it only a transient position (two years)?
- What is the age of management?
- Has the company had EEO problems?
- How will the candidate's performance be evaluated?
- How do you coordinate the work of generalists with specialists?

- How do you upgrade the fitness, ability, and skills of your people?
- What is the role of the personnel department in the public relations operation?

With the answers to these and other questions in hand, the consultant begins the search.

While each firm conducts its searches differently, we all have in common the need to know who's who, and where. In our firm, we have developed a proprietary information retrieval system which, coupled with our knowledge of the field and its key people, rarely fails to produce candidates meeting the precise specifications. Bear in mind that the Public Relations Society of America lists approximately 11,000 practitioners on its membership roster. Of this universe, and within that group, we consider only a few hundred to be the real stars of the business. In our system, these professionals are analyzed and coded by 162 different criteria including aspects such as professional skills, specialized experience, outside interests, personality traits, and so on. Our "key executives" list is updated weekly, and our senior consultants make it their business to be in personal touch with everyone on that list at least once a year.

While I don't intend to be cavalier on this element of our activity, it should be clear that with the essential information already in our hands, the actual search for talent almost takes care of itself. That is, the obvious candidates for the position "surface" quite rapidly and almost mechanically.

Then begins the interviewing and screening process, the consultant's most important contribution since it saves time and avoids problems for the corporate personnel executive.

From this point on, almost all our effort is concentrated on determining the personality, attitude, and temperment that will best complement the company and the person to whom this position reports.

How do we accomplish this effort? First and foremost, we listen to and then ask questions, visiting and sensing the hiring executive.

Professionals who have been forthright with us and do not insist on "mirror hiring" maximize their chances for long-term success in public relations staffing. "Mirror hiring" is one of the more destructive errors that executives at high levels can make; no professional organization can flourish when populated by a cadre of act-alikes and think-alikes. Simply stated, in such cases the hiring executive seeks to add a younger edition of him or herself. Yet after serious thought, most executives quickly recognize they neither need nor could get along with a clone.

A careful search, of course, also may avoid the cost of a bad decision. Our studies have shown that an unsuccessful hire can cost as much as 130 percent of the salary involved. It's only prudent to get it right the first time.

After our client has successfully hired the "heavyweight" person it sought, it must examine whether the match will last for the desired period of time. This leads to my next geometric pattern: "the maintenance triangle." Employee satisfaction and retention take care of themselves if three basic opportunities are in place:

- Freedom of creativity. If a creative person is afforded the respect and environment in which to do the things he or she does best and, in fact, was hired to do, the professional has to be satisfied.
- Freedom of growth—emotionally and intellectually. Give a person encouragement to grow and room to do it in, and he has to be satisfied.
- Recognition in the form of remuneration based on performance. Pay a person well and increase that pay as his contribution to the company warrants, and he has to be satisfied.

If an employee possesses these three satisfactions and incentives in his professional life, why on earth will he want to change? Perhaps this analysis is simplistic, but I have found it to be true, especially when I have sought to convince a "star" employed elsewhere to take a look at employment with my client company. If his stardom is acknowledged and rewarded where he now works, he simply will not consider moving; he's already satisfied.

If we work on a continuing retainer basis with our clients, we have the opportunity to help them develop and operate the "maintenance triangle." This is one of the most rewarding aspects of our work.

Public relations professionals all too often feel ill-perceived or misunderstood by their employers. With our long-term knowledge of these people, coupled with our deepening involvement in their companies, we sometimes function as objective surrogates for management and ombudsmen for their public relations staffs.

I have given a great deal of thought to the problems of hiring the very best available public relations talent and, an ever-greater challenge, keeping that most valued employee. What would it take to increase success in these two tasks? My experience suggests an orderly approach to the problem. First, I recommend a structured process of interviews in five specific circumstances. Each of these circumstances require communication with valued employees. They are hiring, evaluation, promotion, relocation, and exit. To meet these circumstances, I recommend six kinds of interview:

1. The hiring interview
2. The job evaluation (or annual review) interview
3. The exit interview

(These three types of interviews are fairly standard operating procedure in most large organizations, although rarely are they done well.)

Also, I have developed the concept of three others, which although, not standard, I regard as essential to round out the program.

4. The job satisfaction interview
5. The promotion interview
6. The relocation interview

A number of corporations have told me that they employ most of these "critical six." Yet, in my more than fifteen years as an executive search consultant in the area of corporate communications, I have never met a single practitioner who has ever experienced all six types of interviews on a formal basis. Nor do I know any executive who knows anyone who has. I don't consider light conversation such an interview; my reference is to in-depth interviews in all six situations.

If these critical six interviews are done properly, I firmly believe that they would go a long way toward eliminating the phenomena described as "burnout" and the "Peter Principle." Such careful interviews would also increase productivity for the organization. They might even give us a happier and healthier society.

Without getting into the specifics of interviewing techniques, consider how, through the proper use of the critical six interviews, a company can substantially lower its burnout statistics and help eliminate problems caused by the Peter Principle.

THE HIRING INTERVIEW

Essentially, this interview determines the candidate's qualifications and personality fit. It is usually the initial contact between the employee and the employer. The basic problem with this interview is that it usually takes the form of a sales situation. The employee is trying to sell himself, and the corporate executive is selling either the job or the advantages of being a member of his organization. Neither wants to raise negatives, or expose his or her weaknesses or problems. The interviewer certainly does not want to air the organization's dirty laundry. And so we have a situation where getting down to the issues and to the unveiled reality rarely occurs.

It's my contention that such a hiring interview, with its inherent lack of candor, sets the stage, unintentionally, for potential burnout. It is most important that the candidate understand the goals that are expected of him within the first year, the second, or even the third year, so that he or she can decide if those goals are realistic. Does the candidate believe he or she can accomplish all or part of what is expected?

What obstacles should the candidate expect to encounter from a hostile staff member who resents his entry at a higher salary or position? Which department, if any, will be uncooperative because it doesn't want to relinquish authority? Which, if any, executive will feel threatened by the hiring of another executive with greater strength and skills, but who will report to him? And so on.

If these sensitive areas are aired, the candidate can determine whether he or she wants to take the position in the face of those obstacles. If he opts to join that organization, after learning the facts, the potential for burnout will be reduced because the *reality* was known prior to accepting the position. Management causes burnout by lack of cooperation in one form or another, or by avoiding full disclosure of important information to the candidate.

THE JOB SATISFACTION INTERVIEW

I recommend that this interview be conducted approximately four to six months after a candidate has begun his or her new position. In my concept the intention of the "job satisfaction interview" is exactly that, to determine how the person feels about the new position. Questions should include: "What do you think of the job?" "Is it pretty much as it was described?" "Do you have any questions?" Now you have firm grounds for discussion, if necessary. If any problems have developed or are beginning to surface, this is the time to identify them. I recommend this type of interview to be conducted at least once a year for all employees, regardless of their length of service with the organization.

If management takes seriously this interview and follows through with the information it receives, it will find fewer dissatisfied employees, fewer burnouts, and obviously less turnover.

Don't confuse the job satisfaction interview with the job evaluation interview.

THE JOB EVALUATION INTERVIEW

This interview, also known as the performance review, has become the second most common interview (after the hiring interview) in most organizations. Of all the interviews, the job evaluation interview has the greatest potential for raising resentments and hostility. In other interviews, management is seeking information from the employee. In this interview, management is giving information *to* the employee, information which the employee may not want to hear, may resent, and may feel is completely erroneous. At the same time, the employee will want to give information *back* to the manager that he or she may not want to hear, may resent, and may feel is completely erroneous. Not only are professional relationships at stake in this interview; so, too, are egos. That is a recipe for trouble.

Managers who undertake these interviews should have some kind of training in conducting them, and perhaps even some role rehearsal. More than one department has been destroyed by badly done evaluation interviews, and many careers have ended unnecessarily because of them. Evaluation interviews should take place only when a mutually agreed upon job description exists. That, at least, will provide both the manager and the employee with an objective basis for discussion, criticism, and agenda for improvement.

THE RELOCATION OR TRANSFER INTERVIEW

The relocation or transfer interview is a necessity for an organization wanting to keep its best talent. Often, the best and most productive employees are those to be transferred to a facility that requires their skills and talents. Similarly, an organization will select one of its outstanding producers to relocate geographically.

Seldom is an executive allowed to choose whether he or she would like to relocate. Many times employees fear to decline transfers because they believe this will cause them to be downgraded, terminated, or at the very least, have their career jeopardized in their company. Unfortunately, this is often exactly what happens.

I have difficulty understanding the rationale of companies who identify their best employees for very important positions and fail to interview them to find out if severe problems may result from the move. Some employees would welcome the change; for others, it may be a traumatic experience. The only way to determine the probable impact is to interview the employee.

If reluctant to relocate, the productive employee has but three choices: to relocate, to stay in the hope he will not damage his career, or to seek out a new position as soon as possible. A good percentage of those candidates who seek our services are often the best talent who cannot relocate, in some cases for very good reasons. Except in a few circumstances it doesn't make sense for any organization to force its better employees to leave. But that is the result of not taking the time to interview those employees.

Indeed, even if the reluctant employee does willingly relocate, the company will probably be the loser. If the spouse or children are terribly unhappy in their new environment, they will, even unknowingly, put pressure on that employee. These circumstances add to the potential for causing job burnout or family breakup.

The end result for the organization is a pathetic waste of the hard-to-find executive and of the dollars and effort that went into his development.

THE PROMOTION INTERVIEW

It is my concept that this interview could be the beginning of the end of the Peter Principle.

The "Peter Principle" is the point at which an individual is promoted from his level of competency to that of ineffectiveness.

A promotion offers one of the more exciting rewards of an organization.

It is granted on the basis of past performance. Usually, an executive assumes because someone has been in one position for a period of time and has done a good job, he or she should be promoted in salary and in position.

Let's examine the wisdom of this reward process, which often becomes almost automatic when one has done his or her job well and the next position above becomes vacant. Is he or she entitled to be elevated and given more responsibility? Perhaps. Should he or she be rewarded with additional responsibility? Not necessarily. Does the person to be promoted really understand the responsibility and the new skills that will be essential for success, or the additional hours that will be required to meet the new responsibility? Has he or she given enough thought to how that responsibility and the tension associated with it will affect his or her life? Does the person really know what the new boss expects? Does he know the idiosyncracies of his new superior? The questions go on and on. There's only one way to make sure each person is right for the new job: the same in-depth interview that the company would go through if it were hiring from outside the company.

The thorough interview I suggest rarely takes place when the number-two man is already on the scene. The assumptions have been made. The person has been waiting a long time for this opportunity; he'd love it. It is company policy always to promote from within. "Anyone inside the company already knows our policies, the structure, the politics, etc. So an interview is not really necessary." And so the company may lose another solid employee to job burnout or the Peter Principle.

THE EXIT INTERVIEW

Many large organizations, small companies, and public relations firms have told me about the effectiveness of their exit interviewing.

Yet just about every public relations professional who has gone through an exit interview jokes about the absurdity of a company expecting to get accurate information from such an interview. The standard answers to why one is leaving are moving for better opportunity, more money, greater responsibility, family reasons, etc. You would not expect a departing employee to answer, "my supervisor is terribly weak, paranoid, ineffective, comes in smashed almost evry day after lunch," or that "he's abusive, insulting, and vicious." Those are some of the reasons we hear in our offices when a candidate begins aggressively to seek a new position, while currently still employed.

During his exit interview, the employee is usually wise enough not to jeopardize his or her future by being honest and losing a reference. The employee also knows that a former superior could surface again, perhaps even with his or her new employer.

Yet the exit interview is critical to learning the real reasons for departure. Paying attention to those reasons will add strength to an internally weak organization. The process can be effective only if it is done by an outside person who will treat all comments under strict confidence. Based on our experience, the majority of executives who move to new positions do so because of limited growth opportunities, restrictions that limit his or her capability of accomplishing good work, or personality problems—*not* money.

These six interviews are needed to keep open and honest the channels of communication among all levels of public relations employees. The importance of such openness cannot be overestimated, for the public relations people in an organization are responsible for nothing less than the nourishing of the organization's reputation.

Henry Fiur, a corporate vice president of public relations firm, offers his public relations premise: "Behavior makes impressions; impressions yield reputation." If it is true that a chief executive has the major responsibility for managing the corporate reputation, it follows that his public relations people control the strongest set of tools at his disposal, the tools of communication.

Corporate public relations exists primarily to counsel concerning a company's behavior, and then to communicate that behavior on a consistent, credible basis. Those audiences whose recognition, understanding, and approval are central to maintaining and expanding the organization's franchise are the ultimate arbiters of corporate reputation. The CEO, through his public relations function, is responsible for securing their approval.

On that basis alone, it is clear that defining, finding, hiring, and maintaining the right people for corporate public relations work must be done professionally and accurately. In the most subtle and the most visible of ways, the organization's reputation depends upon it.

V WHERE PUBLIC RELATIONS IS GOING

An Overview

Merton Fiur

President
Center for Public Communication

T he future for public relations promises a rich agenda of opportunities and needs, challenges, and rewards.

The opportunity is to establish public relations clearly and permanently among the higher functions of organizational management and, in that process, position top public relations managers as peers of, and contenders for, chief executive positions. Contributing to that opportunity are the environmental changes that are expanding the protective and anticipatory dimensions of the management role. As organizations move toward uncertain futures, values and missions are being reassessed and new policies and messages are being formulated—activities that fall largely, if not totally, within the public relations responsibility.

If public relations professionals are to capitalize on their opportunity, however, they must still acquire demonstrable knowledge and understanding of the full spectrum of business functions and management considerations and, thereby, pull public relations into the business mainstream. This

---

Merton Fiur has spent more than 25 years in the public relations field, including 15 years as a counseling firm principal. His current management consulting practice, as well as his extensive teaching and writing activities, also encompass marketing and corporate planning. Mr. Fiur also is the founder and senior associate of the Center for Public Communication, which uses a computerized system to analyze public policy issues for various corporate planning functions.

requires making public relations more accountable in traditional organizational terms.

Major challenges await the practice of public relations as well. Primary tasks of the future include: changing the way organizational and management performance are judged; mediating new conflicts in society; fostering "people cultures" within the organization; and shifting to global strategies. These tasks will also demand new skills, such as: developing future-oriented research and analysis capabilities; mastering new communications technology; and dealing with new social, economic, and political configurations.

In this transition, public relations will redefine itself as the function of mediation and anticipation and grow beyond its limiting communications origins.

PUBLIC RELATIONS FACES THE 21ST CENTURY

Merton Fiur

President
Center for Public Communication

At any moment in history, society is confronted by alternative futures—different versions of what our world may be like some number of years down the road. Right now, the alternatives being explored in futures planning can be categorized into four broad clusters of possibilities:

1. *The American Dream*—in which our society is characterized by continuing growth and success. We overcome problems, maintain economic superiority, and prosper in social harmony.

2. *The American Disaster*—a "hard-times" scenario, in which problems overwhelm us, causing economic hardship and social dislocation.

3. *The Disciplined Society*—much like Orwell's *1984*, in which we trade in our freedoms and accept controls to keep society running smoothly and insure our comfort and security.

4. *The Transformational Society*—in which we adjust our values and priorities, focusing primarily on the individual. Fulfillment of human potential and quality of life are dominant.

Each of these alternatives is regarded as a legitimate candidate to represent our future because the seeds of each can be found in the events and trends that are visible today. Of the many forces of change currently discernible in our environment, the following most clearly—and powerfully—will shape the future of public relations:

- Awareness of, and concern about, change itself, which is shifting management priorities increasingly to protection of the organization's franchise and extending planning horizons well beyond the traditional three-to-five-year period.
- The rejection of traditional structure and hierarchy, seen in the decentralization of organizations and avoidance of institutions in favor of the individual.
- The political movement away from party ideology and government process to issues and informal networks.
- The demographic shifts in age and income distribution, creating a larger and disproportionately affluent elderly population.
- Economic and social globalization, breaking down borders, superseding national interests and drawing together individuals everywhere around shared ideas and information.

Each of these dominant trends is irreversibly changing our world and the way we live in it, individually and collectively. Within the next decade, we will see these changes significantly altering the positioning, practice, and management of the public relations function.

PERCEPTION AND POSITION

Like all trends, those just cited as having most significant impact upon public relations have been in the making for years. The fact that they are just becoming clearly visible to us only means that they are at or near their peaks and are being acted upon with increasing volume and intensity. That action should impart a sense of urgency for change to every serious public relations professional.

Largest and most critical on our agenda for change should be the fundamental premise for the existence of public relations—our statement of mission, if you will.

From its earliest stirrings as an organized body of activity, public relations has been communications oriented. Its definitions describe communications. The codes of our professional organizations focus on rights and wrongs of communication. Public relations education—graduate and undergraduate—reside in departments of communications at colleges and universities.

How and why public relations began with that orientation is easily understood. The first practitioners were mostly journalists who moved around to the other side of their desks to create, modify, and delete editorial coverage of their new employers.

They became press agents or publicists.

If press agentry or publicity originally was the whole dog, today it is only the tail, and a diminishing one at that. Yet it is still perceived as the operative appendage of the animal.

The reasons for this counterproductive perception, and how it should have been and could be changed, are worth at least a couple of chapters on their own. But in another book. What's important in addressing the future is a redefinition of public relations. A new statement of mission.

It should be something like this:

Public relations is the management function primarily responsible for shaping and implementing policies of mediation among social, political, and economic interests capable of influencing the growth and/or survival of an organization's basic franchise. To this end, the public relations function has responsibility also for identifying the forces and effects of change in the organization's environment so as to anticipate potential new needs for mediation and to inform all other anticipatory activity within the organization.

Only by creating a new paradigm for itself will public relations get out from under what has grown to be the bone-crushing weight of its communications origins. Unless our body of professional activity becomes generally perceived as essential to the management of organizations into their new futures, our franchise will be completely lost.

For better or worse, public relations lacks the institutional status that has protected from extinction such other functions as law and medicine, which were totally unresponsive for so long to the changing world around them. And not even institutionalization has protected the legal and medical franchises from life-threatening "credibility hemorrhages" which still have not been stopped.

The point is that no franchise, however once esteemed or entrenched, is safe from the potentially devastating effects of change. It's not difficult, therefore, to contemplate a considerably less secure franchise, such as public relations, vanishing almost overnight, like a beach house washed away by heavy storms. Public relations must seek higher ground.

Part of that elevation of public relations involves adopting a larger view of the world—a view that will be shared increasingly by the most senior managers of all organizations.

The latter also are rushing to shift their orientation to a more valid one. They're turning away from the monumentally destructive short-term, bottom line fixation to a longer-range philosophical approach based on people and simple principles. Obviously, this approach is hardly new, but it does seem to have been forgotten in the post–World War II rush to material superiority in the world. Now we are seeing the return of understanding that values and people are what produce qualitative and enduring financial results, not demand for financial results per se.

Inherent in this management reorientation process is an epidemic among organizations of reappraising their reasons for being. In reaffirming, or modifying, the essential purpose of the organization, management becomes better able to protect as well as enhance its franchise. Such focus sharpens management's ability to identify the aspects of change that will affect the organization, to recognize their implications, and to develop appropriate strategies in anticipation of problems and opportunities.

The management changes now taking place are filled with the stuff of which the highest public relations aspirations have long been concerned. For years our most serious professionals have been articulating the philosophies and concerns that now bid to become management's new priorities. If public relations can consciously move its weight to this high end of its spectrum, its integration into the uppermost reaches of management will accelerate tremendously.

Also reinforcing the concept of top management status for the function is the trend to more informal peer management, in contrast to the military-like hierarchy and bureaucracy that grows more anachronistic by the day. With chief executive concentration being diverted to softer, qualitative considerations in peer group settings, the best public relations professionals not only will have a place alongside the CEO, but will also find it increasingly possible to aspire to that number one spot itself.

Standardization

The concept of public relations as a true peer of the highest management function also will be the most forcing aspect of long overdue standardization of structure and practice in our field. That standardization will closely resemble the organization of this book.

Categories of public relations will be clearly labeled according to their respective roles in the organization's life.

Public Affairs

Public affairs will drop many activities inadvertently and inappropriately patched into it over the years and emerge clearly as "keeper of the flame," concerned exclusively with long-term protection of the fact and image of the organization's well-being. Specific activities within this area will be confined to:

- *Policy Planning*—heavily emphasizing such "soft technology" as environmental research, issue tracking, trend projections, cross-impact analysis, scenario writing, and crisis strategy.
- *Government Affairs*—enhancing and protecting the organization's legitimate interests affected by public issues that will be decided by formal jurisdictional process.
- *Policy (or Strategic) Communications*—coordinating all images and messages reflecting basic organization policy or strategy, both ongoing and timely, incorporating traditional activities of corporate identity, media relations, and crisis management.

Corporate Relations

Ongoing programs of communication and related activities designed to deliver specific messages consistently to permanent constituencies will be identified neatly within the area of corporate relations or a comparable label now being used as a catchall. Target groups within this area already are defined well and cultivated sophisticatedly. They include investors, employees, customers, community, industry, and hosts of special "publics" (i.e., educators, clergy, legislators, etc.).

Marketing Support

The pervasiveness and blatancy of publicity to help effect transactions in the marketplace perpetuates two unpleasant situations:

1. It keeps such activity inextricably linked to public relations rather than to the functions it directly supports; and
2. It regularly repaints publicity with the stigma of irresponsible press agentry, which it sometimes resembles, and automatically transfers the blight to public relations.

The ideal would be to sever this area completely from public relations, stripping it of any labels remotely associated with our function, and send it off in pieces to be added to promotion, fund raising, event management, and whatever other functions it most directly serves. That's too much to hope for. But we can look for some other shifting about that will align market support more closely with its real masters while elevating its objectives, messages, and visible activities to coincide with corporate relations programs aimed at the same audiences. This particular change will happen as a result of natural forces that are pushing public relations and marketing ever closer to each other.

THE MARKETING-PUBLIC RELATIONS CONNECTION

The same management reorientation process that is clearing the path for public relations' ascendency to the top line on the organization chart has created an environment in which it must join forces with marketing (already on that top line). In particular, the important analytical and communications skills of the two disciplines will become increasingly essential to each other.

Public relations works from the environment to the marketplace. Marketing generally moves in reverse. This tends to give public relations a defensive posture. Marketing's posture is aggressive and opportunistic. In short, the public relations glass is half empty. Marketing's is half full.

In general, marketing is closer to where client management has been. Its function is familiar and comfortable. It emphasizes enhancement of the franchise—a marketplace orientation. Marketing is characterized by action and immediacy.

Public relations is closer to where management is moving. It is much more focused on change and the future—concepts that are less familiar and comfortable. Public relations' priority is protecting the franchise, which requires sensitivity to the business environment. Its principal characteristics are anticipation and concern with long-term public policy.

In planning and evaluating their efforts, marketing and public relations both rely heavily on research and analysis, but each does so from a different perspective:

- Marketing strives to look at its functions objectively, with extraordinary emphasis on quantitative measurement. Public relations tends to be subjective and qualitative.
- Marketing focuses on target customers and their demographic and psychographic profiles. Public relations looks at multiple audiences and their relationships, as well as at the environmental factors influencing their characteristics and interactions.
- Marketing uses established techniques to produce countable transactions. Public relations operates on generally accepted principles to improve the climate for the franchise so that all desired transactions can take place.
- Marketing builds on what has happened to influence what is happening now. Public relations extrapolates from what is happening now to prepare for what will, or might, happen.

In program implementation, we see heavy reliance on communication for both marketing and public relations. Here, too, the differences in each function will contribute much to the other:

- Marketing seeks memorable impact. Public relations has credibility as its primary goal.

- Marketing deals heavily in emotion for immediate response. Public relations relies largely on information to modify behavior over time.
- Marketing concentrates on achieving and strengthening a fixed position in the marketplace. Public relations dwells on maintaining an accurate, consistent corporate identity in all places.
- Marketing activities are fairly well defined and structured. Public relations activities are much less so.
- Marketing communications follow relatively rigid guidelines. Public relations communications are extremely flexible.

Combining the respective techniques of marketing and public relations will improve the effectiveness of both.

Public relations efforts, as required, will have heightened interest and impact. Stronger and more actionable communications will produce more visible and dramatic results. And public relations will acquire new skills in creating thematic, consistent, and memorable messages. Those messages also will be more targeted in terms of appealing to audience segments, as well as in reaching those segments efficiently via expanding and increasingly fractionalized media outlets.

Marketing, on the other hand, will be able to do a better job of consistently relating its messages to a basic statement of corporate mission through imagery and delivery. It also will acquire the more varied communications skills it needs for diverse new media, such as teletext, where longer messages require editorial interest, rather than stretched-out sales pitches.

These brief "laundry lists" of compatible attributes of marketing and public relations only begin to suggest the scope and importance of the working relationship that will develop between the two functions. Sooner, rather than later, that relationship will include routine exchanges of specialists. Some of the more significant benefits will be:

For public relations . . .

- Public affairs research and planning will draw profitably upon quantitative and qualitative marketing research, as well as standardized tools and techniques, for marketing analysis and strategic planning.
- Corporate communications will benefit enormously from the input of ad agency creative and media departments, each of which enjoys the luxury of substantial investment in state-of-the-art techniques.
- Marketing support public relations will refine the efficiency and effectiveness of its efforts through utilization of advertising research, particularly copy testing, and sales promotion, in which important methodologies have been honed to a science. The latter also applies to direct marketing, which will hold great value for corporate communications, too.

For marketing . . .

- Advertising account management and marketing research will be elevated significantly through involvement with public affairs futures planning, environmental scanning, and issue analysis capabilities.
- Creative output will be strengthened at various times by the perspective, knowledge, and skills of print and broadcast publicists, financial and consumer relations specialists, speechwriters, and corporate graphic designers.
- Sales promotion efforts will accomplish significantly more as they are plugged into such public relations areas as special events, corporate support of the arts, or charitable contributions.

None of this proposed togetherness is meant to suggest that marketing or public relations should usurp, or even encroach upon, each other's primary responsibilities.

As we noted, marketing needs greater orientation to alternative futures and greater sensitivity to the environmental activity creating an increasingly fluid context for its activities. It also needs closer identification with the corporate mission and the franchise built around it.

Public relations needs a more businesslike approach, particularly including quantitative evaluation, as well as leading-edge communications capabilities for better messages to new audience configurations through changing media.

Each function can deliver what the other needs to maximize its role in guiding companies effectively into the uncertain future.

THE PROFESSIONAL AGENDA—WHAT WE DO

Given the environmental trends that are creating tomorrow's world and, with it, a new positioning for public relations, it's axiomatic that significant changes will be made in our professional agenda. These changes will be found in the same two broad categories that define this book—what we do and how we do it. First the "what."

The Corporate Report Card

By far the most urgent and straightforward new task for public relations is to assist in forcing the radical change that must be made in the criteria upon which the performance of organizations and their managements are judged.

The dominant criteria today still are based on short-term financial performance reflecting the "get rich quick" mentality, not only of shareholders and the financial community, but also of employees at every level. In time, of course, the continuation of present trends will slowly move these criteria to enlightened long-term values.

But that's not fast enough for the growing number of managers who are striving urgently now to adjust to longer-range strategies and to redefine their organizations' missions and values. Public relations help will be needed increasingly to build understanding and support for those organizations trying to make the best decisions for future survival and growth at what may appear to be, or may actually be, the expense of immediate, albeit temporary, gain.

New Mediation

With change comes conflict. Some inevitably arises from dislocation of the old until it catches up with the new, such as we have just discussed in the previous section. Other conflict comes from new or exacerbated differences that create significant adversarial relationships. Public relations in the coming years will face a number of the latter, some of which are being recycled from the Industrial Society into our Post-Industrial Society. Three of these "reheated" conflicts will top the public relations agenda:

Technology versus Human Values

Originally seen at the onset of automation, this conflict is stimulated anew by the fact and rapid sequence of computers and robotics. One dimension of the conflict is public acceptance of the use of technology, described by John Naisbitt in *Megatrends* as "hi-tech, hi-touch," meaning that people won't use technology that strips them of human contact. So, even though new electronic media make it possible to work or shop without leaving the home, people will still go to the office and the shopping center to preserve their humanity.

The other dimension is technology's replacement of human labor, particularly by robots. According to a newsletter on robotics, every time wages go up a dollar an hour, 10,000 more robots become economically practical. In a sluggish world economy, marked by high unemployment and aggravated in the United States and other industrialized nations by the shift of labor-intensive manufacturing to the Third World, potential loss of even more jobs to robots is a time bomb.

These and other technological advances pouring in on society (genetic engineering, satellite broadcasting, artificial organs, etc.) pose monumental policy and communications challenges to public relations professionals in helping to identify and articulate tenable positions for employers and in modifying constituent attitudes driven by inappropriate information and values.

Old versus Young

Last seen as the "generation gap," this conflict is back on the agenda as the "money gap." Projections indicate that by 1990, the 50-plus age group will account for 25 percent of the population and will represent 50 percent of $35,000-a-year-plus income. The younger generation is being forced to lower its material expectations and accept the hard reality that it may not be able to have more than its parents did—a gross violation of the American Dream. At the same time, they will be shouldering a larger tax burden to support federal programs for the aged.

Public relations will be called upon to help avoid and ameliorate potential young-old conflicts in the work place and the marketplace. In the latter, public relations will have to join forces with marketing to help build acceptance for a "less can be more" mind set, and foster preferences for quality vs. quantity.

Haves versus Have-Nots

The young-old conflict, as noted, will expand and aggravate the enmity between haves and have-nots that seems to have existed since the beginning of time. What gives this conflict special significance for public relations in the years immediately ahead are new aspects of the problems that will confront the public and private sectors as a result of current trends.

In the world that may emerge over the next decade or two, it appears that the chasm between haves and have-nots is likely to be enlarged while opportunities to bridge it are being reduced. Further, this conflict may be expressed in many polarities other than young-old.

The most significant new expression of the conflict, and the one which will most tax our professional skills, will be the information-rich vs. the information-poor. As the dominant commodity of our emerging society, which should become increasingly oriented to qualitative values, information will grow in importance as a wealth-equivalent. Public relations will have a critical role, not only in its traditional areas of producing, packaging, and distributing information, but in helping to assure equal opportunities for access and utilization among all segments of society.

People Culture

We have only just begun to realize that complex structure, large size, bureaucracy, authoritarianism, and other organizational characteristics typically associated with the military are antithetical to change. The most successful corporations of recent years are those that have ignored or abandoned such characteristics and cultivated other values that have enabled them to anticipate change and remain responsive to their marketplaces on a timely—and profitable—basis.

Studies of these successful companies have produced a catalog of simple values they have adopted in varying combinations and formats. One value, however, is universal in presence and simplicity among these organizations— focus on people.

Motivated internally by successful examples of people orientation and externally by society's growing rejection of hierarchy, organizations are rushing to trade in their "bureacracy is king" buttons for ones reading "people who need people." And the change, of necessity, will be more than cosmetic.

In committing to concern, respect, recognition, encouragement, and appreciation of the individual, corporations will find it essential to implant and nurture a culture that genuinely reflects and thrives on that commitment. As the corporate function uniquely equipped to help promulgate philosophy within the organization and communicate it to constituencies, public relations will play a key role in this transformation.

Global Interdependence

Shifting from inner-to outer-directed concerns, another major trend shaping the future of public relations is the increasing interdependence of our global society. Narrow national interests are being superseded by international considerations of finance and trade balances. Parts and products are manufactured and assembled in whatever countries have the most appropriate and efficient labor, technology, and facilities.

If economics can be seen as the warp of world togetherness, then communications is the woof. Computers, satellites, microwaves, cable TV, teletext—these and other technologies are advancing and converging to create breathtaking communications possibilities. Information and images can be, and are being, delivered electronically around our planet virtually at will. We can communicate with one individual or millions, with barely noticeable difference in time and effort.

These factors will escalate in importance to public relations professionals as our organizations participate in the global exchange of goods, services, and information in greater number and intensity. Here again, we will find ourselves having to work in harmony with the marketing function in helping companies negotiate a transition from their fragmented culture-bound multinational approaches to unified transcendent global strategies.

Inherent in such strategies will be the same key characteristics found in what we previously described as the general management orientation of the future—focusing on the company's mission, promulgating simple values, and anticipating change. This is public relations' turf; and we will have to know it better, and be more skilled in cultivating it, than any other function if we are going to fulfill our own mission effectively in the future.

THE PROFESSIONAL AGENDA—HOW WE DO IT

Changing the way organizational performance is judged, mediating new conflicts, fostering people cultures within the organization, shifting to global strategies—these major additions to the public relations agenda of the next couple of decades will demand the best skills we have...and more. New strategies, as well as new tools and techniques, will be added to the public relations function to meet these specific emerging needs.

Additionally, basic responsibilities of public relations within the organization will have to be expanded and upgraded. A number of new skills will find their way into the "how" of our function.

Custody of Image

As the changes we have been discussing make their impact upon our organizations with growing frequency and force, new self-images will become epidemic. Organizations will be scrambling to redefine their new selves and to articulate their fresh visions to all internal and external constituencies— locally and globally, to customers and employees, for financing and sales, from janitors to board chairmen.

Public relations will inherit a useful opportunity to take firm control of the organization image. Every message, every impression, regardless of form or purpose, will come under the jurisdiction of public relations. With that authority will come responsibility to develop thorough working knowledge and relationships in every major aspect of the organization's life.

We have dealt often and at length with the marketing connection. This may be the most intensive relationship to be cultivated by public relations, but it is only one of several. Of equal urgency will be knowledgeable involvement with finance, human resources, operations, administration, and, where pertinent, research and development.

The kinds of images we're concerned with here cannot be fabricated or imposed artificially with clever campaigns; they will be grown and perceived properly only as a result of a philosophical imperative that is willingly absorbed into every fiber of the organization.

The perspective needed to manage the development of these new images will be nothing less than that required of the CEO, and successful implementation will require the best instincts and skills a public relations professional can command.

The most significant distinction to be made between *image growing*, as we are discussing here and more traditional public relations approaches to *image building,* is the difference between process and program. We have considerably more experience with the latter. Yet, in its purest sense, public relations is process, and it will be perceived as such more clearly through its new image management responsibilities.

Communications Skills

Technology, information access, and social restructuring pose special considerations for public relations in the years immediately ahead. Not only will developments confront us with new policy decisions, but they will force the development of new communications skills, as well.

New Media

Technology, as we have noted, is exploding the possibilities of communications channels, outlets, and formats. Fresh knowledge and facility, much of it quite complex, will be required of public relations to bring us up to speed in the new media. In this context, we will do well to remember how long it has taken us to achieve demonstrable and acceptable levels of performance with the media we have been dealing with routinely on a professional basis for nearly four decades. A comparably slow learning curve with new media is likely to be considered both inadequate and unnecessary to endure, particularly with other disciplines, such as marketing, doing their future communications homework now and positioning themselves to assume more responsible roles in the organization.

Access

Affluence and education rise and fall together as demographic qualifiers of the general public. This correlation holds special significance for the packaging and distribution of information in the society that is emerging.

The new media just referred to will not be as ubiquitous as telephones or TV for some time, if ever. This is primarily a factor of cost, both in making the technology physically available and in being able to afford it. The latter, already discriminatory in the extreme when one contemplates the importance of connecting to the world around us via telephone and television, will further disadvantage and separate from society those in the lower economic strata. We also can anticipate great disparities based on education in the ability to utilize information among the population segments with relative equality of technological access. These inevitabilities must become dominant concerns of public relations professionals.

The primary concern, which we hope all society will share, is how to bring the have-nots into the new information network so as to avoid, and possibly reverse, their disenfranchisement and polarization. At the more mundane and pragmatic level, while society wrestles with the larger issues, public relations will have to learn to segment and orchestrate the organization's communications to maintain information quality and consistency. The task conjures up an image of rain filling up a hole in the ground and spilling over in rivulets in every direction. That same process is dispersing and fragmenting communication channels, outlets, and audiences. Public relations will have to stay on top, and preferably ahead, of this process in its efforts to provide state-of-the-art communications capabilities.

Networks

Paralleling the communications explosion now under way is the rapid proliferation of networks that is creating a new social infrastructure. These networks represent alternatives to the centralized bureaucracies that have been dominating people's lives. Although perceived as "fuzzy" because of their lack of formal structure and hierarchy, networks are a growing force in the reshaping of social and political institutions.

Some observers describe networks as the first step toward a more democratic way to form action-oriented groups. Others go further and see it as a future mechanism for global management. These networks are built around information, interests, and ideology. A directory published by Doubleday in 1982 listed networks for programs for the elderly, community alliances with prisons, exchanging information about home schooling, options within holistic health, opposing nuclear power, saving endangered species, creating a computerized community bulletin board, structuring a local skills bank, forging a mountain commune, establishing a food co-op, starting a growth center, and building a windmill. The directory lists several thousand such organizations—all operating on the same underlying values, which are doing what isn't being done and changing what you don't like.

If these groups have no visible hierarchies, they do have peer leadership that is virtually indistinguishable and interchangeable at any time for any reason. They connect to similar organizations and grow horizontally around information sharing. They seem to act almost spontaneously, but with skill and effectiveness.

There are a number of loud and clear messages here for the future of public relations. Most obvious seems to be that yet another layer, still somewhat alien in nature and configuration, is being inserted into society to further expand and complicate the job of identifying and communicating with target audiences. More subtly, and ominously, we are being put on notice that effective and less manageable (from our perspective) organizations can appear at our gates almost instantaneously and without warning, fully equipped to change what they feel needs changing.

Those organizations among our own employers that have adopted simpler and more enduring values, or are genuinely striving to do so, will find themselves very much in harmony with the new networks. In this situation, our task will focus on innovative methods and means of communicating philosophical unity and support. For those of our organizations that will be unwilling or unable to respond in a positive, timely manner to the reemergence of our oldest values, networks promise to impose frightening new adversarial conditions upon the public relations job description.

Anticipating Change

If there is a single overriding mandate in all of the considerations presented for the future of public relations practice, it is: *"Anticipate Change!"*

Unfortunately, the technology available to assist us in this task is young, scarce, and extremely "soft." On the bright side, however, the principles of this technology are in place and operative. The systems into which they have been incorporated are performing, in acceptable measure, the tasks to which they have been dedicated. These tasks include:

- *Environmental Assessment (Monitoring, Searching, Scanning, etc.)* — primarily by analyzing media to spot events, trends, and issues of potential significance to the organization.
- *Issue Analysis*—identifying issues and analyzing activity around them to determine their relative significance, stages of progress, and projected outcomes.
- *Scenario Writing*—exploring long-range decision choices by "scripting" stories of possible futures based on projectable hard data ("drivers") and incorporating possible quantitative and qualitative changes in the environment.
- *Cross-Impact Studies*—combining expert judgment and statistical techniques to project and rate probabilities of events and their likely effects.

Public relations professionals must become conversant enough with these and other emerging approaches to know when and why to call upon them and how to use their output. The prerequisite for this working knowledge is an understanding of change itself.

For example, change is not serendipitous; it has a progression and a pattern that are eminently "readable." We also know that change is both advanced and reflected by media. Further, there is an established process by which society acknowledges and responds to change—sometimes legally, sometimes behaviorally, but always definitively and visibly.

As stated in the suggested redefinition of public relations at the outset of this chapter, public relations should be assuming primary responsibility within the organization for the anticipation of change. In that capacity, professionals will be working with current and emerging technology dedicated to that task. The best professionals will be able to go even further by upgrading and refining the state of the art and, it is to be hoped, advancing the technology through their own innovation.

Public relations must be able to work across the business spectrum at all levels, to be able to play an effective role in building a new organizational culture. But that is only one of many internal and external policy considerations.

The larger implications for public relations in protecting and enhancing organizations in the coming years will demand that those who manage the function bring virtually the same general business knowledge and perspective to the job that will be required for any senior management slot, including that of CEO.

In the past, the cycles of organizational leadership have been task oriented, shifting periodically to respond to popular perceptions of most needed skills—engineering, finance, marketing, etc.—reflecting quantitative values. The leadership paradigm of the future, however, will be qualitative—focused on people and the changing world. Discipline and productivity will emanate from sense of purpose, rather than rules and statistics. Involvement and quality will be achieved through information and encouragement, rather than devices and lip service.

In short, organizational success will be a function of mission and culture, not bottom line orientation. If the qualitative is there, the quantitative will follow.

PUBLIC RELATIONS MANAGEMENT

To this point, we have been exploring the future role of public relations in the management of organizations. We have repositioned our function so that it can make its optimum contribution to the organization and, in so doing, draw fully upon the highest aspirations and capabilities of the best professionals in the field. And we have just explored the functional implications revealed in our elevated horizons.

It's heady stuff, filled with wonderful visions and challenges for every serious professional. It sets the mind racing and the juices flowing. And well it should.

But let's not overlook nuts and bolts considerations that come under the heading of management of the public relations function. A few considerations are critically essential for the future.

Business Decision Process

In discussing public relations' custody of the corporate image, we touched upon the need for better working relationships with other management disciplines—finance, administration, operations, marketing, human resources, research and development. The message there was the need for

organizations adopting better values to be able to plant and grow new self-images and project them from the inside out.

Again the emerging organizational ethic will create de facto top management priority status for public relations. It will be an integral part of the decision-making process. The only question is whether the public relations professional also is included in the process.

There have been a number of instances, generally among the more successful organizations, where public relations has been elevated to the top management echelon. In most of those instances, however, the function was placed in the jurisdiction of another discipline already at the top, leaving the professional manager at the implementation level.

The major reason for this situation has been management's perceptions that public relations professionals are not in the mainstream of business decision making, lacking both the attitudes and aptitudes necessary to share in that process. Part of that perception is real. The other part is the stigma of the press agent stereotype, which public relations has been unable to eliminate despite decades and myriad opportunities to do so.

Change now is providing the public relations professional with a unique, and probably final, opportunity to modify the old perceptions. Just as new values are moving the organization's needs closer to public relations capabilities, so will professionals be forced to upgrade their business capabilities to meet the organization's needs.

As for losing the old stereotype once and for all, those who seek to manage public relations at the top will be able to find new identity in becoming the organization's agent for change.

Businesslike Approach

Implicit in the public relations management mandate for the future is the development and application of basic business skills, not only for participation in organizationwide management, but also to enable the public relations function to be seen and understood throughout the organization in more traditional business terms.

The absence of this understanding, more a result of failure in transmitting than in receiving, also has played a large part in limiting the effectiveness of public relations and the management progress of its practitioners. Public relations will have to do a better job of communicating why and how it does what it does, and in teaching and demonstrating how well it does it.

Standardization of public relations activities according to the organizational needs they fill will go a long way to creating the needed understanding. But a lot more ground will have to be covered.

- *Planning* will have to parallel other strategic and tactical planning within the organization. Public relations will have to work from the common information base and utilize the organization's standard analytical tools

and techniques to set objectives and determine programs of implementation.

- *Objectives* will have to be framed and articulated to be consistent with those of the organization. Further, they will have to be defined specifically enough so that the business benefit is clear and the degree of achievement is measurable; that is, "increase awareness and conviction among the sales force of the company's commitment to quality," as contrasted with a traditional, "promote a quality image for the company."

- *Research* will have to be used with infinitely greater frequency and skill to refine objectives, target program efforts, and measure the effectiveness and cost efficiency of results. Public relations will have to become research-fluent, moving easily and appropriately from primary (original) research to secondary (available); qualitative to quantitative; and pretesting to postassessment.

- *Programs* will have to be thoroughly detailed with schedules; allocation of budget, people, and other resources; responsibilities; and approval procedures. Above all, program activities must be clearly responsive to objectives and include rationales built around available data.

- *Controls* will be required to determine measurement methods and criteria for evaluating relative achievement and to build an ongoing data base for future planning and evaluation. Also needed will be strict record keeping and reporting procedures.

- *Contingencies* will have to be built into planning so that alternative scenarios can be implemented if desired results are not achieved or if program considerations change. Contingency considerations will have to include zero-base planning and procedures, effectively imposing "sunset" laws on activities that should be dropped for lack of performance or to make way for newer or higher priorities.

If public relations is to fulfill its mission for the future, it must acquire the attributes of sophistication and accountability inherent in the planning, execution, and evaluation areas just described. Even more, these attributes must be seen as fundamental to the function, and not just cosmetically applied to gain credence.

Bigger Budgets

For years, public relations has envied the budgets of advertising. The enormous discrepancy in the allocation of funds to the two functions has been rationalized in many ways ("Advertising costs more." "You know what you're getting.")—none of which has ever been explored thoroughly or challenged successfully.

This, too, will change. For several reasons.

The institutionalization of public relations on the top management line

automatically will insure easier access to and acceptance of larger budgets for public relations. There will be fewer layers to go through for budget approvals and, therefore, far fewer people and occasion for sniping and snipping at activities and expenses.

Dollars allocated to public relations also will expand naturally as the function's mission grows larger and more sensitive and sophisticated. All of the major changes projected for public relations practice over the next couple of decades create new opportunities and dictate new requirements that will add significant costs. Some of this already has been seen in the fragmentation of media and audiences that has been taking place in recent years.

Another big budget factor will be the greater involvement of public relations with marketing. The substantial additional costs of incorporating the latter's techniques into our function will be accepted quickly and easily because they are proven quantities. Also, certain marketing activities for which public relations may assume or share primary responsibility eventually could find their way into the public relations budget.

Finally, and most basic, is that a businesslike approach to the management of public relations will put the function on a tangible cost-benefit basis. The lack of such a basis has long been troublesome to those managers who see the function as an act of faith, in which they play the role of high priest. No more. Managers of public relations will be accountable for their existence, activities, and the resources they consume. Or they will give way to those who are ready and willing to make the function accountable, and who may or may not be public relations professionals.

Like all things, public relations budgets will eventually get back to basics. If we assume that the function does good things for the organization, it follows that we should want to know that if we can accomplish a measurable quantity of our mission for X dollars, we should be able to accomplish some specific additional quantity for $X + Y$ dollars.

We also should want to know our points of critical mass and peak efficiency in an activity so that we can make rational budget decisions and move funds around to expand and refine efforts. We should want to test alternative approaches to find optimum cost-benefit points. And we certainly should want to figure out how to be more efficient with available dollars.

Who's to say today that in 10 years, a $50 million annual budget for public relations won't be as good an investment, or a better one, for the organization than $50 million for advertising? It's not unthinkable.

"THE PUBLIC RELATIONS DREAM"

In case you haven't noticed—what we've spelled out here is an alternative future for public relations that reads a lot like the "American Dream" alternative described at the outset of this chapter.

We see public relations elevated to new heights of importance and receiving the social, political, and economic support to which it aspires within the organization. We see the professionals in the field being given every opportunity, albeit without guarantees, to grow and prosper as a result. We see the function overcoming traditional problems and achieving significant new levels of effectiveness in helping the organization similarly overcome and achieve.

As is generally true with alternative futures, this one for public relations has put down roots in our present. In fact, all of the assumptions for the operative scenario are in place, giving our future more of a quality of reasonable expectation than conjecture.

Expectations, however, always remain to be filled. Those for public relations, as noted, will not be realized automatically. There are conditions— large, but able to be met without inordinate difficulty. Yet, there is a cloud on the horizon.

The conditions for achieving the "Public Relations Dream" essentially are no different than they have been since some of the pioneers in the field had their first great visions of its future. Identify with the highest organizational goals. Develop professional working knowledge of finance, marketing, operations, administration, etc. Be businesslike and accountable.

It is troublesome to contemplate that these long-standing conditions have not been met in the past. Whether those upon whom they were first imposed couldn't meet them, or opted not to, is now moot. A new decision point is at hand.

New and larger needs and opportunities, and a new generation of professionals are converging on that point. The issues will be revisited. There are good reasons for optimism about the outcome.

APPENDIX

PUBLIC RELATIONS/ PUBLIC AFFAIRS JOB GUIDELINES

Bill Cantor

INTRODUCTION TO THE GUIDELINES

Good public relations depends entirely on the quality of the people who plan and execute it. True, new technologies and techniques, a sound organizational structure, good planning and budgeting, and solid research can all enhance a communications program. Nothing, however, can replace the effective use of qualified people. Without them, little is possible; with them, few things are out of reach.

As in every other job, every other human institution, there seem never to be enough good people. It follows, then, that among organizations that recognize the value of good public relations, there is competition for the best people. There is concern, too, about how to evaluate a job candidate or an employee, about how to organize good people to gain the maximum benefit from their talents. And, all too often, these critical managerial functions are left to those who are not familiar with this business, this profession.

For that reason, I have prepared this section. It will help you in selecting the right people for your communications organization. It gives field-tested and time-tested guidelines for most of the key jobs in public relations. They are the result of more than 15 years spent working exclusively as an executive recruiter in public relations and public affairs on behalf of corporations, public relations/public affairs agencies, and other clients. Not only can you use these guidelines to develop your organization, they will also help you get cost-effective service from your executive recruiter.

I have also prepared a glossary of public relations/communications terminology (following the guidelines). There is a reason for its inclusion. The language of public relations has and continues to have practitioners in the field who do not agree on nomenclature. That lack of agreement is a source of consternation and frustration for those in the field; it is often a source of bemused irritation for those who look on.

I have, therefore, imposed my own sense of what the terminology means—and, occasionally, what it ought to mean. For example, I use the term "public relations" in   401 the classic sense to cover the entire gamut of disciplines used in the corporation and/or institution as it relates to its various publics. I use it because it best describes, as corporate communications or corporate relations do not, the two-way process that the discipline seeks to create and maintain on behalf of its institutions.

On the other hand, I use the term "issues management," when that term clearly does not describe the function. One cannot "manage" issues; one can only manage one's responses to issues. However, the term, once created, has stuck. To fight that losing battle is to sweep back the sea.

With the job guidelines and glossary in hand, then, you should be able to better identify and evaluate the people you need for the jobs that you must fill. To do so, however, with a good chance of success, means following a number of steps.

First, you should have a goal and mission statement for the public relations/public affairs department. It should be written by, or approved by, top management. Few companies actually seem to have such statements, though corporate statements of policy and purpose are not uncommon. However, it has always seemed ludicrous to me that corporations and institutions spend large sums of money on public relations without having any clear idea about what public relations is supposed to accomplish. And if you don't know what you want accomplished, how can you find and hire the best people to accomplish it?

So, obtain a goal and mission statement.

Second, you should be able to answer the following general questions:

1. What is the purpose of the public relations/public affairs department?
2. What is to be accomplished? By when? Is the timetable reasonable? Is it logical?
3. What are the functions and responsibilities of the individual you want to hire, as well as of the department? Is management in accord?
4. Is management committed to the function? Will it truly be supportive? Is there or will there be hostility from the financial, legal, or other departments because some of the functions to be performed by this new person, or the broadening of the department, could or will impinge on these other departments?
5. Has anyone done an internal audit to ascertain weaknesses as well as strengths of the department?
6. If you do not have the internal capability to do an audit, have you considered outside assistance?
7. Are you prepared to take full advantage of the executive search firm that specializes in public relations, or are you trying just to locate lists of names and piles of resumes? If the latter, you are wasting your time and money. You are probably better off running your own recruitment advertisement.

Accept the fact that even the greatest professionals in public relations are only as good as their management allows them to be. If they are not privy to the short- or long-range goals of the company, if they do not sit in on the strategic planning committees, if they do not have an opportunity to give their input, then management is indeed wasting a most valuable human resource. Do not hire a manager when you only want a technician. Do not hire a top flight counselor when you only want an order taker.

Third, in selecting people, there are five basic ingredients you should consider:

1. Administrative skills
2. Creative or action skills
3. Basic skills (writing, editing, photography, etc.)
4. Personality and attitude
5. Demonstrated judgment and common sense

With these steps taken, you are ready to begin the hiring process. Review the following sample job guidelines in relation to your own situation and adapt them to your needs.

JOB DESCRIPTION (SAMPLE FORM)

CORPORATE NAME _____

Title of Position   Grade Level   Salary Range

Division/Group   Department   Location   Approved by

Reporting Relationships

Reports to _____
(Title)

SUPERVISES

Directly   Indirectly

QUALIFICATIONS

Education:

Experience:

Special knowledge or skills:

PERSONALITY TRAITS

MISSION AND GOALS

(For this department or individual; short and long range):

SPECIFIC ACTIVITIES

(Please describe in detail on the following pages, as per the categories on the next form.)

SPECIFIC ACTIVITIES OF THE POSITION

(Please describe in detail.)

A. *OBJECTIVE*

B. *BASIC FUNCTIONS*

C. *MAJOR DUTIES AND RESPONSIBILITIES* (Rate in order of Importance)

GUIDELINES FOR PREPARING JOB DESCRIPTIONS

1.   Vice President-Public Relations/Public Affairs

2.   Director of Public Relations (or Communications)

3.   Director of Public Affairs (or Governmental Relations)

4.   Director of Investor Relations (or Financial and Shareholder Relations)

5.   Director of Employee Communications

6.   Director of Community Relations

7.   Director of Media Relations (or Publicity)

8.   Director of Issues Management (or Public Policy)

9.   Director of Special Events

10.   Director of Executive Presentations

11.   Director of Editorial Services

12.   Director of Public Relations Research (Corporate or Agency)

13.   Director of Institutional advertising

14.   Director of Consumer Affairs

15.   Director of Customer Relations

16.   Director of Public Relations (Nonprofit Organization)

17.   Director of Public Relations (Trade or Professional Association)

18.   Account Executive (Corporate or Agency)

19.   Account Supervisor (Usually with an Agency)

20.   Director of Client Services (Usually with an Agency)

21.   Director of Creative Services (Usually with an Agency)

1.   VICE PRESIDENT—PUBLIC RELATIONS/PUBLIC AFFAIRS

Objective

To establish and maintain sound relations between the Corporation and its various publics, producing a business climate in which the Company can operate most effectively.

Basic Function

Should be responsible to the president or chairman for assisting the chief executive officer (CEO) in the formulation of overall planning for present and future public relations; providing input to and implementing approved policies; and directing and coordinating the Company's plans to achieve established objectives. The Vice President-Public Relations/Public Affairs is responsible for interpreting the Company's corporate character to the public and for analyzing, interpreting, and evaluating public opinion to its executives.

Major Duties and Responsibilities
(Rate in order of importance.)

1.   Advise the CEO of public relations policies and procedures calculated to ensure maximum possible understanding and acceptance of the Company by its various publics, thus aiding the Company's progress.
2.   Direct the development of and recommend short- and long-range public relations and public affairs objectives, plans, and programs for the Corporation.
3.   Advise and assist the heads of operating divisions and subsidiaries in the development and execution of public relations programs consistent with the overall Corporation policies and objectives.
4.   Advise the CEO on the public relations effects of proposed policies, plans, and activities.
5.   Establish and maintain favorable relations with all media: newspapers, news services, newsletters, trade journals, professional journals, radio/TV, consumer and business magazines.
6.   Assist directors of community relations, employee communications, and investor relations in maintaining relations with the plant cities' business/financial press.
7.   Develop publicity programs to support the marketing efforts of divisions.
8.   Assist all divisions of the Company in maintaining the Company's graphic standards and enforce these standards when necessary.
9.   Act as corporate spokesperson to the news media, except when otherwise directed; write all nonfinancial news releases.
10.   Review all public statements of the Company for accuracy and consistency.
11.   Write position papers, testimony, reports, public statements, and speeches for attribution to Company executives as required.
12.   Write, produce, and distribute other corporate communications of a public relations nature: corporate brochures, position papers, speech reprints, plant dedication booklets, etc. Create radio and television publicity and programs.

13. Arrange public or news conferences, meetings, or speaking engagements for corporate executives.
14. Supervise production of audio-visual presentations.
15. Supervise and direct corporate contributions, giving, activities in the arts, foundations, etc.
16. Conduct such other communications or public relations activity from time to time as required.
17. Exert administrative and budgeting control over and supervise the activities of the staff.
18. Improve ability of Company to recruit top executive talent.
19. Assure that proper liaison with civic and community-oriented business organizations is maintained with such organizations as deemed appropriate.
20. Determine the kind and extent of political involvement the Corporation should have with employees and develop appropriate programs.
21. Provide counsel and assistance to subsidiary companies as needed in their efforts to build good relations with their publics.
22. Provide input to management as to the feedback from the public reflecting their reaction to the Company's policies and actions.
23. Prepare monthly reports on activities for top executive management.
24. Develop a budget to cover the Corporation's communications, Public Relations/Public Affairs activities and closely supervise the disbursement of such funds.
25. Carry out administrative or special project functions as might be directed by the top executive management, as assigned.
26. Maintain close liaison with outside public relations counsel if and when such is retained.
27. Develop methods for determining shifts in public opinion as related to the Corporation and report findings to executive management.
28. Monitor the Corporation's advertising themes and content to make certain they reflect favorably on the Corporation.
29. Develop themes and copy platforms for corporate or institutional advertising on issues of concern to the Corporation.
30. Coordinate and direct administrative staff services of this operation.
31. Draw up plan for public relations department to enable staff to perform functions effectively and efficiently.

2. DIRECTOR OF PUBLIC RELATIONS (OR COMMUNICATIONS)

Objective

To assist the Company's executives to manage in the public interest and to create public programs to further knowledge, understanding, and acceptance of the Company's policies and to achieve public support.

Basic Function

The Director of Public Relations is responsible, under the supervision of the Vice President-Public Relations/Public Affairs, for developing, establishing, and carrying out public relations policies, procedures, plans, and programs which will generate and maintain favorable attitudes by general and specific publics toward the Corporation and its operating divisions; and for advising and making recommendations in the determination of Company objectives, policies, and plans insofar as they affect or are affected by public relations considerations.

Major Duties and Responsibilities
(Rate in order of importance.)

1. Develop short- and long-range public relations objectives, plans, and programs for the Company.
2. Assist heads of operating companies and divisions in the development of programs consistent with overall Company policies and objectives.
3. Plan and direct such public relations research as is necessary to evaluate the understanding by various publics of the Company; keep the president and operating division heads advised of public opinion trends.
4. Maintain current information about the public's opinion of the industry and the Company, and project trends in public opinion as the basis for planning and executing public relations and public affairs programs.
5. Initiate a planned program of communication to all concerned publics.
6. Assist top management and key executives in the preparation and review of speeches, statements, reports, and testimony for delivery before industrial, legislative, industry, governmental, civic, professional, and other groups.
7. Maintain media mailing and contact lists.
8. Develop and maintain effective relations with various groups whose acceptance or influence is of special interest to the Company.
9. Direct relations with all public information media and release information concerning the Company to those media.
10. Work with organizations such as the Conference Board, U.S. Chamber of Commerce, and other groups on areas of common interest.
11. Coordinate the public relations activities of the Company's domestic subsidiaries and divisions.
12. Coordinate and review the public relations activities of the international department and participate in the activities of the international public relations staff of the Company.
13. Advise Company executives on all phases of Company and division identification and graphics.
14. Represent the Company as spokesperson before public groups and organizations.
15. Supervise and direct the staff necessary to implement programs of the public relations/public affairs division, including general public relations, investor relations, employee communication, community relations, etc.
16. Conduct such other relationships as the CEO of the Company may from time to time specify.

3. DIRECTOR OF PUBLIC AFFAIRS (OR GOVERNMENT RELATIONS)

Objective

To maintain open communications with government agencies, legislators, and individuals whose actions may impact on the Company, and to communicate the Company's policies fully and fairly.

Basic Function

Responsible for maintaining two-way channels of communication between the Company and legislative, governmental, and regulatory bodies and individuals. Responsible for analyzing and interpreting economic and political changes affecting the operation of the Company; for developing, establishing, and implementing present and future plans, policies, and programs to enhance the Company's position vis-à-vis government and regulatory agencies; and for directing and coordinating the Company's plans to achieve its legislative objectives.

Major Duties and Responsibilities
(Rate in order of importance.)

1. Supervise the Washington public affairs operations and those in state capitals.
2. Maintain two-way relationships with federal, state, and local officials.
3. Monitor state and federal legislative actions, issues, and trends; analyze and interpret this information; report it to appropriate Company officials; and formulate and implement action programs.
4. Conduct such research as required to determine public opinion as it relates to legislative matters.
5. Arrange for meetings between Company executives and government officials; arrange for and write testimony when appropriate; counsel Company executives on their relationships with government.
6. Arrange seminars, speeches, and the like to keep Company executives abreast of public affairs.
7. Produce communications directed to public officials as required: statements, white papers, position papers, booklets, audio-visual materials.
8. Encourage all employees to be informed on issues, candidates, governmental and·political processes.
9. Work with all appropriate associations and organizations to further Company's objectives in the legislative and executive areas of government.
10. Execute general responsibilities common to all executive and supervisory positions.
11. Work with counterparts in other corporations on solving industry problems or refining industry regulations.
12. Conduct such other public affairs activities as the Vice President-Public Relations/Public Affairs or the CEO may from time to time specify.
13. Coordinate work with that of other public relations/public affairs staff members.

4.   DIRECTOR OF INVESTOR RELATIONS (OR FINANCIAL AND SHAREHOLDER RELATIONS)

Objective

To establish and maintain effective relations between the Company and the investment community, particularly with shareowners, analysts, financial community, and the financial news media.

Basic Function

Works with the Vice President-Public Relations/Public Affairs, Treasurer, and/or Vice President-Finance in assisting them in Company's overall planning for present and future investor relations; implementing approved policies; and directing and coordinating the Company's plans to achieve established objectives.

Major Duties and Responsibilities
(Rate in order of importance.)

1. Formulate objectives and long-range plans for investor relations and submit them to Vice President-Public Relations/Public Affairs for incorporation into division plans.
2. Study, analyze, and interpret trends and developments in investor relations field.
3. Recommend to Vice President-Public Relations/Public Affairs revisions of existing investor relations policies, plans, and programs.
4. Supervise studies of shareholder opinion and analyze share ownership.
5. Maintain an up-to-date knowledge of Securities and Exchange Commission (SEC), disclosure requirements of the stock exchanges, seek legal counsel when needed, and monitor the Company's compliance with these requirements.
6. Write the narrative text of the annual report to shareholders, and supervise its graphic and printing production and distribution.
7. Write and produce other shareholder communications as required: quarterly reports, dividend stuffers, shareholder correspondence, special mailings to analysts or shareholders, audio-visual communications.
8. Produce the Company's financial fact book and other materials for inclusion in press kits and presentations.
9. Arrange for the annual meeting, including special audio-visual presentations or exhibits.
10. Establish and maintain relationships with the financial press; develop and distribute financial news of the Company; and develop special feature articles on the Company for business and financial publications.
11. Write speeches and presentations for the CEO or financial officers of the Company for analyst or business audiences; publicize these appearances and handle reprinting and distribution of these presentations, when appropriate.
12. Supervise the planning, production, and placement of financial advertising.
13. Assist the Vice President-Treasurer in establishing and maintaining relationships with security analysts and others in the investment community:

specialists, investment bankers, brokers, underwriters, institutional research firms, statistical services.

14. Arrange for visits by analysts to Company headquarters, for plant tours; visit analysts in their offices; arrange analyst meetings for the CEO and Vice President-Treasurer; and respond to routine telephone inquiries from shareholders or analysts.

15. Prepare contact reports summarizing visits to financial community people and send to executive management.

16. Distribute financial information periodically to security analysts.

5. DIRECTOR OF EMPLOYEE COMMUNICATIONS

Objective

To establish channels of credible communication with executive management and employees in order to develop mutual loyalty to the Company, and to develop understanding of Company policies and activities so employees can become spokesmen in their neighborhoods and peer groups.

Basic Function

Employee communications is responsible, under the direction of the Vice President-Public Relations/Public Affairs, for developing, producing, and implementing programs of internal communications.

Major Duties and Responsibilities
(Rate in order of importance.)

1. Write, produce, and distribute a company newspaper (or magazine).
2. Write speeches, correspondence, and statements directed to employees by management.
3. Prepare exhibits, audio-visual presentations, and other communications directed to employees; arrange meetings and seminars as directed by management.
4. Write, produce, and distribute the management newsletter.
5. Write and produce the employee handbook and other brochures and general communications requested by management or the personnel department.
6. Work closely with various employee organizations and assist with their activities.
7. Send retired employees information distributed by the Company.
8. Prepare letters from management periodically to be sent to the homes of employees to keep the family informed.
9. Develop a system for measuring employee accomplishments.
10. Improve employee performance, morale, and support of company programs.
11. Improve employee understanding of the Company and its line of business.
12. Develop internal communications media such as bulletin boards, in-house television, pay envelope stuffers, letters to employee's homes, etc.

6.   DIRECTOR OF COMMUNITY RELATIONS

Objective

To create favorable public opinion in the community toward Company by monitoring social trends, analyzing, and interpreting them to management, and advising them on policy changes intended to bring the Company's policies into harmony with public opinion.

Basic Function

The Director of Community Relations is the Company's "social responsibility and goodwill officer." The basic function is to formulate and carry out programs to eliminate or reduce frictions between the Company and the communities in which it operates, also between Company and any activist groups working on local or national scale.

Major Duties and Responsibilities
(Rate in order of importance.)

1.   Monitor social trends by maintaining communications channels with academics, community leaders, activists, and organizations; maintain close relationships with appropriate editors and writers; analyze these trends and formulate action or nonaction programs.
2.   Serve as staff director of Company's contributions program and/or secretary of contributions committee; as such, investigate requests for assistance and make recommendations to the committee.
3.   Maintain inventory of Company's and Company officers' memberships in civic and business-related groups, and recommend extensions of these, if appropriate.
4.   Maintain relationships with press in plant cities and arrange for distribution of corporate news releases directly or through operating personnel to this press.
5.   Supervise research as required on community attitudes toward the Company.
6.   Arrange for exhibits, audio-visual demonstrations, speeches, and direct mail to community leaders as appropriate.
7.   Execute general responsibilities common to all executive and supervisory positions.
8.   Conduct such other community relations activities as executive management may specify from time to time.

7.   DIRECTOR OF MEDIA RELATIONS (OR PUBLICITY)

Objective

To present information about the Company and its various operations to news media for the purpose of increasing public knowledge and understanding of Company through continued identification of Company policies and activities with the public interest.

Basic Function

To analyze, develop, and implement the Company's external communications with all print and electronic media, including newspapers, magazines, television, radio, films, theater, and individual writers and photo-journalists, etc.

Major Duties and Responsibilities
(Rate in order of importance.)

1. Analyze objectives, policies, and standards for corporate components and identify media to generate the greatest exposure.
2. Counsel executive management on the impact of policies, decisions, courses of action, and public statements on relations with the media.
3. Develop and implement effective two-way communications programs with news media, which are mutually beneficial to media and to Company and its successful operation.
4. Prepare news releases and publicity programs on information released by the executive office.
5. Provide information about Company in response to news media inquiries.
6. Promote appropriate participation by Company personnel in public activities and associations to generate visibility in the news media.
7. Plan and implement national media strategies which get Company's views on particular issues known and accepted in timely manner by specific target audiences.
8. Obtain exposure for corporate position on public issues impacting on its business.
9. Maintain close contacts with representatives of news media.
10. Develop special feature articles for placement with the print media.
11. Develop special materials for use with broadcast media.
12. Undertake special assignments in areas of public, news media, and community relations for corporate and division managements.

8. DIRECTOR OF ISSUES MANAGEMENT (OR PUBLIC POLICY)

Objective

To project and articulate Company policy as far as possible into the future.

Basic Function

To research and closely monitor issues of interest to top management which impact the corporation's activities: (1) Identify issues affecting Company; (2) prioritize them; and (3) develop creative program to bring Company message to the public. This position interfaces with top management, and provides information and consultation for decision making.

Major Duties and Responsibilities
(Rate in order of importance.)

1. Identify the basic issues which impact the Corporation and monitor them closely, prioritizing the issues.
2. Develop contacts with futurists in various areas and work with them.
3. Review and evaluate political, social, and economic issues, trends, and conditions which impact the Corporation.
4. Evaluate Company's future needs and opportunities, and recommend appropriate action.
5. Participate in periodic review of Company's policy positions in relation to key issues.
6. Develop close contacts with academic institutions and the recognized authorities in corporation-related areas.
7. Develop positions for the Company on various issues for public pronouncements.
8. Attend conferences, seminars, etc., where advance information on future trends might be secured.
9. Work with top management in projecting their thinking into the future.
10. Maintain close contacts with legislative and regulatory authorities relative to areas of interest to Company.
11. Conduct outreach program to get more exposure of Company to appropriate publics.

9.   **DIRECTOR OF SPECIAL EVENTS**

Objective

To use special events and create situations as a vehicle of communications to enhance the goodwill and reputation of the Company or to promote its products.

Basic Function

Responsible for formulation, development, and execution of special activities to create greater visibility, positive understanding, and goodwill for the Company, its products, and services.

Major Duties and Responsibilities
(Rate in order of importance.)

1. Create and develop events to showcase the Company's products or services (e.g., bake-offs, recipe contests, fashion shows, beauty demonstrations, financial forums, author appearances, energy fairs, brownstone revival programs, etc.).
2. Assist with charitable events held in local facilities to enhance Company's reputation.
3. Plan, assist, and advise on programs designed to create goodwill and public

understanding in various communities (e.g., Little League, 4–H, Junior Achievement, etc.).

4. Plan and execute sporting events participation of Company, where appropriate.
5. Conduct annual facilities visitations (e.g., family day, wives' visits, open houses) to corporate facilities. where appropriate.
6. Arrange for plant or facilities tours by educational and other groups.
7. Create special events and opportunities for top management to tell Company's story.
8. Participate in such civic and professional activities as might be important to Company communications efforts and Company interests.
9. Render whatever assistance possible in crisis public relations situations.
10. Offer use of Company's auditorium or meeting room to local civic groups (e.g., planning boards, charitable organizations without large facilities of their own, etc.).
11. Create major sporting events for public goodwill.
12. Develop and manage budget for these activities.

10. DIRECTOR OF EXECUTIVE PRESENTATIONS

Objective

To favorably influence public policy affecting the Corporation's business, and build its reputation as a sound investment and an ethical, credible, statesmanlike organization providing a major contribution to every community in which it does business.

Basic Function

This position exists because it may be in the Corporation's best interests to have a single person and section responsible for centrally coordinating, writing, clearing, and finalizing the pronouncements by the top executives directed to the Corporation's diverse publics. Centralizing these executive communications (i.e., speeches, testimony, financial reports, by-lined print media articles, public policy letters) assures their accuracy and consistency with corporate policies.

Major Duties and Responsibilities
(Rate in order of importance.)

1. Research, write, and obtain approval for speeches, executive correspondence, information responses, and by-lined articles for the chairman, president, and executive and senior vice presidents.
2. Write key policy communications from top management to middle management and employees.
3. Maintain consistent adherence to approved public positions on major issues.
4. Help identify and seek forums for speech topics that meet corporate objectives.
5. Screen speaker requests to identify specifically the organizations, their reputations and positions, the message being sought, the audience and its interest and

knowledge level, the community and news media opportunities, as a basis for accepting or rejecting the request.

6.   Maintain a reference file and familiarity with opinion-leaders' speeches and positions on public issues.
7.   Maintain familiarity with current events and literature appropriate to the development of high-quality written and spoken communications.
8.   Coach speakers and writers to improve effectiveness of presentation, using professional coaches and videotape practice sessions.
9.   Write message of the CEO for annual report and quarterly reports.
10.   Draft letters for the CEO's signature upon request.
11.   Assist with preparation of special reports as requested by top management.
12.   Maintain regular contact with members of top executive management.
13.   Produce a regular "Speeches in Print" report for top management.
14.   Make certain that every major executive communications pronouncement is consistent with the Company's position on the issue or subject.
15.   Monitor the quality and style of all Company's written communications.
16.   Attend conferences on subjects of interest to the Company to keep abreast of developments.
17.   Supervise and coordinate activities of staff writers under his/her direction.
18.   Oversee the activities of the corporate speakers bureau.

11.   DIRECTOR OF EDITORIAL SERVICES

Objective

To give Company the capability of producing excellent written materials and editorial assistance while maintaining quality control of materials prepared and distributed by the Company.

Basic Function

To act as principal editor and writer for public relations/public affairs department. To initiate, research, and write speeches, policy statements, newspaper and magazine articles, and other materials for senior management; also, to prepare news releases, bulletins, background papers, and presentations as required or assigned.

Major Duties and Responsibilities
(Rate in order of importance.)

1.   Research and write basic background memorandum on the Company.
2.   Research and write news releases, feature articles, and other printed materials.
3.   Develop a copy clearing procedure to make certain materials are properly cleared by the executives involved, legal department, executive management, etc.
4.   Handle special projects and requests as assigned.
5.   Develop a style book for use by all preparing written materials for Company.
6.   Keep abreast of all public developments affecting the Company.

7. Assist with the development of presentations as needed.
8. Assist with the ghost writing of speeches for senior management.
9. Periodically review all Company publications for style and accuracy consistency.
10. Maintain appropriate news media contacts.
11. Provide for the creative input and production of audio-visuals, motion pictures, sound slides, etc., as required.
12. Assist in production of annual and quarterly reports, and other financial statements.
13. Provide consultation and assistance with preparation and placement of technical articles for specialized publications.
14. Function as Company's literary specialist available for consultation with top executive management.
15. Maintain list of free-lance writers and photographers, and contact them when needed.

12. DIRECTOR OF PUBLIC RELATIONS RESEARCH (CORPORATE OR AGENCY)

Objective

To provide a reference file and corporate intelligence system accessing whatever information is needed for decision making and for achieving corporate objectives.

Basic Function

To develop and operate a research capability and delivery system to support efforts of the public relations/public affairs personnel, and especially executive management.

Major Duties and Responsibilities
(Rate in order of importance.)

1. Determine informational needs of the Company as related to its activities.
2. Develop a basic research plan containing essential elements of information for presentation and approval of executive management.
3. Review all possible sources of present and future information needs of the Company'(e.g., Library of Congress, etc.).
4. Research impact of Company communications efforts in various areas and issue reports.
5. Develop a permanent system of quickly measuring attitudes and opinions of various publics in relation to a given issue.
6. Study various issues of interest to Company and determine public reaction to them.
7. Develop a basic research file for use by Company personnel on special projects, such as speechwriting, etc.
8. Make arrangements to access information retrieval systems such as those of Dow Jones or the *New York Times*.

9. Establish archives for Company and develop a history.
10. Engage clipping services and broadcast reports to monitor coverage received by Company and its competitors.
11. Subscribe to appropriate publications for Company needs and reference.
12. Fill requests for information from authorized personnel.
13. Supervise and conduct attitude and opinion surveys.
14. Keep current on new equipment, technological developments, etc., in Company's industries of interest.

13. DIRECTOR OF INSTITUTIONAL ADVERTISING

Objective

To make certain the themes reflecting corporate advertising conform to the content of other outlets used by the Company, such as news media, printed materials, etc., and that entire efforts of all are coordinated and properly timed.

Basic Function

To provide input, direction, and supervision for advertising campaigns not concerned with promoting products or services, but designed to enhance corporate image and identity, or present its point of view in answering attacks or launching Company defense positions.

Major Duties and Responsibilities
(Rate in order of importance.)

1. Direct and coordinate the entire corporate advertising effort.
2. Supervise the work of advertising agencies involved with the effort.
3. Develop the budget and monitor the expenditure of funds.
4. Maintain close liaison with public relations/public affairs personnel.
5. Responsible for the preparation and distribution of conference reports on various meetings with agencies, suppliers, etc.
6. Monitor all advertising agency activities in the area of print and broadcast media pertaining to the creative and billing functions.
7. Responsible for obtaining clearance of all advertising copy from the law department, executive management, etc.
8. Implement advertising, promotional, and publicity campaigns conducted by the Company.
9. Develop and research special interest advertising for minority groups and other publics.
10. Supervise advertising staffers in preparing institutional advertising.

14.   DIRECTOR OF CONSUMER AFFAIRS

Objective

To identify with the concerns of consumers and the public, and to create understanding for and represent interests of the Company in this special field.

Basic Function

To advise top executive management of trends of consumerism and concerns of individuals communicating with the Company; be prepared to offer solutions in the best interest of the Company and the consumer; and be responsible for Company's consumer response system.

Major Duties and Responsibilities
(Rate in order of importance.)

1. Follow all legislation concerning consumers and impacting Company's products or services.
2. Monitor implications of Consumer Products Warranty and FTC Improvements Act of 1974 as it affects the Company.
3. Monitor rules and regulations passed by Federal Trade Commission, Food and Drug Administration, Federal Communications Commission, etc., which impact on any of the Company's products or services.
4. Develop a strong consumer affairs operation with clearly written plan of action.
5. Establish policies and develop procedures for analyzing and utilizing the data generated through consumer communications.
6. Develop system for alerting management of impending consumer problems.
7. Develop guidelines for evaluating essential factors for management in the area of consumer affairs.
8. Make constructive suggestions for improving Company's products and services.
9. Develop with other departments a program which meets consumer needs and increases sales.
10. Develop and evaluate field training programs relating to consumer affairs.
11. Maintain contact with organized consumer groups and activist organizations.
12. Be prepared to offer solutions to objections on issues relating to advertising, packaging, labeling, instruction manuals, etc., to avoid criticism.
13. Communicate information concerning consumer affairs to all levels of management.
14. Develop meaningful and constructive testimony to be given before federal and state regulatory agencies.
15. Where pertinent, develop a plan for effective, rapid product recall.

15.   DIRECTOR OF CUSTOMER RELATIONS

Objective

To enhance the reputation of the Company's products and services with present customers and to significantly broaden the customer base and support.

Basic Function

To manage the Company's interface with its customers, making certain any and all contracts or complaints are handled properly, and to develop a system of two-way communication with customers.

Major Duties and Responsibilities
(Rate in order of importance.)

1. Assume managerial responsibility for all customer affairs representatives and contacts.
2. Manage the daily functioning of the customer response procedure and make certain the customers are contacted without delay.
3. Where pertinent, research shipping procedures—whether internal or through external services—for Company's products. Make modifications where constructive.
4. Where pertinent, research and develop a policy for return of defective or damaged products throughout entire distribution chain—department stores, appliance centers, franchisees, dealers, etc. Initiate needed changes.
5. Maintain high quality of communications standards, both verbal and written, with present customers. Develop instructions for telephone board complaint clerks.
6. Participate in development and execution of special customer affairs programs.
7. Maintain close contact with marketing research and exchange information.
8. Develop procedures for handling customer complaints in accordance with legal and other departments.
9. Send advance copies of ads, promotion brochures, special offers to all customer affairs representatives.
10. Conduct periodic audits of customer complaints and how they are handled.
11. Study Company's insurance liability policies for protection adequacy against customer complaints concerning defects (spoiled food, defective cars, or machinery, etc.).

16.   DIRECTOR OF PUBLIC RELATIONS (NONPROFIT ORGANIZATION)

Objective

To plan and carry out a program designed to create and maintain a favorable public image for the institution or organization and to encourage public support for the institution's mission, programs, and accomplishments.

Basic Function

Responsible to the chief executive officer and to the board of trustees for formulating plans for, and for implementing, diverse programs, activities, and efforts that meet the needs, objectives, and policies of the institution in the public arena, as well as for interpreting programs and policies to the public, and public attitudes and opinions to the institution.

Major Duties and Responsibilities
(Rate in order of importance.)

1. Consult with, and counsel, the chief executive officer and the trustees on policies and programs that involve the various publics and the institution's public image.
2. Define long- and short-term public relations goals, and recommend public relations programs and activities designed to meet these goals.
3. Prepare a budget and organization chart, with job descriptions, for carrying out the public relations program and activities; maintain budgetary controls.
4. Advise and assist administrators of other departments, as well as constituent groups (trustees, alumni, students, volunteers, etc.) in handling activities that may reflect on the institution's public image.
5. Serve as communications liaison between the chief executive and trustees, and the institution's various publics or constituencies.
6. Establish and maintain good relations with both the print and electronic media, keeping them informed of the institution's activities.
7. Maintain institutional mailing and contact lists.
8. Produce institutional publications, including annual reports, newsletters, magazines and journals, brochures, catalogs, posters, invitations, etc.
9. Work with the head of development or directly handle fund-raising activities, possibly including the preparation of grant applications.
10. Plan and handle arrangements for special events, including guest lists, physical arrangements, invitations, programs, publicity, etc.
11. Assist the chief executive, trustees, and other top officers in preparing speeches, position papers, testimony, and other official institutional statements.
12. Work with governmental and community groups to help achieve institutional goals.
13. Serve as the institution's representative to local, state, regional, and national organizations.
14. Plan and implement public relations programs for employees.
15. Represent the institution as speaker before community and professional groups and organizations.
16. Develop a history and achievements background of the organization.
17. Where pertinent, highlight any research projects or educational activities or awards won by students or researchers in organization.
18. Publicize the board of directors, trustees, and executives, etc., to secure more recognition for the organization.

17.   DIRECTOR OF PUBLIC RELATIONS (TRADE OR PROFESSIONAL ASSOCIATION)

Objective

To create goodwill for the industry and members represented by the trade association.

Basic Function

To develop and implement a program of public information and action to create a climate of goodwill.

Major Duties and Responsibilities
(Rate in order of importance.)

1. Develop and plan for the collection of information and statistical materials on the industry and its members.
2. Maintain close relations with other trade associations covering the industry.
3. Maintain close contact with academic institutions which have an interest in doing research on the industry.
4. Publish a newsletter reporting items of interest to Association members and on Association members' activities.
5. Conduct opinion polls on industry customers and report on the results.
6. Work with appropriate personnel in developing and maintaining membership in the Association.
7. Each year, report on election of Association's officers and localize the releases.
8. Arrange for press conferences and publicity during Association's annual convention.
9. Recruit competent public relations personnel and develop a staff.
10. Publicize various aspects of industry to make it better known in a favorable way.
11. Work closely with public relations personnel in other industries in areas of common interest.
12. Maintain close relations with government regulatory authorities and congressional committees in areas of the Association's interests, and prepare testimony and position papers for public hearings.
13. Work in unison with other public relations directors (of Association industry or profession) for greater impact.
14. Maintain a clipping and publicity monitoring service to keep abreast of developments in the industry.
15. Develop a speech source material file for ready reference when Association officers or member executives require speeches written.
16. Develop a series of films and audio-visual presentations to make the industry better known.
17. Develop, write, and produce background brochures for use of Association's membership development officer.
18. Write and distribute informational bulletins regularly to Association members.
19. Develop and administer the annual public relations budget.

20. Advise Association members on contacting their legislators when necessary.
21. Develop sample public relations programs for use of Association members who do not have public relations staffs.

18. ACCOUNT EXECUTIVE (CORPORATE OR AGENCY)

Objective

To assure maximum performance of the agency on behalf of the client while maintaining a reasonable profit.

Basic Function

To maintain liaison with and be responsible for all the agency's work on behalf of the client, functioning essentially as the primary point of contact between the two whether within a public relations agency or the Company.

Major Duties and Responsibilities
(Rate in order of importance.)

1. Develop key contacts with management of the client and facilities, and keep up the two-way communication.
2. Supervise the work of all agency staff people on behalf of the client.
3. Secure approval of copy, news releases, feature articles, etc., from the client.
4. Hold periodic conferences between the agency and client representatives, and prepare written conference reports.
5. Write and distribute monthly projections of future activities to executive management of agency.
6. Require weekly work reports of the staff people working on account.
7. Assist in developing annual budget for client; closely monitor such expenditures.
8. Assist in reviewing monthly bill for staff time and out-of-pocket expenses, and convey to the client.
9. Monitor all clippings and radio-TV reports, and send to client.
10. Lead client's management in public relations activities.
11. Seek out public relations problems with client and suggest ways to solve them.
12. Arrange periodic review meetings between agency and client's top management.
13. Develop annual public relations program for client and secure approval.
14. Keep account supervisors informed of activities affecting the client.
15. Develop and maintain lists and files relating to client activities.
16. Conduct each account as if it is a business.

19. ACCOUNT SUPERVISOR (USUALLY WITH AN AGENCY)

Objective

To manage, supervise, and coordinate the activities of various account executives while maintaining an awareness of needs of clients and their importance as profit centers.

Basic Function

Constantly to review the activities of the account executives, their staffers, and specialized departments, keeping top management informed of pertinent activities and potential problems.

Major Duties and Responsibilities
(Rate in order of importance.)

1. Develop a spirit of teamwork and high morale among the people working under his/her direction.
2. Develop a system for account executives to report in writing each week a summary of their activities. Review weekly staff reports and summarize for top management.
3. Develop contacts with clients' executive management and maintain two-way communication. Also hold periodic review meetings between agency people and clients.
4. Lead the account and client staff personnel in the conduct of public relations activities, but manage the accounts rather than working on them directly.
5. Enhance the creativity of the staff people under his/her direction.
6. Work to increase the volume of business from among present clients by promoting additional activities, always managing and supervising the accounts under his/her direction for maximum profitability.
7. Develop a system of monitoring the publicity produced for each client and report results on a monthly basis.
8. Seek to anticipate public relations problems before they become major issues and bring solutions to top agency management rather than presenting problems only.
9. Make certain as much account executive, account supervisor, and staff time as possible is billable to clients.
10. Make certain activities on behalf of clients are executed within budget estimates so accounts do not run out of funds prematurely.
11. Supervise each account's use of the agency's specialized departments and their personnel.
12. Search for opportunities for new clients and new business.
13. Prepare for agency top management an account-by-account profit and loss statement.

20. DIRECTOR OF CLIENT SERVICES (USUALLY WITH AN AGENCY)

Objective

To review, keep under surveillance, and direct the activities of account executives, account and group supervisors, on behalf of clients and act as an objective counselor to increase efficiency and solve problems.

Basic Function

To make sure that the full range of services of the agency are being properly managed and used by the staff on behalf of clients and, if possible, to expand use so that agency billings and profits increase.

Major Duties and Responsibilities
(Rate in order of importance.)

1. Function as a key assistant to the general manager or whoever is the agency's chief executive officer.
2. Assist with the management and supervision of account and group supervisors.
3. Make certain clients are utilizing to the fullest the entire resources of the agency.
4. Seek out and develop new areas of activity for client services.
5. Function as a salesman for various agency services to the client.
6. Conduct department as if it was his/her own business.
7. Seek out new business for agency and write presentations.
8. Counsel, upon request, on any special problems clients might have.
9. Lead clients in public relations activities, rather than simply following their directives.
10. Frequently review staff time to make certain the maximum hours are billable to clients.
11. Prepare periodic situation reports for top management. Make recommendations for improvement of operations.
12. Participate in new business meetings and presentations to articulate agency's capabilities.
13. Write articles on various aspects of public relations for professional journals.
14. Enhance the capabilities of the agency's specialized departments.
15. Review all written reports prepared by the account supervisors and executives and constantly evaluate.
16. Develop ideas for research projects which might be of value to clients, to be conducted either by the agency or outside sources.
17. Keep abreast of important developments in various client industries.
18. Conduct public opinion polls when useful or necessary.
19. Be aware of the capabilities of corporate intelligence and how it could be applied for the benefit of clients.
20. Develop an annual review and analysis system on the public relations status of each client.

21.   Conduct periodic audits of the various public relations programs and activities on behalf of clients.

21.   DIRECTOR OF CREATIVE SERVICES (USUALLY WITH AN AGENCY)

Objective

To provide a source of new, original, imaginative, and creative ideas which account personnel working with clients can utilize and to provide consulting to make full range of agency creativity available to all clients.

Basic Function

To make available superior creative services beyond the capability of typical account personnel in the form of suggested programs and activities which they can help execute on behalf of clients and to study, refine, and make workable creative ideas submitted by staff members.

Major Duties and Responsibilities
(Rate in order of importance.)

1.   Participate in new business meetings/presentations to articulate some of the recent agency success stories that demonstrate agency capabilities.
2.   Organize staff discussions to generate workable program ideas and marketing strategies and to identify trends, planning, etc.
3.   Be available as agency's creative resource to participate in brainstorm meetings called by others in the agency.
4.   Write programs in response to new business opportunities.
5.   Act as "final filter," screening and reviewing written programs before they are submitted to prospective clients.
6.   Make presentations to staff on "creative PR," how-to sessions designed to encourage more agencywide creativity.
7.   Write articles about interesting agency case histories for trade publications.
8.   Take the lead in involving other in-house resources, such as graphics, research, etc., in program implementation (showing creative uses of such specialties).
9.   Lead by example. The day-to-day work of this executive should be laced with consistent standout creativity that gets superior results.
10.   Initiate new agency profit centers. Identify areas of opportunity that can be developed into new agency capabilities and services.
11.   Foster a climate within agency which encourages creation and flow of ideas.
12.   Develop procedures for the creation and production of slides, motion pictures, video, multimedia, etc., productions on behalf of clients.
13.   Maintain contacts with outside producers and providers of creative services. Keep abreast of new developments in these areas.
14.   Set the quality control standards for the agency's creative output.
15.   Remain abreast of promotional activities of client's competitors and developments in client industries.

16. Develop ways of expanding agency business on behalf of clients (new activities, etc.) to increase billings to clients.
17. Organize internal training programs for staff development.
18. Maintain a reference file on available courses, seminars, workshops, etc., for benefit of staff members who wish to upgrade their skills.

GLOSSARY

Bill Cantor

ABC Audit Bureau of Circulation. The organization sponsored by publishers, agencies, and advertisers for securing accurate circulation statements

abstract a summary of the essential points of a document, usually presented to executive management

acceptable risk the potential loss that a business, individual, or community is willing to accept rather than provide resources to reduce or eliminate such a loss

acceptability the ability to inspire belief—an essential element of communications

account a client of a public relations or advertising agency; also refers to internal groups, units, divisions, etc., which corporate public relations personnel might be serving

account executive a representative of either a public relations or advertising agency who is assigned to function as liaison between the agency and client. Also in some corporations one who functions similarly between an in-house agency and its internal clients, divisions, or subsidiaries

account supervisor individual, usually within an agency, in charge of and responsible for the activities of several account executives' work on behalf of clients

adjustment a primary element of good public relations, which recognizes that people, groups, and organizations must adjust to one another in a stable and orderly society

advance copy a report of a speech or announcement circulated to news media before an event has taken place to give them time to prepare their coverage for dissemination at the time of the event

advance man an individual who proceeds ahead of a speaker or group to a given locality and makes all arrangements to pave the way usually before a speech, special event, etc.

advertisement a sales message intended for delivery to prospects of a not-for-profit organization or customers of a commercial firm or vendor, generally by means of paid space or time in newspapers, magazines, radio, television, direct mail, or billboards, with the form determined by the medium

advertising presenting persuasive materials to the public generally via paid space or broadcast time, usually to promote a concept, individual, or company product or service

advertising agency an organization devoted to creation, preparation, and placing of advertising materials

advertising manager the executive who is in control of and responsible for advertising

advocacy advertising the persuasive presentation of an idea, concept, or point of view (not products or services), generally through paid advertising

agency a business service usually retained by, and authorized to act on behalf of or represent the interests of, others

alphanumeric data that can be composed of numbers, letters of the alphabet, punctuation marks, and symbols for computers

ambassadorial relations the efforts of the leading diplomatic representative of a country to create goodwill and improved public relations with the representatives and people of another country

analog something that is analogous or similar to something else

analog communications a system of telecommunications used to transmit information by electrical currents

analog computer a computer operating electrical currents representing the mathematical problem to be solved

angle a certain aspect of a story used as an introduction to gain the reader's attention, interest, and immediate awareness. It has the same meaning as "slant"

animation making inanimate objects apparently alive and moving by setting them before an animation camera and filming them one frame at a time

annual report a yearly financial report required by the Securities and Exchange Commission, usually summarized and translated into layman's terms for distribution to stockholders and financial news media

area probability sample a very accurate mathematically based method for selecting a sample (people to be interviewed) for opinion research

ASCAP American Society of Composers, Authors, and Publishers. A performing rights organization of authors and publishers which protects the copyrights of its members

association an organized body of people who have some interest or purpose in common—civic, legislative, charitable, or business—for which they work together

attitude in general, the operation of emotion, reaction, and pro-and-con tendencies with regard to a particular object, concept, or person

audience The group or groups to which an organization's public relations program and activities are directed

audio-visual aid any mechanical form of aid that assists a speaker to communicate more fully with his audience, such as sound slides, films, videotapes—usually involves a screen

audio-visual communications the process of communication by means of electronic devices, which usually involve a screen and visual images, as contrasted with printed materials

author's alterations changes made in subject matter by author after the type has been set and submitted in proofs

automation in general, the combination of machines and electronic devices that handle rapid services or the mass production of goods, usually on an assembly line

bandwagon reinforcing the public's natural desire to be on the winning side of an issue or conflict, usually by presenting a position as irresistible and victory inevitable

banner head headlines set in large type and usually extending across the top of the front page of a newspaper

basic fact file information collected by the public relations staff of a corporation to facilitate dissemination of news to the public

behavior modification changing the way people think and act, usually without their awareness of what is happening

behavior pattern the recurrent manner of acting or responding to a given situation and/or set of stimuli

blow up to enlarge the size of any visual item by photographing and producing an enlargement

blurb non-news statement issued to the news media, but containing only generalities instead of specific facts and intended for promotion

BMI Broadcast Music, Inc. The world's largest music licensing organization which protects the performing rights of its writer and publisher affiliates

booklet a printed piece, usually six pages or more with a paper or self-cover, prepared as a bound unit usually by stapling

boomerang effect whenever an individual or organization reacts in a way unanticipated by the planners of a public relations campaign

brainstorming the creative process of group thinking about and articulating of ideas on a given subject or problem, often recorded for future evaluation and use

break when the story or events the PR personnel have arranged climaxes by attracting the media coverage that was calculated

breakdown a break in the communication chain which can occur between the encoder (which prepares information for communication) and transmission (the method of transmitting the information); or between transmission and the decoder (translating the information for the receiver's use)

briefing book a book compiled for use by the executive so he can have all the pertinent information on a given subject for study and review prior to an interview or appearance at a news conference

broadcast the dissemination of programs or messages by radio or television waves, usually received by an antenna

broadside a single sheet printed on one side designed for quick reading and stimulation to immediate action

brochure A printed piece containing six or more pages and more elaborate than a booklet

build up the preliminary activities in a publicity campaign to promote a person, product, or service

bulk mail a quantity of third class mail that must be delivered to the post office in bundles, sorted by state and city

bulldog edition a morning paper's early edition, printed the preceding evening and sent to readers on the night train or plane

bulletin boards a potentially effective medium, used as a part of the public relations programs of many corporations, for contacting employees and others

business publications newspapers and magazines produced specially for the business and financial community and for special business interest groups

by-line name of the writer positioned under the headline at the beginning of the story

cable usually a bundles of wires protected by a lead or other type of sheath completing electronic circuits between two points

cable TV distant and interference-free images received on a TV screen by means of a pair of wires rather than by means of an antenna receiving signals from a broadcast station

campaign a highly organized effort made through a specific plan over a period of time to influence and alter the opinion of a group or groups on a given subject

caption descriptive copy, usually short, placed adjacent to or under illustrations

card-stacking the deliberate selective omission of facts so the communicator can present a view in the best possible light. Usually omits important details

cathode ray tube (CRT) the input/output display of a computer terminal similar to a small TV set

CATV Community Antenna Television. A term used interchangeably with cable-casting

center spread the two center facing pages of a publication (also double spread)

central processing unit (CPU) the place where data actually gets processed, which is the heart of the computer

CEO chief executive officer. Usually of a publicly held corporation

channel a band of frequencies assigned to a given radio or TV station

channel noise technical term for interference in the transmission between the encoder and decoder

characteristic an attribute, description feature, or identity

cheesecake illustrations, also known as "leg art," usually photographs, depending for their effects on the display of feminine sex appeal

chips minute pieces of silicon which contain numerous electrical circuits and which are used in computers

circuit a means of two-way communication between two points comprising "go" and "return" channels, thus completing the circuit

circular a free distribution item or mailing piece, usually one sheet, intended for inexpensive widespread distribution

client the organization or person retaining an outside or house agency for specialized services

client copy materials written solely for and slanted to please the client, rather than slanted to the requirements of the news media

clippings or clips stories or features taken from various printed publications mentioning an individual or organization, usually obtained from a clipping service charging a flat rate per clipping

clip sheet several news releases, usually printed on a large sheet, sent to editors at the same time

closed circuit live videotape or film material transmitted by cable for private viewing on a TV monitor

combination publication a publication distributed by an organization to both its members and/or employees and outside individuals

commercial a television, radio, or film advertisement slotted into programming and paid for by the advertiser

common carrier an organization which provides communications services to the general public and which is regulated by appropriate local, state, or federal agencies

communicate to pass an idea from one person or audience to another, registering the desired effect on the opposite side; to transfer ideas from one mind to another

communications the art of transmitting information, ideas, and attitudes from one person to another through verbal and/or visual symbols. Requires sender, message, and receiver (from Latin, "to make common," to share)

communications center in larger corporations, usually means place where the audio-visual communications are technically centralized and directed

community adjacent geographical area which could be affected by a company's policies or operations. Also a group of people tied together by a common interest

community relations the sphere of public relations which covers enlisting the cooperation and support of civic authorities and local citizens of the area in which the organization is located

conciliation a procedure under which a neutral third party attempts to persuade the parties concerned to settle their dispute without seeking to impose one's own terms of settlement on them (similar to mediation)

conference report a summary of the points discussed, actions taken, and decisions made with, and assignments given to, members of an organization; also may include members of an outside advertising or public relations firm

congruity, theory of the theory that in any argument or debate special interest groups will always support themes reflecting their own beliefs and interests

consultant a person who gives advice and information on a professional basis

consumer one who uses goods or services to satisfy personal or household wants rather than for resale or use in business or industrial corporations

consumer affairs activities involving maintaining good relations with the organization's consumers; also the appropriate regulatory and legislative agencies concerned with consumer protection and similar issues

consumer publications newspapers, magazines, and periodicals, published for the general reader as opposed to the special interest reader

contact someone the public relations practitioner personally knows and works with, frequently with the news media

content analysis the technique of reading publications for reference to an organization, then coding and analyzing the content to determine trends and opinion

contingency plan a preconceived written plan involving public relations activities to be put into effect

control group a group of people selected for their characteristics or opinions, often used as a test group against which to test the results of research

COO chief operating officer

cooperative advertising any form of advertising in which two or more organizations or individuals combine their efforts in a single campaign

copy written materials or a manuscript which is to be set in type or used by broadcast media

copy clearance the approval of written public relations materials for publication by appropriate persons in executive management

copy desk point where all materials written for publication are reviewed and edited. Now found in many public relations departments and agencies.

copy platform statement of the basic ideas for an advertising or publicity campaign—basically the themes to be projected

copy writer a person in an agency or corporate public relations department who specializes in writing various types of materials as assigned

corporate art   collection of art objects of corporations which collect art for display on their premises and as an investment

corporate contributions   financial support many corporations give to what they consider worthy causes, such as scholarships, research, civic organizations, employees' colleges, and prep schools

corporate mission   a single, clear-cut goal of management created so all aspects and relationships of the corporation can be brought to bear on achieving basic objectives

corporate public relations   the entire gamut of public relations for a corporation as a whole rather than for any of its primary individual functions

corporate social responsibility   recognition of the relationship between business and society, and the conscious planning of corporate actions taking this into account

corporation   a body of persons granted a charter legally recognizing them as a separate entity having its own rights, liabilities, and privileges separate from those of its members—usually publicly owned via shares of stock

correspondent   a reporter who contributes to a newspaper or magazine; usually from another place

cost-benefit   a term used to express the value of a benefit-producing system. Can be expressed as a ratio of cost (negative value) to benefit (positive value) when both are in equivalent terms such as dollars, man-hours, etc.

counselor   a person who gives advice and counsel on a continuing basis and is usually on a long-term retainer

coverage   the extent of press and media publicity obtained for a given story or activity

created event   an event or situation created by public relations personnel to elicit news coverage

creative services   original, imaginative, unique approaches to situations or problems and available from specialized personnel

credit line   a line of copy acknowledging the source or origin of a news story, photograph, or artwork

critical issue   an important emerging trend or problem that is reaching its resolution point and will affect the organization

crowd   a group of people who think and act in unison without apparent direction or leadership

crystallization   the act of bringing previously subconscious public opinions and attitudes into public consciousness

current system   the procedures and systems in use at present

cursor   a special indicator on a display screen used to point out the position on the screen that is the object of attention

customer relations   the status of relations between a corporation and its customers—one of its publics

data   raw facts or observations; factual material used as a basis especially for discussion or decision information

Dataphone   both a service mark and trademark of AT&T and the Bell System. As a service mark, it indicates transmission of data over the telephone network

deadline   the day and hour in which news copy must be in the hands of the editor of a newspaper or broadcast program director

decoding in the communications process, the act of translating the information received for one's use—a critical phase of the operation

demonstration a coordinated public activity, either planned or spontaneous, which could engender news coverage

depth interview a lengthy interview technique requiring skill; elicits both conscious and unconscious personal dynamics and motivations

design studio place where graphic designers and artists work to create visual materials

development fund-raising activities of nonprofit and educational institutions

digital communications system of telecommunications often used in telemetry or signaling; employs a noncontinuous or pulse signal

digital computer a calculating device which represents data in the form of pulses and operates on them mathematically (e.g., adding machines, electronic computers)

direct mail the promotion of ideas, products, or services by letter writing

disc a flat, hard, rotating plate for use in computers to record and retrieve information magnetically (similar in looks to a music record)

disclaimer a statement to qualify or repudiate a claim made in printed materials

dissonance theory the psychological difference between knowledge and action, attitude and behavior—inconsistencies between what people know and how they act

distribution publications to which a release to news media was sent; the destination of any company communication to the public

dividend payout proportion of earnings available for cash dividends to holders of a company's common stock

donations money given to worthy organizations and causes to create goodwill. Company donation policy usually comes within the scope of the corporate public relations program

draft preliminary or working state of a news release, feature, script, or any other written material before final approval

earth station a TV receiving station designed to capture signals from satellites for relay to broadcasting stations

ecology the physical environment in which an organization and its individual members function

editorial an expression of the views and opinions of the management in control of a publication or broadcasting operation

editorial credit mention of a company or its product in an editorial feature (e.g., a particular bank supplying information for story on housing costs)

editorial services the function of conveying information by providing assistance with preparation and creation of materials involving the written and spoken word

educational program the efforts of an organization to provide information and instruction to specific groups by various means, such as booklets, owners' manuals, package instructions, reference materials, sound slides, films, etc.

eleemosynary institution a not-for-profit organization, not working in behalf of any industry; usually tax exempt and dependent on charity and contributions

embargo a deliberate request to delay publication of information sent to newspapers until after a predetermined date. The warning usually appears at the top of the first page of the news release or statement

emergency program   a written public relations plan to go into effect in case of an emergency or disaster. It includes plans for dealing with news media, possible product recall, etc., and should be updated periodically

employee communications   the two-way transmittal of information to and from management and employees by various media—letters, newsletters, magazines, brochures

employee relations   activities involving maintaining good relations with employees (fringes, salaries, pensions, etc.); usually but not always conducted by personnel department

encoding   the primary stage of any communication in which a person or source encodes information for transmission to another person or source

engineering of consent   an attempt by provision of information, persuasion, and adjustment to engineer public support for an activity, cause, movement, or institution

environment   the complex of social and cultural conditions affecting the nature or surroundings of a person, organization, or community

evaluation   measuring the success of a program or concept

exclusive   a story offered by a public relations practitioner, writer, or reporter to only one newspaper, magazine, or radio or television news program, excluding all others

executive presentations   especially prepared materials (e.g., speeches, policy statements, pamphlets for use of top executive management) for both internal and external communications

expense account   funds provided to the public relations practitioner by the corporation or client to defray personal expenses such as travel, maintenance, lunches, etc.

exposure   the extent to which the public becomes aware of a person, activity, theme, or organization, from the efforts of public relations or advertising

external piece   document prepared by an organization containing pertinent information for external distribution to those outside the organization

external publication   magazine or newspaper published by an organization specifically for people or groups outside of the organization

facsimile   an instantaneous method of transmitting by electronic means printed materials and photos to outside points

fact sheet   usually a one-page summary of the organization or an individual; in effect, a profile giving highlights

feature article   a newspaper or magazine article which discusses and interprets the significance of a news event or trends, as opposed to simply objectively reporting the news

feature syndicate   an organization which produces features and articles or other materials for sale of reproduction rights to publications

feedback   the information and reaction which is communicated back from receivers to the source of the message

fees   money paid a public relations consultant at the beginning of each month to cover consultation and advice. Staff time and out-of-pocket expenses are usually billed separately at the end of the month.

fiber optics   the transmission of messages by means of light waves through fiber, rather than electrical waves through metal wires

fillers journalistic slang for short pieces dropped in between major news stories or articles to fill layout holes

films basically motion pictures—and the most effective of all audio-visuals. Used for everything from providing information to straight promotion

film strip a visual aid consisting of a short strip of film on which are printed individually projected pictures; generally used for educational purposes. Often synchronized with audio-tape or verbal presentations

financial public relations the efforts of a publicly held company to communicate with shareholders, the investing public, the financial community, and business and industry in general

flack slang term used by old-time newspaper and wire service reporters for press agents

flyer a direct mail or handout piece prepared to announce or promote new merchandise, a sale, or special event—usually one page

folder a printed piece, usually four pages, containing information

format the size, makeup, and general appearance of a publication

fourth estate derived from England where the monarch, the House of Lords, and House of Commons occupy the three estates of the realm. During the 18th and 19th centuries, it became recognized that the press occupied the fourth estate

free-lancer self-employed journalist or writer who sells stories and articles to editors and accepts commissions for special assignments

front an organization deliberately established to appear as an independent third party supporting the aims of an individual or organization in controversy

fund raisers specialists in raising money for an organization or cause, usually making use of communications techniques

function (or functional characteristic) something a program, individual, or system does; an activity

fund raising the process of raising money by or for a nonprofit organization client for charity or similar purposes, often using sophisticated public relations techniques. Sometimes referred to as "development"

futuristics activities related to the organization's long-term plans, projecting into and anticipating operations for the future

gatekeepers a form of psychological slang meaning people or groups which filter information in a communications network (e.g., editors). They can accept or reject a message before it reaches the public, therefore exerting great influence

generalist one who interrelates and is familiar with all public relations services, but is highly skilled in perhaps only a few

ghost writer a writer who is engaged to prepare materials which will be attributed to another person

glittering generalities words or phrases so closely associated with commonly accepted ideas or beliefs that they carry conviction in themselves without benefit of reason or supporting facts

goal the general end toward which an effort is directed, whether it be that of an individual or department. The final objective of a public relations effort

gobbledygook long and involved prose incomprehensible to readers, often found in materials prepared by government agencies

going public a privately owned company issuing stock to shareholders, thus converting it to a publicly held company

goodwill   the favorable feeling, attitude, or opinion of people or groups toward a person, institution, organization, or group

grapevine   slang term for information passed among employees, not officially issued by the company; usually based on rumors

gross revenues   the total of all income of a corporation

ground rules   previously agreed upon conditions under which two or more organizations can collaborate on a given project; can also refer to method of the company working with the news media

hack   one who hires himself out to do routine writing, usually banal and hackneyed

handbill   a small printed announcement usually delivered by hand on the streets to passersby

handout   slang term for news release to media

hard news   objective reporting of timely events of common interest, such as international conferences, congressional debates, elections, etc.

hardware   the physical components of a computer system

herd instinct   the tendency of people to mindlessly follow the will of the majority and to do what everyone else does

histories   usually a description of the origin and development of a company or organization prepared for distribution to the public

hold for release   a warning that the information in a news release cannot be published until a certain time and date, usually indicated on release. Similar to embargo

hometown release   special releases prepared for the local weekly press concerning a local resident or organization

horizontal management   system in which members of management team have different skills and enjoy equal status, all contributing whatever they can to achievement of company's objective, in contrast with the vertical structure consisting of a hierarchy of rank and chain of command

house journal   a company publication designed for employees

house magazine   a magazine circulated within an organization forming an essential part of personnel relations; in some instances includes customers

house organ   a publication issued by an organization, directed at one or more of its publics and at helping it to achieve its public relations goals. It can be internal, external, or a combination

identification   the psychological process in which the receiver of a message mirrors the sender of message, usually a leader; an effect sought in communicating

image   the impression, the feeling, the conception which the public has of a company; a consciously created impression of an object, person, or organization

industrial relations   corporation dealings with personnel, labor relations, working conditions, employee benefits, and sometimes including employee communications

information center   an office or booth positioned at a critical location to provide information to visitors or tourists, etc.

information programs   an integral part of any public relations program which makes use of various media of communication

information retrieval systems   method of accessing information as needed from that which is stored, usually in the memory of a computer

infomercial the promotion of a product or service as a integral part of a documentary or visual presentation and woven into its content, as contrasted with a conventional paid commercial

in-house processing data is processed as it occurs into a computer physically located on-site

input information fed into a data processing system. Also information received by and subjected to analysis and review by individuals

insert an item which accompanies letters, bills, or other mailings

institutional advertising paid advertising which promotes the company and its ideas or policies rather than its products and services

institutional holdings usually means all the shares of common stock held by institutions (insurance companies, banks, funds, etc.), but excludes individuals' holdings

interactive television basically two-way communications through television in which the viewer can respond to what appears on screen, sending messages to a central source

internal piece usually refers to a document conveying pertinent information prepared for internal distribution only

interviewer the individual who asks respondents the questions specified in a questionnaire of an opinion attitude or market survey

investment community includes security analysts, brokers, bankers, underwriters, investment bankers, and similar organizations or persons in financial community

issues analysis the process of studying issues and projecting their long-range impact on the corporation

issues management the function of identifying and prioritizing the variety of issues that impact on the company and of developing programs to influence the desired audience(s)

joint statement a situation in which two organizations each separately but simultaneously issue the same or similar statements on the same subject (e.g., a merger or union settlement)

kill to stop working on a news release or news story because a new situation or development divests the story of any value; also applies to public relations projects

kinescope (TV) a recording on film of a live or videotape television presentation

labor relations an important aspect of industrial relations which deals primarily with the labor force, including the union

layout plan of a particular page of a newspaper, magazine, or other publication showing the relative position of stories and illustrations

lead (*pronounced leed*) the beginning, usually first sentence, of a newspaper story. Frequently summarizes the entire story

leaflet a printed piece, usually four pages, for inexpensive distribution

leak to slip tentative ideas or information to the news media or others (e.g., financial community) in an effort to gauge public reaction. Similar to "trial balloon"

legislative liaison maintaining contacts with state and national legislators, and expressing the corporation's views on key issues

leg man an on-the-spot reporter who telephones or cables the latest news to the newspaper, where it is rewritten by a rewrite man for publication

letters to the editor   a section of a newspaper or magazine for reader comment. Frequently used by the public relations practitioner as an outlet. Generally considered as part of any campaign to influence public opinion

leverage   the force developed by joining a company or organization with others whose interests coincide and applying combined strength to shift public opinion

libel   generally consists of printing or broadcasting a false or defamatory statement that injures a person or adversely affects his/her life

light box   box topped by electrified, see-through, magnifying glass panel through which the details in negatives and contact prints can be viewed

lobbies   essentially pressure groups which practice the art of making useful friends and influencing people—usually legislators and government regulatory agencies

low profile   a condition sought by some companies in which they want as little public visibility as possible, especially in the news media

made news   a situation or event especially created to generate news coverage

magnetic tape (*Mag Tape*)   a magnetic Carrier for an inexpensive recording device used to store large amounts of data in a computer

makeup   the general appearance of a page on which an advertisement and/or editorial materials are to appear

managed news   technique of some government agencies involving release of news in order to benefit the agency or department and not necessarily in the public interest

management   the people charged with the responsibility of determining organization or corporate policies, and planning and directing corporate operations

manual   a compilation of directives, policy statements, or instructions into a booklet or book form

market   where a product, service, or idea is to be sold

marketing   the function which organizes and directs all the business activities involved in researching and converting customer purchasing power into sales for the company. Usually not part of public relations, but often strongly supported by it

marketing communications   the support given to the effort to market products and/or services indirectly, making use of the news media rather than paid advertising. Often referred to in publicity as "product publicity"

market research   gathering facts and information needed to make marketing decisions

market share   the percentage share of optimum selling opportunities achieved by a single company promoting a particular product or service in a given market

mass behavior   the response of crowds, mobs, rioters, or groups—generally, but not always, unstructured, unpredictable, and irrational

mass communications   delivery of information, ideas, and attitudes to a large and diversified audience through the use of media developed for that purpose (i.e., printed and broadcast media)

mass medium   a medium directed at and reaching a wide variety of people, rather than directed toward a specific audience

measurable terms   a description of something that can be measured

media   the mass communications outlets available for the delivery of a message, including newspapers, magazines, radio, television, etc.

media relations   the relationship between a company and all the various media of communication, including print and electronic

merchandising amalgamation of methods used for selling a product or service

microwave the transmission of information by means of ultra low frequency directional radio waves between line-of-sight terminals

mileage a slang term denoting the number of column inches obtained in the print media on a given subject being publicized

misquoted an error in reporting—taking something out of context which can give an incorrect view of what was said

mission the strategic long-term objective of a public relations department's efforts to cope with public opinion

mobile exhibit a specially designed exhibition stand which can be easily transported and erected on various sites. It usually is handled by one or more persons who contact the public

model release an agreement, actually a signed document by the model, that a photograph in which person appears can be used for promotional and publicity purposes

monitoring services these are essentially media watchdogs which check the news media (press and also broadcast) for mentions of the company or client. They are engaged by the public relations practitioner, usually for a monthly fee

morgue journalistic slang for the library of a newspaper where clips and other reference materials are filed for use by staff members

motivation research psychological attempts to discover exactly what makes people respond to given stimuli, such as promotion or advertising; relies heavily on understanding subconscious impulses

muckrakers journalists who specialize in exposés, and confessions of corruption and sordid activities in high places. Muckraking was very prevalent at turn of the century and is still somewhat used

multimedia show a presentation which makes use of a variety of audio and visuals simultaneously projected on several screens accompanied by sounds combined for maximum impact

multiple number of times cost of a share of common stock is divisible by stock's pershare annual earnings

multiple channel approach disseminating information concerning a given subject on the target audience by utilizing several types of media and methods of communication to surround and inundate audience with content

narrowcasting telecasting to audiences specially segmented, either geographically or by special interest

net income the amount remaining from gross revenues after payment of all business costs, expenses, property charges, interest, and taxes

news information or details of recent events or original reports on opinions or discoveries of interest

news agency an organization which gathers news for dissemination to newspapers, magazines, radio and television editors, usually by teletype

news conference a gathering of members of the news media, both print and broadcast, to cover an announcement usually too complicated to convey in any other manner and sometimes split into two sections—one for print and the other for broadcast media

newsletter a printed sheet or small newspaper issued at regular intervals and devoted to a particular subject, giving details and inside information to its readers. Frequently published by public relations departments of corporations. Newsletters can be either internal or external. A commercially published newsletter charges subscription fees

news release   a written communication usually containing information of a timely nature sent to all news media and often to others outside the press

news syndicate   an organization which disseminates news and announcements to the various news media in exchange for an established fee

no comment   a "stonewalling" technique of refusing to comment or respond to questions from the press or government investigators. Although it can stop the press from getting information, it usually dos not prevent them from commenting

nonactive public relations   in a given situation or set of circumstances, doing or saying nothing, since to do so might create an even more negative reaction

nonattributable   often used by politicians, public figures, and sometimes corporate executives who are prepared to issue information with the strict understanding that they are not to be quoted by name or implicated in any way

not-for-profit   status granted an organization by the Internal Revenue Service under the terms of which nobody profits and so it pays no income taxes

numeric   data can be composed of numbers for computer use

objectives   specific aims or goals—a key aspect of every public relations program. Objectives should be precisely defined in order to give focus to the activities involved

off the record   a comment which means that the information being given is not for publication, by mutual agreement of the subject and the media representative

on-line processing   data entered into a remote computer via telephone communications as it is ready to be processed

on the record   a statement made deliberately for attribution and to be included in the record or printed in newspapers

op-ed   the newspaper page opposite the editorials in which various opposing points of view are presented, frequently on controversial subjects.

open house   an occasion when a company invites its employees, customers, suppliers, or neighbors to visit the factory and/or offices to see its facilities. Senior management circulates among the guests; refreshments are served and souvenirs offered

opinion polls   polls frequently conducted by a number of organizations using techniques based on theory of probability; usually conducted with questionnaires to access the attitudes and opinions of a particular section of the community or public

optimum   most desirable result under implied or specified conditions. Not necessarily either maximum or minimum

PAC   *see Political Action Committees*

pamphlet   almost synonymous with booklet or brochure, but originally meant several sheets of paper stitched together

panel interview   one person is interviewed by a selected number of journalists at the same time; usually occurs on radio or television

payola   a term used to refer to bribes of any kind. Most often applies to payments to disk jockeys for playing a particular record on radio or television

personal press agent   an agent engaged by one person to act on his/her behalf in dealing with the news media. Usually employed by actors, dancers, musicians, executives, etc. Might also be employed to keep a client's name out of the newspapers

personalization   the device of identifying a personality, such as chairman or president, with an institution or organization so that the public will think of it as being human

photographs   basically, news photographs used heavily in most public relations operations to tell an organization's story

photo journalism   a form of journalism in which the reporter and his notebook is supplemented by the camera. Pictures, more than words, report the news

pitch   the salient bit of information management wishes to communicate to the print or broadcast news media in a news release, feature, or presentation. Management's point of view. Also, presentation of an agency to a client

pizzaz   slang for making more exciting, lively, or increasing impact

placement   presenting or "placing" a news release, feature, or other materials with a news media writer or editor. Usually done through personal contact

plain folks   an approach designed to win the confidence of an audience by communicating in a style or manner more comfortable to the audience

plant   a stage-managed question designed to bring out the right answers at a press conference or panel discussion. Also, a suggestion resulting in news coverage

plant tours   a guided tour of the corporation's local manufacturing facilities, usually conducted for the community. Sometimes conducted for students

plugger   a press agent who seeks to obtain free mentions of his client, products, or services on radio and television shows. Also refers to one who seeks "puffs" in newspapers and magazines

policy   the basic tenents and views of an organization which determine its attitudes, activities, and positions on a given issue. A "statement of policies and purposes" is often written and approved by top management

policy bulletins   issued by many large corporations to inform personnel of important company actions and decisions. Prior to announcement of an event, bulletins are issued to managers with instructions to inform their supervisory and rank-and-file employees

political action committee   a group of people organized by business, labor, professional, and other groups to raise political funds voluntarily from members to be contributed to favored candidates, political party committees, etc.

political relations   the contact an organization has with professional politicians and government regulators

position   a situation, state of circumstances, or point of view of a person or organization relative to a given event or issue

position paper   a document issued by an organization to officially articulate its posture or position on a given set of circumstances, event, or issue

postage meter imprints   stamping all mailings with a message which appears on envelope next to stamp. Both impressions made simultaneously by mailing machine

posture   the position or attitude corporation assumes relative to a given controversy, situation, or issue

presentation   a talk covering facts, ideas, suggestions—and often illustrated—for a public relations program or campaign given by a public relations practitioner to a present or prospective client. Some public relations firms will do presentations only if paid by client for them. Also used in advertising

press book an expanded and enlarged clipping sheet which is frequently circulated among executive management

press conference a gathering of the press called to announce important and complicated company news, and to elicit news media questions. Usually involves preparation of press kit, including company statement, which is distributed at time of conference

press junket a special tour for news media representatives in which transportation and accommodations are provided so they can view a special event or facility. In return for the trip, they are expected to provide coverage. Now being used increasingly less because of the expenses and ethical considerations

press kit usually a folder containing background material, photos and illustrations, news releases, etc., and distributed at a news conference, plant opening, or some special event as reference material for news media

press relations the two-way link between the organization and all media—a vitally important aspect of any public relations program. Press relations are deeply involved with publicity

press release information in printed form, written in newspaper style, issued especially to press by press officer of an organization or a public relations agency

press room a special room established at a convention, conference, or exhibition hall exclusively for use by the press. It usually contains desks, paper, telephones, typewriters, etc., plus background information about the event. Entry usually by badge

press showing carefully planned event for press in order to introduce a new product, service, or seasonal line of merchandise prior to publication date

press table special table set aside for the media at a luncheon, dinner, or important meeting; generally set up near the speaker's dais. Public relations representatives are present to provide information

prestige advertising advertising that tends to build an image or reputation rather than sell a specific product or service

preview presentation of a television production, motion picture, or audio-visual show before general transmission or release to the general public

price/earnings ratio (p/e) the mean of the high and low of the price of shares of stock divided by the per-share earnings

privacy, invasion of violation of right of a private citizen to keep his or her personal affairs from being made public without his/her permission. Does not apply to those seeking publicity or operating in the public domain

private sector that portion of a community which is not a part of the governing or public service body; generally a synonym for citizen groups and private industry

proactive public relations anticipating events, circumstances, or situations, often through the execution of advance plans—basically offensive and aggressive public relations

product publicity any form of promotional activity to obtain publicity for a company's products

profile a detailed study of a specified audience, classified by size, age, sex, income, education, etc.

profit the monies remaining with a business enterprise after it has paid all of its bills and expenses (overhead, salaries, taxes, rent, etc.), and the reward for risk by investors

projected looking toward the future: forecast on the basis of present information

proof an inked impression of composed type or of a plate for inspection, approval, or filing

propaganda promoting of ideas to make converts. Originally it meant simply the spreading of a belief

proposal brief written analysis of the public relations needs of a potential client, prepared by a counselor or by a public relations practitioner for his/her organization

props abbreviation for properties—the inanimate background objects used in a film set or studio during shooting of a film, commercial, or photographs

proxy written authorization given by a stockholder to someone else to vote his/her shares of stock

proxy fight the efforts of a stockholder or shareholder group to win the voting support of the stockholders controlling the majority of the outstanding shares

proxy solicitation the process of contacting shareholders of a publicly held company to secure permission for management or a brokerage house to vote their stock during a meeting of shareholders

proxy statement a document required by the Securities and Exchange Commission (SEC) and the stock exchanges, detailing for stockholders and investors all information pertinent to a request for their vote or proxy on any question or group of questions to be acted on at a meeting of stockholders

psychological warfare the planned use of propaganda and other actions by the military to influence emotions and opinion, attitudes, and behavior of groups to support the accomplishment of national aims and objectives

public (plural: publics) any group of people bound together with a common interest which a public relations program seeks to influence (e.g., stockholders, customers, legislators, regulators, media, etc.). The need to define the public(s) is a primary function of a public relations operation

public affairs usually, an organization's relations with governmental and legislative bodies; but increasingly used as a synonym for the term "public relations"

publicity information concerning a person, organization, event, issue, or product disseminated through the various media of mass communications to attract attention and influence opinions

public information officer a public relations practitioner with the government or the military

public policy the position of an organization, governmental agency, or legislative body, regarding a given set of laws, situation, trend, or development

public relations planned and organized program of policies and conduct to develop public confidence and increased public understanding

public sector that portion of a community which belongs to the public at large; generally used as a synonym for governmental agencies

public service advertising advertising with a message in the public or private interest

puff a term used to indicate favorable editorial comment included with the text of a news release to please the client. Also, a deliberately flattering mention of a person or of an advertiser's product in the news media

quarterly report   statement of a company's sales and earnings for previous three months and issued four times a year. Often contains information about the company's operations

quota sample   a term widely used in opinion research to indicate the breakdown of the group of people under study or queried by opinion research experts

radio-TV reports   services which monitor the broadcast media for references to an organization, and send out clips and/or transcripts

random access   the ability to access from a storage device in a computer, in an equal amount of time and effort, specific data from among many

reactive public relations   responding to a given set of circumstances, situation, or event after the fact. Basically defensive public relations

real time   a real-time computer system may be defined as one that controls an environment by receiving data, processing them, and returning the results quickly enough to affect the functioning of the environment at that time

redundancy   repetition of the main idea of the message to make certain it gets through even if part of the message is lost

reinforcement   bolstering the attitudes and opinions of those who already tend to agree with or be committed to a given cause

release date   the day and time on which information issued to news media is to be exposed to the public. It is usually noted on front page of news release

remote device   a terminal connected to the central processing unit for transmission of information

reporter   one who gathers news, and writes accounts of matters and events for a newspaper or a broadcaster

reprint   taking a story or article which has been printed in news media or an advertisement and photocopying it for further distribution

respondent   the individual who is questioned and who responds to survey questions

response time   the length of time required to respond, generally to a crisis or emergency. Response time is usually measured from time of emergency to the time message or response has been received

risk   possibility of loss

risk element   anything which produces or poses an uncertainty

robot   a piece of machinery or an artificial being which can perform functions normally performed by humans

roundup story   an article in the press quoting several companies or persons on a given subject

rumor   a widely circulated, unverified, and usually inaccurate story from an unknown source passed around by word of mouth. Frequently prevalent when accurate information is unavailable

rural   of or pertaining to the country, country people, or life outside of cities

sample   the portion of the total population involved in a survey. Although relatively small, this portion is representative of the total population involved

satellite   an object placed in a fixed orbiting position in space in relation to the earth and by means of which messages are relayed to and from earth stations

selective attention   singling out specific objects from among many on which to focus the public mind

selective reinforcement the tendency to select from several ideas or messages those which confirm an attitude or opinion already held by the individual

semantics the theory of signs which deals with words or human response to verbal symbols or the meaning of meaning

service fee the amount or percentage of commissions paid by a client to an advertising or public relations firm for undertaking a particular job

shareholder relations activities in a publicly held corporation involving maintaining good relations with shareholders, stockholders, or investors (other than institutional investors)

shares outstanding number of shares of common stock at year-end, exclusive of treasury stock

simplification favorable generalities providing simple answers for complex social, political, or economic problems

sinking fund a fund set up and accumulated, usually by regular deposits, for paying off the principal of a debt when it falls due, or to replace something that will wear out

slander the spoken or verbalized communication of false or defamatory statements which injure a person or adversely affects his or her life

slant *see angle*

slides a form of visual aid making use of still pictures projected onto a screen. Excellent for teaching or instructional purposes

slogan a catchy and easily recognizable phrase, frequently set to music, used to communicate an impression of an organization. Mostly used in product promotion or corporate identification, and must therefore be easy to remember

SMSA Standard Metropolitan Statistical Area. Unit by which the Census Bureau presents population information

social psychology the study of individuals in interaction and in relation to their environment

software all of the programs (i.e., instructions) that run on a computer telling it what to do

sounding board a group of people representing a cross section of an audience; used to get a reaction to ideas or materials presented to them

sound slide visual illustrations flashed on a screen simultaneously with a record or sound tape

source a person who has important information to communicate and who is contacted for that purpose

space grabbing obvious publicity stunts created to elicit press coverage, hence space, which normally would be devoted to news

speakers bureau a service provided by most larger organizations as part of its public relations program to provide speakers on various subjects of interest, usually upon request from local or community groups

speaker's kit a collection of suggested talks, with various openings and conclusions provided. These materials are usually prepared by the public relations department

special event a situation or happening designed to influence opinion, such as an anniversary, reception, grand opening, sporting event, product introduction, etc. Usually it results in publicity

spokesperson   the individual in the public relations/public affairs department who delivers or issues statements to news media for attribution on behalf of the company

sponsored book   a prestige method of publicizing the history and development of a company or organization. It can be privately printed and issued by the company or, if especially good, by an established publishing house

sponsored film   a motion picture produced, paid for, and distributed free of charge by an individual or organization, usually informative, entertaining, and soft sell

spot news   a spontaneous event in the news—like a flood or airline crash—which demands immediate coverage by the news media

stakeholder   an individual or group which has a direct "stake" or interest in the organization, such as employees, stockholders, suppliers, dealers, distributors, politicians, etc.

standing operating procedure (SOP)   method of handling a given situation or conducting operations, usually described in a manual approved by top management

statement of objectives   a written statement issued by an organization to the public outlining its public relations posture—basically a social contract with the public it serves

statement of policy   usually a one-page, simple description developed by top management of the goals, objectives, and mission of an organization

station   one of the input or output points (e.g., telephone set in a telephone system) of a communications network

status report   a formal report to executive management on a given project or event as of a specific point in time

stereotype   preconceived mental notion or concept people have which does not necessarily conform to reality

storyboard   a collection of drawings of the main incidents or action changes for a motion picture or television commercial; also includes dialogue and the main camera and sound effects

strategy   the basic policy decisions in the conduct of a long-term campaign to achieve its objectives

straw man   setting up what might be a phony issue and then knocking it down

stringer   a part-time correspondent for a newspaper, usually working some distance from the publication. He/she covers spot news and assignments, and is paid space rates

studio   the chamber used for producing art creations, or film or television productions

stuffer   a broadside or pamphlet inserted into a pay envelope or sent with bills or other materials to customers

stunt man   a press agent who specializes in producing stunts which will elicit coverage by the news media. Looked upon with disfavor by many public relations practitioners

style book   a booklet produced by an organization for staff use outlining rules for capitalization, spelling, references to dignitaries, governments, etc., in order that all editorial material will conform to same pattern. Many public relations departments have style books

subliminal communications theoretically influencing human behavior with images or symbols beyond one's perception or awareness

support functions in a public relations campaign the activities which contribute to the overall attainment of the objective

symbol visual representation of a theme, policy, or point of view

synergism the action of two elements which, when mixed, work so that the total effect of both is greater than the sum of the two acting independently

tactics the methods and actions of achieving the short-term objectives of a campaign within a strategic plan

targets any primary groups to be reached with a message such as farmers, laborers, government employees, intellectual elites, etc.

teleconference meeting at various locations, each with speakers and/or TV screens, making it possible to talk with and see each other, thus saving travel expense and time. Increasingly used by corporate management

telemetry the process of detecting and gathering information at one location and relaying it to another automatically

teleprocessing a form of information handling in which a data processing system utilizes communication facilities to connect remote points

teleprompter important technical aid for speakers. A speech is typed in very large letters on a roll of paper which is inserted into a specially designed lectern. As speaker gives his talk, lectern drum rolls at speaker's pace insuring that he can look at prompter screen to read speech text

teletype typewriter operated over telephone circuits

telex service a dial-up electronic service which enables its subscribers to communicate directly and temporarily among themselves worldwide on circuits of a public network

tender offer an offer to purchase a designated number of shares of a corporation's stock at a specific price by a specific date. Person making offer is usually, but not always, intending to acquire enough shares to control the company

10-K report a detailed financial report required of publicly held corporations by the Securities and Exchange Commission (SEC) annually, and available to the shareholders and the general public. A portion appears in the annual report

terminal a device capable of sending and/or receiving information over a communications channel such as telephone, teleprinter, cathode tube, etc.

test campaign a limited publicity or advertising campaign in certain area to assess reaction and results before deciding to go nationwide with campaign

testimonial an expression of appreciation or esteem, most frequently used in promotion and advertising. An opportunity for a company to present its case through a third party. The testimonial often benefits from sanction of a respected or well-known authority who testifies

text the body copy of any written material, usually after publication

themes salient messages reflected in copy repeatedly in an effort to achieve the goals of the campaign and to influence public opinion

threshold of consciousness the point at which a given object passes from out of the mass of unperceived objects into the awareness of the individual

tie-in a promotional technique between two organizations cooperating on a joint venture which will benefit both

third-party technique   very similar to the front technique, in which a presumably impartial and disinterested third party acts for a client in a controversy

timely disclosure   a requirement by the Securities and Exchange Commission and stock exchanges that publicly held corporations whose shares of common stock are listed on an exchange practice "timely, full and complete disclosure" of any and all pertinent information which might affect the price of the shares, simultaneously to the financial news media and community

time sheets   a report of executives and staff members accounting for time spent on various activities; most frequently used by agencies as a basis for billing hours to clients

trademark   a word or design used on an article of merchandise to identify it as the product of a particular manufacturer (e.g., Kodak, Coca-Cola); but it might also be used for goods and services such as transportation, insurance, and entertainment

trade press   usually refers to all the business publications covering a given business, industry, or profession

trade publication   any publication aimed at special interest readers of a certain industry or profession

training films   films used to teach a variety of subjects visually. They can be more effective than the instructors in the classroom

transfer agent   the firm which records and transfers shares of common stock from one person to another when shares are bought and sold

transmitting   the method of relaying information between an encoder and decoder; like a transmission belt for information

trend   general direction of activities or events in a given area of interest

trial balloon   a planned miniature campaign or series of events conducted immediately before the launching of a major campaign. It is used to assess opinion and public reaction. If public reaction is adverse, the campaign can be postponed

two-step communication   the theory of persuasion that provides for a middleman or opinion-leader to influence the masses

video display terminal (VDT)   screen on which data can be viewed

videophone   a combined telephone and television transmission by means of which the voice and sight of the two parties are received at each end

visibility   public prominence calculated to engender press attention and comment. It implies frequent public attention

volunteerism   the giving of personal or corporate time and resources other than money to nonprofit service organizations, or similar units, for the public good

word processing   a combination of keyboard, computer memory bank, cathode ray tube, and printer used to write, edit, and store written copy

working capital   the excess of current assets over current liabilities, really a measure of the capital needs for running the company

NAME INDEX

SUBJECT INDEX